Glorious John

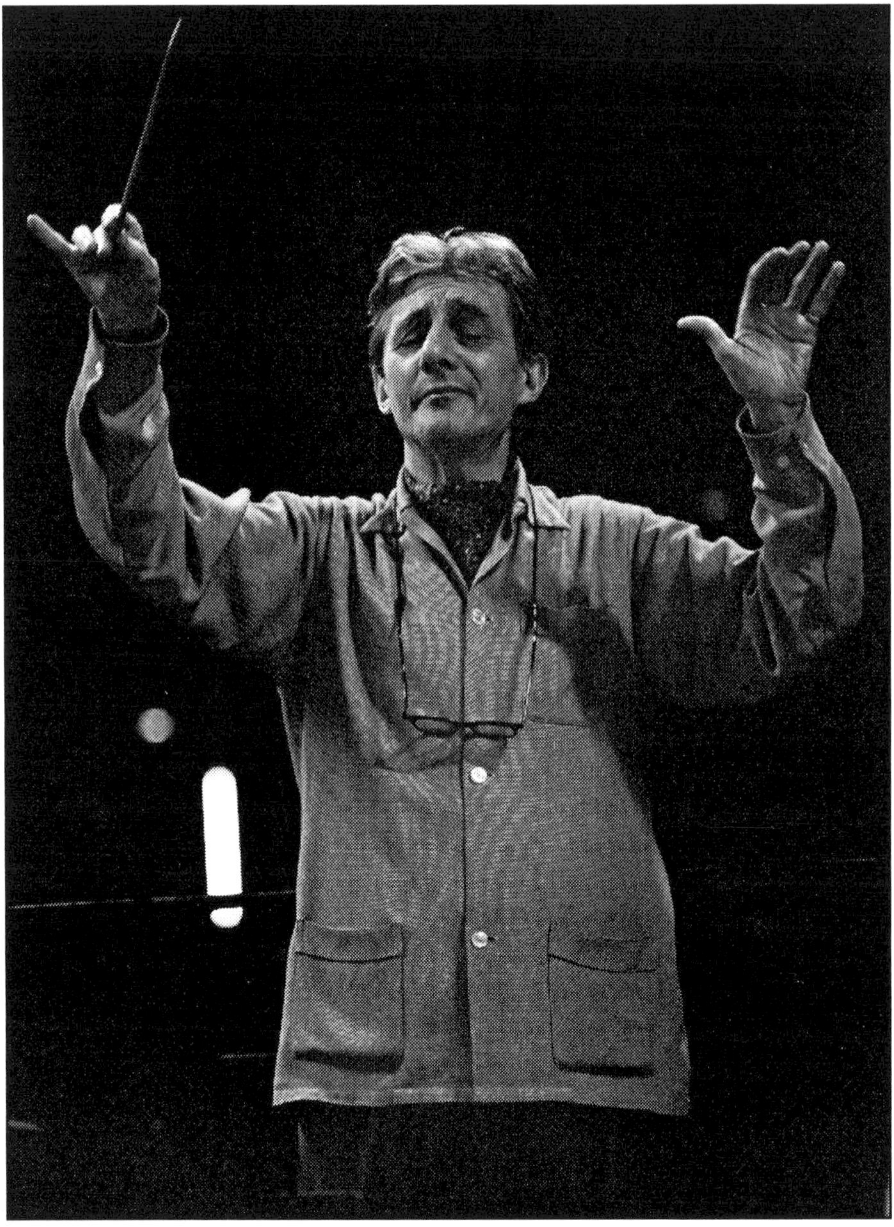

GLORIOUS JOHN

A Collection of Sir John Barbirolli's Lectures, Articles, Speeches and Interviews

Compiled, Edited and Introduced by
RAYMOND HOLDEN

The Barbirolli Society

Royal Academy of Music

First published by The Barbirolli Society, 2007

The Barbirolli Society
2 Cedar Close, Uttoxeter, Staffordshire ST14 7NP

www.barbirolli.co.uk

© The Barbirolli Society, 2007

All rights reserved

This book is sold subject to the condition that it shall not, by way of trade or otherwise, be lent, resold or hired out or otherwise circulated without the publisher's prior consent in any form of binding or cover other than in which it is published.

ISBN: 978-0-9556710-0-5

Pagesetting and design by
Design and Print, Oxford

Printed in Great Britain by
Marston Book Services Ltd.

For Evelyn

In Memory of Professor Cyril Ehrlich and Sir John Pritchard

EMI recording session for Schubert's Symphony No. 9

Contents

Preface	xii
Editor's Note	xiii
INTRODUCTION	14
PART ONE: On Barbirollli	
'A Few Reminiscences'	21
'50 Not Out': a Draft Copy of Speech Given on Barbirolli's 50th Birthday	24
Acceptance Speech on being Awarded the Gold Medal of the Royal Philharmonic Society on 13 December 1950	24
Draft of a Speech by Barbirolli to the Board of Directors of the Royal Philharmonic Society, London	25
'Memories of the "Proms"'	28
Foreword to *Gods or Flannelled Fools?*	29
'The Present and Future'	30
'Music and Cricket'	32
'Christmas'	34
Interview with Michael Kennedy: 'My Twenty Years with the Hallé'	35
Extracts from 'The Young Sir John Talking–on the eve of his 65th birthday	43
'The Maestro Remembers...'	43
Speech given on the occasion of Barbirolli being made a Companion of Honour	47
On being made Freeman of King's Lynn	52
Extracts from 'Barbirolli at 70'	54

PART TWO: On Composers and Compositions

'The N. G. S. Orchestral Records'	63
'Notes for a Lecture on Smetana's Opera "The Bartered Bride"'	65
'Strauss and "Der Rosenkavalier"'	71
Lecture on Verdi's *Don Carlo*	85
'*Pelleas and Melisande* Preamble'	91
'Article on Richard Strauss for Hallé Magazine October 1949'	94
'Forty Years with Elgar's Music'	96
'Elgar, the Man'	97
'Jean Sibelius 1865-1957'	99
'V.W. – A Tribute'	100
A tribute to Vaughan Williams	101
On the death of Vaughan Williams	102
'The Noblest Traditions of Italian Art'	104
'St Matthew Passion'	107
'Barbirolli talks about the Elgar Second'	108
'The Dream of Gerontius: a Personal Note'	110
An Interview with Ronald Kinloch Anderson	113
Some Reflections on Mahler	114
'Memories of "Otello"'	116

PART THREE: On Conducting

Speech given to the New York Philharmonic-Symphony League	125
'Becoming a Conductor: a Conference with John Barbirolli'	128
Speech to the New York Philharmonic-Symphony League on 1 November 1938	133
Preamble to a lecture on conducting given to Hallé Club	142

PART FOUR: On Orchestras, Organizations, Administrators
              and Performing Musicians

Speech given in Glasgow	151
Speech given before the Lord Provost of Glasgow	153
Radio broadcast concerning the Scottish Orchestra	155
Second speech given before the Lord Provost of Glasgow	157
Third speech given before the Lord Provost of Glasgow	161
Fourth speech given before the Lord Provost of Glasgow	163
Lecture given at the New York 'Philharmonic Symphony League Luncheon'	167
Speech given on behalf of the Musician's Emergency Fund, New York	168
Second speech given on behalf of the Musicians' Emergency Fund, New York	169
'On the Training of Young Musicians: National Orchestral Association Speech'	170
'Statement to be used by the Little Symphony of Montreal'	172
A Tribute to Leslie Heward	172
'My First Season with the Hallé'	174
Speech for the Inaugural Lecture of the Hallé Season, 1944-45	175
Notes for a speech given at an Edinburgh reception on 25 June 1946	178
Unidentified speech dated '4th July, 1946.'	178
'Message of Greetings for the "Hallé" Magazine', dated '13th July, 1946'	180
'Observations by JB on Corporation Grant Issue', dated '28th September, 1946.'	181
'Lord Mayor Reception after return from Austria Tour 1948'	182
Speech for the '1949 Hallé Committee Dinner'	183
'Foreword' to *Sir Charles Hallé: a Portrait for Today*	184
'Chivalry lifted up her lance'	186
'A Memorable Visit'	189
'Kathleen… The Last Years'	192

'Her Last Festival Performances: a Tribute to Kathleen Ferrier'	202
'Sir John Barbirolli writes…'	203
'The Centenary Season'	204
'Foreword' to *One Hundred Years of the Hallé*	207
'The Welfare State Calls the Tune'	208
'George Weldon'	210
Congratulatory letter to the Vienna Philharmonic on the occasion of its 125th anniversary	211
'Sir Malcolm Sargent'	212
Draft of an entry for the Israel Philharmonic's Artists' House Guest Book	212
'A Message from Sir John Barbirolli'	213
80th birthday greeting to the bassoonist, Archie Camden	215
Interview with Michael Kennedy	216
Barbirolli's draft foreword to the autobiography of Rachel Morton	218
'South Place Sunday Concerts'	219
Ninetieth birthday greeting to Sir Robert Mayer in 1969	220
Homily written on the death of the tenor, Giovanni Martinelli	220
Interview in *Nihon Keizai Shimbun* (27 August 1969)	221

PART FIVE: On Programming and Audiences

'The Musical Highbrow Menace'	229
Untitled speech given during Barbirolli's tenure with the New York Philharmonic-Symphony Orchestra	231
'The Re-Opening of the Free Trade Hall, Manchester – 1951'	233
Programming for the Trafalgar Day Concert, 1958	234
'Musings from the Maestro'	234

PART SIX: On the State of Music

Article for the *Daily Telegraph*, London	239
'Speech Given at the Re-opening of the Henry Watson Music Library'	243

PART SEVEN: On Technology and Music

'The Lighter Side of Orchestral Accompaniments'	249
Speech given at the Contemporary Club, Philadelphia	251

PART EIGHT: On Music, War and Politics

Easter statement from New York	263
Centennial Address to the New York Philharmonic-Symphony League	264
Draught article concerning Barbirolli's fourth season with the New York Philharmonic-Symphony Orchestra	265
Speech given at the Authors' Club, Hollywood	265
'Colonels and Privates Queued Together'	270
Script for a broadcast on 'Music Magazine'	273
On the death of President Roosevelt	275
'Impressions of Vienna: the Revival of Music'	275
'Message for the British Council'	278
'Speech to [a] Lanc[ashire] Trade Union at Belle Vue'	279

Illustrations	305
Index	309

Preface

Sir John Barbirolli has been a source of interest and inspiration to me for much of my life: his recordings were some of my most treasured possessions as a teenager; his interpretative style shaped my understanding of the recreative process as a performing musician, and his professional artefacts have been a valuable research source for me as a performance historian

Because of my continuing interest in Barbirolli's sound world, some years ago I began to investigate his distinctive Bruckner style and, as a direct result of those investigations, I was invited to teach at the Royal Academy of Music, London. There, I learned that Lady Barbirolli had given to the Academy in the early 1970s a large number of her husband's professional papers and some of his scores for research and teaching purposes. As is often the case in busy conservatoires, where the day-to-day demands on librarians and archivists are often overwhelming, the artefacts lay largely undisturbed for a number of years. But with the help and encouragement of the Academy's Librarian, Kathryn Adamson, I began to investigate these materials more carefully. After opening this historical treasure chest, we soon realized that the Barbirolli collection was a rich source of information for musicians and historians alike and that it should be collated and prepared for publication.

But as the project progressed, it became clear that the documents held at the Academy were incomplete and that they would have to be supplemented from materials held elsewhere. These were kindly provided by the Hallé Orchestra's Archivist, Eleanor Roberts, and by Paul Brooks, David Jones and Pauline Pickering of the Barbirolli Society. Throughout the collation process, I received the enthusiastic support of the Academy's Vice Principal and Director of Studies, Professor Jonathan Freeman-Attwood, its Head of Research, Dr Amanda Glauert, its Registrar of Collections, Janet Snowman, and its Director of Conducting Studies, Colin Metters. Lady Barbirolli was also an enthusiastic supporter of the project, and without her advice and interest the book would never have been published. Together with the above, I would like to thank Professor Sir Curtis Price, Kim Perkins, John Woollard, Malcolm Gerratt, Dr David Patmore, Michael Kennedy and my wife, Mary, for their assistance in completing this book.

Editor's Note

Barbirolli was a natural communicator, both on and off the rostrum, but some of the texts for his public lectures and speeches are telegraphic in nature. Although there is a temptation to make those manuscripts flow more naturally, such manipulation would inevitably diminish the impact of Barbirolli's characteristic style. Where the text is particularly problematic, however, such as at the beginning of '50 Not Out', I have simply moved the fragments of material to a footnote. If a small addition to the script has been necessary, this is indicated by square brackets. The texts have been ordered according to issue and, within each of those sections, they have been listed chronologically.

Raymond Holden, who was formerly an orchestral and choral conductor, is a Research Fellow of the Royal Academy of Music, London, where he teaches on the post-graduate and undergraduate programmes. He is also a tutor-in-music for the University of Oxford's Department for Continuing Education. As an author, he has been published by Yale, Oxford and Cambridge University Presses.

Introduction

Sir John Barbirolli was small in stature but a giant of the podium. His charisma, warmth of personality, good taste and outstanding musicianship meant that he left an indelible impression on all whom he encountered. Stories about him are legion and his impact as a social, economic and musical figure was important not only to Manchester and the Hallé Orchestra but also to music in Britain as a whole. Born at the beginning of the age of recording, he has exercised influence well beyond the grave, with the release of each newly-discovered live performance on CD, his cult status grows from strength to strength. But the high regard in which he was held was not won easily, because he rose through the ranks of the music profession, working variously as an orchestral player, soloist, chamber musician, arranger and jobbing conductor. Consequently, by the time he had become a podium star, he had gained a global perspective of music which resulted in a personal style that moved comfortably from the mechanics of score preparation to the practice of performance. That said, his response to the printed musical text was neither simple nor immediate, and it stood in sharp contrast to the approach of Sir John Pritchard, who 'could read the most difficult of scores like he could read *The Times*'.[1] As Barbirolli lacked the keyboard facility necessary to study scores at the piano and the benefit of perfect pitch, he turned to solfège as his principal study tool. Although laborious, this method meant that he was able to build his interpretation meticulously, using every weapon in his musical armoury to create his own distinctive sound world.

Born in Southampton Row, London, on 2 December 1899, Barbirolli was the son of a French mother and an Italian father.[2] With music firmly in his ears from birth – his father and grandfather were violinists who had played in the same orchestra as the young Arturo Toscanini for the première of Verdi's *Otello* at La Scala, Milan, on 5 February 1887 – Barbirolli was introduced early to music with violin lessons. But his habit of wandering around the house while playing the fiddle soon annoyed his grandfather, who decided to root him firmly to the one spot by buying him a 'cello.

Having transferred to the 'cello at the age of seven, Barbirolli progressed quickly and in 1910 he won a scholarship to the Trinity College of Music, where he studied with Edmund Woolhouse. His impact at the College was immediate and, on 16 December 1911, he played the Cantilena from Goltermann's 'Cello Concerto Op. 14 with the Trinity College orchestra at the Queen's Hall. In 1912, Barbirolli became a pupil of Herbert Walenn, under whose tutorage he won the Ada Lewis Scholarship to study at the Royal Academy of Music. Walenn's influence was profound and, in later life, Barbirolli always referred to his former teacher with admiration and respect. On leaving the Academy, Barbirolli joined the Queen's Hall Orchestra and later gave his first solo recital at the Aeolian Hall in New Bond Street on 13 June 1917. That year, he joined the army and it was there that he conducted for the first time. After leaving the army, he again worked as a freelance 'cellist, taught at Herbert Walenn's London Violoncello School, was the soloist for a performance of Elgar's 'Cello Concerto with the Bournemouth Symphony Orchestra and joined the Kutcher Quartet.

Although Barbirolli seemed destined to become one of Britain's leading 'cellists, his ambitions lay elsewhere. After forming the John Barbirolli Chamber Orchestra in 1924, he soon became known as a conductor and, much like Sir Thomas Beecham before him, used his orchestra as a means by which to gain performing experience. Clearly talented, he quickly came to the attention of the singer and impresario, Frederick Austin,[3] who engaged him as a conductor of the British National Opera Company in 1926. Unable to meet its costs, the BNOC ceased trading in mid 1929 but was reformed later that year as the Covent Garden Opera Syndicate. The change of management had little effect on Barbirolli, who was re-employed as a staff conductor with the new company. His years in the theatre were central to his musical development because he was able to explore much of the standard operatic repertoire and to experience the rigours of touring for the first time. By performing works by Wagner, Strauss and Verdi with little or no rehearsal both at Covent Garden and in the provinces, he was able to develop a flexible conducting style and an immediacy of approach that stood him in good stead for the rest of his life.

During those early years, Barbirolli published his first articles in *The Gramophone* magazine. These pieces allowed him not only to promote some of his most recent recordings but also to consider the difficulties of working as a conductor in the recording studio and to ponder the way in which audiences from different backgrounds respond to particular repertoires. These texts offer a fascinating insight into the pioneering years of the record industry and the way in which Barbirolli interacted with both the music that he was interpreting and the audience for whom it was intended.

As a member of the Covent Garden Opera Company's conducting staff, he had a role that was both didactic and interpretative. When performing in the provinces, he was often dispatched in advance to the towns the company intended to visit to deliver lectures illustrated with music examples. At Halifax in the early 1930s, for example, he gave talks that balanced synopses of the operas with critical analyses of the works as a whole. The lectures were also a forum for Barbirolli to challenge existing notions of music and society and to champion his belief that music was an egalitarian art form that should be accessible to all and not the province of the few.

From Covent Garden, Barbirolli moved to the Scottish Orchestra in 1933. As the orchestra's Music Director, he faced a steep learning curve. Although he famously deputised for an indisposed Sir Thomas Beecham at a concert with the London Symphony Orchestra at the Queen's Hall on 12 December 1927 and had given his first concert for the Royal Philharmonic Society on 17 January 1929,[4] his experience as an orchestral conductor was limited. Nevertheless, he accepted the Scottish post with confidence and set about preparing a schedule of concerts that would have unnerved even the most experienced of conductors. Having previously conducted only a handful of compositions for symphony orchestra, he quickly tackled multiple works by sixty-nine composers ranging from J. S. Bach to Gershwin. Amongst this exhaustive exploration of the orchestral literature were the complete symphonies of Beethoven, Brahms and Elgar, composers who later formed the basis for his mature performance aesthetic.

As Music Director of the Scottish Orchestra, Barbirolli was expected to participate actively in its financial management. In his speeches before the Lord Provost,[5] the question of funding was ever-present. From the artists engaged and the works programmed, it is immediately obvious that the Scottish Orchestra was experiencing a golden age under Barbirolli. This golden age did not come cheaply, however, and the need to motivate audiences to attend concerts and the necessity to encourage guarantors to dig deeply into their pockets were essential if his plans were to succeed fully. But Barbirolli also realized that to achieve his goals the mass-marketing of music was necessary. By the nature of its construction, the concert hall was a limiting factor, so to overcome this he began to exploit the BBC as a conduit to a greater listening public. Unlike Wilhelm Furtwängler in Germany, Barbirolli recognized the importance of radio for the dissemination of music and was keen to develop the Scottish Orchestra's links with the Corporation. In any case, while developing those links, he was careful to ensure that the broadcasts would not reduce audience numbers in the concert hall and that any relationship with the BBC would work to the Orchestra's advantage by acting as a form of free advertising campaign.

Although the impact that Barbirolli made with the Scottish Orchestra was important locally and nationally, it was his work in the recording studio that brought him to the attention of the wider musical world. Having begun to record for HMV in 1927, he came into contact with some of the world's leading soloists, including Artur Rubinstein, Arthur Schnabel, Fritz Kreisler, Frida Leider and Mischa Elman. After he took up his Scottish post this list was supplemented by such figures as Vladimir Horowitz, Adolf Busch, Jacques Thibaud, Solomon, Bronislaw Huberman, Emmanuel Feuermann, Alexander Kipnis, Jascha Heifitz, Walter Gieseking and Florence Austral. All were well-connected musically in the United States and all recognized his outstanding musicianship. Consequently, when Arturo Toscanini resigned as Music Director of the New York Philharmonic-Symphony Orchestra in 1936, Barbirolli was engaged by its General Manager, Arthur Judson, to fill the Maestro's shoes, initially as guest conductor in 1936 and later as Music Director from the 1937-8 season.

Much has been written about Barbirolli's tenure in New York and much has been misinterpreted. Although popular with players and audiences alike, Barbirolli never managed to convince fully the critic of *The New York Times*, Olin Downes, of his outstanding musicianship. As one of the principal barometers for musical taste in America's largest city, Downes wielded considerable power. If an artist fell short of his expectations, it was almost certain that their New York career was doomed to failure. Such critical power was not unknown elsewhere in the United States and when Rafael Kubelik later fell foul of the *Chicago Tribune*'s critic, Claudia Cassidy, in the 1950s, his tenure with the Chicago Symphony Orchestra ended after only three years. But to make matters worse for Barbirolli, Downes was a fanatical supporter of Toscanini and unwilling to accept any other conductor as head of New York's principal orchestra. That being so, Barbirolli's tenure with the Philharmonic was always going to be fraught with danger, even though it was clear to many that he was an interpreter of importance and a performer with charisma.

As Music Director of one of America's leading orchestras, Barbirolli regularly tackled the thorny questions of finance and programming in his lectures and speeches. Although the culture of funding in Britain and Europe was markedly different from that of the United States, he was happy to work with the system of private subsidy if it meant that he could pursue his musical objectives. That said, he was more than willing to make financial concessions if funds could also be released for the training and welfare of the players. In his speeches on behalf of the Musicians' Emergency Fund and the National Orchestral Association, he spoke passionately about the need for sponsors to act philanthropically. It is clear from the tone of these talks that he never lost touch with the needs of jobbing musicians and that his sympathies were the result of his own early experiences and those of his father and grandfather. But Barbirolli did not restrict himself to musical matters in his American speeches; he also used them as a means by which to alert Americans to the privations suffered by the British during the Blitz. In a tone that was often Churchillian, he left no doubt that he expected America to join the fight against fascism and to reject isolationism. By adopting such a provocative stance, he often alienated his listeners. Nevertheless, he felt passionately that it was the moral duty of all Americans to support the war effort and to make sacrifices where necessary.

With war raging in Europe from 1939, Barbirolli longed to return to Britain 'to do his bit'. With the help of the First Lord of the Admiralty, he crossed the Atlantic by convoy in 1942 and gave concerts with England's beleaguered orchestras. Shocked by the level of devastation that he witnessed and the degree of misery that was being endured, he was determined to return permanently to his homeland and to stand shoulder-to-shoulder with his fellow countrymen. It is hardly surprising, then, that when he received a telegram in 1943 inviting him to become the Permanent Conductor of the Hallé Orchestra in Manchester he leapt at the chance. But on taking up the post, he was confronted with an orchestra of barely chamber proportions. Undeterred, he set about rebuilding the Hallé from scratch and eventually moulding it into a personal instrument that responded easily and quickly to his unique performance style.

Barbirolli's name soon became synonymous with the Hallé Orchestra and he led them from triumph to triumph. Part of his performance strategy was touring. Although travelling from city to city in Britain was a financial necessity for the orchestra, Barbirolli also insisted that regular international tours were essential. By plying their trade at home and abroad, Barbirolli and the orchestra were able to enhance their reputation both nationally and internationally. With his profile firmly in the ascendant, many commentators wondered why Barbirolli remained in provincial Manchester. They argued that the Hallé lacked the virtuosity of orchestras such as the Berlin Philharmonic and the Cleveland Orchestra and that Lancashire was hardly a suitable place for a musician of his ability and standing. But they failed to understand that the Hallé had been trained by him to be flexible and responsive and that those qualities were seminal to his performance style. They also failed to understand his personal commitment to the players and his love of Manchester and all things Mancunian.

Because of the sheer length of his tenure with the Hallé Orchestra, it was almost inevitable that the majority of his speeches, lectures and articles were written during that period. As in Scotland and New York, many concern finance, programming and management. There are, however, also texts of a more personal nature, such as those concerning the deaths of Kathleen Ferrier and Philip Godlee. In these, Barbirolli recalls vividly and touchingly Ferrier's and Godlee's personalities, idiosyncrasies and musical qualities. With their loss and the gradual onset of old age, tradition, history and a sense of place became increasingly important to Barbirolli. In particular, he loved to recall Edwardian London with its unique combination of sights, sounds and smells and he always described himself proudly as 'Cockney John'.

While Manchester and the Hallé were dear to him both personally and professionally, Barbirolli began to widen his sphere of influence during the 1960s to include other orchestras. Principal amongst these were the Houston Symphony Orchestra and the Berlin Philharmonic. With the resignation of Leopold Stokowski from the Houston orchestra in November 1960, Barbirolli was appointed its Music Director from the 1961-2 season. Although he remained with the orchestra until 1967, he made no commercial recordings with it. Because of the lack of sound documents from this tenure, some commentators have underestimated his relationship with the Texas orchestra. But he was deeply committed to it and, when he conducted it both at Houston and on tour, he lavished on it the same care and attention to detail that he did with the Hallé in Manchester. Similarly, when he worked with the Berlin Philharmonic he felt a personal and musical connection that went beyond the ordinary. Having conducted it first at the Edinburgh Festival in 1949 and again in Berlin in 1950, he worked with it annually from 1961 until his death on 29 July 1970. Ranging from one performance in 1962 to fourteen performances in 1967, the importance of these concerts increased not only in number over that decade but also in emotional importance for Barbirolli. The love and respect that he had for the Berlin players was reciprocated and, after his death, the Intendant of the orchestra, Wolfgang Stresemann, wrote that '... [he was] one of the most beloved guest conductors of the Berlin Philharmonic ... [and] a heroic interpreter of heroic music.[6]

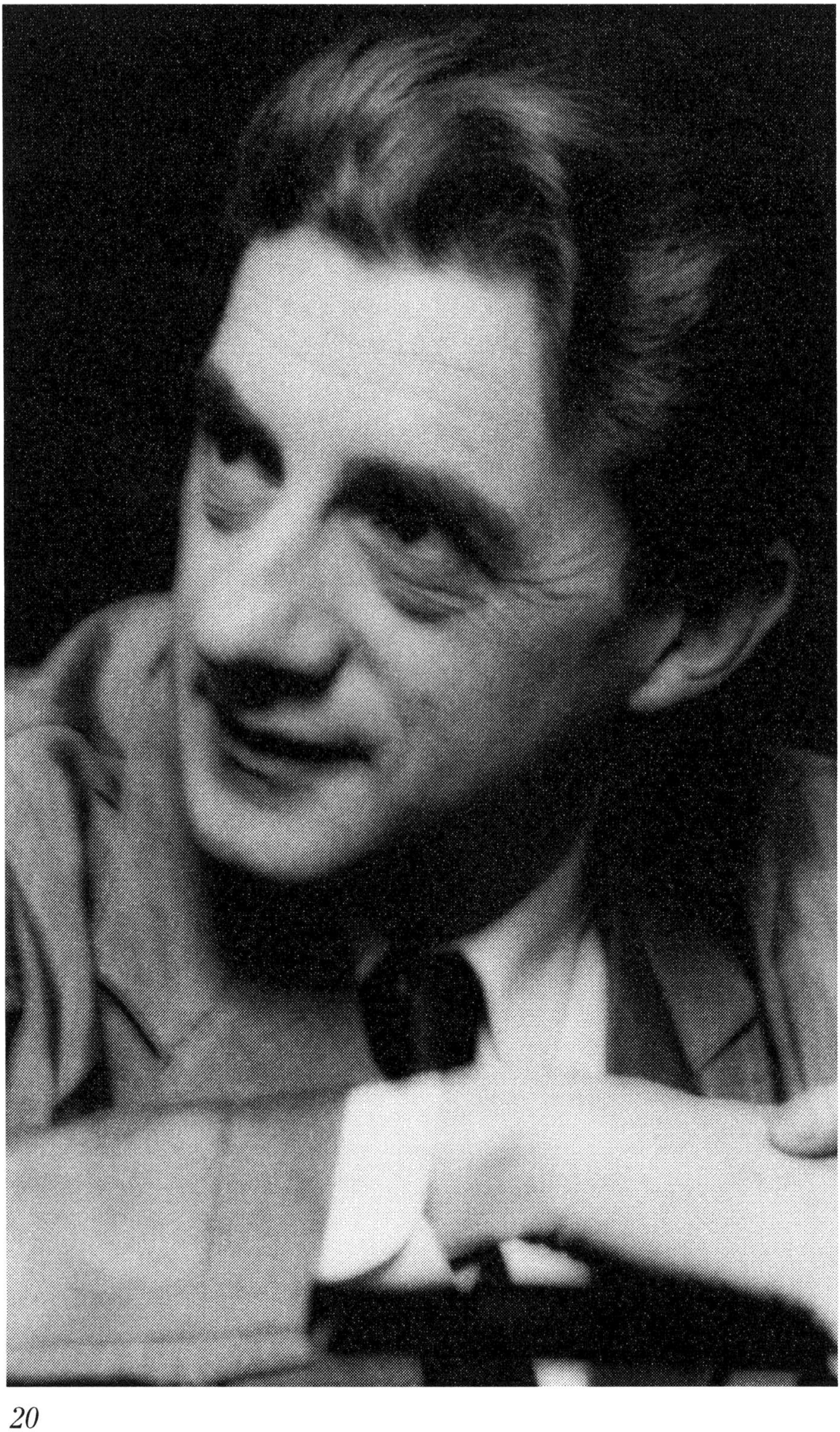

PART ONE

On Barbirolli

'A Few Reminiscences'[7]

'Although I have little time for writing articles at present, I was unable to refuse the invitation of *The Gramophone*, which was responsible for my first orchestral recordings in the days of the National Gramophonic Society. Proud and happy as I am at the compliment which New York has paid me, I am deeply aware of the hard and difficult task which lies before me, and I hope that I shall not prove too unworthy of the honour which has been paid to British Music through me

Please let me deprecate at once any talk that I am going to be Toscanini's successor. With his going closes a great era in the history of the New York Philharmonic, and an official of the New York Philharmonic Society put the position in this way to a reporter in an interview. He said: "We feel that in inviting Mr. Barbirolli we are making what may prove an interesting experiment. We realize he is young but we are faced with the necessity of discovering fresh talent, and from what we have heard of his conducting in England we have every reason to believe that our choice will be a happy one."

I hope so. Strangely enough this year is my Silver Jubilee as a public performer; it is almost exactly twenty-five years ago that I, a small boy of eleven, played the solo part in the Saint-Saëns Concerto at the Queen's Hall.[8]

I continued my studies as a 'cellist, but my real ambition had always been to conduct. Bandmasters in parks were my heroes when I was a youngster. When I was about six or seven, a small band used to play in Lincoln's Inn Fields: we lived near by in Drury Lane at the time, and it was the greatest treat I could think of, to be taken there to watch the bandmaster. Meanwhile I practised and practised on the 'cello and was earning my own living long before most boys had left school. When I was fourteen I set out on my professional career and it was not long before I had played everywhere

Glorious John

except in the street! – theatres, music halls, cinemas, in opera orchestras, and in chamber music. I went right through the mill. I think now that it was the best possible thing that could have happened to me.

A conductor must be a good psychologist, he must know how to handle the different personalities which make up an orchestra. Living among orchestral players and knowing them so well was to be a great help to me later on.

When I was sixteen I became a member of the Queen's Hall Orchestra, and it was a good schooling to work my way through such a large repertoire of orchestral works. Round about this time I also played in the Carl Rosa Opera Company Orchestra, and soon joined the Beecham Opera Company at Drury Lane: in fact I scorned no avenue that would teach me something about my job. In those days mechanical music was unknown in the theatre; wherever plays were performed there would be a small theatre orchestra. I played in one of these. There was not much to do, incidental music to plays had fallen into disuse; all we did was to play the people to and from the bar in the intervals. In the long waits between the act-intervals I studied scores. When the time came that I had the opportunity to conduct, all these early experiences, this knowledge of playing inside an orchestra were to stand me in good stead.

Actually the first conducting I ever did was when I was in the Army. The Colonel of the Suffolk Regiment, with which I served, was an enthusiastic amateur fiddler, and after the Armistice he found that a number of us could play, and formed a small orchestra. I played in the orchestra and we used to have some very good evenings. But one night the regular conductor was unable to turn up, and at the last moment I took his place. I have always maintained that the stick technique of an efficient conductor was a natural thing, and I can with truth say that as far as "stick facility" (if I may use such a term) is concerned, I conducted as naturally then as I do now. Anyhow, I enjoyed myself that night.

My first professional effort was in 1925 when I founded a chamber orchestra under the auspices of the Guild of Singers and Players. The orchestra was small but of fine quality, and it soon made some reputation for itself. It was with this orchestra that I made my first gramophone recordings for the National Gramophonic Society with some Purcell and Delius pieces.

About this time Ethel Bartlett and I had enjoyed some success playing piano and 'cello sonatas from memory – everybody seemed to think it rather wonderful that should play without music, but it was merely the result of very intensive rehearsing in which we used to indulge. Ethel Bartlett was the soloist at my first Guild orchestral concert, and she and her husband, Rae Robertson, are to be my soloists at the concluding concert of my season in New York.

A few months after the Chenil Galleries were opened a chamber orchestra was formed, and through the offices of John Goss, the conducting of it was entrusted to my care.

John Goss, always a good friend and a believer in me, was, in a way, responsible for my debut in opera. He engaged me to conduct a concert he gave of Van Dieren's works. Frederick Austin, then the artistic director of the BNOC, was in the hall, and was sufficiently impressed to engage me to go on tour with the BNOC. Within a year I was conducting at Covent Garden.

My first big concert opportunity came when, through the sudden indisposition of Sir Thomas Beecham, the London Symphony Orchestra sent for me, giving me forty-eight hours' notice to conduct the Elgar Second Symphony. Casals was the soloist in the Haydn ['Cello] Concerto,[9] and one incident I remember vividly. At rehearsal, after the first few introductory bars, I stopped the orchestra and made a few remarks. Casals leaned forward in his chair and said: "Listen to him. He knows". I was only a boy, and those few words coming from such a great artist touched me deeply. It was a wonderful thing for a man of his greatness to do: I shall never forget it. But then I have always cherished the thought that all really great men are simple and generous, and very rarely have I been disillusioned. It is certainly true of Casals and Kreisler, to mention but two.

The Queen's Hall was packed that night, and a memorable evening for me. Coming off the rostrum, after the closing bars of the Elgar, I found a little man on the platform who accosted me with the words: "Don't sign any gramophone contracts. See me to-morrow at ten. My name's Gaisberg – HMV". And that was the beginning of my association with HMV, and a very delightful friendship with that great man, Fred Gaisberg, an association that has lasted ever since.

I would not like to go to New York now without acknowledging my very real debt to my friends, the orchestral players of this country. From the day I left my seat among them to stand before them, our relations have been those of mutual respect and affection, and in the great honour that has come to me, I would like to feel that they have a share'.

Glorious John

'50 Not Out': a Draft Copy of Speech Given on Barbirolli's 50th Birthday[10]

'...50 Not Out.[11] Not a bad score & by wars of the Roses[12] timetable not so slow either! 50 in 50 years! Anyway hope that they have been good ones, with a few sides & without the help of no-balls. Unless [*sic*] most cricketers tho[ugh], I have no wish to complete my century, I'd rather treat you to a few more years for hard hitting & leave you to your memories. I see with great pleasure here L[aurance]. T[urner].[13] my partner between the wickets also reached ½ cent[ury] & with fine Lancashire caution I don't think we are likely to run each other out. I w[ou]ld just like to say how proud I am to be honoured by the presence of one who[14] is already a legend in the annals of cricket. Wilfred Rhodes.[15] Present in 1926.[16] Tell story if not too late. Pitches a bit rougher. Ken. Not been an easy road, but your dear trust & affection [illegible] all [illegible] words light to you etc.'.

Acceptance Speech on being Awarded the Gold Medal of the Royal Philharmonic Society on 13 December 1950[17]

'Your Majesty, Dr. Vaughan Williams, ladies, and gentlemen, - Some little time ago it was my privilege to be present in the Manchester Town Hall when Mr. Winston Churchill received the freedom of the city, and he said in one of his first sentences: "There are some things that a man should not hear till he is dead." And I feel I rather qualify for that. Then he went on to wipe away a none too furtive tear, and I feel that I could do that too, for my heart is very full. But there my emulation of this great man stops, because he went on to give a most magnificent oration with which, I am afraid, under the stress of the emotion that I feel tonight – if not for other reasons – I cannot compete.

Dr. Vaughan Williams, if such a thing were possible I feel that the great honour that has been conferred upon me tonight has been intensified by the pride and pleasure I feel in receiving it from your hands. I hope that by our performance, whatever its shortcomings, of your symphony you have felt something of the gratitude and – may I say? – the affection we have for you and for all you have done to enrich our lives by the study and the performance of your music.[18]

Part One

And not only have you enriched the lives of conductors and orchestras, but of musical communities the world over, as I can say with a certain amount of truth, for I have conducted this symphony in various parts of the world, and parts of the world where perhaps its tragic quietness could not be so well understood. But it is a wonderful thing that wherever I have played this work the greatness of it has been apparent immediately and due honour has been paid to its inspiration.

Now what can I say of the Royal Philharmonic Society? In its 137 years of existence it enshrined many historic and moving events of our musical life. Indeed some memories are bound to fill us with awe, because one of its finest moments was when it put out the hand of warm friendship to the mighty Beethoven in his hour of distress. And it is a wonderful thing to know that such a great and noble society exists in our midst in this time. It is something that we should nurture and treasure more than ever before in this difficult and shifting world of ours that we have this great society that has existed for so long, that has meant so much to us. If I may be permitted a comparison that is perhaps not out of place, I feel a lot more confidence in this rather unstable world, as they must have felt at Lord's when they saw W.G. Grace about.

Now I am sure no greater honour will ever come to me than is being given to me by this great society tonight except perhaps the honour, that I hope may be mine for many years to come, of continuing to serve this society with the Hallé at my side or in front of me.

I say this because, as perhaps you know, we are somewhat bound together, and if I may be permitted a purely personal note for a moment it is a particular happiness for me to receive this distinction standing in their midst. I have still some strenuous work to do, and you some strenuous listening to do, so will you forgive me if I try to express my gratitude to Dr. Vaughan Williams and the society by just repeating the words of Sachs in the last act of the 'Mastersingers.' 'Friends: Words light to you, bow me to earth. Your praise is far beyond my worth.'"

Draft of a Speech by Barbirolli to the Board of Directors of the Royal Philharmonic Society, London[19]

'...I have already spoken of the excitement etc of my first concert with T[homas]. B[eecham]. (although already played under him in some operas).[20] Scanning thro[ugh] old programmes there are some things I remember the Mozart Concertante with those two English artists & Sir Thomas' prog[ramme] included the Prelude "on the Cliffs of Cornwall" from Ethyl Smyth's "The Wrecker" which I was to revive myself as conductor at C[ovent]. G[arden]. some 15 years [later.] She was a formidable etc box load of letter, wish I c[ou]ld quote from one particular one, thrown out for obscenity & indecency. The sentence c[ou]ld appear quite innocent, but I sometimes wonder she didn't enjoy writing with other intent.[21] 1st experience of Landon Ronald,[22] with his great affinity with the music of Elgar "Falstaff" (George Baker) & too great charm. He was a gentleman Trés Soignér. Perhaps too much so like me. In another programme appear the names of 3 great English singers, after got to know with greater intimacy. Frank Mullings, Norman Allin & Edna Thornton.[23] Tell Aida story (very [illegible] or accessible) After that rather domestic little interlude then I recall the 1st time I heard [Albert] Sammons[24] play the Delius Concerto, an experience of such exquisite loveliness that will never fade. (Good fortune many times later) Then Bob Radford,[25] a unique figure of great artistry, comradeship & benevolent humour, and generosity as I was to discover when I joined the B[ritish]. N[ational]. O[pera]. C[ompany]. Tribute to Fred Austin & tell Balfour [illegible], Fred & [Delius][26] Bax.

Cortot, whose pupil Ruth Fermoy was to become for many years in the Cesar [sic] Franck Variations, & with whom I had the honour of playing the Franck Quintet a few years later. [illegible], plays like Ysaye.[27] …Suggia. Jacky.[28] Played at her [Suggia's] Memorial Service in Oporto (Cavatina) Op. 13. Siloti. Perhaps rather an irreverent memory. An old man then played faster than anybody I have known. My old & kind friend Allen C. known in the profession as a "speed merchant) [sic] not unpopular for this dash[29] enabled a host of my thirsty musicians to get one down before they closed. But Siloti won the [illegible] "Derby" by a short neck, but I am afraid we were never level throughout the race.

Lamond.[30] Beethoven – Weingartner[.] Decided to go my own way.[31] Then dear Lionel [Tertis] again. In the Bax Violin Concerto,[32] between music and performance for me a bewitching experience. Jacques Thibaud too, with his inimitable style, grace & charm w[ou]ld be a good attribute to many violinists we have to listen to to-day. The more names & performances or I do go on forever.

Harold Bauer, great [& beloved][33] friend of my beloved teacher Herbert Walenn.[34] Bauer played the 4th Beethoven. A performance still indelibly imprinted on me. The slow mov[emen]t particularly, played with a beauty of sound, intimacy and depth of expression, that are engraved on my mind

Part One

after 45 years.

For [being a member of your]³⁵ orchestra, & enabling me to hear so many great artists³⁶ & taking part in the first performances of V[aughan]. W[illiam].'s Pastoral, Delius' Requiem & Holst's Perfect [Fool] Ballet music³⁷ was a wonderful experience for so young a man. I have dealt at some length on my memories as a member of the orchestra, because I thought it w[ould] be interesting for a [younger]³⁸ generation not fortunate enough to have heard some of these great artists of the past & perhaps unbecoming for me to dwell too long on my concerts as a conductor.³⁹

In years between leaving the orch[estra], chamber music etc I was co-opted at Committee for players etc so in the interval before beginning to conduct, I still served the Soc[iety] in some capacity.

In 1929 honoured [by]⁴⁰ my first concert with them.⁴¹ My next concert a year later will ever be memorable for 2 things. A most ravishingly beautiful performance by Casals of the Schumann Concerto, which sounded as if he was improvising it as he went along. This experience has remained with me all my life; to play like that greatest, illimitable reserves of technique. The second thing was entrusted with two 1ˢᵗ performances by two great English composers, Bax & V[aughan]. W[illiams]. Fantasia on Sussex Folk Songs cello & orch (Casals) and the Overture, Elegy & Rondo of Bax. Tell story of lost scores. Nobody noticed not even the composer. Bax autobiography. The next concert brought me the joy of accompanying⁴² the superb & very kind and sweet person Elena Gerhardt in the Kindertoten Lieder [sic] of Mahler & some songs of Wolf orchestrated by Nikisch: The one conductor in the world I had always wanted to hear, but to the world's great loss he died soon after the end of World War I in his early sixties. Only a few months before [E[lena]. G[erhardt]. died]⁴³ I spent a lovely evening with [her]⁴⁴ at a friend's home holding hands, recalling our concert together & my egging her on to tell me about Nikisch.

This is neither the time nor the place to go into details of the many programmes I have conducted for the R[oyal]. P[hilharmonic]. S[ociety]., but there are just 2 more I w[ou]ld like to mention. I am⁴⁵ particularly happy to remember I played my first Mahler Sy[mphony] in London under the auspices of the Society (9ᵗʰ) & since I see him here debt of gratitude to Sir N[eville]. C[ardus]. for having led me to the study of his symphonies.⁴⁶ Remember him saying written for you etc, Mémé & Mahler.⁴⁷ And the last and greatest of them all when that great⁴⁸ (I was going to say Old Man of, but I must [illegible] to that great young man,⁴⁹ presented with the Society Gold Medal in the presence of H. M. The Queen (now our beloved Queen

27

Glorious John

Mother.) Tell of how you just heard news. The Hallé on this occasion played what I regard as at least one of his masterpieces the[50] 6th Symphony. In a speech of much charm eloquence & wit[51] he quoted Wagner's Dictum of the ideal of a conductor is one who c[ou]ld find the "Melos" in the music,[52] then with a chuckle "He even managed to find the tunes in mine"[.] I sometimes wonder if that evening ever really happened, but the medal in my treasure chest at home is always there to re-assure me. My heart is to full to thank[53] Mr Chairman & all your colleagues on the Board of the Soc[iety] at all adequately for all y[our] kindness & the great honour you have paid me this night & with your permission I w[ou]ld like to propose a toast to the R.P.S. may its great traditions &[54] beneficent maintenance of them, last for such time that in those magnificent words of Abe Lincoln "not even the silent artillery of Time can ever destroy".[55]

'Memories of the "Proms"'[56]

'"Proms"! What memories the word conjures up for me, and what a musical education I received from them. People who frown upon such plebeian pleasures, and talk of them airily as having done a great deal to educate the "masses" are apt to forget that it is the masses who originally determined the destiny of works that are now strangely termed "classics". I must have first visited the "Proms" in 1910 or thereabouts. (In case anyone should imagine from this date that I am in my dotage let me just remind them I was then 10 years old!). In those good (bad?) old days a ticket for 60 concerts cost £1 and in addition every member of the orchestra had a free pass which he could hand on to any friend, relative or acquaintance he cared. My father, who was at that time the Musical Director of the Queen's Hotel in Leicester Square, had had most of the rank and file string players of Sir Henry's orchestra of that time through his hands, and so the little cockney urchin who was at that stage door in Riding House Street punctually half an hour before the concert, was nearly always bound to cadge admittance. My attendance was generally inspired by thought of hearing a full orchestra play the works I had grown to love when listening to my father's String Quartet (which, of course, contained a piano!) including, believe it or not, such pieces as Tchaikovsky's "1812".

But this brings me to the real point of this little message of welcolme and blessing to my old friend George Weldon's series of "Proms" in our magnificent new Free Trade Hall (surely with its warmth and friendliness an ideal setting for such a venture). The time is a little later, 1912, to be correct, and I had again managed to effect an entrance to those magic seats behind the orchestra where the orchestra's guests were accommodated, primarily to hear one of my real red-blooded favourites, "1812" or "Freischutz [*sic*] [Overture]" – I forget which. The programme contained an item I had never heard before, Dance Rhapsody No. 1 by Delius. I resigned myself to what I thought was certain to be inevitable boredom before another favourite came along: but when the music began (and 40 years ago it was stranger music than it seems now) I was transported to a world of exquisite loveliness which has never ceased to be. Surely my experience was not unique and must be repeated time after time. Four years later, in 1916, I was myself a member of the orchestra, at the tender age of 16. But already I am become garrulous in my memories, and my allotted space is already more than exhausted, so: Bless Sir Henry! and Hail, George Weldon!'.

Foreword to *Gods or Flannelled Fools?*[57]

'When Mr. Keith Miller first approached me to write a short foreword to his and Mr. Whitington's latest book, he told me that two of my predecessors in this "genre" had been Duleepsinjhi and Mr. Menzies. This I suppose was put out as an inducement to me to consent; little does he know how very nearly it acted as a deterrent, for apart from my love of the game I have very little qualification to appear in such distinguished company.

Many musicians are and have been addicted to the great and lovely game (though sometimes recently one has had cause to wonder if it is still a game), and even in the Hallé we have a fair team of which I have the honour to be the President. The players are equipped with caps suspiciously resembling those awarded to English test cricketers, and one would be tempted to remark that the similarity ends there were it not that the inconsistency of some recent England elevens make the resemblance slightly tragic. I have not yet had the opportunity to read more than the opening chapter of what promises to be a lively, stimulating and searching appreciation of modern cricket, but I liked immensely the title of this first part, "Gods or Flannelled Fools?", and its contents. Fools was the title my father (an Italian) chose for most English-speaking races, since he could but wonder how a bat and ball was capable of arousing such passions in men that sterner issues left cold. The culmination for him of this incredible inconsistency was the sight of a newspaper placard one afternoon, "England Collapses". Fearing the worst, and wondering what on earth had induced him to choose a country on the verge of disintegration as his adopted land, he bought a newspaper. He soon found reassurance but never ceased to be stunned by the implication.

I don't think this little story is irrelevant, for this intensity of feeling for cricket has never really left us, and that is why there will ever be a public eager and willing to watch, play and think about it.

There is much I would like to comment on in this first chapter, but I will confine myself to the remarks regarding the delay in the announcement of teams chosen to represent their country, and what the authors rightly call the "excruciating suspense" imposed on the public and particularly the players. I myself sometimes have to be a one man Selection Committee in the recruiting of young blood for important posts in my Hallé Orchestra and would with great and humble deference venture to suggest that my approach to this vital question would not be out of place in the realm of cricket policy and politics. My general rule has always been to pick the youngster, and, having picked him (unless you have no confidence in yourself), have faith in him; don't expect him to "deliver the goods" straight away, but give him a chance to adjust and gear his gifts to his new and rather isolated position. If he is at all conscious that after an initial failure he is likely to be dropped, that failure is almost a foregone conclusion.

For ten years I have had ample reward in this patient encouragement of truly gifted youngsters, and since the future depends on them I feel it a vital question whether they are destined to be Fools or Gods.

In Music and in Cricket I feel there is still a need of great personalities, not only for the good of both these arts, but for the inspiration and enthusiasm they engender in the younger generations that are to follow.

At present there seems to be a shortage of these in both fields, but in Keith Miller, however, is one of the most colourful personalities the cricket world has ever seen.

John Barbirolli[58]'.

'The Present and Future'[59]

'Being by nature an energetic and restless person, my long period of enforced rest was the most difficult thing I have ever had to face. At first I was so depressed that even my nightly ration of sleep deserted me; but a gradual realization that I can deem myself fortunate to begin work at the end of November after such a serious operation is making things easier.

Part One

And, I must confess, I have not been *entirely* inactive. I underwent the operation on a Friday, and by the Monday a pile of scores and centenary folders was by my bedside!

But, by the nature of things, progress was extremely slow and painful. It was some time before I listened to any music, the longest period without it since I was a very small child. This may surprise some people, but the fact is that I have always been averse to listening to music except when fully concentrating, and therefore find it tiring as yet, In any case, here was a wonderful opportunity to just lie back and think.

It has enabled me, too, to achieve a great ambition of mine: for a long time I have been wanting to begin a serious and exhaustive study of the mighty *St. Matthew Passion* (I am the proud possessor of a first edition of the Bach Gesellschaft full score, presented to me by me dear friends of the Hallé Choir on the occasion of my fiftieth birthday and Knighthood).[60] Surrounded by various editions, literature on the subject – Schweitzer, Parry and Sandford Terry are an inspiring mine of elucidation and information on it – and with a special invalid music stand over my bed, it is the most wonderful way of whiling the weary hours away. Perhaps, who knows, and without making any promises, I shall be ready to give a *complete* performance of the work in 1959. My ideal would be to give the first part on Holy Thursday evening, and the second on Good Friday afternoon.

My operation was really the culmination of a long period of ill-health, but I am sure, and so are my doctors, that when I have recovered fully from this I shall be fitter than I have been for a long time. As will be known, I am going to Italy to convalesce. As some may be aware, I am of Venetian ancestry and still, indeed, speak the Venetian dialect. Lady Barbirolli and I will go to the district known as the Veneto, stay with our cousins in Rovigo and visit at our leisure Padua (where my father was born, and which contains the oldest university in Europe, if not the world),[61] Verona, Vincenza and, of course, my beloved Venice.

I am being allowed to start conducting again about November 20th, when I have concerts in Italy booked a year ago and for which dates guest conductors had already been engaged for the Hallé.[62] I return to my beloved orchestra for our annual performances of *Messiah.*

I shall never forget the kindness, concern and affection expressed on my behalf by friends known and unknown in all parts of the world, during these weeks. It has been an overwhelming experience, and I wish, most sincerely, to thank you all'.

Glorious John

'Music and Cricket'[63]

'On his first walk around the West End, in the 1890's [*sic*], armed with his Italian-English dictionary, my father was particularly intrigued by the street-corner newsboys and their placards. As he made his way from Piccadilly to Leicester Square, however, he noticed that each placard carried the same inscription and it seemed to him that he should consult his dictionary. Imagine the feelings of one who had just uprooted himself and family from the comparative security of his native Italy, when he read – "*England Collapses*". It was many years before he recovered from this shock and discovered that a sovereign was still worth a sovereign.

As a schoolboy, I hardly covered myself with glory on the cricket field, although I developed a passion for a game which completely mystified my parents when they came to watch. But apart from my lack of talent, I encountered a further difficulty, namely, that scorers found it difficult to spell correctly the name "Barbirolli". I experimented with a change of name – Bob O'Reilly[64] – only to find that Irishmen were considered to be quite beyond the pale where cricket was concerned.

My grandfather came to live with us in London, and taught me the Venetian dialect which was his only language. I, in turn, tried to interest him in cricket and actually took him to the Oval on one occasion. His response was to tell me that he had always considered Englishmen to be lunatics and he had now been finally convinced of it. I, on the other hand, was very proud of my Anglicisation to the extent that I was able to drop the aspirate just as well as my cockney schoolchums and to refer to 'Obbs, 'Itch and 'Ayward. I became, and indeed remain, a great Surrey fan.

In 1926, I got my first chance to conduct opera. As is now history, England that year had a chance for the first time since the war to regain the Ashes. The first days of the final Test coincided with my opera rehearsals. Between chunks of Puccini, I received news of the great stand Hobbs and Sutcliffe (probably their greatest), which put England in with a good chance. When the fateful morning arrived for Wilfred Rhodes (recalled in his 50th year) to try his luck at mowing down the Aussies, the whole thing was too much for me. Instead of making my way to the final rehearsal, I sneaked off to the Oval. Rhodes may have bowled well, but he was assisted by a force which he did not know about until I first met him twenty-five years later. Much of the demolition of the Aussies can be attributed to my grandfather, who, in teaching me Venetian, had seen to it that I had a complete repertoire of the strange imprecations known only to Venice. As each Aussie came out

Part One

to bat, I muttered these imprecations over and over until he arrived at the wicket. The combination of Rhodes and myself was irresistible and the day was finally won for England.

After 1926, I had little chance to watch cricket, although I still remained an ardent devotee. As conductor of the New York Philharmonic [-Symphony] Orchestra from 1936-1943, I tried occasionally to interest the Americans in my passion. But great a country as is the United States, the American lack of interest in cricket is to me a sign of immaturity. However, when I came home in 1943 to re-form the Hallé Orchestra, I was able to live a full life again – a life without cricket or music is very dull indeed. This was not because I was able to attend County and Test Matches (my conducting duties generally prevented this), but because my own musicians formed a team, and over a period of years played many charity games on their travels. It is well known that Mr. Stephen Potter invented Gamesmanship, but I sometimes wonder whether my Hallé cricketers acted as his advisers where cricket was concerned. Their favourite ploy was to hold a conference with the opposing team prior to the match to explain how a cricket ball, flying off a hard surface could, by splitting a finger and damaging a mouth, destroy for ever the livelihood of a violinist or wind player. It was then agreed that the groundsman should be instructed to saturate the pitch just before the match and whichever captain won the toss, the Hallé Orchestra, in the interests of their safety, should bat first. In this way, the Hallé players were able to get a few runs on the board (let us face it, even a musician can score runs when the ball is bouncing only four inches high). If the sun was shining, the pitch would, of course, gradually dry up and the opposing team went in to bat, one of my horn players and a double bass player, both fast bowlers of reasonable ability, would let fly at the bemused opposition. When all else failed (as it frequently did, despite this chicanery) a secret weapon would be produced. A photograph of this weapon can be seen facing page 177 of this book.[65]

I think that I have a reasonable knowledge of the laws of cricket and that I am qualified to act as umpire in friendly matches. In the Hallé matches, however, it was of course, necessary to add one or two new rules. For instance, no Hallé batsman could ever be given out l.b.w., and should he be bowled out, I was under instruction to shout, somewhat belatedly, "No ball". When the opposition were getting on top, it was customary for our bowler occasionally to bowl one too wide of the wicket for the batsman to get at it, and there was always a look of amazement on the batsman's face when, instead of seeing a wide being signalled, he found an up-raised finger

33

signifying that he had been caught behind the wicket.

I have always been interested in the affinity between cricket and music. There are a few musicians who are not devotees of the game. I am told that when a conductor walks out to the rostrum to begin a concert, the atmosphere is similar to that of the famous batsman walking out to the wicket. It has always occurred to me, however, that there is one vital difference. Once a conductor is on the rostrum he is there willy-nilly for at least two hours. Even the greatest of batsmen, however, occasionally experience the dismal trek back after a few fleeting seconds before the public, glancing ruefully at the scoreboard as the scorer hangs up the dreaded sign – "Last man – 0".

I wonder if conductors would benefit from an occasional removal to the artist's room after a bad start to Beethoven No. 5 ?'.

'Christmas'[66]

'The Reverend Austen Williams has done me the honour of asking me to write something for the Christmas Matinee brochure.

Apart from the desire to contribute – however unworthily – to so wholly admirable a cause, a reason which made me say "yes" when commonsense said "you really haven't the time" (I am writing this in a few moments of peace flying over the Atlantic) – is that the Festival of Christmas has become such a puzzling and uncomfortable one in certain ways, and I really fell I would like to say a word about it. Has it not become a bit of a financial racket? And, although it is by no means a recent innovation, I have always rebelled against the abbreviation *Xmas*, when one has the privilege of writing the word *Christmas*.

When I was a small boy the Festival meant all the excitement of the pre-Christmas shopping with Mummy in the Berwick market, the auctioning of turkeys, and the Soho shops full of special sausages, cakes and delicacies – for we were essentially a Latin family. My father was Italian and my mother French, so our Christmas dinner was a magnificent compromise of Latin and French customs. Another abiding memory, the kerbside sellers of little toys and decorations, all at a penny or twopence. We were not poor, but all these Christmas extras were a *treat*. But above all, Christmas in those days was a religious and family festival, and in the main I hope and like to think it has remained so. For us there was the thrill of the Midnight Mass, the sense borne upon us that we were participating in great event.

Part One

I travel a great deal, but whenever possible my wife and I plot to be *home* for Christmas, and by home we mean with our families. Sometimes we have not managed it, and then in some places we have found a joyous humility and understanding of the Holy Day – and I mean really joyous. In others we have found an insane orgy of spending and dissipation which has sickened us. On the last occasion that we were separated from our families, we found ourselves – through musical commitments – in a great metropolis. The atmosphere could hardly be called Christian though it was all done in the name of Christmas. We received invitations galore but steadfastly refused them all. Not having the stomach to face organised revelry in hotels and restaurants, we had a very happy Christmas Day: Midnight Mass and then a Christmas Dinner out of tins in our locked hotel bedroom (for fear of being found out!) We felt very happy, close to each other and our far distant families, and not unmindful of the Glory of this Day'.

Interview with Michael Kennedy: 'My Twenty Years with the Hallé'[67]

'How many times had you conducted the Hallé before you became it full-time chief?
Only twice. The first time was in January 1933 while Sir Hamilton Harty was in America, and the second was exactly a year later when I deputised for Elgar in a programme of his own works because he was ill – in fact he died a month later. I was then conductor of the Scottish Orchestra where I remained until I was invited to go to the New York Philharmonic in 1936.

Anyone in Manchester aged thirty or under must regard you as a established part of the scene and perhaps does not know how you came to be there in the first place. To a slightly older generation it is a famous story which you would perhaps like to relate?
I confess it had not occurred to me that there must be many of my young and faithful followers who regard me as part of the "establishment" and yet are unaware of the exciting and almost dramatic element in the story of my coming to Manchester to reconstruct the Hallé, which with *The Guardian* (in *that* order G[eorge] B[ernard] S[haw] liked to say) had made the name of Manchester famous throughout the world. In full detail it is rather a long story but some essentials are necessary for a full comprehension of the situation. At the outbreak of war in 1939 the Hallé and the BBC worked

closely together and the BBC Northern Orchestra consisted of Hallé players. If this arrangement had not existed, the Hallé might have gone out of existence. But with the "boom" in music in wartime it soon became obvious that the Hallé was having to refuse engagements because so many of its players had BBC commitments. So eventually that remarkable and charming man the late Philip Godlee, chairman of the Hallé Concerts Society, decided to break with the BBC, to establish the orchestra for the first time in its history on a yearly contract basis and to engage a permanent conductor, something it had not had since Hamilton Harty left in 1933. Philip always said that he thought of my name as he lay waiting for his early morning cup of tea to arrive. He rang up R. J. Forbes, then the Principal of the Royal Manchester College of Music, who knew me, and without telling the rest of the committee, Forbes cabled to me in New York asking if I would be interested in the post. A visit to Britain in 1942, when I came over in a convoy which was subject to U-boat attacks, had made me long to return to my home country. So this telegram was the chance I was waiting for although I don't think that at the time I had much time to speculate on what this call might mean to my future life.

Were you surprised, when you arrived in Manchester, by what you found?
I can only answer "By God, yes". I had been led to believe I would find an orchestra of 70 or so and I found 26. I arrived on 2nd June, the first concert was booked for 5th July, so I had a month to find and train players at a time when many of the best were in the Services. Some of those to whom I gave auditions and then engaged had never played in a professional orchestra. Forbes had written "There are sufficient funds available in the form of guarantees to make the venture a sound one". At a committee meeting soon after we began when I inquired what the reserves were I was told there were enough for two weeks unless we earned the rest. Earn it we did, as there was no kind of subsidy in those days. I also remember soon after my arrival in London finding myself at some sort of cocktail party at Novello's at which representatives of various London orchestras were present. Discussing the task I had been entrusted with, their only comment was "The thing's impossible". I like the impossible. Perhaps that is why I am still there.

Nevertheless you knocked those inexperienced players into shape and the orchestra won widespread critical acclaim. What do chiefly remember about that first Bradford concert?
The acrimonious arguments that went on in the Northern Press when I

Part One

refused to subscribe to what I can only describe as the "piano racket" that was prevalent at the time. It seemed decreed then that no orchestral concert was possible without a piano soloist playing one of three concertos – Grieg's, Rachmaninov's second and Tchaikovsky's first, though I believe Beethoven's fifth and Schumann's were allowed to infiltrate insidiously. It was something of a dope racket. How well I recall Godlee and Forbes meeting me on arrival at Manchester on a rather murky day and driving me in all haste to the Midland Hotel so that I shouldn't be too depressed by the prevailing conditions and while we were awaiting the arrival of the inevitable tea, hearing the rather ominous mutterings of "You tell him"; "No, *you* tell him". I sensed trouble somewhere and finally one of them blurted that for the Bradford week of concerts six, or it may have been five, pianist had been engaged, including, I remember, Myra Hess, Moiseiwitsch and Clifford Curzon. I was a fiery young man in those days and my Italian blood leapt to the surface: "If I was enticed back from the USA to become a piano concerto accompanist, I would return immediately to a more civilised musical atmosphere, etc., etc., etc". I agreed to retain one pianist and the sole survivor was my old friend Clifford Curzon and when it came to the centenary concert in 1958 I asked him to be the soloist on that great evening as a memento of that first occasion. I cannot forbear to add, however, that such was the "power of the pianist" at that epoch neither Forbes nor Godlee could steel themselves to announce this catastrophic news to Mrs. Tillett (of Ibbs and Tillett)[68] so it was left to the Maestro, who accomplished his mission with particular pleasure. The upshot was that, as far as J.B. was concerned, the piano racket was broken; and, to be serious for a moment, a great benefit to the financial and artistic future of what I will call my Hallé. Ninety-nine per cent of my out-of-town concerts with the Hallé are without soloist. The audience come to hear the orchestra and the music. Incidentally, the first concert of the new "Hallé" coincided with the fourth anniversary of my marriage to Evelyn Rothwell, a good omen, for both institutions are still sturdily surviving.

When the war ended and musical life in this country developed on a hitherto unprecedented scale, it soon became apparent that municipal financial aid would have to be forthcoming if orchestras were to survive. Many battles were fought, especially in Manchester. What are your views on this subject?
I am confident that it is now an established principle in town halls that financial support for the symphony orchestras of the great cities of this country is essential. My "battles" in Manchester were because it had always

Glorious John

appeared to me that my orchestra was penalised for being so successful with the public. The more we earned ourselves the less we received by way of financial support – support that would have enabled me to enlarge the orchestra at that time and create better conditions for the players. Until only recently the funds generally available for music were inadequate and inequitably distributed. Slowly but surely progress has been made, and, though my own city has always given me less financial support than other cities offer their orchestras, they have never failed to give a sympathetic hearing to our pleas, and to be conscious of our problems, and in the practical terms of actual money their contributions to our funds now has never been so high. In my years with the Hallé great progress has been made. There still remain many things to be done, but I think I can look forward to the future with confidence.

The Hallé, of course is not a municipal orchestra. It is run by a private committee in trust, as it were, for the spirit of Sir Charles Hallé. Do you think the Hallé would benefit if it became a municipal orchestra, the Manchester Philharmonic?
Definitely NO, and I would always advise – and indeed I deem it absolutely essential for its confirmed greatness and growth – that it should retain it independence as a society.

How deeply have financial considerations affected your programme policy? In other words, are there particular works which you have wanted to conduct but which you have had to exclude because of the box-office risk involved?
Perhaps fewer than one would think, though of course we have taken box-office risks during these years that have since paid dividends, but this I will only do with works which I believe to be great or of considerable merit, such as the Berg violin concerto. When I first took the Hallé round the country, Debussy's *La Mer*, Ravel's *Daphnis and Chloë* etc. were still connoisseur pieces to the general public. Now they are Sunday "populars", not only in Manchester but in all places we visit. I can play the big Elgar works that were considered box-office "death" in the 1930s and after. I have risked quite a bit on Walton. The critics, who live day in and day out with music often forget that to the man who pays for his ticket a concert is not just another job to do, have decided that Walton is old-fashioned, but to the ordinary concert-goer in Middlesbrough or Preston he is a bit of a risk, a "modern". Britten since the *Sinfonia da Requiem* doesn't seem interested in the orchestra *per se*. All these things must be looked at in historical

Part One

perspective. It was quite something when I did complete cycles of the Sibelius and Vaughan Williams symphonies. All in all, I think we in Britain are the most catholic-minded musical public in the world to-day. People are often surprised when I tell them how little of Dvorak (apart from the New World) is known outside his own country and England. Just over a year ago I gave the first public performance in Berlin of Dvorak's D minor symphony (No. 2 or No. 7, whichever numbering you prefer). None of the orchestra had played it, and did they love it! And the public went wild. What a *novelty* for them! But publicity ventures of the Musica Viva type are a waste of public money, for they lead nowhere and have already died what I would call a timely death.[69] Reference to the Sibelius and the Vaughan Williams cycles brings to mind the critical reaction that has consigned these two great men to limbo – or thinks it has – and yet when I have begun to revive such things as the Vaughan Williams 5th symphony it was obvious that this great benediction in music *effortlessly* spread its power and magic without the aid of unintelligible and meaningless verbiage in expensive periodicals. The same with Sibelius, and that other great composer so condemned to-day for his lusciousness etc. Richard Strauss. I remember so well the denigration that started at once in certain circles when he died fifteen years ago. But it is the same in literature. Galsworthy might have been a novelette writer to judge from some of the obituaries, but was he not as great a chronicler of his times as Dickens was of his? The only answer to this sort of thing is in the lines from *Titus Andronicus*:

      The eagle suffers little birds to sing
      And is not mindful what they mean thereby.

Do you think that a permanent conductorship imposes too much of a dictatorship of personal taste on a provincial city which relies on one orchestra for its series of concerts and has not, like London, a wide range of choice?
I don't see how I can answer this without sounding conceited so I will just have to take that risk in the cause of honesty. My general reply is "No", though of course it depends greatly on the quality and catholicity of taste of the permanent man. There can be no great orchestra, with a *style* of its own, unless it has a regular conductor of high quality both as a teacher and as an interpreter, and by style I mean not only a particular characteristic, but a suppleness and variety of style that can attune itself to music of all kinds and periods. The late Ernest Newman often referred to my quality as a string player which enabled me to produce certain "stylistic" sounds from an orchestra. The Hallé are even taught to play with different kinds

Glorious John

of vibrato for different kinds of music (every first-class player should be equipped with this quality). There are, of course, also different types of portamenti, though few are aware of these, and there is also the important question of *no* vibrato and *no* portamento which in any case must be used only to stress certain melodic and emotional elements, as Mahler well knew. I cherish a letter from Stokowski, who attended a Hallé concert and wrote to me that he considered the Hallé *one* of the great orchestras of the world (there is no greatest anything) because it had such a variety of style. This is a long way from the tale I was told by old Charles Collier, who played the harp for me in Manchester when he was over 80 and had played in the first performance of Elgar's *Gerontius*. He remembered that at Birmingham in the early 1900s, when Sarasate was playing Beethoven's violin concerto, he insisted on the drum notes which open the work being in the right key. This was apparently revolutionary, and Charlie remembered the timpanist muttering darkly afterwards "Tuning the timps! What will they want next?" As for the dictatorship of personal taste, I don't think Manchester has been too unfortunate in having a conductor who has been acknowledged as a conductor of opera, a considerable interpreter of the German classics, the French impressionists, who started conducting Berg in the mid-1920s, who has made a special study of Elgar, Bruckner, Rubbra, Bach's *St. Matthew Passion*, Handel, who gave the first performance of Britten's *Sinfonia da Requiem* and violin concerto, and of Fricker's first symphony and the symphonies of John Gardiner and Arthur Benjamin.[70] I can't think that such a man is a great menace to the musical development of a city's public. As regards London's "wide choice", apart from the BBC Symphony which happily for us all can afford certain things we can't, I don't think there is much that London hears that Manchester doesn't. And Manchester doesn't get a choice of two 1812s every week-end!

Since 1958 you have reduced your engagements with the Hallé and twice a season in Manchester you are away in Houston, Texas, for a six-week period. This has been criticized on the ground that the orchestral standard deteriorates in your absence because there is no regular conductor to maintain the quality. What are you views about this?

People are rather inconsistent. If I'm there all the time it's dictatorship of taste; if I'm away, that's wrong too. The difficulty is to find a regular conductor for the absentee period who quite frankly is of real class and would be willing to accept this rôle. They don't grow on trees. The Hallé management and I always try to get the very best guest conductors but

Part One

these are usually with their own orchestras and not available at the time we want them. I have tried time after time for [Carlo Maria] Guilini and [Nino] Sanzogno but they are fully committed elsewhere. One thing I must point out as I did after similar criticism in Houston. In Manchester and Texas I conduct more concerts with my own orchestras than does any other permanent conductor of international status. This has been checked on the basis on an average of the number of concerts in the series. When I conduct other famous European orchestras it adds to Hallé prestige and has led to invitations to the Hallé for foreign tours, such as our recent Scandinavian tour. In this way the Hallé can justify its claim to be an international orchestra. In any case, up to 1958 I always went away for several weeks during the season.

Not everyone regards Manchester as the haven where they would be. When you were made a Freeman you called yourself a "Franco-Italian-Cockney-Mancunian". Why have you been happy to stay here for a third of your lifetime?
This is not so difficult to answer as some people might think. I suppose some may be right who regard me as a fanatic as far as music is concerned. From the age of 7 or 8 it absorbed all my time and become even more absorbing. For instance to feel, after conducting it for 30 years, that you begin to understand, and can communicate to others, something of the might of Beethoven's 9th is to feel life is worth living. And it seems to me Manchester must be good for fanatics i.e. workers who can be oblivious of surroundings provided they are content in their work, for think of the scientists, doctors and journalists that Manchester has nurtured. But another very potent factor – one which sophisticated people may scoff at, but which nonetheless exists – is the loyalty and affection that the people of that great city and all over Lancashire have shown me. It can all be summed up in what I said to Evelyn at Belle Vue after I had refused the offer of another conductorship: "If I had accepted, I could never have faced these people again".

There must also be disappointments, things which you wish had been different or had been left undone.
Curiously enough, no. There is nothing left that rankles, or troubles the conscience, though of course minor ones there must have been.

What are your outstanding musical memories of your 20 years with the Hallé?
The first time I conducted *Messiah* and the *St. Matthew Passion*. Performances

Glorious John

of *Gerontius* and of Chausson's *Poème de l'amour et de la mer* with Kathleen Ferrier. The centenary concert. The night I conducted Elgar's second symphony in memory of Philip Godlee after speaking at his Memorial Service earlier in the day – the symphony might have been written for him, it was so appropriate. What a friend he was. And the performance at Belle Vue of Verdi's Requiem in memory of Ginette Neveu when the rain beating on the roof, far from being a distraction, added an element to the already elemental music.

For one who began his career in opera, it must be frustrating that Manchester and the North have no established operatic life. The North produces great singers, yet its chief operatic ventures are now by students. Have you ever thought you would like to develop a Covent Garden of the North, based on Manchester, with the Hallé in the pit?

It has been a dream of mine for years, though the vision of the idealist must be seared by practicability. It almost breaks my heart to hear the words "with the Hallé in the pit" for there is no pit in Manchester. When I first appeared in Manchester as a conductor with the B[ritish] N[ational] O[pera] C[ompany] in 1926 there was a pit at the Opera House which held 50 players or so, but even that modest "hole" which meant having percussion and brass protruding from the stage boxes has been filled up or so greatly reduced that the Covent Garden company removed to the Palace Theatre where, even on a level, they play with a much smaller orchestra than that which appears at the Garden although the taxpayers of Manchester maker their contribution to the great subsidies which produce such splendid sights and sounds – which alas have never been seen or heard by Mancunians and which we now know we shall never see as the Covent Garden no longer tours. In Houston, the Music Hall, an all-purpose theatre, has a pit holding 75 players which can be used at various levels and can go as deep as the Bayreuth pit. Two short seasons of all the great operas, including Wagner and Strauss, are given ever year, with the Houston Symphony in the pit and of course heavily subsidized by local opera enthusiasts. So far, my time-limit at Houston has not allowed me to accept invitations to conduct some of these. Have Manchester and other provincial cities in Britain realized that they have never heard an opera with a full-scale opera orchestra (by which I mean an orchestra of the size designated by the composer) in a properly constructed orchestral pit?

Part One

Do you intend to stay another 20 years with the Hallé?
I hope so, for the late 70s and the early 80s seems to be regarded as a very promising age for a conductor these days and I am only 63!

Extracts from 'The Young Sir John Talking – on the eve of his 65th birthday'[71]

'Sixty-five? That's no great age these days. It's trite but true to say you are as old as you feel, and musically speaking, I feel no different than I did 30 years ago... Music is a tremendously revitalising thing, you know. If I ever feel a bit tired I soon revive when I start conducting. You have only to ask the orchestra about that ... People often ask me how to stay young and my answer is hard work. If you have an extremely arduous responsible and dedicated job like mine, and a job you love, it's the most wonderful thing in the world for keeping young. When I was in Texas I met four of the American astronauts. Awfully nice lads. Scott Carpenter said to me: "After seeing you tonight I might introduce a conductor's course into the space training curriculum to keep our boys fit. ...I am a traditionalist and I love [Manchester]. I have been with the Hallé for 21 years and enjoy the family atmosphere. By that I mean succeeding generations of families have come to listen to the orchestra since its inception. Manchester is an invigorating place in which to work. It is a city of great traditions and the tremendous loyalty of the audiences here is something I value greatly. ... [I will celebrate my birthday in] the best possible way – by a rehearsal and concert with my Hallé. I'm giving myself a birthday present by playing Elgar's First Symphony.[72] It is one of the works I love and it was first played by the Hallé on December 3 1908'.

'The Maestro Remembers...'[73]

'If old Scrooge were alive today, his thoughts and feelings about Christmas could hardly be expressed better than in that glorious, one-word outburst of his – humbug! Maybe it is because I'm getting older, but the good, old-fashioned Christmas seems to have resolved into an orgy of over-spending, drinking and dangerous driving! Frankly, I find it hurtful that this beautiful festival should be turned into a vast exploitation of the seamy side of some people's characters.

Glorious John

To me Christmas has always been essentially a religious festival; above all, a time for family reunions and the personal joys which such things bring. Some of my happiest recollections are of the Christmases of my boyhood in London. How well I remember walking through the exciting bustle of Holborn with my mother – she always took me to Gamages to choose toys and, of course, meet Father Christmas. It was all wonderful: the dazzling lights, the great array of cockney characters in the street, stretching along the kerb and offering, in their own inimitable fashion, every kind of toy. It was quite extraordinary what you could buy for a penny or two-pence in those days – toys which would cost many shillings now and not be half so attractive.

But, apart from all the excitement of those expeditions, I suppose it is not unnatural to connect Christmas with feasting; and, although my parents had lived in England for many years, they always insisted on a traditional Italian dinner on Christmas Day. Mind you, in true 'when in Rome' fashion, we always tacked good old English Christmas pudding and mince pies onto the many continental delicacies. We used to start this great Christmas banquet of ours with cappelletti, a kind of ravioli, made in the shape of little hats to give it the necessary touch of gaiety. These were filled with bits of chicken and veal boiled in chicken broth. Then followed zampone, a pork sausage, highly spiced, and made in the shape of a pig's foot, served with a large piece of boiled beef and spinach. Finally, we had to find room for turkey, Christmas pudding and mince pies. And I can assure you my mother was liberal with the brandy in the pudding – she could afford to be lavish, too, for a bottle of brandy cost a mere 2s. 3d. in those days.

But it was the shopping for all those delicacies which was so exciting and fascinating. It was a job in which my father revelled. It gave him a happy feeling of nostalgia for his native country to go shopping in Soho; for a walk down Old Compton Street was like taking a trip along an Italian street – and, I'm glad to say, it still is.

Father always took me with him on these excursions. Many of the traders knew him and after the usual exchange of greetings – always in Italian – he would ask about the varying qualities of the foods they had to offer. Whereupon, they would invite *Caro Professore* to have a taste. As a result, he would have a good lunch just buying the hors d'oeuvres!

In those days, London was largely Georgian and when I was about six or seven we lived in pleasant old Georgian house in Grenville Street, close to Russell Square. Around the corner lived Lionel Monkton[74] [*sic*], who wrote, "The Quaker Girl". I used to see him going out in the morning, cutting quite

Part One

a figure as he strode majestically along the street in his top hat and frock coat.

Music has always had a place of great importance and influence in our family record. Both my grandfather and father shared the first desk of the violins at the old Empire Theatre in Leicester Square, from where Dad later migrated next door to the old Queen's Hotel. Those were the days of nine-string bands and the hotel was a favourite calling place for actors who used to enjoy the operatic selections which my father and his fellows played. The hotel was run by the firm of Nicholson's who are still renowned for their gin. A bottle of this spirit in those days cost 1s. 9d. and Nicholson's Special Scotch was 1s. 9d. a bottle! They called it "N.S.S."; but the English members of my father's orchestra always used to say it, "Never Saw Scotland"; and the Italian members christened it, *Nostro Santo Signore* – Our Blessed Lord. What generosity flowed from the Nicholson firm! Every Christmas Eve they presented my father with a pheasant, turkey and a bottle each of scotch, gin and port, which he promptly brought home by hansom cab to a very excited family.

And then there was the joy of going to the midnight mass on Christmas Eve. It was celebrated at the French church in Leicester Square – destroyed during the war but since rebuilt. This church, in fact, was my first school, a kind of kindergarten which I began to attend when I was about five, journeying there by horse bus – the old green bus which plied between King's Cross and Victoria.

It sounds almost incredible today, but such was the leisure of the time that my father and grandfather (who always saw my sister and myself safely on the bus) would stand on the step for a few minutes to give a cigar to the conductor and driver and exchange pleasantries with them before we went off on our journey.

So much then for Christmas at home. There have been occasions when my music engagements have taken me out of the country at Christmas. And for me it was then always rather sad and nostalgic – I never really felt like celebrating. Generally we had a concert on Christmas Day, for which I was very relieved since it gave me something to think about and do.

Last Christmas I was in Belgrade.[75] When I arrived there, I found that they still abide by the Orthodox Calendar, so that *my* Christmas Day wasn't theirs. But thanks to the kindness and understanding of the people, I was able to fulfil my wish of going to a church on my Christmas Day – even though we didn't finish rehearsing until eleven o'clock that night.

Hearing about my desire, the good people who were arranging the concert got in touch with the priest of a local church. He met me there half-an-hour later and, in the stillness and peace of the night we knelt and prayed together – close to a manger depicting the Nativity scene. It was all very wonderful and made me so happy.

Maybe I'm sentimental, but that is what Christmas has always meant to me, as indeed I think it does to millions of people, especially families with young children.

In England, Christmas is always, of course, associated with the Messiah – the great oratorio which, through the years, has never lost its appeal in city, town, village hall, or churches throughout the country. Indeed Messiah means much more to the people of this country at Christmas time than it does anywhere else in the world. A few years ago, I was conducting the famous Dublin Choir of Our Lady in Italy. We were appearing at the Sacred Umbrian Festival which specialises particularly in choral work and is held at Perugia, not far from Florence. We gave the Dream of Gerontius and the Messiah. It was the first time they heard Messiah and the impact it had on the audience was unforgettable; it hit them like a thunderbolt!

Later, we went on to Rome, and there came one of the most memorable occasions of my life – a special performance we gave before Pope Pius XII.[76] He was on holiday at his lovely palace, the Castel Gandolfo, and there the choir from Dublin sang the whole of the first part of the Dream of Gerontius. Afterwards His Holiness and I chatted together. "*Figlio mio,*" he said, "*questo e un capo lavoro sublime.*" "My son, this is a sublime masterpiece." He was a great lover of music, had a fine collection of records, and few people knew that, as a young man, he played the violin.

The Pope had been ill, suffering from a terrible hiccough complaint. Two days after our performance he had a recurrence of the affliction and ten days later, died. The last live music he had heard was the voices of a Dublin choir singing, "Go Forth Christian Soul", which ends the first part of "The Dream", I sometimes think what a sombre joy it would give Elgar and Newman to have known this.

In England, it has become a tradition that I conduct the Hallé and Sheffield Choirs in Messiah. And they always combine to give a great performance at Belle Vue, Manchester.

During the war years, the place was never hot and to rehearse there in freezing temperatures was always a perishing experience. When peace came, the circus returned to Belle Vue and I remember going there shortly before Christmas to rehearse; I was agreeably surprised to find the place beautifully warm. To an official who happened to be passing down a

Part One

corridor at the back of the King's Hall I remarked that it was most kind and considerate of the management to get the place so cosy and warm. "Well, you see, sir," he answered, "we've some very valuable animals here!"

I could not resist replying: "You're not referring to the members of my orchestra by any chance!"

It was after one performance of Messiah at Belle Vue that I met the Russian composer Kabalevsky. He had come over here on a mission to study manuscripts and find out all he could about the English way of life in concert halls. After the performance, we talked together in French.

"Do you know, I must tell you, my dear master," he said to me, "this is the most profoundly moving thing I have ever seen and heard in this country. This wonderful chorus of amateurs, some of them workpeople, and then this marvellous audience – children, grown-ups, people of all kinds... It has made the most profound impression on me of anything that I have seen since I have been in this country."

Meeting Kabalevsky and hearing him talk so movingly, and obviously sincerely, about this performance of Messiah, is a memory I shall treasure all my life, for it showed that great events, and great music, transcend all political faiths and ideologies'.

Speech given on the occasion of Barbirolli being made a Companion of Honour[77]

'-1-

A few years ago in 1961 to be exact, I celebrated my golden jubilee as a public performer by having at the tender age of eleven played my first concerto in our dearly beloved, and ever to be lamented, old Queen's Hall. I wonder sometimes if there ever has been such a medical monstrosity as a pre-natal prodigy, I must have been one.

-2-

My parents whether consciously or not cleverly contrived that I should enter the world [in the] month [of] great musicians. It seems extraordinary what a great importance the month of December seems to have assumed in my life.

December 2 My birthday and official opening of Queen's Hall (1893) Sibelius, Mascagni, Cesar Franck, Berlioz, Beethoven, Kodaly [sic], Scarlatti, Weber, Puccini, Casals, Tertis. Puerto Rico

December 16 1911 First Concerto

Glorious John

December 12 1927 First L.S.O. Casals. for Beecham
December 13 1950 R.P.S. Gold Medal. V-W Queen Mother
Tell story father on phone. Casals remark to orchestra. Learnt Elgar 2 in 48 hours and which started incidentally my long and happy association with H.M.V. Tell Gaisberg story. And again in December this august and famous body is graciously honouring me on my 70th birthday!

-3-

There must be many amongst you who either have to talk or have to listen to other people talk (I don't know which is the worse or more painful) as part of your professional lives, and these orgies of oratory in which we as a nation, seem to like to indulge, and perhaps part of the Spartan discipline we have imposed on ourselves, and which have enabled us to survive some fearsome national ordeals.

-4-

Any attempt at formal speech making on such an occasion is I think out of the question; and in its place I must ask you to bear with me and brace yourselves to listen to some random and perforce nostalgic ramblings.
It must be very difficult for anyone not of my generation or those born in the 20's [sic] to realise the magic, beauty and overwhelming personality of pre/14 London.

I suppose that having achieved such an early musical maturity and going about a great deal with my father I have retained a much more vivid recollection of pre/14 London than would a normal schoolboy of my age.

-5-

London in 1911. The year of the coronation George V. and the birth of my Evelyn. The siege of Sydney Street and Scott reached the Pole (recently flew over the other month on my way to Los Angeles).

To return to the Coronation of George V how well I remember the beauty and grace of the street decorat[i]ons and illuminations, and before that of course the death and funeral of Edward VII. (standing outside shop)

Mother and father of course had seen the Jubilee and funeral processions of Queen Victoria (of which mother retails [sic] a rather unfortunate anecdote (tell and add Sir Charles Wheeler[78] episode).

-6-

It was also to be the last year in which my beloved horse buses were to run regularly in the streets of London. Earlier my sister and I used to go to school (in Leicester Square) in the green bus which plied between King's Cross and Victoria. Tell about Nono and father – exchanging greetings. Smokes etc. Might introduce here Archbishop Lang, story Bishop of Stepney.

Part One

Recrimination. Greatly increased vocabulary.

My life about /07 to /11 was to me always full of interest for I was treated almost as a grown up; and there was always the treat of an occasional theatre (in the Gods, here I have had the thrills never to be recaptured in the comparative affluence of my later years such as queuing up and all the buskers (all for free) acrobats, and nigger minstrels – two hours of entertainment before the curtain went up. It was either in 07 or 08 during the original run of the "Merry Widow" that I had the supreeme [*sic*] good taste to fall in love with Lily Elsie (a Manchester girl) a taste in female loveliness I am happy to relate I have retained to this day.

-7-

Of course went to school – (story of becoming 'cellist) H.E.G.S. Tuck shop London School of Economics. Since when economics etc. Homework, 2 hours practise. Before acquiring my first really good private teacher, I remember a strange German who gave me a few lessons, of certainly a very original character. Book of folk songs, Blue Bells, change his socks. Main recollection was that I wished my very expressive rendering of the aforesaid Blue Bells would have conjured up some of the perfume of these Scottish blooms; to counteract the prevailing aroma distilled by my teacher's strange activities. A few whispered words dad. Saw him no more.

-8-

All my early life was lived in that charming part of London known as Bloomsbury. With its lovely peaceful squares and Georgian houses. Lionel Monckton and the whistler in the Belle of New York. Frank Lawton and dear adorable Evelyn Laye[79] (Boo) born in Southampton Row (50 yards – Senate House – Mus. Doc. Queen Mum. High class confectionary – only sign of snobbery in my beloved Meme.

We soon moved to Drury Lane and the house where I was destined to have my first cello lesson still stands. It is extraordinary how vivid some memories of that time remain. The little toy shop – cum – sweet shop, tobacconist, etc. (whips and masks) the old mo; Mogul Music Hall practically opposite to us, and of course the great theatres of Drury Lane and Covent Garden.

-9-

I suppose I became very theatre conscious at the tenderest of ages as my father and grandfather (1st desks at Empire and Golden Age of Adelon Genee [*sic*]) would take me to rehearsals there, where the first seeds were planted in me that I one day would be a conductor – tell white gloves etc – and I also think this early contact with the sights sounds and smells of a theatre

Glorious John

– particularly that most obnoxious and fascinating one of size, which cannot be dignified by the [name][80] of odours, implanted in me that instinct which was to serve me so well when I started my conducting career in the opera house.

-10-

Another enchantment of this period for this little boy of 5 or 6 was the long street of Long Acre itself which led to St. Martin's Lane. Here was the home of nearly all the great carriage makers in London and behind huge plate glass windows stood the most beautiful array of carriages of all sizes and orders; this was sometimes a favourite evening stroll of my Italian granny and I never lost the fascination of looking at these beautiful things. And of course in the same street and streets adjoining were the saddle and harness makers, which gave that quarter of London a very distinct leathery smell. A curious thing this, the smell of cities; Paris Venice and the lilac in Russell Square.

-11-

At about this time too came my first contacts with Covent Garden. First Falstaff in England[.] Counting the sovereigns. Pessina. Meme. Granny, etc. All keen opera goers and they heard the very first performance of Butterfly in London. Giachetti. Of course the gallery was the limit of the family purse and great occasions like this involved long queueings [*sic*] and I would with my sister at certain intervals (we lived literally a minute or two away) bring food to sustain the waiting and hungry enthusiasts, little thinking that only thirteen years later I was to enter that stage door myself as a 'cellist and a matter of 21 years later as a conductor.

-12-

I look back sometimes, and think of the great people music has enabled me to come into close contact with, names that even though I have not yet reached the age of (complete) decrepitude are already becoming legendary. As a very young student at the R.A.M. I had a prize presented me by a man whose godfather had been "The Iron Duke"[.] Corelli sonatas. As a little boy of 11 I remember playing at a charity concert in Aylesbury, and being introduced to Lord Roberts (and thinking we were about the same size) and a few years later playing some chamber music at Lady Cunard's where I also remember Churchill

-13-

Looking rather bored – when a man of exquisite courtesy and charm came and chatted to me. We had just played the Franck Quintet, and this led to ideas of an analogy, between the religious element in Franck's music and

Part One

that of Handel, of whose music my companion seemed to have an intimate knowledge and understanding. That man was Arthur Balfour.

-14-

Of course that was in my 'cellist days. And I think now of the first time I ever raised a baton. Tell story – scrubbing fatigue.[81] Suite de concert. But it was not until several years later that I was to raise a baton once again. Then there are all the great artists I have been associated with; an era that includes such figures as Ysaye [sic], Kreisler, Thibaud, Casals, Rachmaninov, Chaliapin, Gigli – and if I may be serious for a moment I would like to dwell on how much we seem to have lost in this age of super technical efficiency. Style, dignity, grace, charm –particularly grace and charm.

-15-

Difficult to describe[.] Lump in throat[.] Ask this of all great artists[.] Ysaya [sic][,] Fidelio[,] Kreisler [and] Thibaud[.] Artists['] sense of humour. Rachmaninoff [sic][,] Kussy. Especially orchestral players. Some great characters amongst them. Influenza germ. Diagholeff [sic] season. Answermet [sic] and his little song. Brilliant commentary Les Sir. Interludes. Only enlarged music hall orch. Terrifyed [sic] of what they might find on the stand. Great leader Catterall[82] and that fabled harpist Charlie, favourite of Richter, 52 years in Halle [sic] and played in the first performance of the Dream, and I had the sombre privilege of playing the Dream under Elgar himself the last time Elwess was destined to sing it. An imperishable memory for me. Charlie was very fond etc. Bad sight. C.B. Fry. Bring in N[eville].C[ardus]. here. Gratitude for his leading me to Mahler. And since we are actually talking of Mahler and the Dream, that gay and gallant spirit rises before us of my beloved Katie [Ferrier] with

-16-

whom I shared some of the most beautiful moments of my musical life. Shakespeare who always knew and understood everything has described with sheer perfection various aspects of her imperishable art. He might have been thinking of her when he penned the words in Henry V "there is witchcraft in your tips Kate"[.][83] I have rambled on, I hope not too inconsequently, of events and influences in my life and there are indeed times when I wonder if it is not all a wonderful dream, though a dream which in terms of sheer hard unrelenting application towards achievement even in terms of almost physical and mental exhaustion has seemed almost a nightmare. I owe a great debt to my dear father (a beautifully natural musician) for never letting me be exploited as a prodigy for gain, and to my great teacher Herbert Walenn, whose serene wisdom and unobtrusive

51

Glorious John

guidance of his rather fiery young pupil played a great part in my formative years.
-17-
To musicians of all grades and degrees of eminence with whom I have worked all over the world I owe a great debt of gratitude for their constant faith and affection and indeed think of them as my companions of honour'.

On being made Freeman of King's Lynn[84]

'Little did I dream when I came to Lynn for its second Festival in 1952 that I should one day stand within these venerable walls to have conferred on me the highest honour it is in the power of this historic borough to bestow on anyone, and when I realized that the only living "Freeman" are three "Freewomen", our beloved Queen Elizabeth the Queen Mother, Ruth the Lady Fermoy, and Mrs Alice Fisher, you can imagine how great is my pride[,] pleasure and gratitude for me to know that my name is to be added to the list of many other distinguished predecessors since 1292.

At one moment it seemed that I might be the first musician Freeman but one (fortunately or otherwise) has recently been discovered, a certain Richard Beck, in the year 1646-47.

When the Halle [*sic*] first played in Lynn, my principal cellist was Harold Beck, and he might even conceivably have been a remote descendant of your first musician Freeman. It is rather surprising that even such an illustrious figure as Charles Burney, who was organist at Lynn from 1751-1760? [*sic*] was never made a Freeman of the town, though the town does have a long history of music both sacred and secular, and supported by the town authorities.

This long history has, of recent years however[,] been greatly revivified and brought to new heights by our adorable and richly gifted Ruth Fermoy. This leads me to venture the thought that perhaps I might be considered the second musician Freeman but perhaps the 3rd Dr Burney to whom I referred just now and was generally referred to by Dr Johnson as "that clever dog", was also an author of great scholarship and experience and who knew all the great composers of his day by such as Handel, Gluck, Mozart and Haydn must have contributed greatly to the cultural life of the town during his stay. His daughter Fanny, the diarist, has left charming descriptions of her father's musical gatherings, [in one][85] of which she used the rather ambiguous phrase that "the performances were promiscuous". I wonder if

52

Part One

by any chance this might have been an 18th century allusion to what is I now believe known as the "permissive" society.

To return to "the clever dog", those who plead or long for what they call the authentic performances of 18th century music, might with advantage and perhaps amusement, peruse the three volumes of his revealing and fascinating journeys through Europe. In these you will find the rather astonishing statement that Mannheim possessed the most famous orchestra in Europe as it etc. I have grown to love Lynn, its treasures, its people, and its generosity to me personally as a musician, culminating in the very high honour that you are bestowing on me this very day. As you know, I am a Freeman of my adopted city of Manchester and a Freeman of the City of London, but I must qualify this by saying it is only in virtue of my being an Honorary Liveryman of the Worshipful Company of Dyers. But neither of these cities confer as far as I can gather, anything but great honour.

You however in your generosity go further in conferring not only great honour but considerable material advantages. I find that now I can save on my coal bill if I have one. Also if I had any children they could qualify for free education if they learnt Latin. If times become hard for me I could do one of two things. Either borrow on the gift of Mr John White, which I believe is £20 for 20 years without interest though I dont [*sic*] think that with my advancing years this would put too much strain on the gift. Finally and atractive [*sic*] of all I can have a stall at your most fascinating Lynn Mart with profit, for I pay only 6d a foot groundage instead of a shilling.

Meat balls.
Now if I may be serious for moment.
Your restoration activity gladdens the hearts of all those who love our fair land, (which is being done to my beloved London is a source of great sorrow to me, just as what Hitler did in destroying and desecrating so much of its beauty, can be and is a source of pride to many of us cockneys for it showed the innate dedication of our people to the cause of decency[,] dignity and honour. Would that such a spirit were alive today. But it will come back). And may the traditions and beauties of Lynn embedded in the Norfolk soil of its great past, continue to flourish in the soil of its so genial and comforting present, and may all our your activities whether architectural, artistic or otherwise, be consecrated to the continued loveliness and renown of this borough, of which I am so proud to be a Freeman.

Milano 12/10/69'

Glorious John

Extracts from 'Barbirolli at 70'[86]

'...If anyone thinks that because I'm seventy I'm going to sit on my arse in the garden and fade away like a dying fall, they don't know me. . .

What would I do? I wouldn't want to go on living if I were inactive. I'm never sleepy. I like the late nights, but when I lie in bed in the mornings, I'm working all the time. It's not the money that drives me. Gawd, the Government takes most of it. Music was my first, and still is, my greatest happiness.

I realised I have mellowed. This can be put down to age and experience. But seventy is a time to take a fresh look at life. You reach a stage at which, with God's help – yes, I am a religious man and often pray – you are eager to go forward, not to win more laurels but to get satisfaction from doing what you feel you must, and driving yourself to maintain standards without which there is no point in going on.

Nelson is one of my heroes. His life has always fascinated me. I am also a hero-worshipper of Lister and Irving. And ah, Frank Woolley,[87] the best batsman I ever saw – the Kreisler of the bat, I call him. These men, in their different ways, set out to achieve success. What they did was an example to be followed.

With me, it must be perfection, and nothing less. I can "kill" an orchestra, first rehearsing with the wind, then the brass and the strings, until I am satisfied.

And, I can be a taskmaster, a martinet. If one player errs, I can use good old Saxon language, although I am careful when lady players are about. If they're in an English orchestra, I lapse into Italian so that they shouldn't understand, yet they know what I am getting at. I will not tolerate music shoddily played.

In Italy, when I let go, it's something of a tirade, believe me. Italian scene shifters have often said, "Come hear the maestro, he's on top of his form"...

Mind you, I'm not a snob. I adore the jazz of Paul Whiteman and Duke Ellington, and Jerome Kern's compositions. One of my favourites is "Smoke gets in your eyes"...

As I move around I perform for audiences made up of parents who were children when they first came to my concerts. Now I am also playing for their kids. ...

In a way I miss a family of children. I love kids, but with the life Evelyn and I lead we wouldn't be able to give much time to them. I don't believe in

Part One

sending them to boarding schools from which they come home estranged from parents. Yet I am daddy to so many children, and that is a wonderful thought...

My dad lived long enough to see me conduct at Covent Garden... And my beloved mother, in her ninetieth year, saw the Queen Mother conferring on me the degree of Doctor of Music at London University'.

Glorious John

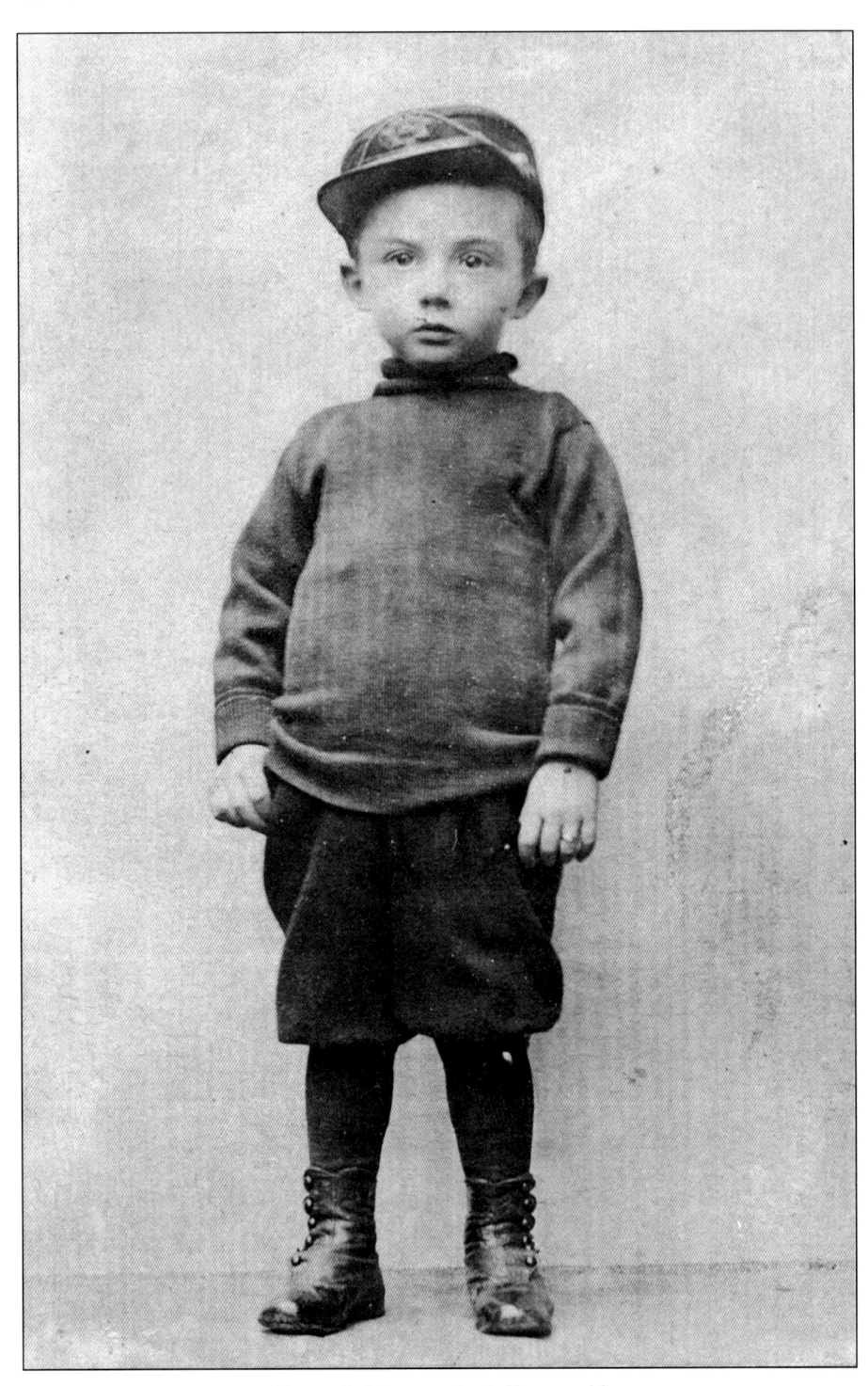

Giovanni at three-and-a-half years old

Giovanni with his sister Rosa, 1907

Glorious John

Barbirolli in 1924

Liverpool 1930

Covent Garden Opera Football Team, c. 1930

Glorious John

Percy Heming and Barbirolli, Cologne 1930

Evelyn, Paul Kilburn (viola player, Scottish Orchestra) and Barbirolli, 1937

Barbirolli and the New York Philharmonic-Symphony Orchestra, 1937

Barbirolli conducting the Vienna Philharmonic, Musikvereinsaal, 1948

Glorious John

PART TWO

On Composers and Compositions

'The N. G. S. Orchestra; Records'[88]

'I must first of all tender my apologies to the Editor and readers of The Gramophone for the non-appearance of my notes on recent orchestral records of the N[ational].G[ramophonic].S[ociety]. promised last month, but my work with the B.N.O.C. is of necessity very arduous during the first few weeks of a tour. I must also confess to being rather awed by the idea of having to write an "article" (this being my first essay in the art of journalism), and when, feeling tired at the end of a long day, I thought of making a start on the dread thing, the word "article" loomed large and terrible and completely shrivelled, so to speak, pencil and hand. However, the London Editor, though very kind and compassionate, is adamant, and so here goes, and I can only beg for your indulgence and hope these few notes may be of some little interest to those who possess the records.

The Haydn Symphony, though not one of the best known, surely contains some of the loveliest tunes in the Haydn Gallery, and the clear texture and rhythmic vitality of the music combine, I think, to make this a very happy choice for recording.

This particular symphony will also, for me, always have special memories, as it was the opening item of the concert at which I had the honour of deputizing for Sir Thomas Beecham with the London Symphony Orchestra. The memory can be pleasant, as happily Sir Thomas's indisposition, though painful, was not serious, and he was conducting again within a few days.

PURCELL SUITE
This is made up of various pieces taken from incidental music to plays, with the exception of the Adagio on the second record, which was originally a five-part Choral Anthem, written for the coronation of Charles II. I was first shown this piece by my friend Herbert Dawson (organist at St. Margaret's with Dr. Roper), was much struck by the originality and beauty of the

Glorious John

harmony, and immediately seized with the idea of transferring it to a string orchestra to savour to the full the richness of the harmonic scheme. It is but 16 bars in length, but whenever I have played it at concerts, it has never failed to make a deep impression. Another piece in the suite worthy of especial notice is the Hornpipe from "The Married Beau," on the following ground bass:

It is, perhaps, interesting to observe that the first four notes of the theme (1) make up the Bell Motif in "Parsifal." This may be of no particular importance, but I am personally always much struck by the similarity when I hear this piece.

MARCELLO, ALLEGRETTO

This little piece, which might be described as an elegant trifle, has a personal history which I may perhaps be allowed to relate. Many years ago (I was twelve at the time) I was laid low by a distressing and unpleasant complaint, which I believe is commonly known as "shingles," which brought in its train considerable feelings of depression; and for want of anything better or more exciting to do, one day I scored a movement of a little sonata by Marcello for violoncello (being something in the way of a 'cellist at the time) which I was rather fond of – afterwards laying it by and forgetting all about it. Three years ago, when I began conducting the Chenil String Orchestra, and had to make programme after programme of purely string music, I bethought myself of this arrangement, and wondered whether, if found, it might prove of any use. It eventually turned up among some old music, and, at a rehearsal, I "tried it on the orchestra." I confess to being rather pleased with the effect, and when something was needed to complete the hornpipe record, this happening to be the requisite length and in the same key, seemed very apposite. I hope it will give pleasure to readers who may possess this record.

ELGAR, INTRODUCTION AND ALLEGRO

We now come to the Elgar work, about which I will permit myself the remark that it is without doubt the finest modern work written for string orchestra, and a superb example of Elgar's genius. I cannot conceive any musical person failing to be thrilled by the spaciousness and loftiness of these lovely tunes, and as to the mastery of the writing that almost leaves

Part Two

one breathless.

Though it is not for me to pass judgment favourable or otherwise on these records, there is one feature which I am sure will attract especial notice, and that is a remarkable advance made in the reproduction of the double bass.

I shall not easily forget my surprise and delight when I heard for the first time the third part of the Elgar record, to find a real balance in the fugue section and also the typical thickness of the bass tone. Again, in the Purcell Hornpipe record, the splendid foundation of tone seems to give a feeling of real live string playing.

John Barbirolli.'

'Notes for a Lecture on Smetana's Opera "The Bartered Bride"'[89]

'[*Ladies and Gentlemen. I must apologize to you if the voice does not prove a model of beauty but the fogs of Scotland and the music of Wagner (I conducted Tristan last night)*[90] *have played havoc with my constitution, and I am afraid you have but a lesser lecturer, and croaky conductor before you to-night. Also I can't help saying I do wish my friend T.M. would not keep on sending me press notices of the splendid lectures he gives you, accentuating as they do my considerable sense of inferiority in this line, and believe, it is only a very strict sense of duty that enables me to sum up enough courage to give myself the pleasure of addressing you to-night. I have really a very pleasant task to perform, that of helping to acquaint you with a very delightful opera, but as is often the case in this country with works that are not heard every night for a hundred years running, the public fight rather shy of it. In a search for causes, I have thought it is perhaps the title they fight shy of The Bartered Bride. Perhaps our national sentimentality sees in any unorthodox proceeding connected with a bride something of a tragedy and I quite understand it must be very vexatious to pay your money to see a tragic opera (arriving armed with all the tears at your disposal) to find yourself confronted with a richly comic work but I think it is a well established fact that laughter can produce tears, so your supply will not have been wasted and this kind will probably do you the most good. Now I think we can proceed to the more serious business of the evening.*][91]

It has constantly been said that if composers in this country would only turn their hand to comic opera, for which their talents are commonly thought to be most suited, they would have the complete sympathy of a

Glorious John

grateful public and [we should][92] quickly become as enthusiastic a nation of opera lovers as any in Europe. There is possibly a certain amount of truth in this; but first of all we must know exactly what we mean by comic opera and what standard of achievement our composers should aim at when it has been decided what is the type most acceptable to [our][93] audiences. We must decide, too, whether we should stress the comic element over the musical, or vice versa; whether acting or singing is the more important; whether comic opera and grand opera can exist in the same repertory, and whether both types should submit to the same methods of presentation. Shall our authors and composers base their future work on Gilbert and Sullivan, for example; are we waiting for an English Offenbach; can we hope for a modern Figaro or Barber of Seville, or do the larger public want [works such as][94] The Geisha,[95] Véronique,[96] or The Merry Widow? [Delightful works all][97] Almost every type except the last is represented in the repertory of the Covent Garden Opera Company, and there is no question but that the genuine comic opera of every kind is acceptable to the opera going public, provided it is musically distinguished and efficiently performed. The Mastersingers and The Rose Cavalier are in their was as popular as The Barber of Seville, Figaro, [and Die Fledermaus][98] while Gianni Schicchi only needs further familiarity to make it equally so.

But unfortunately there are no operas, and particularly no comic operas, by British composers amongst those we are now taking on tour. It is not that there are none in [the][99] complete repertory, but there is not one that we could perform before you which can be said by the most biassed [*sic*] to equal in merit the half-dozen best in the world – and our stay in each city is so short and our visits so infrequent that it would not be fair to give you anything but the best we can find. We are therefore compelled to depend upon established favourites of proved high merit, and to confess that while comic opera may actually be the particular field of British composers there is little that we could put before you to prove it. [Here I must make it plain that G&S[100] are only allowed to be performed by the D.C.[101] (illegible)][102]

Many of the best of the European comic operas have been known to the British public almost ever since there [*sic*] were first written, but you will scarcely be surprised to learn that there are still a number which, though long established in the firm affection of European audiences, have never yet been put on the stage in this country. [We][103] have not yet heard Johann Strauss's Gypsy Baron, which some consider even finer than his Die Fledermaus [musically there is also][104] Schwanda the Bagpiper, [and][105] others. The list of comic operas with which we are still unfamiliar is a long one. Yet there is no obstacle in the way of their performance other than the attitude of the public. That attitude is one of the things the Covent Garden Company is in business to test. What the public wants the public shall have.[106]

Here, for example, is a case in point. It will serve very well for a test. An opera we are about to present to Halifax audiences for the first time is on trial. Or rather not the opera itself – it is the [public][107] who are on trial. The Bartered Bride is a comic opera, a real comic opera, one of the best of its kind, and one of the most successful, too. Now, countless comic operas have been written, but when one comes to count them up there are not very many genuine comic opera masterpieces in the repertory. Indeed there is a lamentable lack of them. We could do with a great many more. For this lack there are, doubtless, good reasons. In the first place a really good comic opera book is one of the rarest things in literature, and almost equally rare is the type of composer who has the musical wit to set a good book in a masterly way, even if he is ever lucky enough to get it. For the making of first-rate comic opera demands a peculiar and exceptional genius. Merely to be an operatic composer of more than ordinary talent, merely to have been successful with lyrical opera, tragic opera, or any form of grand opera, is not nearly enough. Many a composer – one can think of half-a-dozen straight off – has jeopardised a considerable reputation by trying to write a comic opera and failing miserably. Then again, [a very vital point this][108] of all the human manifestations of emotion that of humour is the most localised. What is witty in one country is often tiresome in another, and while the ordinary passions of love, jealousy, anger and hate can be torn to shreds in any language and in any country, a joke or a piece of fun has to be both sound and cosmopolitan to survive the crossing of frontiers.

Frederick Smetana, the composer of The Bartered Bride, had then the necessary something which so many others lack, and by virtue of it he was able to join the very small company of those who have written comic operas achieving world-wide success and apparent immortality.

He was born in Bohemia in 1824 and died there in 1884. After a successful career as a young man in various European cities he returned to Prague on 1862 and there founded a national Czech Opera, of which he was the director, and for which he wrote a whole series of operas – some of them comic operas as is his masterpiece The Bartered Bride, and others graver and more dramatic, but all of them on national subjects and imbued with traditional Bohemian ideals. I need not remind you that Smetana was a master composer, not only in opera but as a symphonic writer, and the

Glorious John

acknowledged father of Bohemian music, to whom Dvorak and later Czech composers owe a profound debt. So that we approach this opera, The Bartered Bride, with the knowledge that musically it is impeccable. That does not necessarily mean that because certain music is written by a master it makes good operatic music, but in this case it happens that the two things go together. The music of The Bartered Bride is operatic music of the very highest order. Partly to prove that point I need only ask you to recall the wonderful overture to the opera with which you are all familiar and which has adorned our concert programmes for half a century. It has the verve of the Figaro Overture, and is, in its way, the modern counterpart to that immortal work. And, in passing, there is something extraordinary, something, perhaps, not altogether creditable in the fact that, knowing the overture, we did not sooner investigate what lay beyond it, and put The Bartered Bride on our operatic stage sooner tha n we did. It was first performed in Prague in 1866, had an immediate success – indeed a triumph – and spread through Germany within a few years of its première. Since then it has never been absent from the German operatic stage. True, it was produced over here in German at a Covent Garden Summer Season early in the century, but, apart from a few [special][109] performances at Oxford about three years ago, and two studio broadcasts, it was performed before the British public in an English translation for the first time last year – 65 years after the première in Prague. Today it is in the repertory of the Opéra Comique in Paris, it is one of the half dozen first favourites in Chicago, and is performed in Germany as frequently as ever. In Prague it is still, of course, the first of all favourites.

The opera is in three acts, composed to a libretto by K. Sabina and performed by the Covent Garden Opera Company in an English version, originally made for the broadcast performances, by Felix Goodwin. The English libretto is published [and will be on sale in the theatre.][110]

The scene of the opera is a village in Bohemia in fair time, the plot is one of typical Bohemian life, and Smetana's music is essentially Bohemian in spirit. This briefly is the story.

Through the agency of Ketzal, a marriage-broker, a marriage has been arranged between Marie [& daughter of Kathinka & Kruschina the latter a name with a rather familiar ring],[111] a girl of the village, and Wenzel, the [to say the least,][112] dull-witted son of Micha, a well-to-do-farmer. Marie, however, loves Hans, a lad without prospects and a stranger to the village. The lovers take comfort from one another and resolve to upset the intrigues of Ketzal. Wenzel has never met Marie, so it is easy for her to hoodwink

Part Two

the stupid boy and pretend to be someone else who is really in love with him. Hans meanwhile has another plan, and unknown to Marie, bargains with Ketzal to give her up for a sum of money, and subject to the strange condition that she shall marry no other than a son of Micha. That Hans has something up his sleeve is clear from his gay, triumphant manner, but, for a time, Marie feels that she has been cruelly thrown over and all because of the shameful bargain. Wenzel makes matters worse by becoming hopelessly infatuated [with][113] the pretty dancer of a circus troupe which is performing that evening in the village. Marie is thus at her wits end, heartbroken by Hans' callous conduct. But a happy surprise is in store for her. Micha suddenly recognises Hans as his long-lost son by a first marriage. He is therefore persuaded to agree to Hans' marriage with Marie, so that Hans wins not only the bargain money but the bride as well.

As you can observe for yourselves, the plot is not a new one. Indeed, in many ways, it is conventional, and completely unsophisticated. But, dramatically, it is well constructed; it moves forward without halting; it is witty, full of incident, and consistently amusing. Moreover it gives scope for a varied and contrasted musical setting of which the experienced Smetana has taken the fullest advantage.

Musically, the opera is Mozartian, for Smetana, a profound worshipper of Mozart, was influenced by him and doubtless modelled his operatic procedure on Mozart's. Just as in Figaro, The Bartered Bride is divided into scenes, arias, and concerted numbers, connected by accompanied recitatives, with prolonged and elaborate finales to each act. Yet there is no apparent division, and the music swings along without pause from the beginning to the end of each act with easy but swiftly moving dramatic action. It is difficult to say which are the best numbers, or which is the best act. In the first act, for instance, Marie's [1st][114] song 'Is my heart not yours' which follows the opening chorus is a little gem; [added text illegible] the succeeding duet of Hans and Marie is dramatically just right[115] [Next comes][116] the Trio with Ketzal, the marriage-broker, arguing with Kruschina and Kathinka about the eligibility of the lad he is offering as a husband to their daughter is a rollicking piece of fun.[117] This scene, with Marie joining the group towards the end of it, is brimful of delicious tunes and occupies nearly all the rest of the act, which concludes with a chorus and dance by the returning villagers.

The second act which, on the whole, is perhaps musically the finest, begins with a drinking song and a dance leading to the entrance of Wenzel, the half-witted boy whom Ketzel has arranged shall marry Marie. He sings

Glorious John

a stuttering song – one of the most comical moments in the opera, and the scene which follows when Marie makes mock love to the [a]mazed but delighted simpleton is a perfect piece of comedy set to the most sparkling and often lovely music.[118] But even this is a little overshadowed by one of the most scintillating passages of musical wit in all comic opera. The cunning overweening Ketzal strikes a bargain with Hans, who, however, knows what he is about, and the encounter is a sheer delight from beginning to end.[119] The musical character drawing of Ketzal is unbelievably subtle, and there are enough musical gems in this scene alone to make the whole of the opera unforgettable. Hans later has his opportunity to display his voice in another beautiful, but very simple, little aria, and the act concludes with a spirited finale – [worthy of Mozart himself][120] – in which Ketzal gives Hans away as having sold his bride[, to the great anger of the][121] horrified and scornful villagers.

[The third act opens with a solo for W. pathos, Chaplin][122]. The scene is a village fair, and a circus troupe provides much fun. [Here we have acrobats, wrestlers, jugglers, weight lifters, circus (illegible)].[123] Then follows a series of complications providing extended concerted numbers, towards the end of which comes he now famous quintet. There are some operatic ensembles, such as the quintet from The Mastersingers and the quartet from Rigoletto, which, apart from the operas, stand out as indisputably immortal. One must concede to this strangely beautiful quintet of Smetana's like immortality. One does not say it is the loveliest thing in the opera, for its is so essentially a part of the opera, but for all that it is of an exceeding loveliness.[124]

The next scene between Hans and Marie contains another duet[125] – this time a kind of bickering match[126] – but Smetana never permits his music to suffer for whatever motive. Indeed he seems to be stimulated by what other composers would be in difficulties about. This duet just flashes and sparkles like a [pretty][127] firework, and nothing [more charming & (illegible)][128] could be imagined.[129]

The finale which clears up all the complications and ends the opera is just as spirited as all that went before, and so inexhaustible does Smetana's flow of delightful melody seem to be, that one can believe he could have gone on for still another three acts with equal ease.

It only needs that the public shall see this opera once to want to see it again. It is because I am so firmly convinced that it is destined for a permanent place in the repertory of British opera companies, both professional and amateur, that I cannot too emphatically ask you to come and see it during the coming visit of the Covent Garden Company to Halifax.

Part Two

Please remember what I said earlier in this talk. The Bartered Bride is not on trial. It is the public that is so, and, given a fair opportunity as we are giving it to you during the next two weeks, I have no doubt whatever what the verdict will be. The public will leave the theatre without a stain on its character.[130]

(About 2,600 words).'

'Strauss and "Der Rosenkavalier"'[131]

'Richard Strauss, of whose work I am here to speak tonight – like other great composers before him, notably, Bach, Mozart, Beethoven, Brahms, and our own Elgar[132] - comes of a musical family. His father, Franz Strauss, who lived to a great age, and was thereby able to rejoice in the fame of his son, was a noted horn player in his day, and was the author of a standard tutor for that instrument. It is said that no less a person than Wagner was glad to consult him, with regard to the ultimate shape of Siegfried's famous horn-call. At Munich, the capital of Bavaria, there was – (round about the middle of the last century) – already a considerable artistic life and culture, much of which centred in the Court Orchestra, an organisation due of course, to Government support. Franz Strauss occupied the post of principal horn there, and having taken to wife a lady belonging to a well known brewing family, - their son, Richard, the composer of the Rosenkavalier, about which I am going to speak to you tonight, was born, in this artistic centre, in the summer of 1864. Great things were astir then in the world of music, for in this very town, only four years later, before the boy Strauss learned his alphabet, Wagner's great comic opera "The Mastersingers", which I expect many[133] of you have seen and heard, was produced under the direction of Hans von Bulow [sic]. This same great conductor and pianist was one of the earliest to encourage Strauss' youthful efforts in composition. Though the works of the later and more mature Strauss often set the musical world agape at their seeming audacity and revolutionary daring, the early works of the youthful Strauss show a close adherence to strict classical models. One work after another betrays various classical influences, Beethoven, Mendelssohn, Schumann, Mozart.[134] I should like to stress particularly in connection with "The Rosenkavalier" – the influence of Mozart. One of those early works of Strauss, a Serenade for thirteen Wind-instruments – though not often heard nowadays, was played quite recently by our B.B.C. and those who listened to it must have been struck by certain Mozartian affinities in its grace and serenity. Some idea of the powerful headway that the quality of Strauss' music ensured for itself quite early in his life, is seen in the surprising fact that a youthful Symphony of his was taken across the Atlantic to be heard for the first time in New York, when its composer was only twenty years old.

In his twenty first year young Strauss was appointed by von Bulow [sic] to succeed him in the Conductorship of the famous Meiningen Orchestra,[135] with which Brahms at that time was often closely associated. From this time onwards Strauss has held – (almost throughout all his life) – a number of increasingly important posts as Conductor – at Munich, at Weimar, and, – just at the end of the Century – at Berlin,[136] and, since the war, at Vienna for a number of years, but this side of his activities need not detain us here, except to add that he has conducted his own works in this country at various times and on many occasions, over a great stretch of years, beginning in 1897 and extending to the B.B.C. Symphony Concerts of the present Season. To return to Strauss' earlier compositions, though they are still worthy of admiration as a very young man's works, it must be said that had he continued throughout his career on those lines, I should not be here tonight discussing them, nor – if I were – would you think it worth while to come and listen to a talk about them. Through most of the latter half of last century, the musical world was divided into two well defined camps. There were, first, the upholders of the old tradition of what we may call pure absolute music, based on the powerful examples furnished by the greatest masters of the past, such as Mozart, Haydn, Beethoven, and Mendelssohn. In the other camp were found the adherents of what was then called "the music of the future", which we may roughly class as music that was intended to be pictorial and dramatic in aim, and possessed a definite explanatory programme. Brahms, and his intimate friend the great violinist Joachim, were two of the leaders of this first, conservative group. The second group, that considered themselves the advance guard, pinned their faith to the problematic works of Liszt and Berlioz, and the rich revelations afforded by the genius displayed in Wagner's operas, though Wagner himself was – it must be said – never anything else but very lukewarm on the subject of programme-music.

At this distance of time, all this is rather taken for granted by us, but 40 or 50 years ago, the issue was regarded a very vital one, and all concerned were ready to shed their last drop of ink on behalf of the side they favoured. At this still early, but crucial period of his life, the young Strauss fell under the influence of a man, many years his senior, Alexander Ritter, who was

Part Two

a violinist, a composer, a writer on music,[137] married to a niece of Wagner, and was moreover a strong adherent of this new programmatic school of musical thought. Under his powerful guidance the young Strauss gradually shook off the severely orthodox musical views of his early training and turned eagerly, but, at first, with apparently only tentative steps, to explore the new paths of music that were to lead to the further extension, of its use for vivid dramatic and pictorial purposes, and sharply defined characterisation. The result of this exploration of new ground is seen in the next twelve years, say, roughly from 1887 to the end of the century, during which short time, Strauss created a group of big Symphonic Poems for Orchestra – (each of which is undoubtedly a masterpiece) – which have caused his name and fame to spread the wide world over. Let me briefly recall to your mind the names and general characteristics of these familiar works. First comes "Don Juan", with its riotously exuberant picture of the head-strong seeker after the ideal woman, ultimately closing his career in disillusionment and death.[138] [T]hen, the following year, we have "Death and Transfiguration", a harrowing portrayal of the fevered imaginings in the soul of a dying man, and the soul's final release into some higher, nobler sphere of being. Next comes that ever fascinating delineation of rascality "Till Eulenspiegel" and his merry pranks, wherein wit, humour, pictorial and narrative power, and with it all, pathos, are combined in a quite extraordinary degree. Close on the heels of this comes the great exposition of Nietzsche's[139] philosophy of the superman, "Zarathustra", wherein we see traced the whole course of mankind's spiritual journeying. This is followed by "Don Quixote" with his high-souled idealism which is contrasted with the garlic-laden humour of Sancho Panza and his homely proverbs, and the unerring realism of the bleating of sheep, the fight with the windmill,[140] the journey in the enchanted boat, and many other extravagant adventures of the immortal Spanish hero. At the end of the 1890's [*sic*] comes "A hero's life"[141], wherein Strauss boldly bodies forth the aspirations and struggles of a hero – (most probably himself, judging from the internal evidence supplied by the music) – and his final renunciation of the world and its uncomprehending ways. Interspersed with these immense works are a number of smaller ones, in themselves sufficient to create an enviable reputation for any man, but these I shall not touch on here. Towards the middle of this long spell of Symphonic works – to be exact, in 1892 –comes the first of Strauss' operas "Guntram", and though we are gathered here tonight to consider one particular Opera of Strauss', "The Rosenkavalier", I think you would like to know briefly something of the Operas that led up to it. "Guntram", this first opera, is still occasionally played in the composer's own country, but it has never been mounted on the stage here, the general public's knowledge of it being confined to one or two excerpts[142] sometimes heard at Concerts. Strauss followed Wagner's example and wrote his own libretto.[143] "Guntram" has other affinities with the work of Wagner, for there is a decided slowness of the dramatic action in many places, besides many touches of mysticism, and the music itself shows strong traces of Strauss' great predecessor. It is notable, too, in Strauss' own career, for the fact that shortly after the production the composer married the singer who had created the part of the heroine.[144] The closing year of the century brought Strauss' second opera to light. This was a one act comedy opera called in German "Feuersnot", and known in England as "Beltane Fire", when it was produced by Sir Thomas Beecham in London in 1910. There is a strong satirical vein in this, for Strauss here takes it upon himself to rebuke[145] his fellow townsmen of Munich in no uncertain terms, for their long neglect of Wagner. This Opera has many charming moments, some delightful choruses for children's voices, and a very beautiful love scene, at the close, which last is fairly familiar to English audiences on the Concert platform. 1905 saw the production of "Salome", Strauss' third Opera. This set the whole musical world by its ears, with its voluptuous oriental colouring, the severed head of John the Baptist – all gory – on a silver platter, the wild ecstasy of Salome's dance, and, finally, the dazzling brilliant mastery displayed in the handling of the colossal orchestra it employs. After this, we find Strauss handling another old-world story imbrued with blood and slaughter, going to ancient Greece this time, for the legend of "Elektra". This Opera may be said to mark the climax of Strauss' indulgence in emotional violence, with its references to foot-steps slipping about in a bath of blood, the night-mare visions that beset the disease ridden Clytemnestra, and the heroine's long pent up desire for revenge, venting itself, (after satiation,) in a dance of exultant joy, at the close of which she drops dead. Much magnificent music, some of it of a rare nobility, goes to the illustration of this old tale, and in the writer of the libretto, we come upon Strauss' first association with the great German poet, Hugo von Hofmannsthal, who was to collaborate so successfully with the composer in his next Opera "The Rosenkavalier" and two later Operas, "The Wife Without a Shadow", and "The Egyptian Helen", which I shall not touch upon now. But having arrived – (in this brief review of Strauss' operas) – at the "Rosenkavalier" – before going on to deal as fully circumstances will permit with that work, I should like to say something in general about the man who writes the book of words for an opera[146] – and also in particular,

Part Two

to tell you a little about the man who wrote the remarkable libretto of "The Rosenkavalier", and of how the poet and composer worked together.

As most of you know probably know, Opera has existed in something like its present from – (that is, a story presented on the stage by means of acting and singing, combined with an Orchestra large or small) – for about three hundred years. In countries [where][147] opera is sedulously cultivated and has therefore been able to take hold on the national taste which nothing can shake – countries such as Italy, Germany and France – the librettist, good, bad, or indifferent, abounds. You will remark, perhaps, that I did not say he flourished. There were in the past, and still are in the present, many reasons that might be given to account for the slightest esteem in which the librettist would often be held. The first of these is the sad fact that not one out of a hundred Operas produced out of any given period is a lasting success. Then, the librettist was only too often some kind of literary hack who happened to be on hand and could supply the composer with a peg on which to hang his music. Often a noted Opera House would have a librettist almost on the premises – a kind of tame Theatre poet – and if the composer wrote for a particular theatre, he had, [whether he liked it or not][148] to take the poet – save the mark – that they provided for him! This is one of the principal reasons why so many good composers have ploughed the sand in mating their fine music to poor librettos. A few modern composers[149] have been more fortunate than most of their predecessors. Gounod, Massenet, Verdi[150] and Puccini have each written more than one successful Opera in collaboration with the same librettist. To this list of the illustrious dead there is only one living name to be added, and that is Strauss, with his several successful Operas to the texts by Von [*sic*] Hofmannsthal. Now, we are in the fortunate position of knowing a good deal as to how Strauss and his great librettist have worked, for a large volume of the letters that passed between the two men, has recently appeared. This throws a flood of light on their methods of collaboration. In one place we see the librettist suggesting some new ideas, or a novel turn of events; in another place, it will be the composer. He has to provide the music that is to irradiate[151] everything, so he surely should be allowed HIS say. What this can result in, when you have a composer naturally gifted with an eye for what is effective on stage, we see in the case of Verdi. Those of you who have seen "Aida" will remember vividly the last scene in the Opera, where the stage is divided into two parts; above is the life and light of the sacred temple of the priest: below, the death and darkness of the subterranean crypt. Now, these two scenes were originally devised by the Librettist to occur consecutively. "No!" said

Glorious John

Verdi, with his keen dramatic intuition "We will have the two together". And the striking result you will remember. In this case Verdi had to deal with a man of only mediocre ability, a mere writer of verse for music, the kind of person I described to you a moment ago. But Hugo von Hofmannsthall [sic], the librettist of the Rosenkavalier, was no tame dangler round the back doors of an Opera House. He was a man who had already achieved a considerable reputation as one of the greatest of modern German poets some while before his association with Strauss was to carry his fame far beyond the borders of his own country. Hofmannsthal, who died about two years ago – was extraordinarily precocious. As a mere youth he had published several dramas and written a deal of maturely accomplished verse. He sprang into fame in the 1890's [sic], and much of his work is characterised by the same qualities as that of some of our own writers of this period such as Oscar Wilde, Ernst Dowson, or the drawings Aubrey Beardsley. Among Hofmannsthal's stage works are dramas on the subject of Oedipus, Elektra – (on which Strauss afterwards based the powerful Opera I have already referred to –) and a version of our old Morality Play, "Everyman". The collaboration of Strauss and Hofmannsthal is among the most extraordinary contacts ever made between poetry and music. Nothing can be cited as resembling it, except the collaboration between Gilbert and Sullivan; and the parallel, (distantly though the lines may be drawn,) is not without its suggestive points. Surely there hardly ever was any writer of words for Comic Opera but Gilbert, whose words can be read for their own sake, and there never has been any librettist of any serious Opera but Hofmannsthal, who had sufficient confidence in his libretto to print it as an independent book, and afterwards to include it in his collective works.[152] It would be difficult to think of any poet of equal rank with Hofmannsthal who has spent so much of his career and put so much of his best work into this sort of collaboration, or who has been a partner in so many operatic compositions of the first rank. He himself is aware of his own uniqueness. "I know", [in the book referred to][153] he says – "and I speak with all modesty, remembering the imperishable masterpieces of our literature – I know the value of my own work, I know that it is many generations since a distinguished poet devoted himself willingly, gladly, to writing librettos for a composer". Hofmannsthal's first concern, and almost his last, is that the plot should shall run on all fours with a lively dialogue that keeps a clear line, however broken, and if Strauss can set it as it is, well and good; if not, and he wants "lyrics" or some particular Trio or Intermezzo introduced, he can slip them in at any time later. The great point is that the thing must be

Part Two

conceived and written as a play that will really act, (as if there were no music at all,) first. Strauss, on the other hand, takes little interest in all this finesse. He has his big musical idea before him, and writes a good deal of it before even the words are ready. Strauss has not hesitated to mark his appreciation of the work of his colleague, for quite early in their association he writes to him "Your lines are splendid and I have already set them. You are a born librettist, and I mean the compliment; it is much harder to write a good libretto than a good play, though I hardly expect you to think so". I will now return specifically to the Opera you have all come here to-night to hear about. First, a date or two. Strauss did most of the composition of the Rosenkavalier at the same country house in Bavaria in which he wrote many of the great symphonic poems I have referred to earlier.[154] The Opera was completed in September 1909, and took well over a year to publish and prepare for stage production. The first performance took place on January 26th 1911 in the same city in which "Elektra" and "Salome" first saw the light, that is Dresden. It was an unquestioned success from the start, and the passage of twenty years has confirmed its right to rank with the three other great master-pieces of comic opera. The Marriage of Figaro, The Mastersingers, and [my beloved][155] Falstaff. The first of its many performances in this country took place under Sir Thomas Beecham in January 1913.[156] Now, the music of The Rosenkavalier – which is I expect what you have been waiting for some time for me to come to – although in many senses typically Straussian, shows almost a complete change of style from much of the earlier work. The fantastic, the heroic, the violently emotional have no place in this "Comedy of Music", as it is called. Here everything is presented to us with a ripe geniality, and nothing is overstressed. Even a nodding acquaintance with the music of the Opera cannot fail to distinguish three special elements in it. First there is, naturally, Strauss' own musical personality, but subtly grafted on to this are two other elements which we see were specially adopted to convey the period, place and general atmosphere of the Opera, the scene of which is laid in Vienna, in the early years of the reign of the Empress Marie Theresa. The two other elements are a certain affinity with Viennese folk-song, together with a deliberate cultivation of the city's characteristic waltz-rhythms, and a strong [penchant][157] for melody cast in a simple Mozartian mould. Carping voices have been heard to declare that the Waltzes and the Mozartian idiom are both anachronisms! In this matter of mere dates, they are doubtless right, but this should not distress us. (We are not greatly worried by Shakespeare's mention of the clock in "Julius Caesar", nor that he makes Hector quote

Glorious John

Aristotle.) Now then you shall hear the story of the opera. It is a good tale, and I hope I shall not mar it in the telling.

Most of Strauss' Operas have no Overture or Prelude of any sort, but The Rosenkavalier is one of the few exceptions. The Orchestral Prelude to the Rosenkavalier is full of exuberant vitality and youthful ardour. After some while, it quietens down, and the curtain rises showing us the bedroom of the Princess von Werdenberg. [Now I don't quite know whether it will be good for our Box Office for me to dwell on the salacious elements in the story or not but if you go to see one of Mr. Cochran's recent productions you will find a bed on the stage used not merely for the purposes of decoration, but of delectation.][158] But where a serious art-work is in question, we British folk show some queer susceptibilities which it is advisable to bear in mind, and I therefore have to announce that when you see the curtain go up on the opening of The Rosenkavalier you will NOT see the bed! [I hope not too many of you will stay away owing to this (for these times) curiously modest (I almost said, virginal) element in our production.][159] To return to the beginning of the story I am going to tell you, when the curtain rises, you see the morning sun breaking in upon the Princess, who is seen receiving the attentions of her lover Octavian, a young nobleman for whom she has devised the pet-name of Mignon.[160] I will, however, always refer to him as Octavian. The Princess is a lady of the very highest Austrian aristocracy, and accustomed to command and be obeyed; she has a large household of retainers over whom she presides, and – (the last point, this, but an important one for the proper comprehension of the inner motives of the action of the opera) – she is no longer as young as she could wish to be, while, on the other hand, her lover, Octavian, is in his youthful prime. While the orchestra gently hints at bird-song,[161] the lovers bill and coo [I believe that is the correct expression][162] together. They are presently disturbed by the ringing of a bell. It proves to be only the Princess' little negro servant, with bells dangling on his clothes, who brings in the morning chocolate. His entry co-incides with a charming passage in the Orchestra, a piquant little march-rhythm, which can hardly fail to note. When the young blackamoor has gone out, the Princess sits down to sip her chocolate, and the Orchestra then plays the first of the many delightful waltz-tunes which Strauss has sprinkled with so lavish a hand over the Opera. All these waltz-tunes have abounding grace, swing, and a never-failing charm. Some of them are loud, with crashing of drums and cymbals, others are quiet and delicate. This one is quiet and delicate, and you will hear most of the melody on the clarinet. The Princess tells her young lover that she dreamed of her absent husband

Part Two

the previous night [and young Oct(avian) is very annoyed that even that was possible].[163] Presently more noise is heard outside the door. The Princess thinks that this must be her husband returning from hunting, and Octavian hastily hides behind a screen, with the brilliant idea of disguising himself as one of the Princess' maids.[164] The noise outside grows louder and more insistent. By carefully listening the Princess finds that her fears of her husband's return are groundless, for she hears the voice of her cousin, the elderly rake, Baron Ochs von Lerchenau disputing with the lackeys about his right to enter. The music played in the Orchestra when the Baron makes his entry is another instance of Strauss' vivid power of musical characterisation. It is heard quite quietly, and rather low, on the strings, and has a courtly, ornamental grace, every bar of which bespeaks a ceremonial air of bowing and scraping. Octavian comes out from behind the screen, in the fetching disguise of a young chambermaid. Before he can withdraw again from the Princess' astonished but delighted gaze, the Baron comes in at the very door from which the disguised lover had hoped to make his exit. The elderly Baron – ever susceptible to the charms of the fair sex – bestows an approving glance on the supposed chambermaid, who, not being able to get out of the room, tries to make the best of it by pretending to be busy tidying up. Undismayed by the Baron's enquiring looks, the Princess tells him that he is her new waiting-woman, fresh from the countryside, and that her name is Mariandel. This information whets the old rogue's appetite and he straightaway scents the possibility of attempting an intrigue with what he takes to be this fascinating young baggage.[165] Meanwhile, the Baron begins to unfold the purpose of his visit and tells the Princess of a scheme of his to get married, in which he wants her help. The maiden of his choice, he says, is a sweet young thing, barely fifteen, named Sophie Faninal, the daughter of an army contractor who has been lately raised to the rank of the minor nobility[, I should think in return for his lenience towards the remaining public fund.][166]One of the most attractive features of the proposed affair – (in addition to the beauty of the young girl) – is, for him, the [facts][167] circumstances that her father is rich, and doesn't enjoy the best of health.[168] Among the Viennese nobility of that period there was a picturesque custom that an intending bridegroom should send a friend or relation of his to the prospective bride's house, bearing a silver rose, as a love-token. This personage is the Cavalier of the Rose, from which the Opera takes its title. While telling all this, the Baron at every available moment does his best to ogle the disguised Octavian, who – out of sheer love of mischief – leads him on. Presently the head of the Princess' household comes in to tell her

Glorious John

that a crowd of attendants and suitors to her clemency, including a singer and a flute-player, are waiting outside to pay her a respectful morning visit. She tells him to let them wait. Then she turns to the Baron and chaffs him about his all-too-obvious attentions to her new waiting maid, and the Baron justifies his amorous goings-on in a boisterous reply, the three characters presently joining together in a short Trio. [The opening words, "Must I" etc giving a good idea of his mental attitude towards betrothals][169] This Trio, it is worth while noting, was Strauss' own idea; so much so, indeed, that the music was written first, and then the words afterwards fitted on to it by von Hofmannsthal! Returning to the topic of who shall carry the silver rose to the Baron's bride-to-be, the Princess shows him a miniature of Octavian, and suggests that he shall be the rose-bearer, to which idea the Baron gladly consents. The crowd of clamorous suitors and dependants outside are determined to wait no longer, and when the head of the Princess' household opens the door, Octavian, in his disguise, rather thankfully makes a hurried exit, and a crowd of the Princess' hangers on soon fills the stage. A screen is brought, behind which a hairdresser attends to the Princess' morning toilet. The hopeful crowd includes, among many others, a milliner, an attorney, a dealer in pet animals,[170] a widow in reduced circumstances with three orphan girls, an Italian tenor, a Flute-player, and last, but not least, for they have a hand in the plot afterwards, a rascally couple of scandal-mongering Italian blackmailers, Valzacchi and Annina, by name. Amid the crowded stage, all these have their say, and try – in various ways – to work on the good feelings of the great lady of the house. The three orphans sing a brief Trio imploring help, the flute-player tootles on his melancholy instrument, and the Italian Tenor [tightens his throat,][171] sings a song in his native language, holding the music in his hand, [in the passed style popular in the days of ballad concerts].[172] The song he sings is cast in Strauss' most rapturous vein of melody, and, harking back as it does to Mozart, is of quite exceptional beauty.[173]

While much of this is going on, the Baron, mindful of other things beside[174] the prospect of a dainty piece of flesh, is in close confabulation with his attorney, arranging the details of his marriage settlement.[175] When this motley gathering of suppliants have at length departed – all more or less pleased with themselves, - though [perhaps][176] annoyed with each other, – the two Italian blackmailers remain behind, and with a view to extorting money from the Baron, offer to keep a lynx-eyed watch on the Baron's prospective bride. The Baron refuses their help in this direction, but asks them to keep a watch on the movements of the Princess's new

Part Two

chambermaid, Mariandel. The Baron, bent on business, has brought the silver rose with him in a special casket, and leaves it with the Princess after receiving her assurance that she will do her best to get her cousin, Octavian, to undertake the delicate embassy of the bearing of the rose to the Baron's intended. Satisfied with this promise, the Baron takes a ceremonious leave of his kinswoman. Left to herself, the Princess muses ironically on the ways of the world, that gaily permit the mating of a young girl fresh from the convent, with an utter stranger, an elderly man, and a rake, to boot. She hints that something of the same kind befell her in her youth, but all that belongs to the past, and the once beautiful woman will soon be known as "the old Princess". Octavian here re-enters, clad in man's attire once more; his youthful affection for the Princess is as outspoken and demonstrative as before, but now the Princess is saddened by thoughts of the passage of time, and its probable effect on her young lover. She has realized at length that youth and beauty and love do not endure so long as the hearts desire for them. I know of no other Opera or play in which this essentially tragic aspect of every woman's life is set forth, and Strauss's music for this scene has a quiet pathos and tenderness that is very touching[, and make (*sic*) it one of the most moving & sincere passages in all his music.][177] Young Octavian dismisses the Princess's fears with renewed protestations of his unswerving constancy. Nevertheless, the Princess's manner to him seems so strangely reserved that he eventually takes his departure, without giving her a kiss. The Princess sends her footman to call him back, but Octavian cannot be overtaken. So the little black boy is rung for and told to take the casket containing the silver rose to Octavian. The Princess is left alone [with her mirror][178] deep in thought, and the curtain falls.[179]

ACT TWO takes place in the house of Faninal, and we see the worthy army-contractor and his household all agog with excitement at the prospect of the arrival of the bearer of the silver, and all that it betokens. The [fair][180] young Sophy[181] breathes a fervent prayer for the Divine aid, while her old nurse looks out the window. Swiftly the music grows in intensity, and culminates in an ecstatic burst of radiant melody, when Octavian, brilliantly dressed in white, finally comes in, bearing the silver rose. Strauss typifies the odorous fragrance of the silver rose and all that it connotes, by some chords on a fairy-like little piano called a Celesta, (which I daresay some of you remember hearing in the Dance of the Sugar-plum Fairy in Tschaikowsky's "Nutcracker" Suite.) The use of this special instrument here is a marvellous instance of Strauss's feeling for pictorial visualization[182] in music. There is a long pause – as of tense rapture – and Sophy replies in terms of simple wonderment to the formal address of Octavian, as the rose-bearer. The music here is of a sustained beauty, and is moreover kept for so long at such a lofty height of inspiration that we have here, in truth, one of the mountain-peaks of modern music. [Here I may be permitted one quotation.][183]

"Who ever loved, that loved not at first sight."[184]
(Gramophone record here.)[185]

When they, the lovers, and we, and the music all return to earth once more, we find the young pair talking on general subjects, principally about Octavian's formidable array of high-sounding names. As the talk goes on Octavian falls under the spell of the young girl's beauty, and finds himself also greatly attracted by her naïve candour. Soon the Baron himself enters, and the coarse clumsiness of his general behaviour speedily makes a highly unpleasant impression on the delicately nurtured[186] Sophy. The Baron's conduct gradually becomes more and more intolerable, and culminates in his attempting to kiss and fondle his prospective bride before them all. Sophy shrinks in horror from his gross speech and manners, while Octovian [sic], (from his point of view,) is even more revolted. The Baron goes out with his attendant attorney to draw up the terms of the marriage-settlement with Sophy's father. Sophy seizes this opportunity to confide in Octavian and beseeches his aid, declaring that she will never marry so horrid an old creature as the Baron. The conflicting emotions in the two young breasts find an outlet in declaring their love for each other. As they embrace, the two intriguing Italians, Valzacchi and Annina, spring out as it were from nowhere, and seizing hold of Octavian and Sophy, they call out loudly for the Baron. He enters, and Octavian tells him that Sophy will have none of him. The Baron pooh-poohs the idea, and attempts to drag Sophy into the adjoining room to put her signature to the marriage settlement. When Octavian threatens the old rake, the Baron emits a peculiar whistle, and a group of his lackeys enter. Notwithstanding them, Octavian attacks the Baron with his sword, and wounds him slightly in the arm. Everyone connected with the household rushes to the Baron's assistance, though the old wretch[187] is really more frightened than hurt. Faninal is furious at all the uproar in his house and the possibility of the splendid marriage of his daughter being broken off, and tells Octavian so. Octavian deems it expedient now to go, but not before he has the satisfaction of hearing Sophy roundly declare that, come what may, she will not marry the Baron. The old nurse, as indignant as Faninal, bundles Sophy out of the room with her. The obsequious father then

Part Two

turns to the Baron and expresses his deepest regrets for the misadventure. The Baron consoles himself with some wine, and the thought of the revenge he will one day wreak on Octavian. In comes one of the Italian mischief-makers [Annina, to be precise][188] with a note for the Baron. The old rascal's intrigue with the Princess's charming new maid, just fresh from the country, Mariandel, has borne promising fruit, for here is a letter from her, saying she will be free tomorrow night. He sees that the luck of his old family still holds good, and delightedly tells the Italian to come to his room, and he will dictate a reply. The Italian wants her palm greased, and when no money is forthcoming, makes a gesture of indicating her intention of taking revenge on the old curmudgeon[189] for his meanness.[190] But the merry old dog, now once again in the best of spirits, is oblivious to this, and, as the curtain falls, comforts himself with a snatch of song in waltz-time.[191] The third act has an orchestral prelude of a kind of furtive hurry-scurry. When the curtain rises we at once see the reason for this. The scene shows a private room at a Viennese inn. In an alcove, somewhat screened off from the general gaze, is a[192] bed. This, of course, I know will not surprise [*sic*] you, (but I will not venture to bolster up my argument with any further talk on this subject!) (pause for laughter?)[193] Who sleeps in it? [What a lovely big bed Mariandel says][194] You'll know in good time[, replies the Baron,][195] [who][196] has arranged to sup and spend the [night][197] in this inn with his latest flame, the Princess' pseudo-chambermaid. Octavian has connived with the two Italian schemers that they shall be on the spot to plague the debauchee with interruptions of various kinds of sudden apparitions of intruding[198] heads from trap-doors and all sorts of queer windows with which the room chosen for the meeting abounds. As the curtain rises, we see the two Italians and their group of satellites preparing all this, and appointing to each one their post. [For the first part of this act, 2 orchestras are employed][199] Presently the sounds of some entrancing Waltz-strains are heard – (the majority of the famous Waltz tunes in the opera are found in this act, by-the-bye,) – and the Baron enters, leading in the simpering Mariandel. While the orchestra, both in its accustomed place and on the stage, discourses delightful strains, especially ordered for the occasion by the Baron, the oddly assorted couple take supper, or rather, try to.

Now I am deliberately NOT going into exact details of all the amusing by-play that takes place at this point in so many directions; firstly, because it would take up too much time, and secondly, because to tell you all about it in advance would blunt the keen edge of your enjoyment and one of the richest comedy scenes that the contemporary stage can show! As the uproar

Glorious John

increases the Baron describes the situation as "Hell let loose", to the landlord of the inn and the waiters who have rushed in to see what the turmoil is about. The entry of Police officials adds to the Baron's discomfiture. There ensues then, on his part, a lot of those bewildering kind of explanations that don't really explain anything! Octavian, bent on exposing the vicious old Baron to the fullest extent, has arranged that Faninal and Sophy shall be sent for at this juncture. Sure enough, the next moment, in comes the army contractor and his [fair][200] daughter. They have been led to believe that they were sent for at the Baron's request, and are mystified and presently thoroughly scandalised to find him in such a sorry pickle.[201] Octavian retires into the alcove and divests himself of his female attire, thereby bringing the Baron's complete discomfiture a stage nearer.[202] All the turmoil is stilled, however, at the sudden appearance of the commanding personality of the Princess, standing in the doorway. She comes forward and does her best to accept the lame excuses of the Baron, though she can scarcely [conceal][203] her inner contempt for his conduct. The Baron makes one last desperate attempt before leaving to gather together a few remaining shreds of his patrician self-respect, but this is spoilt by the noisy intrusion of a number of servants in the Inn, all demanding payment for services rendered, and the Baron, rushing out in an attempt to evade them, is seen no more.[204] Sophy, Octavian and the Princess, with her ripe feminine intuition, speedily perceives from the demeanour of Sophy and Octavian, that youth, as ever, is calling to youth, and that she must renounce her youthful lover sooner than she had even feared.[205] She accepts the situation calmly, with a touch of half humourous [sic], slighly [sic] ironical condescension, and the three characters combine the mingling of their varied emotions in a Trio, which is probably the finest piece of concerted vocal writing in Opera since Wagner wrote the superb Quintet in the Mastersingers. You shall judge of the quality of this Trio here and now. But, before letting you hear the actual record, I should like as an especial point of interest, to draw your attention to the curious fact that the serenely curving melodic phrase with which the Trio opens, is simply a modification of one of the gay waltz tunes heard earlier.

(Play the Waltz-tune and then the Record)

After this Trio (which you have just heard), the Princess unobtrusively slips out. Octavian [takes][206] Sophy in his arms, and they sing a happy little duet, in phrases almost as simple as a folk song.[207] Faninal and the Princess make a momentary appearance, and give their blessings to the lovers. The Duet is then resumed,[208] after which the lovers go out. For a moment the stage is empty; then the little blackamoor comes in with a taper and searches for a handkerchief that Sophy had just dropped in going out. The same charming little march tune that accompanied his entry in the First Act is now heard again in the Orchestra. He finds the handkerchief, trips out quickly, the curtain falls, and that's the end. In conclusion, I should like to tell you a little story. Someone said to Strauss one day that the Rosenkavalier struck him as an Opera full of beautiful spontaneous melody, and – on the other hand – many carefully calculated discords. "Ah!", said Strauss, "the exact contrary is the case. Inventing discordant passages is an easy matter for me. What DID cost me an infinity of pains was the shaping of the many beautiful melodies that the Opera contains!"[209]

I trust that when you go to see the Opera, you will heartily endorse this last, and realise that the highest art is the art that conceals art'.

Lecture on Verdi's *Don Carlo*[210]

'ACT I.
FOREST OF FONTAINBLEAU. [*sic*]
The scene opens in the Forest of Fontainbleau [*sic*] where Elizabeth is riding escorted by her page Tybald whilst a hunt is in progress. Don Carlo hidden by the trees, has come incognito from Spain to see for himself the Princess to whom he is betrothed and at first sight falls in love with her. [Here comes an aria of real lyric beauty, of which I will ask Mr L(ark) to play you the first phrase, which we can call the theme of Carlos[211] (*sic*) love for E(lizabeth.) This is used again in the prelude to Act III.][212] Aria, [After this][213] Elizabeth and Tybald return having lost their way in the growing dusk and Don Carlo introduces himself as a member of the Spanish Envoy's Suite. The page who has caught a glimpse of the lights of Fontainbleau [*sic*] in the distance is dismissed by Elizabeth, who entrusts herself to the care of the noble stranger. They begin to talk and it transpires that one of the conditions of the peace to be concluded between France and Spain is the betrothal of Elizabeth to Don Carlo. Elizabeth plies the stranger with questions about him. The seeming stranger assures her he can vouch for the sincerity of Carlo's love, and shows her a portrait he has brought of her betrothed. She recognises it immediately and Don Carlo falls at her feet with a declaration of his love.

Here follows a duet of exquisite tenderness, which opens with a phrase

Glorious John

for the orchestra of rather novel [shape][214] for Verdi. [There is not time to sing this duet but, Mr Lark (will) play the opening phrase, and another tune which we can call the Fontainbleau (*sic*) motiv and is also used again later on in the opera Eliz(abeth's). Aria Act V.][215]

DUET.
They are then interrupted by Tybald who returns with [other][216] pages carrying torches. He prostrates himself before [Eliz(abeth)][217] and addresses her as Queen. Philip of Spain has asked for her hand and her father has consented. She protests she is promised to Don Carlo, and during this a crowd arrive, escorting the Spanish Envoy, who tells her Philip desires her full liberty of choice and formally repeats his request for her hand. The crowd anxious for the cessation of hostilities[,][218] urge her to accept, which she reluctantly does amid their blessing, and a cry of despair from Don Carlo

ACT II
SCENE I. This Act opens with the Monks of the Convent of St. [Giusto][219] chanting before the tomb of Charles V, to which Don Carlo has come to try and forget the sorrows of the world (Minor and Major chords) [Charles V motiv used again in (the) Prelude to Act V.][220] Soon to his delight arrives Rodrigo, Marquis of Posa and his dearest friend. Rodrigo tells him the oppressed Flemings are in dire need of his help, then stuck by the anguish on his friend's face begs him for the reason of his sorrow. Carlo confesses his love for his stepmother, meanwhile fearing his friend will recoil from him at this. All Rodrigo does however, is to enquire whether the King is aware of this, and on being informed to the contrary, suggests Don Carlo try and obtain for himself the Governorship of Flanders, where he might forget his woes in the relief of an oppressed people. King Philip and Elizabeth arrive, and she is much moved at the unexpected presence of Don Carlo. After a brief homage at the tomb they pass on leaving Don Carlo and Rodrigo to swear eternal friendship, in a rather trivial and vulgar duet, which is all the more marked in contrast to the rather fine and austere music that has gone before. This one of the poorest themes in the Opera, [& is the one I have previously termed][221] the theme of comradeship and is used again (I regret to say) at the end of the II Scene of this Act and at the death of Rodrigo (end Act 4, Scene II). [Record of Duet. Scotti & Caruso. So that you can be prepared for the work when you go etc..][222]

The second scene is a garden outside the gates of the convent, where

Part Two

the pages and the ladies-in-waiting on the Queen are passing the time in song. It is in this scene that the important character of the Princess Eboli makes her first appearance. Soon after she has sung the "Song of the Veil" (Moorish Love Song) Elizabeth returns and soon Rodrigo is announced. He bears a letter from her mother in Paris, and with it slips another note in her hand[,][223] which in an undertone he begs her to read. Elizabeth guesses rightly it is a note from Don Carlo, in which he tells her to have complete trust in the bearer. She asks Rodrigo beg some favour. He does so, but on behalf of his friend Don Carlo, who is much hurt at the hostility of his Father and begs audience of him. Eboli who is in love with Don Carlo wonders if this is a ruse to see her again, but Elizabeth better understanding the note, wonders if she could [bear][224] to see him again. She decides to send a message she will be glad to receive her son.

Rodrigo manages to keep the ladies at a distance when Don Carlo arrives, so he may speak with the Queen alone. He begs her do all in her power to get the King to send him to Flanders. She[,][225] always keeping her relationship to the fore (Mother and Son) promises her utmost. Maddened by this insistence on their relationship, he loses control and begs a word of pity as a human being. She tells him her reserve is a matter of duty[,][226] and confesses, though they must part[,][227] she still loves him. Carried away he embraces Elizabeth, who tears herself free and with terrible sarcasm asks if he [would care to][228] first murder his father[,][229] and then marry [his][230] mother. He recoils[,][231] and saying he is accursed[,][232] rushes out. The whole of this scene between Don Carlo and Elizabeth, is perhaps the best thing in the whole Act. The variety of moods is admirably translated, and I would draw your attention to the longing so tenderly expressed in the tenor phrase "Perduto ben my sol tesor",[233] which in manner of orchestration (3 flutes and Clar[inet].) and mood is a precursor of portions of the [Nile][234] Duet in "Aida". There are some sweeping phrases and a poignant ending.

DUET.
The King entering is furious at finding the Queen (contrary to his express orders), unattended, and dismisses the lady who should have been in waiting. The Queen bids her farewell in a beautifully pathetic aria with accompaniment of great expressiveness in which the Cor anglais plays a prominent part.[235] The King seeing Rodrigo asks him to remain, and bearing in mind his splendid services and the fact that Rodrigo has never asked the smallest favour presses him beg for one. Rodrigo replies he wants nothing for himself, but begs the King have pity on the desolation and mourning

Glorious John

into which persecution have driven Flanders.[236] The King replies that Peace can only be obtained by Bloodshed. Rodrigo retorts that is the peace of the dead[,][237] [and] The [*sic*] King should give them Liberty. Philip warns him beware of the Inquisition[,][238] then confesses his anxiety about the Queen and Don Carlo. It shall be the duty of his loyal friend to watch them, and grants him the privilege of access to the Queen at all times. Philip leaves him with a final warning to beware the Inquisition, whilst Rodrigo is delighted at the opportunities of aiding his friend[,][239] which chance has put in his way. This scene forms an elaborate duet between Philip and Rodrigo, in which admirable characterization and sensitiveness in the accompaniment is shown.

ACT III[240]
SCENE I. Midnight in the Queen's Gardens in Madrid. Don Carlo is discovered re-reading a letter of assignation for that [hour][241] which he imagines has come from Elizabeth, but has really been sent by Princess Eboli. Soon she enters heavily veiled, and Don Carlo immediately makes love to her. She unveils, and realizing his mistake is profuse in his apologies. (A little more tact on his part at this moment[, might][242] have saved him a heap of trouble). Eboli realises at once he had mistaken her for the Queen[,][243] and in her jealousy tells him to beware of her revenge. Rodrigo at hand watching on his friend, comes forward and begs her not to listen to his words. She leaves in rage. The two men left together, Rodrigo begs Don Carlo, hand over any incriminating documents he may possess. Don Carlo doubting his friend's loyalty hesitates at first, but Rodrigo, soon convinces him and the scene ends in protests of mutual trust and affection.

The only music I shall let you hear from this Act is the beautiful prelude, based on the motive of Carlo's love. (Don Carlo's first Aria, Act I, Scene I). You will note the beautiful and bold harmonic progression (last twelve bars) which is unmistakeably new for Verdi, and savours of the Othello [*sic*] period, but this need surprise us unduly as it belongs to the revised Edition of 1884. (13 years after Aida but 3 years before the production of Othello [*sic*]).[244]

SCENE II. This scene is laid in the great square of the Church of Our Lady of Atocha, where a number of heretics are to be burnt at the Stake. There are crowds and the bells are ringing. While the people sing of the glory of Philip and of Spain the Queen and the court enter and take their places on the steps of the Church, and the monks lead in those condemned to die. Presently the doors of the Church open and reveal the approach of Philip.

Part Two

As he descends the steps six deputies from Flanders presented by Don Carlo beg mercy for their oppressed Country. Philip brands them as traitors and orders their removal. In [the][245] great ensemble [I have referred to][246] the crowds join in their plea for mercy, but Philip and the monks insist they are traitors and heretics. Don Carlo, thereupon begs to be entrusted [with][247] the Governorship of Flanders and his father summarily refuses. Don Carlo draws his swords and swears to avenge the Flemings. Philip commands he be disarmed. No one moves till Rodrigo steps forward and to him the amazed Don Carlo gives up his sword. Philip after bestowing the title of Duke upon Rodrigo leaves the scene, the rejoicings [continue],[248] the flames grow ever brighter and a "Voice from Heaven" consoles the [victims][249] with promises of peace in the next world. [End Act III].[250]

ACT IV (PART I).
The King is found meditating in his study and gives vent to his exceedingly gloomy reflections in the famous aria "Ella [giammai][251] m'amò",[252] one of the most basely treated bass arias in existence. RECORD.[253] [Pinza].[254]

After this the grand [sic] Inquisitor arrives to discuss with the King the punishment of Don Carlo. The Inquisitor assures him the Inquisition will support the most extreme measures, and also demands the sacrifice of Rodrigo. The King protests that Rodrigo is the only man that he can trust, while the other insists he is a far great[er] culprit than Don Carlo. The Inquisitor leaves and Elizabeth enters angrily demanding the return of her casket of jewels which has been stolen. Philip has it in his possession and orders her open it in his presence. On her refusal, he does so himself and the portrait of Don Carlo is found. He is in a fury, but she reminds him Don Carlos[255] [sic] was first betrothed to her. He goes further, taxing her with infidelity and threatens to kill her. [She][256] calls for help and Rodrigo and Eboli arrive. The latter is torn with remorse at the scene she has herself engineered. Elizabeth recovers and laments her exile in France. When the men have gone, Eboli confesses her treachery to the Queen and begs forgiveness, not only for stealing the casket but for allowing the King to seduce her. Elizabeth after giving her the choice between Exile and a Convent leaves Eboli to curse the fatal beauty which has secured her these doubtful pleasures, in the famous aria O-Don Fatele [sic].[257] RECORD.

ACT IV (Scene 2).
The Scene opens with Rodrigo [visiting][258] Don Carlo in prison. Don Carlo's treasonable correspondence has been found in his possession and knowing

Glorious John

he must soon die[259] has come to say farewell. Don Carlo will not accept the sacrifice offered but Rodrigo urges it is Don Carlo's duty to live to save Flanders. During this a man[260] has crept in [unseen][261] and at this moment fires at Rodrigo mortally wounding him. With his last breath he urges on Don Carlos his duty to live, and tells him[262] Elizabeth awaits him at the Convent of St. [Giusto.][263]

The King arrives to free his son but Don Carlo recoils in horror from the man who has murdered his friend. A great noise is heard outside. It is the crowd demanding the heir to the throne. The King orders the gates to be opened and the vengeful crowd rush in. Eboli in disguise is among them, and urges Don Carlo to profit by the confusion and escape. At this moment the Grand Inquisitor enters, and commands them prostrate themselves before their Heaven protected King.

The terrified crowd sink to their knees begging mercy, whilst the King and the Inquisitor advance to meet each other.

The Church has saved the State.

ACT V.
The last Act opens in the Convent of St. [Giusto][264] with Elizabeth praying before the tomb of Charles V. It is night.

Immediately after the introduction (based on the Charles V motiv first introduced by the Chorus Act II (Scene 1) comes a fine aria for Elizabeth in which the Fontainbleau [sic] motive [sic] is quoted [when][265] she speaks of the noble soil of her beloved France, and the happy days [at][266] Fontainebleau. ARIA. [Licette.][267]

Don Carlo arrives to bid her a last farewell and tells her of the strength that has come to him to do his duty in [a][268] manner worthy of Rodrigo's sacrifice and his love for her. She weepingly expresses her admiration, and with the knowledge that only in the next world can they find happiness, take their last farewell. This scene with Don Carlo takes the form of a magnificent duet, in which you will find the lovely phrase of the tenor in Act II (Scene 2) (Perduto ben moi [sic] Sol tesor)[269] treated with a wealth of orchestral and harmonic [device].[270] It is too long to perform in its entirety this evening, but I will ask L. & P. to sing you the closing section, which to my mind is perhaps the most [beautiful][271] thing in the whole [work].[272] In what I may perhaps refer to as its poignant spiritual tenderness you will find one of the supreme examples of Verdi's genius. DUET.[273]

Philip and the Inquisitor enter, the King seizes Elizabeth by the arm and commands the Inquisitor's attendant seize Don Carlo. At this moment a

Part Two

Monk garbed in the habit of Charles V emerges from the tomb. All thinking it is an apparition lose their grasp on Don Carlo who is dragged into the interior by the Monk.

[I hope I have not wearied you much with this perforcedly inadequate survey, but I do hope it has sufficiently aroused your curiosity to make you go and hear the performances that are to be given at C[ovent] G[arden]. this summer. Nobody who professes admiration for Aida, Othello [sic], and Falstaff can afford to miss hearing the work in which more than in any[274] of their immediate predecessors, Verdi explored those paths which were to make the last stupendous achievements possible.

Harrogate London Pullman. 12.3.33.][275]'.

'*Pelleas and Melisande* Preamble'[276]

'Pelleas so rarely performed etc. etc.
Before anything else I would like to say that there is some music that is not always intended to amuse or distract, that to quote Christopher Morley,[277] it sometimes attempts to convey "that strange solitude and homesickness that is the glory and distress of the human spirit". That spiritual solitude and nostalgia are conveyed by Debussy in his Pelleas in music so shadowed by remoteness of suggestion and mysterious of mood that only attentive and confederate ears can know the burden of its song. As we hear Debussy's wonderful score unfold itself, the realization is borne on us that there is no music such as this. For this music seems greatest in those moments when it hints of truths that music had never told. It is touched with an exquisitely pitiful sense of the pathos of human destiny, its falling twilight at the end of all delights, its mystery and its inescapable end. Through all this music of still intensive desperate ectasies [sic], and a tenderness hardly to be borne, ther[e] runs an utterance of commiseration unequalled anywhere perhaps in Bach.

Like all intimate disclosures of the creative imagination, it is unique for everyone who loves it. It permits us to think that we alone possess it.

The excerpts from the score performed at these concerts are drawn from Acts 1, 2, and 4. They are taken chiefly from the preludes to these Acts and from the entractes [sic], or orchestral interludes, that link the scenes of each Act. The entractes [sic], of extraordinary beauty and expressiveness, are seldom heard in the opera house, for the reason that most opera audiences are in tha [sic] habit of regarding entracte [sic] music as a not too

Glorious John

disturbing background for conversation.

ACT 1

While hunting, Golaud, the widowed grandson of old King Arkel of Allemonde, loses his way in a forest. He comes upon the wraithlike Melisande, weeping over the loss of a crown that has fallen to the bottom of the well. Timorous and aloof, she gives Golaud no inkling of her identity beyond her name. But at length, she consent[s] to go with him. Golaud would now take Melisande as his bride. He writes to Pelleas, his half brother, to persuade their mother Genevieve to gain Arkel's approval. Bringing Melisande, Golaud returns to the castle. Melisande and Pelleas are drawn to one another.

The first piece in this Suite begins with the brief orchestral prelude with which the opera opens, and is linked with the entractes [*sic*] which precede Scenes 2 and 3. The music is sombre, brooding and fateful, and is redolent of the sea and of the strange and pitiful figures that are to enact the tragic drama that follows.

ACT 2

The opening scene of this Act is laid beside an old and disused fountain in the park near the castle "the Fountain of the Blind," so called because it once possessed the power to heal the eyes of the sightless. This ancient well under the dense trees that no sunlight ever pierces – this well is almost as deep and as old, they say, as the sea itself. Its mystery and its silence are restorative and so is its water, which is always cool, even when the castle park is hot and oppressive.

The twelve bar prelude to this magical scene is music of indescribable limpidity and freshness, as though the fountain had stirred in its long sleep and spread it murmuring coolness through the instruments.

Pelleas and Melisande enter together. It is a stifling day, and they seek the refreshing tranquillity of the fountain and the silence under the overarching trees. Their talk is dangerously intimate. Melisande, dips her hand in the cool water, and plays with her wedding ring, tossing it high in the air as she leans above the well. Pelleas warms her. "You see my hands dont [*sic*] tremble" she reassures him. But the ring falls into the deep water and is lost. "What shall we say to Golaud", asks Melisande in agitation, "if he asks where it is"? "The truth – the truth" answers Pelleas.

They leave, and the first orchestral interlude of this Act leads, by a transition to the second interlude. This second interlude follows the scene in Golaud's bedroom in which he discovers the absence of Melisande's wedding ring, and, his suspicions aroused, bids her harshly go at once to seek it in the place where she lyingly [sic] tells him that she must have lost it – in the grotto by the sea, where she went in the morning to gather shells fo[r] the child Yniold. The tide is rising, and Melisande says she is afraid to go alone to the grotto. Golaud suggests that she ask Pelleas to accompany her.

The music of the entracte [sic] is linked, in this arrangement, with the end of the third scene of the Act, the scene before the grotto. The place is very dark. But Pellease [sic] describes it to Melisande for, he tells her, she must be able to answer Golaud if he should question her. The moon breaks through the clouds and illumines brightly and interior, revealing three old and white-haired beggars asleed [sic] against a ledge of rock. Melisande is frightened and begs Pelleas to take her away. They leave in silence as the curtain falls.

The third and final portion of the Suite is concerned with the music of Act 4 in the opera. It begins with the agitated music that precedes the meeting of Pelleas and Melisande, in a room in the castle where he tells her that he is about to leave, never to return, and entreating her to see him alone before he leaves, and includes the sublimely compassionate phrase of the old Arkel: "Si Jetais" etc. If I were etc."

The music then goes to the next entracte [sic], the greatest and most tragically poignant of all (which I always feel had some affinity with the tremendous concentration and power of the final scene in Parsifal, though in a much more concise form) and leads to the final scene of the Act, where Pelleas and Melisande speak at last of what they have known for a long time.

(Here speak impromptu of the whole essence of this work: instead of the ravings and the rantings of the usual operatic procedure, these so timid and urgently frightened declarations "Je t'aime: je t'aime aussi". Oh qu'as tu dit M., je me l'ait presque pas entendu".) From this moment all discretion is to the winds, and this sudden release of passionate abandon, is eloquently pictured in the tragic ectasy [sic] of the music.

The scene ends with the rushing in of Golaud (Melisande's husband) who kills Pelleas with his sword. Melisande flees in terror, with Golaud pursuing her through the forest as the curtain falls.

As I said earlier, this may not be the music of the masses, but if th[e] hearing of these extracts have made even a few of you anxious to probe further the haunting and hurtful mysteries of this masterpiece, I rest well content'.

Glorious John

'Article on Richard Strauss for Hallé Magazine October 1949'[278]

'This can in no sense be an article surveying the achievements of this great artist, nor even a reasoned critical appreciation of his work, but just a few stray thoughts which have been in my mind since that evening only a few weeks ago when I read with deep emotion of the passing of the Master. Immediately my thoughts travelled back to an evening in Venice in February 1883 when the news came to the world that Wagner had died, for many must have felt then, as I felt that evening, a feeling of emptiness that a great figure had left us who not only had revolutionized certain aspects of composition, but had given great beauty to the world in doing so. (Not always the accomplishment of all revolutionaries.) Lest this comparison of his importance with Wagner be thought exaggerated in some quarters, let me say at once that on this question I am in complete agreement with Ernest Newman when he wrote soon after Strauss's death, "Let there be no mistake about it, he is in the royal line".

Note for the editor I have not got the article by me but if you want to verify the exact words they can be found in the articles Strauss I and II which appeared in the Sunday Times a few weeks ago.

Then, when I scanned the papers for further news or obituary notices I found, not altogether to my surprise, a fairly widespread attitude of denigration towards him, or attempts to disparage him, through the subtle agency of dwelling more fully on his lesser works rather than his masterpieces. I had noticed much the same kind of thing when Galsworthy and Puccini died; were they too successful and too much loved by the public? An interesting speculation this. Surely, it is relatively unimportant at what period of his career a man does his finest work, it is for posterity to become selective and treausre [*sic*] for all time that which can most help it to ennoble itself. I never had the honour of meeting him though I did have in 1933 the memorable experience of hearing him conduct Parsifal at Bayreuth. Incidentally, he was also perhaps, except for Wagner, the only great composer who achieved real fame as a professional conductor[279] and I wish I had more space here to go into some of his remarkable and extremely sound 'dicta' on this subject. My abiding impression of this performance, (at which, by the way, original scenery for the 1st and 3rd Acts was being used for the last time) was of a masterly mind, with a complete grasp of every essential of the score, coupled with a serene control of every detail. There may have been a kind of detachment there, but it was not the detachment of coldness, rather let us say the supreme tranquility [*sic*] granted only to the greatest. Never shall I forget the exquisite loveliness of the Flower Maiden's Scene, with its unhurried and compelling seductiveness. Strauss the man I never knew personally, but from the sayings handed down to us we can glean glimpses of a man rich in cool selfcriticism [*sic*], and with a sense of humour occasionally tinged with acidity but never malicious. Of his selfcriticism [*sic*] the following is I think a very valuable example: "But I always want to do too much, to introduce a little counterpoint here, to bring in a more interesting harmonic development there, and as a result I often spoil it." Would that some of his successors, even the most gifted ones[,] could survey their work in this spirit of detached and unerring judgement. Significant that after a serious operation recently we read that to help him through the sleepless nights he chose the scores of the Emperor Quartet of Haydn, the Mozart Clarinet Quintet, Beethoven's Second Symphony and 'Tristan'. Of his humour I like particularly these examples: "The metronome marks of the classics are unknown to us, only our music critics have authentic information about them, straight from Olympus", and again "Richard Wagner once said the Allegros of Mozart should be played as fast as possible. True, but not twice as fast as possible."

Of this artistic generosity let us not forget the tribute he paid to Elgar after hearing "Gerontius" at the Dusseldorf Festival, a tribute which made England realise that she must revise her impression of the masterpiece which had so trajically [*sic*] suffered from a disastrous first performance at the Birmingham Festival of 1906. Born the year before the first performance of Tristan, what thoughts must have crossed Strauss's mind these last years as he looked back over the magnificent past and contemplated as he must, the sombre if not indeed, sordid present. This was strongly borne in on me the night when the Halle [*sic*] played the "Metamorphosen", one of his last and greatest works. This noble piece ends with a quotation in the 'cellos and basses of the first four bars from the funeral march of the 'Eroica', under which he has written the words "In Memoriam". He himself has left no clue, but surely it is not rash to speculate that he was probably thinking of the great German culture of the past, a culture so wantonly massacred by the madness of conquest. Richard Strauss, your place in musical history is secure; your name is already enshrined amongst the immortals of our art; VALE'.[280]

Glorious John

'Forty Years with Elgar's Music'[281]

'Ever since I can remember – and my memories go back over 40 years now – I was regularly taken to the Henry Wood "Proms" and Sunday Concerts and from the age of ten onwards the music of Edward Elgar has meant more to me than I can say. I never argue about him with people who try to point out his faults to me – if full-bloodedness, grandeur and nobility of melodic invention, can be termed "faults". He has sometimes been called "vulgar" – and if there be any vulgarity in his music, it is of the kind that belongs to the greatest of artists, and you can find it in the same way at times in Verdi and Wagner.

Elgar's principal choral works are dealt with elsewhere in this brochure. I therefore propose within a short space to roam over the particular fields with which I have been associated as an orchestral player, soloist (I gave one of the earliest performances, after Felix Salmond,[282] of the Cello Concerto with Sir Dan Godfrey[283] in Bournemouth), chamber-music player and conductor.

As an orchestral player it was my good fortune to play under him on many occasions, and although he may not have been a great conductor in the professional sense of the term, anybody sensitive to his music could not fail to glean a wonderful insight into how he wanted his music played – a lesson I hope I have never forgotten, for these occasions made a vivid and permanent impression on me. I well remember the last time he appeared at a Promenade Concert in the old Queen's Hall conducting his Second Symphony in a programme of British works, and how everything else in the programme was dwarfed by it.

Speaking as a cellist who performed his Concerto on many occasions, I can give the assurance that no writer of concertos has ever understood the instrument better, or scored for it with greater understanding and subtlety.

His chamber music, of which again I took part in many performances of the Quartet and Quintet, has never been appreciated at its true value, but I am sure the day will come when it will blossom fully into its own.

Of the choral works, I have so far only conducted *The Dream of Gerontius* –surely one of the greatest masterpieces of religious expression in music that our art can show. This great work is comparatively unknown in Europe despite the enthusiasm with which it was received at performances in Germany in 1901 and 1902. I hope it may be granted me, before I lay down my stick, to remedy that lamentable state of affairs.

John Barbirolli'

Part Two

'Elgar, the Man'[284]

'One of the great mysteries of music to me is why our own great composer, Sir Edward Elgar, is not accepted as whole-heartedly and without reservation as we accept Beethoven and Brahms. I consider him to be the last of the great line of symphonists (I hasten to add that I have not forgotten Sibelius, whom I place in a different category) and as such well worthy of universal recognition.

My own associations with Elgar's music stem from those days when, as a small boy, I used to waylay members of my father's orchestra and beg their complimentary tickets for the Proms, where I stood entranced by the majesty of the music I was hearing. I remember vividly too, my early days with the Scottish National Orchestra, of which the principal oboe was Evelyn Rothwell, later to become my wife. We were walking together one evening and I remarked that there was one thing I would try to do before I die; to make the public realise the greatness of Elgar's music. I am happy that this ambition is beginning to be fulfilled. His symphonies are greeted with enthusiasm, and I am often asked to conduct them; and only a few weeks ago I had the great thrill of seeing the hall at Nottingham packed for a Hallé concert which included his Second Symphony. Elgar's music is also gaining a firm footing abroad now, where not long ago it was unknown, and I have tried to include as much as possible in my guest programmes. Recently in Basle I conducted the splendid orchestra there – which has been in existence for over sixty years – in its first performance of the Enigma Variations! And so, slowly, the barriers crumble.

It has sometimes been wondered why I, a Cockney-born Londoner of purely Latin blood, have such an affinity with what some call a purely English composer. This isolationist point of view I am not prepared to accept, as I think his music has those elements of greatness which belong to all. One might just as well argue that Brahms can only be accepted and understood by the Germans, or Beethoven by the Viennese.

To revert to this curious affinity, though, between a Latin Cockney and the Worcester-born Elgar – it may arise from the fact that I was born just at the end of the Victorian era and was brought up during the Edwardian period which, of course, Elgar expresses so ardently and admirably. Having begun to play in public at the age of eleven, and started to earn my living at fourteen, I suppose I matured rather more quickly than most children of that age, and I have very conscious memories of the splendour of that era. For me it is a London, which, with its horse-buses (on which I went to

Glorious John

school), four-wheelers and hackney cabs – providing the main excitement of holiday trips to the sea-side – I have seen disappearing with deep pangs of regret, reactionary as this may seem.

Without disclosing any political opinion, I still find it hard when making speeches, as I have had to do in many parts of the Commonwealth, not to refer to it as "the Empire"!

A supposed sin which Elgar has been accused of is his extravagance and vulgarity; but as my old friend Neville Cardus said the other day, "since when has it been a sin to be generous and extravagant?"

Elgar was a *man*, who strode the Malvern Hills and breathed into his very large nostrils the good healthy air of that most delectable part of England. Perhaps it is this very cleanliness, majesty, and the deep emotional content of his music which he was not afraid to show, that makes him an anathema in certain circles to-day.

I remember vividly a remark – an extremely perceptive remark – made to me by H.M. the Queen Mother when she was present at the Hallé concert which opened the Elgar Festival at the Royal Albert Hall some years ago. When I had the honour of being presented I ventured to say how happy I was that England's greatest musical son was at last being treated in a manner almost worthy of him. To this Her Majesty replied with prescient understanding: "Yes, I agree; but it is not quite the thing to think so to-day, is it!"

But perhaps the best analogy to make of Elgar, instead of Beethoven and Brahms, is with to me another great composer who is beginning to come into his own in this country – or at any rate in Manchester! – Bruckner. For he has the same sublime virtues and what some people like to call faults, for they indulge in what seems to arouse such deep resentment in the breasts of some musical commentators who utter (or rather, write) the word "sequences" as if it were some foul and incurable disease.

Another accusation is his vulgarity, but then hasn't every really great composer had his moments of this virile commodity? – Wagner and Verdi to mention but two.

Amongst the works we shall perform in Manchester to mark the hundredth anniversary of the birth of this great man, I must place high in my affections the Cello Concerto. As an old cellist myself, who played the second performance of the work under Sir Dan Godfrey at the old Winter Gardens, Bournemouth, I am deeply conscious of the intrinsic value of this composition. Apart from this, it is generally agreed, particularly from the point of view of the orchestration of the accompaniment to the cello solo, that it is one of the greatest masterpieces written for the instrument – it is universally acclaimed and played by all great cellists.

The public of Manchester has shown me great kindness, understanding and indeed affection. If they want to provide me with a debt of gratitude that I can never repay I ask them to pack the Free Trade Hall on the occasion of the actual Birthday Concert on June 2nd, when we perform the immortal *Dream of Gerontius* – a sublime sacred masterpiece which takes second place to no work in that genre.

I had the melancholy privilege of spending an unforgettable few hours alone with Elgar a few months before his death, and he spoke more about his music and himself than I had ever known him do before. Despite all the official honours that had come to him there were dark passages in his remembrances, one of which was the occasion of his 70th birthday concert at the Old Queen's Hall – a hall no larger than the present Free Trade Hall. It had been half empty.

May I beg of you to redress this wrong'.

'Jean Sibelius 1865-1957'[285]

'The Finnish Master had been with us so long that it is difficult to realise that he is no longer here. Although nothing had come from his mighty pen for many years, there was still the somehow comforting assurance musically that the great symphonist was still alive in his beloved Finland.

With his passing a unique era in the development of symphonic music has ended, for he brought to it a power and originality of mind unequalled in his time. We in this country can at any rate take ever-lasting pride in that we were the first outside his own country to recognize his gigantic stature, and have remained faithful to our perspicacity.

When, during the early years of my assuming the direction of the Hallé, I took the plunge and gave for the first time here the cycle of the seven symphonies, I was greatly heartened by the magnificent response on the part of the Manchester public, and I am sure that nowhere will he be more sincerely and deeply mourned than by the music-lovers of Manchester, to whom he brought such deep and everlasting solace by the greatness of his achievement'.

Glorious John

'V.W. – A Tribute'[286]

'It is with a full heart that I set down here a few personal reminiscences of Vaughan Williams, whose recent death has robbed the British musical scene of a great and loveable genius. This is not the place to attempt to appraise or discuss his music in detail for that is well able to speak for itself. Both in this country and abroad his lovely compositions have been accepted as music of great inherent beauty. In recent years, conducting the Sixth, Seventh and Eighth Symphonies in places as diverse as The Hague, Zurich, Prague, Lisbon, Copenhagen and Warsaw, I have been impressed not only by the public's reaction, but by the fact that members of the orchestras concerned – the most searching of critics – have been unanimous in their praise and in the quite obvious pleasure they derived from their participation.

I had been familiar with the music of V-W (as I shall call him) since my student days at the Academy and had played some of his chamber works with the International String Quartet, but the first big orchestral work of his that I conducted was the *London Symphony*. Strangely enough, this also turned out to be the last big work of his that I was to conduct in his presence – at the Cheltenham Festival a few weeks ago. However, my first actual meeting with him occurred when I came back from America in 1943, and HMV asked me to make a recording of his Fifth Symphony. It so happened that he was to conduct a performance himself quite soon, so I was able to go and hear him rehearse the work in the wilds of Walthamstow, I think it was. It was a unique experience in many ways, and it was there that I first encountered an example of his impish sense of humour, for he said to me "Barbirolli, you must not take too much notice of what I do, for I am such a bad conductor that the result is probably the opposite of what I intend!"

It amused him to assume on occasion a technical ignorance, but this was far from being true. A later incident will illustrate this. Towards the end of the first movement of the Sixth Symphony he has that wonderful lyrical passage for the strings where he directs the first violins to play the tune on the G string and the second violins play the identical tune at the same octave on the D string. The effect of this is absolutely magical, for the D string doubling of the G string gives the G string sound an opulence and clarity which I have never before heard. When I asked how he discovered this extraordinary effect, he replied: "Many years ago I used to play the fiddle a bit and I was playing Raff's *Cavatina* to myself one day scaling the heights on the G string, and I found that some of the top notes got a bit woolly, and I wondered whether the merger of the two sounds might not obviate this". It turned out of course that he was quite right! To me the loveliest part of this story is the picture of V-W standing alone in his room playing Raff's *Cavatina* to himself – if only we had a record of this unique performance!

Our meeting at a rehearsal of his Sixth Symphony at Oxford led to a deep and intimate friendship which grew more and more precious to me as the years went by. I have always thought of him as one of the most "complete" men I have ever known, for he loved work, he loved life and he loved good food and wine; and from all these qualities perhaps stemmed his great humanity which is so wonderfully reflected in his scores.

Some of my dearest memories are of the parties after concerts he attended with a few selected friends. Although he was by now in his eighties, he used to astonish all of us by his physical resilience. Attendance at rehearsal on his part was a matter of great concentration to detail and heavy criticism, and he never hesitated to retouch some passages if he felt it was not exactly what he intended. It was amazing how unerring his instinct was, and how much he could achieve with the slightest adjustment. Critical comment on his use of the vibraphone in the Eighth Symphony (which he did me the honour of dedicating to "Glorious John") amused him: "The vibraphone – why not! It makes such a lovely noise." And it was not long before some of the more hasty criticisms had to be revised.

There are many other amusing and endearing stories I could tell if space permitted. V-W was a great composer, a great man and a great friend. The British musical scene is the poorer by his passing and all his friends and the thousands that loved his music will sorely miss him'.

A tribute to Vaughan Williams[287]

'Early on the morning of 26 August there passed from us on of the greatest and most beloved figures in British musical history. I have been privileged to have had his intimate musical and personal friendship for many years; years that were to become more and more precious as they passed. He was one of the most 'complete' (if I may use the word) men I have ever known. He loved life, he loved work, and his interest in all music was unquenchable and insatiable. Only a few weeks ago in Cheltenham at the Festival of British Contemporary Music, he was in his place at ten o'clock every morning to hear us rehearse the efforts of his youngest, sometimes even obscure, contemporaries, and we all marvelled at him.

Glorious John

It is given to few men to touch the hearts and minds of his fellows in such degree as he has done; and only to the anointed is given the genius that can span such opposites as the lovely little 'Linden Lea' and the tremendous Fourth Symphony.

Dear Ralph: we shall always honour, admire and be grateful to you; but above all we shall always feel blessed that we walked the same earth with you'.

On the death of Vaughan Williams[288]

'The first thought uppermost when thinking of V.W. was the bigness of the man. Not only physically, but in mind, heart and thought. This showed in his insatiable curiosity about any new works, and any possibility of utilizing instruments not currently used in, one might say, the classical armoury. I remember, for instance, when he was criticized for the use of the vibraphone in his 8th Symphony; he said to me, with that marvellously subtle twinkle in his eye: "Why not, John? It makes a lovely noise." And there was the care he took mastering the technical possibilities of the harmonica when he wrote that charming piece for Larry Adler.[289]

Then there was his eternal sense of Youth, and his enchanting sense of humour about things and people – not always quotable, for it was salted at times with his own particular brand of Rabelaisian wit. With all his big and shaggy grandeur, there was also a little of the sprite in him. I remember well that adorable remark he made to his wife, Ursula, when they acquired the house in Hanover Terrace. V.W. was in his early eighties. She said: "I'm afraid we can only get a twenty year lease," to which he replied: "Never mind, my dear; we can renew it."

He had great kindliness and sensitiveness towards others. When he had completed his 7th Symphony (the Antarctica), he thought that he would like me and the Hallé – of which orchestra he had become very fond – to give the first performance. I only got to know much later that he was hesitant to show me the score, for fear of the embarrassment it might cause me if I did not like it. Can true nobility of spirit and greatness go much further?

Then came the lovely 8th Symphony, written for me, and its beautiful Cavatina with the first theme announced by the cellos: a charming allusion to my early days as a player. Talking of this I am reminded of an incident which may not generally be known. I had invited V.W. to conduct some performances of his Sea Symphony in Manchester and Sheffield. At the

Part Two

rehearsal in Sheffield one of my cellists (the sub-principal) was ill, and I thought I would substitute, just for my own pleasure. I had no thought of playing in the evening, in case it flavoured of some sort of publicity stunt. But after the rehearsal V.W. came to me and said: "John, would you play for me tonight?" I said that of course I would be delighted, and he added: "I'll tell you why: I once conducted an orchestra with Kreisler in it, and I would like to be able to say I once conducted an orchestra with you in it."

It appears that as a young man he was conducting a work of his at one of the 3 Choirs Festivals; and, terrified as he already was, he turned to the first violin section and to his consternation saw Kreisler playing at one of the back desks. This, he said, completely shattered him; but the explanation turned out to be simple and really very logical. The next item was a concerto to be played by Kreisler, and since there was nowhere to "warm up" in the cathedral, Kreisler had taken the obvious course of joining the first violins to do so.

Very happy memories Evelyn and I have of the V.W. at the Cheltenham Festivals, which I conducted for so many years. He was a constant follower of them, whether any works of his were being played or not. This, I think, showed one of the finest facets of his character. There every morning at ten o'clock was this great old man, eagerly waiting to hear the work of young men, some of them comparatively little known, without prejudice and always with kindly interest. I remember that before each Festival, he would quiz me with: "John, who's the latest wrong note man?"

Evelyn and I always remember with great gratitude the last Cheltenham Festival he attended; it must have been only a month or so before he left us. In fact Evelyn was really the architect of an unforgettable evening. The festival was to close with his "London" Symphony ("which," he always used to confide to me, "is really my favourite." Then with a really gamin look he would add: "But don't tell anybody – I gather it's not quite the thing to say so.")

He had a wonderful ovation that night, and I remember how deeply moved we all were to share the great moment with him. I say that Evelyn was the architect of the occasion because she had had the inspiration of asking him to supper after the concert, at an hotel where we were staying at the top of Cleeve Hill. It was a lovely moonlit night, and coatless and hatless, his hair gently waving in the breeze, V.W. stood up there gazing at his beloved Malvern Hills.

With us were Ursula and his two dearly loved young friends, Michael and Eslyn Kennedy. His affection for these two dear people was touching

Glorious John

to behold, and I am sure all of V.W.'s admirers will be looking forward with the greatest anticipation to the "double" biography, so to speak, which is to appear from the pens of Ursula and Michael.

Not long after that, I looked on him for the last time. It was a glorious summer's morning, with the sunlight flooding the room; and the noble lines of his face, and the beauty of his hands, were just as might be the effigy of some great medieval prelate'.

'The Noblest Traditions of Italian Art'[290]

'To write about Puccini, who is and always has been one of my musical heroes, is not easy. So many memories and so many examples of his musicianship come crowding through. It is only possible, in the short time available for writing, to recall a few of them.

The first time I ever saw him was in 1920, when he was of course world-famous, and when I was at the last desk of the 'cellos in the Covent Garden orchestra. And the occasion was a rehearsal for the first performance in England of his *Trittico* – *Il Tabarro*, *Suor Angelica* and *Gianni Schicchi*.

As a young musical enthusiast I had already bought and studied the vocal scores, and these rehearsals, under Gaetano Bavagnoli, who knew the works thoroughly, were a constant source of pleasure for me. This was not so for many of my colleagues in the orchestra, who resented somewhat the conductor's intense application and care for detail.

We were rehearsing in the Covent Garden crush-bar foyer, where most preliminary orchestral rehearsals are still held. And I can recall to this day my delight when I looked up and suddenly realised that Puccini himself was standing behind my chair.

He was a tall handsome man and we immediately noticed about him one personal idiosyncrasy in dress. He had a passion for English-made striped ties. But when he bought them he was quite unaware that many of them were special ones – either Old School colours or Club ties. And it was rather fun to see him one day masquerading, without knowing it, as an Old Etonian, perhaps the next day as a Carthusian, speculating whether by the next rehearsal he would have "joined" I Zingari!'[291]

Puccini did not speak any English, but he made frequent comments in Italian during the rehearsals. It was obvious that he wanted, from both orchestra and singers, great warmth and subtlety of lyrical expression, allied to an almost constant overall *rubato*.

Part Two

I clearly remember him singing, to the trombone-players, the big phrase in *Il Tabarro*:

[musical notation]

with a tremendously broad *rubato* on the triplet in the second bar. But in the more purely rhythmical elements of his music, as, for instance, in the opening of *Gianni Schicchi*:

[musical notation]

he sought a tight and sharply accented form of playing.

What I said earlier about Puccini's love of warm, lyrical singing brings me to a particular point. His ideal of a tenor was the Caruso-Gigli type of voice. And I think that the tendency in some quarters to regard him as a "light" composer is due mainly – and especially in this country – to a lack of really suitable large voices for his works.

How often have I myself been obliged, when conducting a Puccini opera, to whittle down the sound of Puccini's orchestra to about a quarter of its true size so that puny efforts from the stage could be heard at all. A consummate artist of Puccini's calibre does not write *ff* or even *fff* in unison with voices without a particular tonal concept in mind.

Talking of Puccini's artistry, how many people – including some who ought to know better – realise the skill and the ultimate refinement of his orchestration, and the originality of it?

His beautiful placing of wind chords, and the exquisite and moving quality of his writing for the flute in the lower register, are only two instances that come to mind out of many. But it would need a special article, and masses of musical quotations, to make these points clear. Here is just one example.

At the end of the duet for Marcel and Rudolf, soon after the opening of Act 4 of *La Boheme*, there is a chord of C major which has a soft and velvety quality that never fails to move me and excite my admiration. This is achieved by a most subtle and imaginative blending in the lower part of the chord, achieved thus:

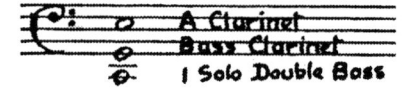

[musical notation: A Clarinet / Bass Clarinet / 1 Solo Double Bass]

Looking for a moment at *Tosca*, I think that anyone who can dismiss this opera as mere "blood and thunder" should have himself seen to.

Glorious John

Take, for example, the opening of Act 3, that miraculous evocation in music of the sound – aye, and even the smell – of Rome at dawn.

Only an absolute craftsman and master of his particular genre could transform his thematic material as Puccini does, and give it varied and pregnant meaning. As I write this I have in mind the gaiety and the tremendous vitality of the four-note figure which opens *La Boheme*. Think of the heart-rending quality this figure acquires in the passage for Mimi and Rudolf at the close of Act 3.

The other day, too, I was looking, reverently, at the score of *Manon Lescaut*, a work rather sadly neglected here except for the performances given recently by the Carl Rosa company. And I was struck anew by the quality and the abundance of musical material in it – enough for most of the composers of today to be able to write a dozen operas.

Recalling *Gianni Schicchi* reminds me of an evening in New York spent with Toscanini, when he dined with me and Evelyn (Lady Barbirolli) and a few well-chosen friends. Mellowed by a long Italian dinner, and the cognac he loved, the old Master was at his most fascinating best.

He talked about Verdi, and he told us how, as a young conductor, he had acquired a personally-autographed photograph of the great composer.

As a young man, Toscanini had conducted *Falstaff* in Milan, and had received a "lambasting" from one of the local critics. Verdi was speaking about this to Boito, and asked "Was it as bad as this says?" Boito replied, "Well, I was there, and thought it one of the best performances I have ever heard." And so, as acknowledgement, and perhaps as some compensation for the critical outburst, came the gift of the photograph.

Then the subject of *Gianni Schicchi* cropped up, and Toscanini related rather sadly how they – Toscanini and Puccini – had quarrelled, so that Puccini would not entrust the premiere of the new *Trittico* to him.

After it had been produced Toscanini happened to be at a performance in Rome, and was particularly moved by the wit and brilliance of *Gianni Schicchi*. He told us how he caught sight of Puccini in the foyer after the performance, and felt a strong urge to go up to him and end the feud, realising that here was still a Master to uphold the noblest traditions of Italian art.

"But," he added, in a moment of rather touching candour, "with my shocking character (*mio brutto carratere*) I could not bring myself to do it. And I have regretted it ever since."

I can only echo my colleague, and repeat: Here was still a Master to uphold the noblest traditions of Italian art.

It is ironic and tragic that the man who put so much loveliness into the throats of singers should have died in such anguish from a malignant destruction of his own throat. But Puccini, who had brought such eloquence to human suffering as expressed in his music, must have had in his last moments the most supreme satisfaction that can come to any creator – the knowledge that all the beauty his mind and heart had created would live.

It will, I am sure, continue to live, to give joy to countless lovers of opera for as long as we allow this world of ours to exist'.

'St Matthew Passion'[292]

'Any musician who contemplates preparing a performance of the St Matthew Passion is faced with an awesome responsibility. Tempo marks and dynamics are practically non-existent in the mighty and noble score, and in the end, even after prolonged and profound contemplation, these can only be the result of deeply personal feelings about the music. The great opening chorus is a very good illustration of this, I have seen editions which conceive it as an expression of idealised grief, strewn with the most elaborate scale of dynamics from *pp* to *ff* (Elgar-Atkins for example). It can also be conceived as purely realistic in intention, depicting a crowd of people excitedly surging through the streets, calling and answering to each other. Schweitzer, to whom I am greatly indebted in my studies on the Passion, takes the latter view, and I agree entirely with him when he says that "the opening orchestral prelude should be played with heavy accents and a certain inward unrest, and that the effect of the chorus should come mainly from the drastic quality of the declamation rather than from factitious dynamic shading".

Bach gives us no indication regarding nuances to be employed in the Arias after the entry of the voice, and I feel that any nuances which give expression to the words and which have a natural musical or poetic justification must be regarded as not only permissible but necessary.

The more I contemplated and studied the vast canvas of this great score, the more I became convinced that I would have to make an entirely new edition of my own. This edition, I must admit, is greatly in sympathy with Schweitzer's, and also Sanford Terry's feelings on the work: namely, that the more dramatically it can be sung the better providing that the dramatic conception is a profound one.

The few dynamics which are Bach's own have of course been faithfully retained, as have all the phrasings which are in many cases meticulously marked (as for instance in the violin obligato [sic] to the Bass Aria "Gebt mir meinen-jesum [sic] wieder") and magnificently and modernly virtuosic they are.

It is obvious that when time pressed, Bach could only hastily look over the orchestral parts, and he evidently felt it more important to mark the phrasings rather than the dynamics (which he would find simpler to indicate to his players as he went along). Schweitzer indeed tells us that many times Bach has inserted ties and left wrong notes unaltered, so the importance of adhering faithfully to his phrasings cannot be over-estimated.

On the purely practical side of performance I have decided to use both harpsichord and organ, but in the recitatives confining the harpsichord to accompanying the Evangelist. In the chorales, and all the recitatives of Jesus accompanied by the orchestra, the organ must always play.

Boys [sic] voices are necessary in certain instances.

The viola da Gamba is used for the Bass Aria "Komm susses [sic] Kreuz", but I have adhered to the violoncello indicated in the score for the obligato [sic] to the Tenor Aria "Gebuld [sic]".

Incredible though it may seem, I began my serious study of Bach's music over 50 years ago at the age of ten, with the Suites and Sonatas for cello: now four years of constant thought have gone to the making of this edition of the St. Matthew Passion.

It is offered in fervent humility and devotion'.

'Barbirolli talks about the Elgar Second'[293]

'[Ronald Kinloch] Anderson: *One composer with whom you have been very much associated for a long time, Sir John, is our great Elgar, and having just finished recording the Second Symphony, following your wonderful record of the First some time ago, I am sure that you must have many memories of these works from your earlier days. Can you tell me when you first conducted the First or Second Symphony?*
Barbirolli: I started with the Second Symphony under very dramatic circumstances. As you will remember, my career as a conductor began in opera at Covent Garden in 1926. The following year Sir Thomas Beecham had been engaged to conduct at one of the famous Monday night concerts which the LSO used to give at the old Queen's Hall. Other conductors who had taken part during the season included Weingartner, Nikisch and others.

Part Two

The programme was to consist of a Haydn Symphony, the Haydn Cello Concerto (with Casals) and the Elgar No. 2. When Sir Tommy had to give up the concert owing to indisposition, the orchestra, remembering that I had in fact played with them many times, said, "Why not give old John a chance?" I was therefore rung up on Friday afternoon. Haydn symphonies I knew inside out; well at least some of them, for there are too many! The Haydn Cello Concerto I had, of course, played many times so this work presented no difficulties. I had played the Elgar No. 2 but had never seen the full score, and when I was asked whether I would conduct the concert I was all for saying no: Friday afternoon – Sunday, first rehearsal – Monday, second rehearsal – Monday evening, concert. I remember my dear old Italian father standing by the phone (we had one of those old fashioned ones in the hall) and whilst I was saying no, he said to me: "Don't be a fool! It is not every day that you will get as opportunity like this!" I therefore capitulated and learnt the Symphony between Friday night and Sunday morning (in less than 48 hours). You remember that wonderful man who was Elgar's closest friend, W H Read[294] [*sic*]...

K.A: *Yes, I knew him very well when I was a student.*
J.B: A great man in many ways, a violinist and a composer as well as a great personality. He was *the* great Elgarian by way of his experience of having played under the composer on many occasions, During the rehearsals he was so kind and such a great help, even though by then I had formed my own ideas about the Symphony. When some of the LSO boys very kindly tried to help me, Bill Read said "Leave him alone! He already knows what he wants to do. You know, Elgar might even like it!" This was, therefore, my introduction to the Elgar Second. And there is a delightful EMI coda to put to the story. After the performance, Fred Gaisberg, that immortal character in the history of EMI, was standing amongst the first fiddles and as I walked off after one of the calls he said: "My name's Gaisberg, don't sign any contracts, I'll phone you in the morning."

K.A: *So as a result of this you eventually started recording?*
J.B: Yes, in 1927.

K.A: *Well I remember your recordings with the then John Barbirolli Chamber Orchestra because it was through your recording of the Elgar* Introduction and Allegro *that I go to know it.*
J.B: This leads on to another little anecdote! Somebody played this

Glorious John

recording to Elgar (I think it must have been Billy Read or one of his friends) and the remark he made was: 'Do you know, I didn't know that was such a big work.'

K.A: *That was certainly a very big compliment. Did Elgar himself hear of your performance of the Symphony?*
J.B: Oh yes! As a matter of fact I forgot to mention that Billy Read must, I think, have phoned or written to Elgar because some two or three days later I received a large envelope with a letter, addressed from the Master of the King's Musick, Buckingham Palace, in which Sir Edward told me about the wonderful things he had heard about the performance and thanked me. This is, of course, a treasure which is framed.

K.A: *I think that the wheel is turning a full circle for Elgar because he is returning to great favour with the public again.*
J.B: It had to come you know. When I was in Helsinki with the Hallé last year, we played two symphonies at the Sibelius Festival, to which the President of Finland came. Afterwards we had a reception at which several distinguished Finnish musicians told me that they were very conscious that there was at present a trend to try and to denigrate Sibelius. I replied that we were having exactly the same sort of thing in our own country with Vaughan Williams. I don't know if you could call it a physical or a metaphysical miscalculation, but Elgar, Vaughan Williams and Sibelius are immortal. And I think it is a physical fact that you cannot destroy immortality.

'The Dream of Gerontius: a Personal Note'[295]

'"Figlio mio, questo e un capolavoro subline." With these words Pope Pius XII raised me to my feet, after I had knelt before him to receive his blessing and thanks for a performance of the first part of "The Dream of Gerontius" given at his summer residence of Castel Gandolfo, by the Choir of Our Lady of Dublin and three distinguished British soloists.

The treasured memory of these noble and sensitively appreciative words is made all the more poignant when we remember that barely ten days were to elapse before His Holiness was to pass from this world, and that this was the last "live" music he was to hear.[296] I have often wondered what the feelings of Newman and Elgar would be if they could know that the last music he heard had been Elgar's setting of Newman's words "Go forth upon

Part Two

thy journey, Christian soul".

But as I recall this, other memories crowd in, and I will go back to one of the earliest of these. Not long after leaving the army in 1919, as a regular deputy with the London Symphony Orchestra, I had the great good fortune (at the last desk of cellos) to take part in the first post-war Festival of the Three Choirs, held at Worcester in 1920. The three Choirs Festival in those days, when Worcester was still a lovely country town, with Elgar's father's music shop still standing, could, I think, well be described as Elgar's Bayreuth.

For a young man who loved Elgar's music, it was wonderful to see the great man, radiantly happy amongst his friends in the Cathedral precincts; more wonderful still to play "The Dream" under his direction, with that great and noble artist Gervase Elwes[297] singing the Soul. I remember that Elgar conducted from memory (the antithesis of Vaughan Williams, who always averred that he could never remember a note of his own music) and although he could not be called a great conductor by the highest professional technical standards, it was extraordinary how he could make you feel exactly what he wanted if you were in sympathy with him.

Now I come to the days when at last I had to study the work in detail for preparation of my own first performance. I began to realise for the first time the great delicacy, imagination and subtlety of much of the scoring. (Alas, this is often obscured by the lack of sufficient preparation. It is a work which has that dreaded reputation "Everybody knows it" so that one rehearsal, or at most two, is deemed sufficient.)

Amongst the many performances I have know conducted, of course some of the most poignantly beautiful memories must be those in which the beloved Kathleen Ferrier took part, including the very last one she was to sing – at the Edinburgh Festival of 1950 with the Hallé Orchestra and Choir. There was an almost prophetic beauty of utterance in her singing of "My work is done, my task is o'er".

The next milestone for me was the opportunity afforded me, through the enthusiasm and indefatigable efforts of Sir Ashley Clarke (then British Ambassador in Rome) to give the first performance in Italy – incredible though this may seem – in the centenary year of Elgar's birth, with the magnificent collaboration of the orchestra and chorus of the R.A.I. in Rome. Never shall I forget the look of joyful surprise and enthusiasm on the faces of the orchestra and chorus at the first rehearsal, when the wonders of the work unfolded themselves. Incidentally, since Italian and English are mother tongues to me, the voluble comments on the work did not escape me.

Glorious John

Such was the great impression created by this performance and broadcast, that the next year I was invited, with the Choir of Our Lady of Dublin, to the "Sagra Umbra" (Sacred Music Festival of the Umbrian Province) to give performances of "The Dream" and also the Messiah, in Perugia, in the lovely old Morlacchi Theatre there; this time with the splendid orchestra of the Maggio Fiorentine.

The Dream of Gerontius has strong links with the Hallé Orchestra. Its first performance, at the Birmingham Festival on 3rd October 1900 was conducted by my great predecessor, Hans Richter, who had taken over the Hallé a year before. Although that performance was a disaster, due to many causes, one of which undoubtedly was Richter's underestimation of its difficulties, Elgar did not blame the conductor. Richter however blamed himself, and he did not conduct it again until he had had ample time to prepare it and to rehearse the choir fully. On 12th March 1903, Manchester heard the work for the first time. A critic of the day who was also one of Elgar's earliest champions, Arthur Johnstone, had attended every performance of "Gerontius" including the two in Germany, and he declared this second attempt of Richter's to be the finest of all. It is particularly interesting to read that Richter attached great importance to the quality and balance of the semi-chorus. Those of you who may one day be listening to these records will, I hope, feel that I share this musical wisdom of my great predecessor.

In fine, it is a work exulting and exalted, written as only lasting masterpieces can be, in a constant white heat of inspiration. In this wise, it is very instructive and amusing to recall W.H. Reed's charming remembrance of a remark made to him by Elgar as they came out of Lincoln Cathedral after a performance of "The Dream". "Billy, I believe there is a lot of stuff called double counterpoint, or whatever they call it in that." Of course, that is the right way round to write "that stuff", when it comes out of the bones and tissue of the music and is not imposed on it from a species of cerebral hangover.

I am profoundly grateful to E.M.I. for granting me the privilege of recording, with such loyal and sensitive colleagues, this great work which I love so deeply'.

Part Two

An Interview with Ronald Kinloch Anderson[298]

'ANDERSON: *Well John, I am happy to say that I had a wonderful experience in Berlin with you when you were conducting the Philharmonic and recording the Mahler Ninth Symphony for us, and as you are now regarded in a lot of places in the world as a Mahler specialist, I was wondering when and how you first came to conduct Mahler symphonies.*
BARBIROLLI: Well, as a matter of fact I owe that entirely to Neville Cardus who (it must be nearly ten years ago now) came to me one day and said, "John, you must take up the Mahler symphonies! They were written for you and you have got the only orchestra in the country that can make the right sound for them!" I must say I became more and more fascinated, and curiously enough I chose the Ninth as my first venture into the field of Mahler.

K.A: *Where was that?*
J.B: In Manchester, and I got Neville to come up and talk about it because it was entirely unknown there.[299] Although it is of prodigious difficulty, I still think, from the point of purely musical content, it is perhaps the greatest of them all. This I felt from the beginning, although I have enjoyed so much all the others.

K.A: *I noticed even in Berlin they don't play a very great deal of Mahler's music.*
J.B: No. some twelve months before this recording I had done the Ninth with the Berlin orchestra when they were not at all keen to do it. Dr Stressemann [*sic*], their General Administrator, said to me afterwards, "You know they are very devoted to you and said if he wants to play Mahler, let him do it!" This is the spirit in which the performance came about and of course they were conquered by it.

K.A: *Absolutely; the members of the orchestra personally told me how thrilled they were to do this work and to do it with you. Your performance of the Mahler Fourth Symphony in the Philharmonic Hall was also an enormous success and a very beautiful performance.*
J.B: And I believe they actually said (I shouldn't really say this myself) that this was the best Mahler heard in a decade – quite a few people must have played Mahler symphonies during that time.

113

Glorious John

K.A: *They were right all the same. It was a most tremendous success. Have you plans for any more concerts in Berlin?*
J.B: I am going back there next June. I can't go there in my usual January period because the orchestra will then be touring America, so they have invited me for June, and I must say I feel very flattered because they have again asked for Mahler and Bruckner. You know for a French-Italian Cockney that is not a bad point to arrive at!

K.A: *That will be a great event – I hope I can be there. Tell me, while we're on Berlin, how do you like the new Philharmonic Hall as a place to play in?*
J.B: Well, I can't say that I like it particularly. These what I call medicinal, orthopaedic, surgical halls that they produce force you to create so much atmosphere yourself when you play. But the architect said a rather nice thing to me after my last concert: "Thank you, Maestro, for putting some blood into my hall!"

K.A: *Well you did it all right because from where I sat it sounded magnificent.*
J.B: One thing I remember very much, talking about that time, is this very beautiful orchestra (I don't think you can use any other word for it). Remember one of the things that impressed you most was their playing of Debussy with me.

K.A: *It did indeed because you got the real French sound from the orchestra.*
J.B: It shows you what instrumentalists of that calibre can give you so readily when you have in mind a particular kind of sound; they are a remarkable orchestra in that way… You know, it's a funny thing to say, but I think in these days it's a great tribute, although it doesn't sound like it, that is a great and beautiful orchestra because it is a very *musical* orchestra.
K.A: *Well that's a nice point to end on, so thank you, John, for a delightful talk.*'

Some Reflections on Mahler[300]

'Q. Your name, Sir John, and the name of Gustav Mahler are almost synonymous to audiences wherever you conduct. Do you feel you have been one of the pioneers of what has been described as the "Mahler Renaissance"?
J.B. Yes, I think I may well have been. Actually the original Mahler pioneer was Bruno Walter, but sometimes he lacked the proper facilities. When I came to Berlin for the first time to conduct the Philharmonic Orchestra,

Part Two

I was very surprised to find that these musicians had previously hardly performed any Mahler at all. I then decided to conduct Symphony No. 9, which I believe is his greatest in musical substance.

It is a source of great satisfaction that in the meantime, Mahler has become one of the most popular composers in England. Even in Italy, at the Scala, Milan, in Naples and Genoa, in each of these towns, they wanted to hear a Mahler Symphony conducted by me – and they did! Just imagine – in Italy! This made me very happy.[301]

Q. Is there a new readiness on the part of the public to listen to this music in a different way, more attentively than before?
J.B. Previously people did not have much opportunity to hear Mahler. However, it may well be a point of interest that it is ordinary people who start loving Mahler, moved by his humanity. Basically it was always the musicologists who have made critical pronouncements on Mahler, on his problems of form and other aspects. At the 1968 London "Proms" I conducted Mahler 6.[302] There we had an audience of nearly 7,000 people, many of them young: the majority of those in the arena stood in silence, for over one hour twenty minutes to listen. The next day in Venice, I conducted Symphony No. 4. Few in the audience had ever heard the work, but such music touches the emotions. This is the uniqueness of it, that everything comes from the expressiveness of these scores. Mahler had so much to say (it is a long time since a composer had anything essential to say) and much of what he wrote strikes one in its language as new music. I think we agree today no really great music is written, but good music, very interesting music that one should hear and know.

One of the most distinguished British music critics is Sir Neville Cardus. Some ten or 12 years ago he came to see me and said "John, my boy, you do not know it, but this music was written for you'. So I began to study the Mahler symphonies – if you want to conduct Mahler well his music must be under your skin and in your bones. Because I subsequently spent two years studying one of these scores, I have, as it were, enriched myself in doing so, and it is a joy to me in my advancing years that I have found something which, apart from the connoisseurs, is new to people and is also of such mighty dimensions. Mahler's name is no longer a mystery – he has at long last become a monument.

Q. What do you regard as the specific details of Mahler interpretation?
J.B: There were people who laughed at me when I told them that I spent

Glorious John

two years studying a Mahler symphony. Of course it does not take me two years to read these scores, but if you prepare for a journey through such immeasurably wide musical spaces, you must know exactly where the musical ideas begin and where they end, and how each fits into the pattern of the whole. In Mahler's symphonies there are many highlights but only one real climax, which one must discover. To do so needs less a simple study of the score than an all-embracing aesthetic reflection – which, incidentally, was also peculiar to Bruno Walter'.

'Memories of "Otello"'[303]

'I have already had occasion to express my gratitude to EMI for making one dream come true in a very literal way, by their recording of the *Dream of Gerontius*, Elgar's great oratorio, in 1965. Now I have to repeat my thanks that I have again had the opportunity to record a work which I have known and dreamt about since I was a boy (and quite a small one at that) – Verdi's *Otello*.

My grandfather (Antonio) and my father (Lorenzo), both violinists, played a great part in my musical life, even although the former died when I was seven. In these few years, however, his influence had been marked: he started me on the violin when I was five and transferred me to the cello two years afterwards. My father, a wise and gentle counsellor, exercised his benevolent influence until his end, much later but still too early, in 1929 when I was thirty. As will be easily imagined, it was a source of great pride and continuous interest in our very musical household, that both my grandfather and father had taken part in the first performance of *Otello* at the Scala, Milan, in 1887. It was of course mainly from my father, in my slightly more mature years, that I heard many – to me – most enlightening memories of this historic occasion. It was a rare privilege for me to hear these, not from some old man searching back in the recesses of his memory, but from a man still in the prime of his life who remembered everything with great clarity.

Of the many memories and incidents which he told us about, his stories of the "band room" talk during rehearsals for the first performance of Verdi's masterpiece have always interested and amused me. We must not forget that *Otello* came as something of a shock to the old school of musicians – "the professors" – of whom there were still many in the Scala orchestra at this time. They had witnessed Verdi's earlier triumphs and now

Part Two

they were faced with something that looked to them almost like Wagnerian music drama and they did not at all approve. The younger men were all enthusiastic and thrilled by Verdi's new contribution to the development of opera. "*Plus ça change...*"

The first conductor of the *Otello* was Franco Faccio,[304] a great friend of my grandfather and very fond of his boy Lorenzo. Like our family he was of pure Venetian origin. He was the greatest Italian conductor of his day and he had already conducted the first European performance of *Aida* and the first Italian performance of *Die Meistersinger.* I am still the happy possessor of many charming notes from him to Antonio and Lorenzo. During rehearsals Verdi had no hesitation in correcting Faccio in regard to any tempo which was not to his liking. Normally rather silent, Verdi would at such moments produce a tremendously loud clicking of his thumb and second finger which resounded throughout the empty theatre and put everyone on their proper course again. One tempo about which he was particularly insistent was Otello's *Ora e per sempre addio* which he used to remind the cast was marked *Allegro assai ritenuto*. My father would illustrate this by singing the passage in Verdi's tempo.

The first interpreter of the part of Otello was the great tenor Francesco Tamagno. Of his voice, temperament and power much has been written; but such voices are difficult to manipulate and my father, to the end of his days, used to shudder at the recollection of Tamagno's inability to sing the A flat at the end of the first act at anywhere neat its proper pitch! Great artist as he undoubtedly was, Tamagno evidently had other weaknesses too; in a letter to Faccio at the time when he was preparing the first performance of *Otello*, Verdi expresses, somewhat ironically, the hope that the conductor will be able to persuade the tenor to sing "something approximating to what I have written"!

My grandfather and father must have taken part in a considerable number of performances of *Otello* at which the composer was present since they belonged to that group of experienced players from the Scala orchestra who went round the more important Italian theatres augmenting the local orchestras in the first performances, with the original cast, of this very new and unfamiliar manifestation of Verdi's art. Certain remarks repeated many times by Verdi were therefore particularly clear in their memories and one of these, which my father often talked about and which has remained vividly impressed on my mind, and to which I have given much thought, expressed the composer's feelings about the interpreter of the part of Iago. I quote this since it seems to me to show a point of view in regard to the

117

vocal interpretation of Verdi's operas which is of special importance. As is well known, the character of Iago was of such paramount importance to Verdi that he originally thought of calling the opera by that name. The first Iago was the French baritone Victor Maurel[305] who, although a great singer, must have had what we might call a fragile and therefore at times unreliable voice. Father used to recall that on certain occasions, although seemingly in normal voice, Maurel would send forth the dread message that he was "*senza voce*". Invariably on these occasions Verdi's reply was the same: "As long as Maurel can *speak* I would rather he did Iago than anyone else".

These few memories were simply heard by me in the normal course of conversation in the family where many legendary names came up. They have never before been written down. I hope they may have been of some interest to those of you who listen to these records. As a closing word, in this cynical and disbelieving world, I would remind the reader again that these are no imaginings of an old man but were heard by me from my father when he was still comparatively young.

Sir John Barbirolli'

Barbirolli – New York, 1942

Glorious John

Barbirolli at Niagara Falls, c. 1940

John and Evelyn, Hollywood, 1941

Celebrating the Centenary of the New York Philharmonic Symphony Orchestra, 1942

John and Evelyn visiting a steel mill, NYPSO tour, 1941

Glorious John

Barbirolli rehearsing the New York Philharmonic-Symphony Orchestra

Barbirolli conducting the New York Philharmonic-Symphony Orchestra

Glorious John

PART THREE

On Conducting

Speech given to the New York Philharmonic-Symphony League[306]

'I am afraid I am but a poor compensation to you for the loss of my brilliant and illustrious countryman, Mrs. Patrick Cambell [*sic*], and I fear I have been brought before you as a speaker on the very insecure basis of an entirely spurious reputation of being able to say what is graphically, if erroneously, described as a "few words." In addition I don't think that even a conductor in the 28th week of a very strenuous season can be expected to be as mentally alert as would be desirable for such a distinguished gathering. I might say quite frankly that I have always thought that one of the obvious manifestations of the courage inherent in the English speaking peoples is the recklessness with which they ask people to make speeches to them – without seemingly reminding themselves that it involves listening to them.

As you know, I have had very little notice of my appearance here, and it is a little difficult to know what to talk to you about. It has been suggested that you might be interested to know something of the labour and strain involved in the preparation of an orchestral concert, and perhaps a word or two on this subject might prove of interest to you.

I do feel that sometimes rather a lot is taken for granted and that the nervous and emotional strain of being a member of a great orchestra such as our beloved Philharmonic is not realised enough by many people. But first there are more routine things to be mentioned. Primarily, or course there is the orchestra itself. It would seem obvious and simple to collect a hundred fine players and expect a fine orchestra. But it is a far subtler and delicate proceeding than this. The best soloists are not always the best orchestral players – too much brilliance can be detrimental to an ensemble and above all it takes years for an orchestra to mature and reach the point of perfection attained by the Philharmonic. The mellowness and rechness [sic] which a body like this acquires can, I think, be likened to that mellowness and beauty which comes to a lovely piece of furniture which has been lovingly tended and cherished for almost centuries. When occasionally through death, ill health, or any cause replacements have to be made it requires not only knowledge but great experiences to find and choose players who will quickly merge into the existing fabric.

Then we come to programmes. Programme making is difficult and dangerous art. In essential, I think it requires three main qualities: catholicity, character, and conviction. The first of these so that the widest possible range is covered. The second, that you not be swayed by sentiments or personal reason, and the third, to arm you against fads and cranks, and thus delay your transference from the podium to the insane asylum as long as possible.

Programme-making last summer. Amount of music read.

REHEARSALS:
1. Perhaps most important and trying features.
2. Preparation for rehearsals – bowings, phrasings[.]
3. Separate rehearsals for complex modern works.
4. Own beauty likened to an experiment.
5. Contrary to belief is musicians' sense of humor [sic] which comes to rescue at tense moments.
6. Example of drummer last week, who had apparently made a slight miscalculation in his estimate of 900 bars, rest or so, and failed to come in. In gently chiding him for his slight misdemeanor [sic], he countered with, "Oh, you want it louder." I know most of the staple explanations and excuses, having used them myself for some years (and curiously, they are the same in most countries), but that was a new one on me. I must add that I had the graciousness to congratulate him warmly on his mental activity, if not his performing one at that moment.

Now I come to probably the least realised fact of all: the nervous and emotional strain on the men, especially the solo men. Liken, the first instruments to principal singers in big roles.

Do not dare eat before a concert
Train like athletes
Pale before important solo

Part Three

Today almost demand infallibility
Let then but make one sour note in a season, and it will be blazoned forth with scorn and horror.
I have the proud privilege of being at the head of a superb body of men whose conscienciousness [sic] and devotion to [music] is alone all praise, and I hope this little insight into their work has not been without interest for you.

Before I sit down, I would like to say this to you of the younger generation present here today, and for obvious reasons I do not use the word "younger" in terms of opprobrium for I belong to you myself. I these days of political upheaval, international strife and hate, grave responsibilities are placed on your shoulders, and amongst them is the one of preserving for generations yet to come all that is finest in the traditions and culture of your great country and your great city.

The Philharmonic-Symphony has a noble history going back nearly a century, and in its history is enshrined the generosity and foresight of the music lovers of this city who helped preserve this magnificent institution for you through what must have been troublesome days in the past. The presence of Mrs. Pratt emboldens me to do something she is probably too shy to do herself and to bring to your notice her wonderful idea for giving a much larger number of people than hitherto have ever done, a personal interest in their own great orchestra.

    Details of League
    Not money making, etc.

Being a musician, I might easily be accused of perhaps stressing too much the importance of music in our lives, but I will even go further and say that the noble heritage left us by the great masters is almost a necessity for the preservation of our sanity in these days. Should my word not be impressive enough for you, I will add that of Shakespeare, for did he not in his infinite wisdom say to us in Taming of the Shrew [rest of text missing]'.

'Becoming a Conductor: a Conference with John Barbirolli'[307]

'Music and Study

An artist who is sincere and serious must have a belief in himself. The musician who is honest with himself, who treads his own path constantly but not obstinately, will come out on top. He should not be too stubborn to listen to others, nor too frail to have faith in his own convictions. I am a great believer in the young artist struggling to develop himself from within rather than aping the tempos and mannerisms of older artists which the facilities of radio and the phonograph have tended to accentuate. One cannot change minute by minute in response to someone else's thoughts. Change comes only with growth and sincerity. There is a kind of beauty in the impetuousness of youth, the richness of maturity and the serenity of age.

In 1936 when, at the age of thirty-six, I took Arturo Toscanini's place at the helm of the New York Philharmonic-Symphony Orchestra, I looked back over my musical life and was infinitely glad of the chance which had been mine to know the orchestra intimately from so many different points of view. I was glad that I had been a member of orchestras during my youth for, among many things, it taught me that a good conductor must also be a good psychologist.

For example, I knew that a conductor has to pull things out of some players, while for others who are sensitive and responsive a flicker of the eye will suffice. The latter type of player just resents being browbeaten. It had been said that certain orchestras had the reputation of being "tough." This was not found to be true of any of them, once they felt that the conductor knew his business. The musicians can sum up a new conductor in fifteen minutes. If he is bluffing, they know it and act accordingly. No orchestra resents sincerity; all will cooperate if approached correctly. The orchestra men are excellent judges of what is or is not worthwhile musically, even if they do not understand a composition at the outset. Their reactions are important and accurate, for they have played so much music that they are able to make just comparisons. Needless to say, struggling to read the bad manuscript of a new work makes them angry and weary. Very often composers are not thoughtful enough to write legibly.

What of the young musician who wants to be a conductor? If he is not born to conduct, he will never make it. People can not be taught to conduct. They can only be taught to beat time, but there is more to conducting than that. A conductor can make the most perfect motions, but succeed in getting nothing from them. One conducts with the mind through the eye. That is to say conducting is a form of hypnosis.

Conductor or Time Beater

There are two sides to conducting, the physical and mental. The first is so easy that almost anyone can accomplish it. Learning the music is at once the most important and the most difficult. Rarely will a good conductor worry about a constantly rigid beat. He will know the music thoroughly and, then indicate what he wants from the players by any means at his disposal. This is determined by the type of the music and the mood of the men at the moment. Sometimes a rigid beat is required, sometimes just the general feeling.

Conducting from memory is a stunt and a fraud if the conductor only knows the high spots. If however, he can write down every note of the score from memory, if he knows the music so thoroughly that his mind is free and he does not worry over what is coming next, if his conducting is equally good without a score, then there is no need for him to use a score if he does not care to. Some conductors discard scores from necessity, because there eyesight is bad. I use scores because I consider it more important to enlarge my repertoire than to spend time memorizing a comparatively small number of compositions. Yet, by the time I have finished studying a new score, I know it so well that there is scarcely any need for the written page. As an illustration, the story of the Bax composition might be cited. I was scheduled to conduct the first performance of a three-movement composition by Arnold Bax with the Royal Philharmonic Society of London. I had been studying it for some weeks. The night before the first rehearsal, the score was lost. I reconstructed from memory a skeleton score, corrected the manuscript orchestral parts and conducted the rehearsals and the concert without the composer knowing what had happened until it was all over.

A writer once described me as being an Englishman with Latin ancestry and temperament. Because my father and grandfather before me were musicians, it was perhaps inevitable that I should adopt the same profession; that I should start to study the fiddle at the age of seven; that I should change to the violoncello and make my first public appearance when I was eleven.

I had tremendous musical opportunities in my boyhood. My father and grandfather, who had both taken part in the first performances of Verdi's

Glorious John

"Otello," supplied a vivid operatic background of reminiscences regarding tempos and other musical habits of the great singers and conductors of that era, while at the Royal Academy when I had a scholarship, I had played all the Beethoven "String Quartets" by the time I was twelve years of age. All this helped to give a wide grasp of musical literature.

When Sir Henry Wood conducted at Queen's Hall every orchestra member had one free pass. I used to turn up outside the hall a half hour before the concert and beg a ticket. I generally got one. At that time I liked conventional music, such as Italian opera, Beethoven, Brahms, and so on. In 1912 in heard Delius' "Dance Rhapsody" and it bowled me over. It revealed a new and unsuspected musical horizon. Immediately I began to spend all my spare pennies buying the music of Ravel, Debussy and other contemporaries. On the instant I decided that Mozart was pretty, but dull; I could not bear Brahms and Schumann, and so on. But my liking for Handel and Bach was never lost. Much later, when my classical development came and when Mozart, Schumann, and Brahms took their correct places in my conception of music, I realized how healthy had been my acquaintance with the music of my own time.

In my early years I was somewhat of prodigy. At the outset I did what other musicians try for years to do: I played concerti with big orchestras. I tried not to let it turn my head, nor to be deceived by the glamour of it. I did not just idly wait for engagements that never materialized – for of course, one always comes to the place where he is not in constant demand; I did not ask always to be a star. There were no patrons. When I had to earn my living I did it wherever and whenever I could, and everywhere I learned something. My musical life, playing in the orchestras at movies and opera houses, in theatre and chamber ensembles, gave me great happiness. I took everything possible from every living moment; I did not spend my time wishing I were doing something else. Toscanini and Nikisch rose from the ranks of orchestra men to be famous conductors. They were unlike those young tyros who consider themselves too good to learn in a humble way, who insist on having fine instruments, plenty of time for meditation and wealthy patrons to make the way easier, and whose horizons are necessarily narrow, their inner selves limited in experience and feeling.

Recognize Opportunity

I do not think there is such a thing as people not having opportunities, nor do I think it possible for an opportunity to the right person. But it is possible for people to be so shortsighted that they are not prepared for real

Part Three

opportunity when it comes. Some are impatient. Some wait for opportunities when they should be working. Some waste time hoping to the greatest or the foremost this or that. Some mope around, fretting at the circumstances in which they find themselves. In the end, they blame their lack of success on lack of opportunity.

While I played in orchestras I was working constantly, hoping that the day would come when I would get a chance to conduct. I bought and studied miniature scores, practiced and prepared myself. I wanted to conduct so badly that even at the age of four I used to shut myself up in a room, sing to myself and conduct by the hour. In my native England a big opportunity seemed to be a long way off, for there were not as many large orchestras as in America, and those that existed were already supplied with able conductors.

In the lives of many people there have been moments when they have wavered. There was such a moment in my life when I decided that I wanted to be a doctor. Now I am glad I could not afford it at the time. But from my brief study along those lines and from my reading, which consists mainly of biography and history, I have learned that youth and innovation will always have their detractors, but those with the right stuff in them will generally manage to survive, and even become ennobled and enriched by the ordeal they have to undergo.

The years, from 1917 to 1919, were lost to music, for I joined the army and went to war. When I returned to England the country was in such a state that there was not money enough for large orchestras and yet, when the need for music was felt, there sprang up many chamber ensembles which delved into little-known music. In 1924 I started to conduct a chamber group which impressed people who heard it so that I was engaged for a series. Soon Frederic Austin, at that time director of the British National Opera Company which succeeded the Beecham Company, heard my group and engaged me, whereupon I was called upon to conduct Gounod's "Romeo and Juliet", Verdi's "Aïda" and Puccini's "Madame Butterfly" – all in the first week with approximately three hours of rehearsal! Within a year I was conducting in Covent Garden in the so-called "Grand" season.[308]

During this time, I was acquiring a repertoire. Those were gruelling days. All day rehearsals went on. Evenings were taken up with performances. Then at five the next morning I would get up to study for a few hours before rehearsal. Since my mother was French and my father was Italian, I knew their native languages, and the knowledge helped in the opera house. Any conductor who wishes to conduct operas with sense should know the

Glorious John

languages in which they are sung. Opera is not just notes, it is also drama. I am one of the few to have conducted opera in Covent Garden in four languages. By 1927 I was conducting the London Symphony Orchestra and the Royal Philharmonic Orchestra.

Musical England

It is strange that many critics comment on how well I play Delius' music, but perhaps this thought comes to them when they remember that we were both born in England. Actually, we are countrymen only through an accident of birth and should be far apart in temperament, for I am of Italo-French descent and he of German ancestry. Very often modern English composer like Delius and Vaughan-Williams [*sic*] are received with suspicion because someone has doggedly kept up the pretense [*sic*] that the English people are "unmusical." Last summer, when I was supposed to be taking a vacation, I scored an "Elizabethan Suite" for strings and four horns, made up of two compositions by Giles Farnaby, one by John Bull, one by William Byrd and one by an anonymous composer. These were all from the old Fitzwilliam Virginal Book, and their original harmonies were left intact. These charming pieces were a product of this "unmusical" England, at a time when anyone who wanted to call himself a gentleman and move in certain social circles had to be able to participate in after-dinner musical performances. In those days, people did things simply because they wanted to do them, not for money, or to create a sensation. It was a classic sincere period from which emerged a classic sincere music, an exciting living music even yet, but it is practically unknown save to scholars. Surely one cannot justly call a country or a people who produce such music, "unmusical!"

Nor is modern England unmusical. A wonderful part of its musical life, especially in the North, in Yorkshire and Wales, are the great voluntary, amateur choral societies, composed of miners, factory workers, and so on. Some of these date back two hundred years or more and membership is by subscription. The members learn compositions like Bach's "B minor Mass" and modern works such as Walton's "Belshazzar's Feast" from memory. Some cannot read music and must learn by Tonic Sol Fa. Even now they're doing this, though in a reduced way because of war conditions. This is an impressive way to use spare time, getting in touch with beauty by learning masterpieces. I do not think we have this to the same extent in America, and an extension of choral enterprise would be a healthy musical sign.

The comparative lack is perhaps due to the fact that there is so much good music on tap that many don't take the trouble to learn it for themselves. They are too content to listen, and then many never know the joys of participation. One should always keep one's respect of fine music. It should never become too familiar. The young musician who is to-day going out into the world must learn to broaden his musical horizon; he must love music far too much to care for its nationality, but at the same time he must learn that there are other masters besides those of German birth. He must explore the great musical literature of all nations and all epochs. The true artist never stops learning; never stoops to hypocrisy or loses his questioning mind'.

Speech to the New York Philharmonic-Symphony League on 1 November 1938[309]

'– Subject: "A few Words on Conducting" –

To me has fallen the pleasure and the privilege of opening the series of lectures to be given by several distinguished musicians on behalf of the Philharmonic-Symphony League, but I would ask you to consider my little talk not so much in the light of a lecture, as of a mild aperitif before the feasts to come. [It is an especial pleasure for me to address some members of the D. A. Society in this country for tho[ugh] I am by blood a pure Latin, I was in a country whose language with slight modifications has become your mother tongue.][310] My first and greatest difficulty has been to think of a subject which might be of interest to you and, secondly, to present it in a manner which will not prove too trying for you, for I am after all a conductor and not a professional lecturer. Besides, I have always held it as a golden rule that conductors should not talk too much (at least at rehearsals). My second difficulty in deciding on what to talk about has also been that I am not sure even now whether I am addressing an audience of seasoned concert-goers or whether there may be some amongst you who have decided to make this pilgrimage to the realms of great music for the first time. But even so, the subject suggested to me finally, "A few words on conducting," might be of equal interest to you all, although when it was put to me I was reminded of an incident related of the late Sir Edward Elgar.

A good many years ago now, a young man who has since won great distinction in his own country, W.H. Reed by name, was so moved on hearing one of Elgar's works for the first time that he waylaid him outside the artist's room of the Queen's Hall in London and begged Elgar for some lessons in composition. Elgar ever modest and truthful, replied, "Well, I

Glorious John

don't know much about that sort of thing, my boy, but come along and we'll have a chat." I feel rather like that, because some of the greater and more vital aspects of the conductor's art are so intangible and elusive, that it would need a far more practised phrase-maker than I to put them into intelligible form. The function of the conductor, and in some cases I might add, the abuse of those functions, have increased so much since their first inception that it might not be without interest to make a brief historical survey of them

CONDUCTING TRACED BACK TO 15TH CENTURY

The history of conducting can be traced back at least to the 15th century by which time it had become customary to beat time at the "Sistine Chapel" in Rome with a roll of paper called a "Sol-Fa." [so that Italy the "cradle of the arts" as Shakespeare once called her, was the cradle of that art too][311] In 1516 we find writings describing performances of concerted vocal music at which "a certain motion made by the hand of the chief singer according to the nature of the marks which motion directs a song according to measure." This rather tends to prove that by the beginning of the 16th century the practice was universal; as does also a passage from Galilei's Dialogo (1583) where he mentions that the ancient Greeks did not beat time "as is customary now."

With the decline of polyphonic music its attendant rhythmic subleties [sic] the time-beater must have become less necessary and as the idea of the conductor as an interpreter as well as a time-keeper was not yet born, the practise [sic] of directing music with the conducting stick seems to have fallen into disuse.

THE QUESTION OF THE STICK

How and when the change came about I am not certain, but by 1740 or so it was customary to direct opera performances sitting at the harpsichord, (at least in Italy and Germany),[312] and we have also of course descriptions of Bach to prove that he in any case was in the habit of directing the music while he himself played the organ. In France, though, the practise [sic] of using the stick seems to have continued [unbroken],[313] for someone (I am afraid I cannot at the moment give the authority) writing in England in 1709 has rather an amusing account of the art as he saw it practised in Paris and apparently copied with assiduous indiscrimination in London. I don't think I can do better than quote you the passage as it stand:

"The Master of Musick in the Opera at Paris had an Elboe Chair and

Part Three

Desk placed on the Stage where, with the Score in one hand and a stick in the other, he beat time on a table put there for that purpose, so loud, that he made a greater Noise than the whole Band, on purpose to be heard by the Performer. By degrees they removed this Abuse from the Stage to the Musick Room (which must mean what we now term the orchestra pit) where the Composer beats the time in the same manner and as loud as ever, but since the Italian Masters (this must refer to the Italian Opera composers who enjoyed great popularity in the town at that time) have come among us, they have put a stop to that ridiculous custom, because the Eye was too much distracted, being obliged to mind the beating of the measure and the score at the same time; besides, (and this will please some of my Metropolitan Opera friends, if not my colleagues there) it kept the singer in too much subjection, and Fear of Errors."

By the beginning of the 19th century, however, the practice of beating time seems to have been firmly established in Germany, though it was not until 1820 that conducting with a stick at Orchestral Concerts was tried and became an institution in London, when it was introduced by Spohr at a Philharmonic Concert. At the rehearsal this daring innovation (until then the orchestra was guided, or we hope it was, by the joint efforts of the principal violin or leader, and a gentleman at the harpsichord who came to the rescue with a few chords if things got a bit shaky) was received, as I suppose all innovations are fated to be, with profound distrust by the directors, but in Spohr's own words, "The triumph of the baton was complete."

THE TRIUMPH OF THE BATON

His account of this historic occasion is very interesting, and I think worth quoting to you: "I took my stand in front of the orchestra, drew my directing baton from my coat pocket, and gave the signal to begin. Quite alarmed at such a novel proceeding, some of the directors protested against it, but the triumph of the baton was as a time-giver was decisive, and no one was seen any more seated at the piano during the performance of Symphonies and Overtures."

The most famous practitioner of the art at this period was probably Mendelssohn who presided over the Gewandhaus concerts in Leipzig from 1835-43. As inspirer and founder of the modern school of conducting, I think we can safely point to Wagner, and a survey of his chief disciples, such as Bulow [sic], Richter, Levi, and Mottl, quickly brings us to our own times.

Glorious John

WAGNER'S TWO PRINCIPLES

Now perhaps I would just say a little as to the practical application of the conductor's art as a means of making orchestral or concerted music more easily intelligible by clarity and eloquence of presentation. This practical application of the art I divide into two sections: The physical with which I incorporate the psychological, and the purely musical mathematics of the art.[314] The possession of gifts of the first-named I regard as essential to the fulfilment of the other; for have we not often had the spectacle of a great musician unable to secure even a mediocre interpretation of a work of his own.[315] Wagner laid it down that the two fundamental principles underlying the art were: (1) Giving the true tempo to the orchestra; (2) Finding the "melos" by which he means the unifying thread of line which gives a work its form and shape. Given these two qualities, of course, we have the conductor in excelsis and most of our lives must be spent in the pursuance of these qualities, more especially the first.

ACCURACY IS NOT ENOUGH

Having stressed the importance of tempo to this extent, I have sometimes advised students as a guiding principle that, "No tempo should be so slow as to make it difficult for a melody to be recognizable, and no tempo so fast as to make a melody unrecognizable," and that composers' metronome marks, though sometimes inaccurate, can be at any rate a guide which would be dangerous to ignore. This is not to suggest that accuracy of this kind alone can make a perfect performance for accuracy without imagination is useless and some small modification of tempo will ever be necessary to a living rendering of any music. From the foregoing, it will be realised that the possession and understanding of these fundamental principals laid down by Wagner can only be claimed by minds of a musically very sensitive nature and endowed with the will, energy, and patience to probe them to the full in the interests of their art.

Now I would say a word on the physical-psychological aspect which is so wholly important because, however, splendid or magnificent a man's musical ideas may be, they will be nullified if these are not present.

When I speak of the physical aspect I mean a natural gift of gesture which should be at once clear and eloquent, and in the term "gesture" is included the beat. I do not personally believe in any standardisation in this respect, but I would ask that every gesture have a definite meaning, and only be inspired by the most complete sincerity toward one's work, oneself, and the public.

Part Three

PSYCHOLOGICAL PROBLEMS

The psychological aspect is the early divination of the types of players with whom you have to deal and your power of making them do their 100 percent-best for you and the music.

This brings us to a very delicate and important problem – the latitude one can allow to players regarding expression in the rendering of their solos. No hard and fast rules can be laid down here as some players need more guidance than others, and the conductor must be quick to realise these points. It is dangerous to worry a very sensitive player too much; on the contrary, during an important and difficult solo the conductor should provide him with a background of sympathy, trust, and help. I have sometimes been approached to explain various interpretations of the same piece due supposedly to "moods" of mine. But the explanation is quite other.[316] This freedom, however, must not extend so as to permit any anachronisms in phrasing, and no "selfish" player, however good, should ever be tolerated in any first-class orchestra.

I think it could hardly be called a digression from my subject, A Few Words on Conducting, if I attempted to tell you something of the general duties and problems of conducting which more or less brings our topic up to the present and immediate time. I wonder if you realise at all that the work the public sees the conductor do is the least of his job. I am not even referring to the continual rehearsals during the season, but to all the work of annotating parts, editing, the one hundred and one points of technical elucidation of scores which has to go on always.

PROGRAMME MAKING

Of course one of the most formidable tasks that faces the conductor of an organization such as the Phil[harmonic] is to make programs, programs that must have as a basis the great classical masterpieces, what we might call a representative selection of modern classics, and such contemporary music as might interest the public to hear – – not forgetting the encouragement which this great Society must extend to native composers of worth. I myself have sometimes spent weeks reading scores of which more than 90 percent must finally be rejected, not because they are all unworthy of performance, but because I have never believed, nor will I believe, that the Philharmonic-Symphony concerts should become an experimental forum. When the program material is all gathered together, I must try to obviate any duplication for the odd and even series, and to insure the retention of some degree of sanity to myself, no attempt must be made to please

Glorious John

everybody. Has it ever occurred to you[317] that one can assemble four of the best pieces of music, and make an abominable program. Also, in a well balanced program the substitution of one piece can completely ruin it. I can say without any exaggeration that it has taken me five months to compile programs for this season, and obviously with the compilation of these programs there must be a constant study. So you can see that the conductor's so-called holiday can hardly be called a rest cure. I personally find that after months spent in research and study the actual period of conducting comes as a blessed release, musical thoughts that have been singing inside one for months at least can be given rein at last.

SEATING AN ORCHESTRA

Some questions which I am often asked, and which I might take the opportunity of referring to here, concern the seating of the orchestra, the type of baton one uses, accompaniment of soloists, and whether it is best to conduct with or without a score. All of these four things are so personal that I can but give my own reactions, though of course we all think we have the best reason for doing what we do. Take firstly the question of seating. The main difference is that of the disposition of the strings. It has become usual of late years both here and abroad to mass the deeper-toned string families on the outside of the orchestra to the right of the conductor in the place for so long traditionally occupied by the second violins. Sometimes the violas are placed immediately on the right of the conductor or sometimes even the cellos, and the first and second violins have been massed together on the conductor's left. This perhaps creates an extra brilliance of violin tone, while the proximity of the lower strings to the outside of the orchestra makes for a deep somber-hued [sic] sonority.

This, however, can have its drawbacks. The main one, I think, is that it tends to a preponderance of the bass parts. An even more vital one, especially in the performance of older classic works where there is often fugal and melodic interplay between the first and second violins, is that when they are massed together it is not so easy to distinguish between the two, and I don't think we can deny the fact that this, what we might call visual, interplay that takes place aids the aural interplay when each section is on either side of the conductor. I personally seat the orchestra in the more conservative way of having the violins on either side which is much in the manner of the Joachim Quartet, because after all the string choir of an orchestra is but an enlarged quartet. I was very interested to find only a few nights ago when visiting some friends who have a collection of Wagneriana

Part Three

to find a sketch for the seating of an orchestra for a concert in Wagner's own handwriting, with the strings disposed of in very much the same manner as the strings in the Philharmonic-Symphony are today. Obviously, as I said earlier, there can be no hard and fast rule laid down, and the conductor in the end seats his orchestra in the way in which he himself feels most comfortable and will satisfy his musical consciousness, which must always be his guide. [Since the notes were made, a notorious colleague of mine, who has almost entirely emigrated to the glamorous world of Filmdom has made even more radical exp.(eriments) need not be discussed here][318]

On the subject of batons, here again the choice is a personal one but perhaps a much more important, sensitive, and delicate choice than is commonly imagined. It is a rather curious fact which I have noted almost unconsciously – some conductors change types of batons in different stages of their musical development. In my own case the batons I find that have suited me best have changed from what might be called a brilliant and flashing period in my youth to the more sedate and sober person I am rapidly becoming. Apart from personal consideration here as in everything, good taste and good sense should determine. It is absurd to use a baton which resembles a diminutive lead pencil as it is to wave a weapon of exceeding length and frailty.

THE CONDUCTOR AND THE SOLOIST
I have taken pardonable pride in the compliments paid me by artists for my so-called accompaniments. I have used the word "so-called" advisedly because with the majority of the great concertos such as the Mozart, Beethoven, Brahms, etc., to call the orchestra and conductor the accompaniment is about as accurate as referring to the piano part of the Mozart, Beethoven, and Brahms Sonatas as accompaniment, and such success as may have attended my labours in this sphere is because I treat a Concerto not as a virtuosic display by one individual, but as a collective musical accomplishment, and I spare no pains to that end. It must not be forgotten that the performance of the great concertos provided during a season is not merely a question of soloists but a part of a definite plan to put before the public as many of the symphonic masterpieces as possible. We must not forget that the great concertos are always considered part of the orchestral repertoire.

THE USE OF SCORES
A still more controversial topic of conducting is the use or not of scores. I would immediately like to say that it is foolish to imagine that a man

Glorious John

knows less about his scores because he uses them. On the other hand, it is just as foolish to accuse those who dispose of them of being bluffers and charlatans. The prime duty of any conductor is to secure the best possible performance of any work with which he is entrusted and to use this end such means as he conscientiously believes will insure the best possible results. To some a score may be an impediment, to others, even though they refer to it very seldom, it is a release from any anxiety which enables them to give a much freer vent to their imagination. At the outset of my career I did a considerable amount of memory conducting, but I placed on myself the extremely arduous demand that what I conducted from memory, I should also be able to write down from memory. As I could not continue to discharge faithfully this onerous conscientiousness, I reverted to the scores. On the last occasion when I conducted "Meistersinger" three or four years ago in London, I amused myself by conducting the dress rehearsal without a score, but for the performance something in me said it was more respectful to have the music before me.

Mention of "Die Meistersinger" brings back one of the most exciting, vivid, and happy evenings in my musical career. One night not long after I had begun my operatic career I was sent for by Covent Garden to conduct a performance of that opera at literally a few hours' notice. While I had conducted many English performances, I had never conducted one in German. But these are opportunities that do not come every day, and in the fiery enthusiasm and impetuousness of youth I accepted almost greedily this task. I shall never forget the wonderful cooperation of everyone concerned, and I treasure to this day a delightful letter of appreciation from Lotte Lehmann who was the Eva in this production.

CONDUCTORS' SUPERSTITION

Perhaps I may be permitted one more personal reminiscence of those intrepid days. It is a story attached to my debut as an operatic conductor. Until that fateful week I had only conducted a small chamber orchestra and was called upon to conduct Aida, Tosca, Butterfly, and Romeo and Juliet within a week with a paucity of rehearsals – – staggering to think of at this time. The directors of the British National Opera which had succeeded the Beecham Opera Company were willing to do their best for me, but with many principal singers travelling about a great deal, it was almost impossible to get the chorus, orchestra, and cast together at one time. However, they did succeed in assembling them on the Friday previous to my debut, which was to be the full rehearsal of Aida. Now I have to let you in on a very grave secret. It is that all conductors [all poor conductors anyway,][319] are very superstitious, and I shamelessly confess that I belong to this select band. We have a superstition in the part of Italy from which I spring that it is very unlucky to begin anything on a Friday, and I remember my old grandmother who was then about 86, on hearing that my first rehearsal in this new sphere of activity was on a Friday, was horrified, and decided we must talk the matter over very carefully. At this, for me, most vital conference it was decided that whether or not I had ever conducted a large chorus and orchestra before, and even if I had to make my debut without a rehearsal, [my new career][320] must not start on a Friday. I had to invent the most formidable untruths to convince the directors of my inability to be present at this full rehearsal. What might be thought impertinence, I thought was almost divine inspiration on my grandmother's part. Perhaps this was not an unwarranted assumption, since, by obviating this Friday rehearsal, I find myself talking to you as the conductor of the New York Philharmonic-Symphony Orchestra.

OPERA AS A STARTING POINT

There is one last point I should like to make and that is I would venture the assumption without any qualification whatever that a conductor is born and not made. By this I am not referring to a music quality, but rather to a purely technical capacity, and I also do not mean that a born conductor cannot find room for improvement. For my own case, from the first I dealt with the most difficult technical aspects, such as [the conducting of][321] recitatives, with the same degree of ease and facility as I do now. Some of the most involved technical problems are to be found in the opera house. I would advise any young man with the opportunity for doing so to graduate from the opera house, and it is an indisputable fact that some of the greatest conductors have come from there. For there the conductor is faced with sudden and curious emergencies of all kinds. He cannot always proceed according to plan, not only because of the performing vagaries of singers,[322] but even [external][323] elements of an unnerving disposition. The number of little things that can happen for which the conductor is technically responsible for surmounting are, I am sure, undreamt of by the audience. For instance, a character has to rush in and sing something and the door sticks – a little delay ensues and yet all must be made to seem as if everything is proceeding smoothly. With choruses singing offstage calculations of distance and sound enter in to make the conductor's task more complicated, yet all must sound entirely unified in the front of the

Glorious John

house. [X ½ tone sharp heard in front.]³²⁴ All these are compiled to equip an artist as a master of his craft.

In think you have listened to me long enough for one evening. In conclusion I would like to say to any young musician who contemplates this most arduous and responsible of careers to [realise the mental & physical discipline & strength required & to make his watchwords]³²⁵ "Integrity and sincerity to yourself and loyalty to the man whose music your are seeking to interpret." Never think "What can I make of this piece?" but try to discover what the composer meant to say. We must bear in mind that the conductor has become one of the most important and responsible personalities in the musical world, and by fine stylistic performances can do much towards a purification of musical perception amongst the general public. On the other hand performances that are merely the vehicle to indulge the vanity of a personality, however talented, can only tend to lead us further from that which should be the goal of all true musicians: Service to that great art which it is our privilege to practise'.

Preamble to a lecture on conducting given to Hallé Club³²⁶

'Preamble

My dear friends of the Hallé Club. My main reason for agreeing to inflict myself upon you, in the guise of a lecturer for this evening, was not that I thought it w[ou]ld be good for you to hear some alleged words of wisdom from me, but on being assured that it w[ou]ld give you pleasure to have me amongst you, I did want to try and show you in some tangible form, my deep and personal appreciation of [what] all you Hallé Club members mean to me and my orchestra, by your warm and sympathetic interest in our great mission. For our work is indeed becoming more and more of a mission. In a world of conflicting loyalties, vast and vital changes, I can claim we stand unflinching, in the relentless and unchangeable pursuit of a great ideal, to bring by worthy performances of all that is best in all kinds of music, a little solace to the sorely tried minds and spirits of all sensitive people to-day.

Now for the matter in hand. What I want to try and do is to trace for you some aspects of the history, general principals, & problems of the [the conductor's art.]³²⁷

When it was 1ˢᵗ etc —...'.

Recording at Abbey Road Studios, London

Glorious John

Belle Vue, Manchester, 1949

Recording session for the BBC's *International Concert Hall*, Free Trade Hall

Barbirolli conducting the National Anthem, Belle Vue, Manchester, 1949

Glorious John

Passport control – on tour with the Hallé, c. 1950

Mémé and Barbirolli, Sussex 1951

Barbirolli – from the family photo album – date unknown

Barbirolli and Kathleen Ferrier, Sussex, 1951

Associated-Rediffusion studios, 1957

Barbirolli and Vaughan Williams, 2 May, 1956

Glorious John

PART FOUR

On Orchestras, Organizations, Administrators and Performing Musicians

Speech given in Glasgow[328]

'Looking [*sic*] Dictionary for definition of "Soroptimist".

[It is a][329] Little [*sic*] difficult to know where to begin [when][330] talking of this great Institution which for so many years has been the mainstay of first class orchestral music in Scotland, and the people whose generosity and passionate belief in the great place which music holds among the arts, have made its continuance possible in the dark days trade and the Arts have been through.[331] Days which happily I think are nearing their end, if the crowds who have been attending our Saturday Concerts [and the improved, if by no means yet satisfactory audiences here in G(lasgow).][332] are anything to go by. But just imagine if that long-suffering race of men and women called "The Guarantors" had not seen the thing through, where would you have been, now that the [audiences seem ready][333] to come back, if the great tradition of your Orchestra had not been maintained and the thing allowed to drop. So may I express the hope that the ever increasing numbers of young people – the most hopeful sign of all this – attending the Concerts will remember the debt they owe to those who kept the Orchestra in being for them. As to the Orchestra itself, I am naturally very happy and proud that in my first year of office as it permanent Conductor it has been acclaimed as possible [*sic*] the best Scottish Orchestra within living memory. But perhaps the [tributes that have][334] [come from two of the most eminently British musicians. My very distinguished colleague Sir L(andon). R(onald). and that great musician Edinboro (*sic*) has honored (*sic*) herself by keeping here, Proff. (*sic*) Tovey.][335]

[As some of you might already know][336] The [*sic*] Orchestra rehearse together or plays daily for 5 hours, or on days when we have sectional rehearsals (that is strings alone, etc.) 6 to 8 hours. You might say, there is nothing very extraordinary in that, but it is extraordinary in this sense that we are the only orchestra of its size in the country who have the

Glorious John

good fortune to do this. Also this continual playing together ultimately breeds a cohesion of tone which we call ensemble, unattainable to other organizations even composed of the finest material, who are unable to work under these conditions. As to the members of the Orchestra themselves, you hardly surmise what a trying [&][337] nervy life theirs is. Apart from the hours spent in the rehearsal room and the concerts, there are the hours spent in private practice, and above all the nervous anxiety as to the playing of various difficult solos. I, who know them all so well, know at what cost certain performances take place. [Then there is the marking of parts, which keep me and my faithful and well beloved Cheetham[338] up to all hours.][339] But these are the mere mechanics of the business and now I would call your attention to the intellectual strain of our work. Particularly do I want to say a word about this, as there is a certain fashion, too prevalent, especially among the more learned members of the law and politics to regard musicians as a rather superior kind of performing animal. These gentlemen who would be ashamed to confess they have never read a book, or that they were unable to tell a Dutch painting from an Italian one, often go out of their way to inform an admiring (and in that case equally ignorant audience,) that they cannot tell the difference between God Save the King and The Campbells are Coming. The basis of all this, is the assumption that music is a purely emotional, and not an intellectual exercise. I can assure you that a Strauss Full Score requires as much brain to elucidate as some statutes, though I would wager it makes more sense in the end.

...Tell them Radford Story[340]... and Asquith letter

To return to the intellectual strain of our labours, I [would][341] ask you to [try and][342] understand the strain of in one day, making the mental adjustments necessary to properly enter into the various styles and moods of such a diversity of Composers as Beethoven, Strauss [Stravinsky][343] Sibelius, Debussy, Mozart, Delius, etc. as we often have to do. The Thing [*sic*] that misleads people most I think, is that we love and enjoy our work so much and in that we are indeed fortunate, for with all its difficulties there is great joy in an Art that has received its inspiration from the best and noblest in Religion, Nature and Literature. I would not leave you without one word of praise and affection for the players it is my privilege to direct. No man could have greater loyalty and devotion, and added to their brilliant capabilities as Instrumentalists is their never failing sense of humour, which always comes to the rescue when most needed.

[After (my)[344] speech delivered (here)[345] in Edinburgh (where I had the unenviable task of tell (you)[346] how good the Glasgow Choral Union was) a gentleman came to me and told me I was a firstclass salesman. Well I will live up to that, and I ask you all who have not yet done so, to do me the honour of coming to hear the S(cottish)³⁴⁷. Orchestra. The great American Orchestras are composed of Germans, Poles, Italians, Frenchmen, Belgians, Dutchmen, and I believe even Americans. Your Orchestra is 100 percent British and 75% Scotch. The audiences this season have (been of fine quality,)³⁴⁸ (and have)³⁴⁹ set a great example, join them (and help this noble and beautiful city to restore the great Art of Music to its rightful place in the cultural life of the land.)³⁵⁰]'³⁵¹

Speech given before the Lord Provost of Glasgow³⁵²

'If I have felt at all reluctant in coming to address your illustrious Society to-day, please believe it is because my proffessional [*sic*] duties have been so heavy of late, as to utterly preclude any attempt to prepare an address even remotely worthy of such a gathering. For instance, this week the orchestra has 8 concerts and 12 rehearsals and an 18 hour day has been my common lot since arrival. To make matters worse I seem to have acquired what is in actual fact an entirely fictitious reputation as one able, and even greater delinquency, one willing to speak. I have had to speak several times in this city and I am afraid I have by now exhausted the small store of latent eloquence I might have possessed, and which was only called forth by the great affection and pride I have for your Scottish Orchestra, and I can only hope any regard you have for me will help temper your attitude towards the few rambling remarks that are to follow. Music as a proffession [*sic*] may appear to some as something pleasant as to be hardly in the category of work at all, yet to succeed to-day, an artist must not only be in the front rank, but harder thing still, be prepared to sacrifice almost all to retain that rank. You must please pardon me if I quote a little from my own career but I am one of those who had the good fortune to begin at the very bottom and in my capacity as a cellist I played in every conceivable branch of my proffession [*sic*] except the street. A source of employment all too common for musicians in London and other great cities at the moment. Although naturally I did not practise for hours day after day to play in circuses & theatres, these did provide a decent living for thousands of musicians, and even for those eventually destined to more serous art, an experience bound to prove invaluable to them in later life. Not merely in terms of musical experience but in terms of understanding of our fellows. A great measure of any small success I may have had as a conductor I attribute to my good fortune in having had the opportunity to live among, and learn to know so well those who were to become such faithful colleagues later on. I am bound to touch on that[353] form of entertainment which has become known as the talkies because like other scientific advances in industry it has meant in some cases greater efficiency with lesser man-power, and undoubtedly the advent of the talkies has meant a distress among[354] orchestral musicians unprecedented in our time. Out of this welter of suffering (and I have known cases among other colleagues too dreadful to contemplate) will eventually come but one thing "The survival of the fittest"[.] The thing to be realised is that all those who were displaced by the introduction of talkies, the majority will never be re-absorbed and the lack of any official aid for serious music, and the resultant precariousness of such undertakings in times of economic stress reduces the chances of employment to this vast army to slender proportions. I have spoken so far only of orchestral players, but the same applies to other branches.

Many of the brilliant young singers who were making names for themselves in the late C[ovent]. G[arden]. O[pera]. C[ompany]. in such work[s] as Falst[aff], Rose[nkavalier] etc. have had perforce to abandon operatic careers because the only two organizations what have remained cannot obviously use all the available talent. I am afraid it is a mournful tale I have unfolded so far, and now I can refer to perhaps what is one of the most delightful features of a musician[']s life. The opportunities which come his way, through this common bond, the love of music, of meeting people it would never be his good fortune to meet otherwise. Particularly am I grateful, if I may again recall a personal experience, to recall a conversation it was my privilege to have with Lord Balfour on the subject of Cesar Franck, with Lord Snowden gentlest & kindest of men, interesting talks on Trade Unions in Music, and a delightful chance meeting with the lovely Queen Marie of Rumania, on the sand at St Briac in Brittany, where the String Quartet of which I was a member at the time was having a rehearsing holiday 13 years ago (incidentally[355] I have had two lots of one week since as my total). We were asked to her modest little villa where we played Debussy & Mozart. Music has this great faculty of reducing barriers, and is perhaps the most democratic of all the arts, though inversely a very expensive one, for the presentation of fine music on a worthy scale costs money. And in this capacity I would like to see a renewal of patronage by the aristocracy. Tell of 16 Cent. Byrd, Gibbons Henry VIII & Elizabeth[.] Glories of English music shone with a radiance we were only to recapture with Elgar

Part Four

& Delius. Brings me to idea of musicians performing animals. Stalinhest [*sic*] Scores Radford tale. Victorian hostess "I do hate that scratching sound".

It is not for me to talk of the place Glasgow holds in the eyes of the world as a centre of shipbuilding & engineering, may I[356] as a privileged guest suggest it could with its recently endowed University Chairs, its excellent Academy & other schools, its fine proffessor [*sic*] Dr Whitaker, and its magnificent orchestra, to say nothing of its fine choral tradition, may I suggest that this could & should in the no distant future occupy a similar position as a cultural centre of Music. You will have gathered I have rather dissuaded any but the more gifted from entering this profession, but once in its clutches, with all its continual hard work and severe nervous strain, great joys come to the musician as is only natural from an art that has received its cooperation from all that is noblest & finest in Nature, Literature, & Religion'.

Radio broadcast concerning the Scottish Orchestra[357]

'Through the courtesy of Mr. Dinwiddie and the B.B.C., I am privileged to-night to have the opportunity of saying a few words to those listeners, and I hope they are many, who constitute what I might term the fire-side patrons of the Scottish Orchestra. To those who have not been present at our concerts during the last two years and who have not had the opportunity of witnessing at first hand the remarkable revival of enthusiasm which has taken place, it is probably difficult to realise to the full extent the greatly increased interest in orchestral music evinced in Scotland to-day. As a very concrete instance of this I have but to call your attention to the extension of our season to fifteen weeks with the possibility of a further extension which, if it materialises, will have been made possible mainly through the scheme of the admirable Carnegie United Kingdom Fund in co-operation with the newly-formed Federation of Music Societies. Originating in the enterprise of the Glasgow Choral Union, now incorporated in the Choral [& Orchestral Union, in 1873, the Scottish Orch(estra), was never in greater vigour than now after functioning without(…)][358] interruption (excepting for the War period) for 63 years. In these days of longevity I like to think of the Scottish Orchestra as a very healthy adolescent. In Glasgow alone our concert season will embrace sixteen Saturday concerts, fifteen Tuesday concerts, two New Year's day concerts. Under the auspices of the Glasgow Corporation it will give eighteen Children's Concerts of which sixteen

155

form part of the ordinary School Curriculum. Under the aegis (to vary the language a little) of the Edinburgh Concert Society fourteen concerts will be given in Edinburgh. In co-operation with the Educational Institute of Scotland, six concerts in the provinces have been arranged of which three will be specially for children and other bookings include thirteen concerts to be given outside of Glasgow and Edinburgh, a total of 84 concerts in fifteen weeks …I really don't think there is any society in the country with a prospect of such a season in front of them. Among the most remarkable features of this revival could be instanced one, the increasing number of young people attending concerts, 2) Recognition by the Glasgow Educational Authorities of the instructive and cultural value of music, and 3) the very material support and encouragement given to the cause of music by the Municipal Corporations of Glasgow and Edinburgh. Reference has already been made to the Children's Concerts promoted by the Glasgow Corporation and they in addition guarantee a considerable sum towards the upkeep of the orchestra. In Edinburgh the Corporation besides being Guarantors for our concerts with the Edinburgh Concert Society, also make a cash grant to the Reid Orchestra which under the direction of that great savant Professor Tovey and the University, is making a great contribution to the advancement of musical education. Before I say a final word of praise to the B.B.C. for the valuable part played by them in disseminating a knowledge of the best forms of music, they will perhaps allow me to say to you, my unseen listeners "Don't imagine for a moment that listening-in can be or was ever intended to be a substitute for concert-going. The B.B.C. have I think given full proof of this, by their very generous contribution to the costs of musical production in broadcasting orchestral performances of various societies in the country. So, that if I say to you that my normally very pleasant voice sounds well,… perhaps, not quite so pleasant through the microphone, I leave the inference to you, [nor will][359] my friends of the B.B.C.[360] I am sure,[361] be offended. Seriously, Ladies and Gentlemen, you have in the Scottish Orchestra an institution of which, I think, you may well be proud, and that in conjunction with all the other splendid musical activities in your midst, and the help and sympathy shown so generously by the B.B.C., it can be trusted to play its part worthily in bringing appreciably nearer that Golden Age of Music which, I confidently assert, is not such a remote possibility as seemed only a few years ago.'

Part Four

Second speech given before the Lord Provost of Glasgow [362]

'My Lord Provost, L(adies). & G(entlemen).,
My first duty is to pay tribute to the Lord Provost for the really magnificent spirit he has shown in placing at our disposal [this][363] beautiful [room][364] (an event I think unprecedented in the annals of the Society) and still a more striking manifestation of his interest, that he should sacrifice what [must][365] be a very scant leisure, to be with us in person. [I venture to][366] suggest that the best vote of thanks the music-lovers of Glasgow can make him, is to heed his eloquent speech at one of our Saturday concerts towards the end of the last season, and prove to him his labours and endeavours have not been in vain.

I have willingly placed myself at the disposal of the Committee for their propaganda, believe me not in any form of self seeking in my professional capacity, and certainly not from any desire to indulge in any exhibition of oratory in a definitely amateurish capacity, but from a very deep inward conviction that a musical regeneration of your great city, entailing as that would, a wider public appreciation of beauty and culture, means greater honour and happiness for you. To the more material-minded this may sound [humbug &][367] nonsense, but I have known men who have had their thoughts turned back to spiritual paths they had long since deserted, through a hearing of the [slow movt. of][368] Elgar['s 1st][369] Symphony, to mention but one concrete instance.[370] Before proceeding further, it would perhaps be of interest to recall [to your minds][371] a few important features [in][372] the history of the Society it is now your privilege to perpetuate.

The Glasgow Choral Union (to which the Scottish Orchestra owes its origin) was founded from two earlier societies in 1855, and the orchestral portion of their choral performances, was then [supplied][373] by an orchestra raised for the occasion. Some years later the need for a more permanent and efficient orchestra was realised[,][374] and in 1873 the Choral Union engaged a large standing orchestra and gave a series of Orchestral Concerts. The first season resulted in a loss of £2,500, but to quote the glorious and beautiful words from the short History of the Society from which these facts come, [(listen carefully)][375] "in subsequent years the results were so satisfactory that the Committee were enabled out of profits,[376] to re-pay to the Guarantors the whole amounts advanced to meet the losses of former years." What has been done once, can, and MUST[377] be done again.[378]

For twenty years the Choral U[ion]. Bore [sic] the entire burden

157

Glorious John

of Orchestral concerts in Glasgow and from 1887 the services of the Orchestra were utilised for concerts in Edinburgh under the auspices of Messrs Paterson. In 1893 a further change came over the scene and [some of the]³⁷⁹ subscribers to the C[horal]. U[nion]., thinking certain radical changes necessary, organised a separate competitive scheme, the orchestra established by them being designated as the Scottish Orchestra. For a season the two schemes worked in opposition, to the financial detriment of both, and eventually in 1898 came the fusion of the two schemes, resulting in the formation of the Glasgow Choral and Orchestral Union as you know it to-day. [This is the career of what is perhaps the oldest unsubsidised institutions of its kind in the country.]³⁸⁰ [The following]³⁸¹ imposing array of great musicians³⁸² have conducted the Society, Hans von Bulow [*sic*], Sir A. C. [Mackenzie]³⁸³[,] [Sir Arthur]³⁸⁴ Sullivan, [Sir Aug(ustus)]³⁸⁵ Manns, [Sir G(eorg)]³⁸⁶ Henschel, [and coming to more recent times]³⁸⁷ Ronald, Weingartner, [&]³⁸⁸ Koussevitski [*sic*] to mention but a few.³⁸⁹ To be in the line of succession to these men is an honour, and imposes a responsibility, I am fully conscious of. [In approaching the scheme for the present season,]³⁹⁰ the Committee wish me to emphasise that their aims are threefold. [Firstly]³⁹¹ The [*sic*] establishment of a [Guarantee]³⁹² fund of so large an amount[,]³⁹³ as to make the burden on each guarantor negligible. [2ndly]³⁹⁴ An [*sic*] Endowment Fund. [and]³⁹⁵ [3rdly]³⁹⁶ and most³⁹⁷ important of all more regular and frequent attendance at the Concerts. [I think I should now give you]³⁹⁸ A [*sic*] few details of the actual figures at which these items stand.³⁹⁹

The [Guarantee]⁴⁰⁰ Fund stands at the highest it has ever been, £6524-16-6, an increase of £2160-2-6 on last year. To all those who have contributed to these splendid figures, our most grateful thanks are due, and I hope it will not be considered invidious if I mention our gratitude to the Corporation[,]⁴⁰¹ and our distinguished and well beloved Chairman Sir Dan S., who shares with the Corporation the distinction of being the largest Guarantor. We are indeed fortunate to have such a man at our head. His experience and counsel have been invaluable, and I was going to add among his other attributes the one of courage, which he must possess to a great degree to remain at the head of an organisation which[,]⁴⁰² like Oliver Twist, must perforce always be coming back for more.

The Endowment Fund initiated this year with such generosity by Mrs. McCloud with a donation of £1,000, stands at £1,819. (I am very happy to have this opportunity of personally extending my thanks [to the lady]⁴⁰³ for [her splendid &]⁴⁰⁴ public-spirited action.) The Committee feel it is a mistake

Part Four

to expect immediate endowment, and confidently take the long view that in due course of time[,][405] Full Endowment will be secured. Their one regret is that the fund was not initiated years ago. Pending full Endowment [*sic*] the Revenue will at least serve to lighten the burden on the Guarantors. [Here I would like to say that my very cordial relations with the Committee in the arduous and difficult task of prog(amme). making etc are a source of much satisfaction to me.][406]

This brings me to what I consider the most vital point of all. The more regular and frequent attendance of the public.

The Lord Provost during the course of his eloquent appeal on Feb 4th. last[,][407] asked the music-lovers of this city a question which I hope you will answer in the right way. He said, ["][408] Are the minds and the souls of the people of Glasgow to be satisfied with Broadcast Music?["][409] In posing this question to you again, please do not construe it as an attack on the B.B.C.. [The musical people of this country][410] [have] a great deal to be grateful to the B.B.C. for, and far from accusing them of damaging Orchestral Societies[,][411] I believe I am right in saying they have in many cases contributed handsomely to help them [to][412] keep on their feet. But my point is that there must be a large number of people who, never having heard an orchestra in the flesh so to speak, imagine it is the same thing which they hear on their machines. When I have with due diffidence put this to some of the more fanatical wireless fiends [of my acquaintance,][413] I am generally met with the reply, "But you haven't heard my set." And when I have gone to hear their set it seems their listening-in takes the form of a paraphrase on Jules Verne, and what I am treated to is something like "Round the World in 80 Seconds."

But far from blaming these people for [our][414] troubles, our real danger is from the apathy[415] of the professed music-lover[,][416] who for some reason or other never manages to go to a concert. I have met them and talked with them in this very city, and when after listening to their protestations of love for our art I innocently express the pleasure I shall have at seeing them at our concerts, an awkward pause generally ensues and excuses of little validity [are blushingly][417] put forward. [(The most that I can say for them is that they do blush)][418] L[adies]. & G[entlemen]. in tremendous seriousness I put it to you that if music is not to be saved by the music lover who the Blazes[419] [*sic*] is to save it?

And [further][420] I put it to you it is an exceedingly improper thing for me or anyone else to have to appeal [for people][421] to attend such a series of concerts as the Committee have put forward [for][422] [The][423] prospectus

159

Glorious John

with [the names of][424] the artists such as would grace [the Prospectus of][425] any Orchestral Society in the world. [*sic*] [contains (*sic*) such names as Adolf (Busch)][426] and [Gerhard (*sic*)],[427] Olszewska, Austral, Ginster, Rubinstein, Solomon, Bartlett and Robertson, [the latter][428] have [been][429] specially engaged also for Boston and New York [and][430] Yvonne Arnaud[.][431] [Further all (are) international artists of the 1st rank][432] [and] do you realise that the Scottish Orchestra is the only really Permanent Orchestra of its size in the country?[433] By that I mean an orchestra which rehearses every day of the week as an entity. It is perhaps news to some of you that the Orchestra and I spend 5 hours a day together and on the days when we have sectional rehearsals I have rehearsed 8 hours. I mention these facts that you need have no inferiority complex[434] in coming to hear your own Orchestra. The personnel has been [examined and overhauled][435] with the greatest care [& where a local appointment have not been possible our new][436] players have come from the L[ondon].S[ymphony].O[rchestra]. the [Royal Opera][437] Orchestra and the Hallé [Orchestra so that there is nothing experimental about our adjustments.][438] Orchestras run on these lines in American involve enormous losses [, &][439] 90,000 [or a][440] 100,000 [is a deficit they commonly budget for over there.][441] Even what seemed a big loss last year is a trifle compare with these figures, but leaving figures aside, we, the Orchestra... [solo][442] artists [&][443] ...myself need audiences, for you may not realise it, but well as we prepare the beacon, yours is the spark which is necessary to set it alight.[444] We are undoubtedly at a critical period in the History of the Society but please realise how simple is the remedy for all our ills. Come to the Concerts. (3 times)[445] They are the cheapest of their kind and quality, and actually the cheapest seat [at][446] the Promenades in London [costs a 100 per cent more (not a seat at all)][447] I have also worked out that (the most expensive)[448] subscription for all the concerts Tues[day], and Sat[urday]s[, spread over the year][449] works out at 4d a day; [the sum][450] people usually spend on newspapers to find out what the concert was like.

For the programmes I claim they have a sanity and catholicity of range and outlook which could not come amiss in other spheres at the moment, though I did have a wild idea at one moment that if we repeated the Plebiscite Programme 54 times we might have 54 large audiences and believe me, I would even do that if it could get people in the concert-going habit again. But [to return to all][451] those people who came and gave me such an unforgettable farewell at my last concert, I remind them of the promise they gave me that they would attend all the Saturday concerts, surely they can't live on one concert a year. [If they can't the logical outcome must be

Part Four

that even their beloved "Pleb" will disappear.][452] To my great regret I have to tell you that though the [Guarantee][453] Fund and the Endowment Fund are in such a healthy state, the subscriptions are Not. ([and stand at][454] under 300 for each series) These I repeat are our most urgent need [& we should have at least another 200 before we begin.][455] To all Guarantors who are not Subscribers I appeal to them to become so [and make their friends become so];[456] it is going to save them a lot of money in the end. And as a last resource I am going to appeal to your pride. [I don't know if you think much of Yorkshire folk up here (but) you must not let them beat you][457] (Tell them about Leeds.) It needs but a few hundred music-lovers to decide to support us to be able to blazon the name of Glasgow all over England and even America as the City which makes its Orchestral concerts pay their way. From this you would have an advertisement for your [great][458] City which could not fail to be of even material benefit, and you would prove that in your great efforts to bring normality to these difficult days you have [not found it necessary to wander][459]from the paths of Culture and Beauty!'

Third speech given before the Lord Provost of Glasgow [460]

'My Lord Provost. L[adies] & G[entlemen].
To express my pleasure at being amongst you all once again is to interpret but mildly the very real and deep feeling of emotion I experience in rising to address you[461] in these magnificent Halls.[462] My first duty therefore is to tender to the Lord Provost and the Corporation of Glasgow my most grateful thanks for making this possible, and to assure them how deeply sensible I am to the honour they have conferred on me and the Orchestra (whose symbol I am for this evening) in so doing. When we consider further the very practical interest they take in our welfare (in the form of a very handsome guarantee [I've got to that sooner than I expected][463]), and above all the personal interest in us so generously displayed by the Lord Provost & Mrs. Swan, our debt to them is indeed great. On the subject of the L[ord]. P[rovost] I could, if Nature had so endowed me wax eloquent, but I will content myself with saying [that we do not][464] under-estimate what the charm & force of his personality has meant to the scheme. The next thing I wish to touch upon is our relations with the B.B.C.[.] My friends of the Press will probably be very disappointed to hear they were never better, and I am afraid I cannot furnish them with any startling headlines by translating

161

Glorious John

their nomenclature to Brigand, Bandit & Criminals. On the contrary I am very happy to pay tribute to their sympathy with our aims as evidenced by an extended measure of co-operation both in Glasgow and in the Provinces. Perhaps it would not be out of place here to mention how delighted I am sure we shall be to welcome their distinguished Musical Director, Dr. A[drian]. B[oult]. to our concerts once again.

Last year I addressed you rather in the spirit of a benign bully, and the almost startling success of our concerts last [season][465] must rob me of my natural inclination to the latter quality,[466] but I renounce it with pleasure. This remarkable revival of interest in the concerts[467] gives us food for serious reflection. Are we really nearing the end of that jarring journey, with jazz and its appendages as our chief companions, natural manifestations as they may have been of the search for gaiety and distraction from the preceeding [*sic*] horrors one generation remembered too well, and [the][468] knowledge of which the older and younger [(generation)][469] thought perhaps to stifle with the dreadful din that for far too long[470] has been allowed to masqueraded as music[?] On all sides I still read advertisements and eulogies of the worlds [*sic*] hottest violinist allied with the hottest banjoist, playing the hottest music, and I can only express the pious hope that they will one[471] day be entrusted to the care of a gentleman who from time immemorial has been reputed to generate more heat than even they can. But seriously I like to think that our audiences of last season, especially the younger members, are symptomatic of a return to the time when relief from everyday cares was sought in the contemplation & companionship of beautiful things, and that they too will come to know the [fragrant memories][472] that only these things can bring. I appeal to you all to your utmost and to extend and intensify this interest as happily displayed, and I make this appeal quite confidently knowing that we have three essential things to offer you.

1stly. Standard of orchestral efficiency which our conditions of work, and the high individual accomplishment of our players make possible. 2ndly. The calibre of our solo artists, [and here I will permit myself to say][473] no comparable scheme of concerts in Europe to-day[474] can show anything like it.[475] In Schnabel, Horowitz & Rubinstein we have probably the 3 greatest living pianists,[476] & Flesch, Huberman, Thibaud[477] must surely be numbered amongst the first six violinists of [their][478] epoch.[479]

It required great courage on the part of your Committee to venture as boldly as this, and I trust their courage will be well rewarded. If not I shall get into trouble too for egging them on. [And here I must tell you we][480] are much indebted to a subscriber who prefers to remain anon, for making possible the engagement of Huberman.[481] Lastly the Programmes. Months of anxious thought has gone to the making of these, and in their general level of interest[482] [and] attractiveness, I think we may without boasting claim to have done our work well. Before leaving the actual concerts, I would like to mention Proff [sic] Sch[neevoight][483] who with Dr. B[oult]. is to be one of our guests. This disting[uished] Scandinavian conductor recently visited London with his own orchestra, the National Finnish Orch[estra], & created a great impression with his readings of [Sibelius &][484] enthusiasts [of the Finnish master][485] here should look forward with interest to his visit.

If any justification were needed in appealing to your support I have but to emphasize the marvel of maintaining such a scheme for so long entirely by private enterprise. I could tell you harrowing stories of great orchestras in Europe, heavily subsidised and yet barely maintaining an existence. Tell of Concertgebouw. This should make you proud, proud that without external aid, but from the depth of your belief in, and affection for your Choral & Orchestral Union you have maintained it whatever the circumstances & conditions have been, proud that you have helped keep the flag of culture flying, & proud that you have provided an antidote to the excessive materialism of our age. From another angle and a far from unimportant one these days, have you stopped to think what a splendid advertising medium the Orchestra is for Glasgow and for Scotland in general. In this connection Mr. Dinwiddie will perhaps allow me to make the suggestion that he would be aiding materially in this Advertisement [sic] Campaign of Scotland if when broadcasting the orchestra he could arrange for it to be broadcast not only in Scotland but throughout Great Britain. (Many of my friends even with good sets have great difficulty in getting a good reception of our concerts.) Thus the world could be made aware of a Magnificent Scottish Enterprise and of the high standard of Musical Culture in Scotland.

And now to [finance].[486] There are 3 ways in which financial aid to the scheme [is][487] possible. The Endowment Fund, the Guarantee Fund, and the maximum amount of patronage by subscription and regular attendance. We will take the Guarantee...'[488]

Fourth speech given before the Lord Provost of Glasgow [489]

'My Lord Provost, Ladies and Gentlemen. To see you, sir, once again on this platform, and once again to have the honour of accepting your

Glorious John

hospitality, is to feel even this premature stage that the success of our season is assured. With such words as I can command I have endeavoured on past occasions to convey to you the realisation of our indebtedness for your help and sympathy, and now if it is not unbecoming to the dignity of the position you hold and adorn, I would like to claim you as a mascot. A mascot, I might add, without which we should very loath to go battle. When I first stood before you three years ago at the inauguration of these gatherings, I recounted to you a strange tale of a singular, moving, and almost incredible beauty. It referred to an ancient and honourable Society [created][490] for the purpose of music making, called the C[horal].U[nion]. of G[lasgow]. which gave concerts, and according to a short history of the Society which has survived, and which has been translated into English for me by persons of impeccable integrity, intelligence and authority (I stress these qualities for I would like to you if possible believe what I am going to tell you). In this history occur these words: words which speak of a state of society so blissful and happy that it is not without great control of my emotions that I can utter them. "In these years the results of the concerts were so satisfactory that the Committee were enabled out of profits to repay the Guarantors the whole amounts advanced to meet the losses of former years." To these words I added with the courage born of despair and[491] rhetorical flourish not without effect, I hope, "What has been done once, can and must be done again." L[adies] & G[entlemen] I am going to continue this little [fairytale][492] of mine[.]

This is perhaps not such a prosaic age as may seen [*sic*] to the insensitive observer, for in the midst of this great industrial city, the art of music, disguised by the good fairy as the Scottish Orchestra, has provided you with a fairy tale almost come true. Last year with the call on the Guarantors brought down to 3/9 the miracle of which we vaguely and bravely talked about three years ago has almost come to pass, and this year which to my great personal regret is the last year of office of our, may I say Sir, dearly loved L[ord]. P[rovost].; this year I think would be a fitting one in which to show a very practical way our gratitude for all he has done for us by making it memorable in the annals of the Society as the first post-war season without a call on the Guarantors at all. There is I think much to warrant that such a thing may come to pass and that the Committee will be amply rewarded for its courage and enterprise in extending the season and putting before you a list of soloists of such unparalleled magnificence. Perhaps it will not be out of place here for me to touch briefly on some of the more important features in connection with the coming season. The

Part Four

extraordinary list of soloists I have already referred to[493] and to their names I would add those of our own Orchestra who are to take part in solo works D[avid]. McCallum, D[avid]. Nichols, C[harles]. Meert, G[eorge]. Maxted and the Misses [Evelyn] Rothwell and [Eileen] Grainger a list of which we can well be proud.[494] I am also delighted to find the scheme of programmes has been well received. I hate to think of the curtailment in the number of years of my earthly existence which the worry and anxiety of this task involves, and of the precariousness which even bonds of warmest friendship assume when these deliberations take place, but joking apart, I am grateful that such small criticisms as have been uttered at any rate show a sympathetic understanding of the difficulties of our task in framing programmes of interest which at the same time must have a general public appeal. We cannot hedge from the fact that however low-brow the admission may seem, we are dependent for our existence on the support of the public; and after the very difficult and lean years we have been through it is not yet the time for experimentation. Add to this fact that the performance of great classical works that may be household words for some of us, are to the more youthful members of our audience voyages of thrilling discovery. Nor can I think we can be fairly accused of having cold-shouldered contemporary music, expensive as some of these programmes have proved, for it is an undeniable fact that some of our most interesting programmes (that is from the point of view of first performances) have invariably drawn the lowest takings. During my period alone first performances have been given of Sibelius 1, 2, 5, 7, Symphonies, "Pohjola's Daughter", Debussy "La Mer", Stravinsky, "Pulchinella" [*sic*] "Petrouschka", Bax, 2 3 4 Symphonies, "[The][495] Tale Pine Trees Knew", Delius Violin Concerto, "North Country Sketches", "Evantyr [sic]", Walton Viola Concerto, V[aughan]. W[illiams']. "Job" and "Tallis Fantasia" and I firmly believe that by giving first, what I might call the classics of modern music we are solidly fostering [a][496] taste for modern music than by the indiscriminate performance of works that can only have interest [for][497] the really serious student of musical evolution. In an ideal state of course provision for this type of music would possibly be made and the B.B.C. with its unlimited resources has rightly rendered a great service in this direction with its contemporary Concerts series. In any case a city which boasts a Saturday night audience which can pack St. A[ndrew's] Halls [*sic*] [as happened last year][498] to hear a Brahms Symphony and [works of][499] Delius and Strauss[500] need not fear comparison with any in its quality of musical appreciation. Before leaving the subject of programmes mention of V[aughan]. W[illiams']. Job has reminded me of a passage in the book of Job

165

Glorious John

which might be applied to all those who attack programmes and repertoires of musical societies and opera Companies without practical knowledge [of their (illegible) difficulties].⁵⁰¹ (Quote) The next thing I would mention is the extraordinary cheapness of the concerts and your Committee faced with an increased expenditure of about £1,200 (which is the sum involved in the extension of the season) your Co[mmittee]. deserve all possible praise for their courage in seeking to meet this increase not by [raising]⁵⁰² the cost of subscruption [sic] but by reducing it, [I suggest there is many an M.P. who would be glad of a rallying cry as effective as that]⁵⁰³ thereby offering increased facilities for all classes of music lovers to hear concerts of the highest quality at a price within the reach of all. Fifteen Sat. concerts, 2/6 equals 1/10,⁵⁰⁴ Total 176. 15 Tues. Concerts 1/9 – 1/5 Total 1.1. 30 Concerts 1/6 Total £2[?]⁵⁰⁵5. Lowest single admission price [1 schilling].⁵⁰⁶ Lowest rate for the B.B.C.⁵⁰⁷ in London £1. 17[.] 6. for twelve concerts. The Guarantee Fund I am proud and happy to announce stands at just over £6,000, (6030 & 9 schillings to be exact,) a sum only once before exceeded in the history of the society [sic], representing 513 guarantors including £360.15 from [53]⁵⁰⁸ new Guarantors. This is one of the healthiest features of our enterprise and symbolic of the widespread affection and esteem in which the Orchestra is held.

In accounting for this hopeful state of affairs there are two public bodies whose assistance to the cause of music must be taken into account. A tribute must I think be paid to the Co[r]p[oration]. of G[lasgow]. for the material support and encouragement they give to the cause of Music. Under their auspices, and with the cooperation of the E.I.S. 18 Children's Concerts are to be given, and [the Corp(oration)]⁵⁰⁹ also stand Guarantors for a very considerable sum towards the expenses of our season. It must be a source of great gratification to them that already we are feeling the benefit of their Children's Concerts policy by the very increased number of young people attneding [sic] the concerts. [Which shows (a) very different state of affairs from 2 years ago]⁵¹⁰ (Charles II tale)⁵¹¹ "Not a woman to talk to and the barbarity of the men such that they consider it a sin to play upon the violin." The other body I wish to refer to is the B.B.C. Each year I have to disappoint my firends [sic] of the Press by having nothing but kind and loving words to say of the [B.B.C.].⁵¹² but unpleasant as the truth may be the fact remains that we continue to get on very well together, and I don't think we ought to overlook the valuable part played by them in boradcasting [sic] Orchestral [sic] performances by the various organisations in the country, thereby not only making a generous contribution towards the cost of musical

166

production, but also disseminating a knowledge and appreciation of the best forms of music to the ultimate advantage I am sure, of the community. I have not yet mentioned perhaps the most important item in the scheme, my beloved Orchestra. I am not going to say very much about them now, it is not at this juncture necessary to speak of their proved skill and devotion to the Society, but I am happy that the spreading of their fame and prowess has not rendered necessary any but very small alterations in the personnel, and I confidently look forward to a year of even greater progress and advancement.[513] For myself I can only say what I hope has already become manifest to you, that you have so enslaved me by your hospitality and appreciation that you have performed the second miracle of making a born Cockney look forward to coming to live in Glasgow for four months. Seriously L[adies] & G[entlemen]. the success of this scheme artistically and otherwise is one of the things nearest to my heart[, but][514] [l]ike all things which we look to, to bring us the greatest happiness, it is not without a certain trepidation that we approach them, lest they should fall short of the ideal we have set them. The ideal I have in mind for orchestral music in Scotland is a high and [a][515] great one, and the trust you have reposed in me is the force that leads me on. In conclusion, I would say that more than ever do I feel now, in these still difficult times, that the regeneration in your midst of an art which has drawn some of the noblest inspiration from all that is best in Life, Literature, and Religion cannot but be of the greatest value, not merely as a cultural asset, but even as a spiritual beacon of hope and comfort in our every-day lives'.

Lecture given at the New York 'Philharmonic Symphony League Luncheon'[516]

'IN THESE DAYS OF NAIONAL PREJUDICE, international discord, religious intolerance, and I would even say, cretinous and murderous stupidity, I have the supreme honour of standing in front of your Orchestra composed of all nationalities and creeds, and in the sacredness of our musical task, comes the understanding of what our real mission in life is and should be.

THE PHILHARMONIC HAS STOOD SINCE 1842, and God willing it will stand for centuries to come. We must face the fact that this may be the only remaining country where such cultural and spiritual necessities of our life will be available. Please believe my disinterested sincerity when I speak of this: Great conductors have come and gone and many others will come and

Glorious John

go, the spirit of the great Masters will remain forever. In the wondrousness of their spiritual and material beauty lies one of the few paths of salving our sanity.

The PHILHARMONIC-SYMPHONY LEAGUE IS NOT HERE JUST TO foster a particular institution, great as it may be, but I believe, to attempt to foster for the people in perpetuity an Eternal Truth – the love of great and beautiful things, without which we must eventually perish.

IF I HAVE SPOKEN MORE FEELINGLY and longer than I had intended, my only daily association with men of all nationalities and creeds has brought me such rare and beautiful experiences through our common devotion to one great art that I would like you to[517] join in our unique experience. I thank you for your graciousness in listening to me patiently, and I would ask you to show any[518] belief in my words by your unstinted devotion to this League and our great orchestra, so that you may bequeath to your descendants, not the savagery that seems to be overtaking some parts of the world, but the solace of some of the greatest minds the history of art has known'.

Speech given on behalf of the Musician's Emergency Fund, New York[519]

'Many appeals must have been made in the past for the M. E. F. and many must have fallen from lips far more eloquent than mine. However, neither Mrs. Astor nor I myself need, I feel, make any apology for the reiteration of these appeals; rather would I regard them as the feeding of a lamp which must be kept burning as a warning and as a reminder of the needs and dangers still to be encountered.

Only yesterday I had repeated to me the cheap, common and vulgar jibe, that it needs a good luncheon table to enable already well fed (if not overfed) musicians to gather and to discuss the needs of their more unfortunate brothers and sisters. Such insinuations I think we can comfortably dismiss as meaningless and unfortunate verbiage. Most of you know the work that has already been done far better than I do, but I wonder if some of you present realise or know how many artists of real distinction have been aided by this fund, artists who through no fault of their own have been plunged into this abyss of despair, brought there through causes bred by the uncertainties created by political and international feuds. Things whith [*sic*] which I assure you, few musicians have any desire to be associated.

Our mission is I hope, & and in fact I know[,] a far simpler and nobler one. To bring to the people through the glories of our literature; and our own heritage finer thoughts and feelings to mankind. Those who would dispute with me the attributing of this particular power to music, I would venture to chide in the words of my immortal countryman Shakespeare when he says in the "Taming of the Shrew" "Preposterous ass, that never read so far to know the cause why music was ordained. Was it not to refresh the mind of man, After his studies or his pain".[520] So you see that even 350 years ago this wizard with his infinite wisdom and understanding had realised that music was one of the healing arts. To those who in their happier days have helped heal the wounds of others, let us know turn, and seek to repay their ministrations, not in charity but in gratitude, and try help raise them from their degradation and despair, towards the dignity which should be theirs, by virtue of their services to the great art which it is my humble privilege to serve'.

Second speech given on behalf of the Musicians' Emergency Fund, New York[521]

'Ladies & Gentlemen:
This is not the first time it has been my (I might almost say) sad privilege to make an appeal on behalf of the Musicians [sic] Emergency Fund. And, ladies and gentlemen, it is a sad commentary on the so-called progress of our lives that at a time when music is within reach of millions more than it has ever been before, never was there such distress amongst professional musicians, of all ages and classes, as there is at the present moment. The causes[522] are many and varied, but it is not my purpose or intention to go into them now. Suffice it to say that whether the causes be mechanical and political, the effects have been to bring underserved and unimaginable suffering to many musicians worthy of a better fate.[523] The Fund, as you know, helps musicians of all classes and includes many who have in their time rendered long and honourable service to music,[524] so I would say to you — please remember them in gratitude rather than in charity.[525] Far more eloquent than any word on mine could be are the following figures which I would like to quote you:

Since the beginning of the Fund in 1932, The Placement Bureau has obtained commercial engagements through which musicians have earned a total of nearly $370,000. The Art of Musical Russia Opera Company organized by the Fund has earned something like $118,000. The Made Work

Glorious John

Department of the Fund has given a total of 5,673 concerts in the public schools since its inception and in 1932 and nearly three million children have heard these concerts. There are at present over 3,000 cases receiving intermittent assistance and 127 cases receiving relief each week.

I think I have told you enough for you to realise the great urgency of our need, and I only want to emphasize one more thing[,][526] [text removed] namely that the Fund receives very few donations and is practically dependent on benefits and these collections for its income. [text removed] With these facts before you, ladies and gentlemen, may I appeal to you to open your hearts (and your pockets) and give as generously as you can so that my poor words will at any rate reap a rich reward'.

'On the Training of Young Musicians: National Orchestral Association Speech'[527]

'It gives me especial pleasure as the Conductor of one of the greatest of our major orchestras to say a few words about the work of the National Orchestral Association, because it is precisely organizations such as the New York Philharmonic-Symphony which stand to benefit most[,][528] ultimately[,][529] from the work of the National Orchestral Association. But apart from this material gain which the major orchestras have from our labours, to me personally, there is another even more important aspect of your work, and that is the humanitarian side of it.

By training and equipping your young[530] artists with the necessary experience and knowledge to take their places in the orchestras, you are easing the path toward finding employment for their talents. Who could deny that in doing this you are helping to solve one of the pressing and difficult problems which the world of post-war music has to face. I have hinted generally at the aims and scope of the National Orchestral Association's work, but if you will bear with me for a moment, one or two more precise details might not be without interest for you. I wonder how many people realise[531] the wide gap between being a good, even first-rate, player of one's instrument and being a good orchestral[532] player of that instrument. A conductor might assemble 50 or 60 brilliant young string players and have a section that would drive him crazy in a week. A conductor of a great orchestra when selecting material for it, must see that it has a certain amount of experience and a sense of discipline involved in making music with perhaps a hundred of your fellows. Even the actual technique of the

Part Four

playing alters. If, for instance, we take a string ensemble and you are playing a solo in a large hall, a player with the requisite experience knows that even in a pp. he must produce a tone which, though soft, must be of fairly full quality to carry well.[533] (He plays soloistically.) Then, on the other hand, he has to produce a pp. effect along with 50 or 60 others, so he has to sacrifice his individual tone quality to help produce the particular effect required at the moment.

In the case of wind players[534] these particular instances do not apply, as they are always playing more or less as solo instruments; but in their case they have to learn, of course, the discipline of ensemble and, above all, intonation. Although wind instruments have reached a pitch of perfection almost undreamt of 100 or 150 years ago, they are still that little short of it that good wind intonation must be a matter of friendly compromise between the players.

So much for the technics of the thing. Now consider the best orchestral literature covered by these students.[535] They are enabled to enter the different orchestras with a knowledge and appreciation of the various styles of playing necessary to display the varying personalities and characteristics of the great classical masters.[536] They also traverse the field of modern music,[537] giving them a wonderful opportunity of cultivating and extending their reading powers.[538] Also, tremendously important in this sphere is the chance given to young composers[539] of hearing what their music sounds like — an opportunity likely to advance their work far more surely and rapidly than would be otherwise possible.

Of the 84 members who have graduated to the major orchestras, 6 are with me in the New York Philharmonic, and of these 84, 30 were Philharmonic-Symphony Scholars under the direction[540] of the first-desk men of the Orchestra.[541] This is an achievement of which[542] you may well be proud, but there is must be no slacking[543] of effort, for even the finest of intentions[,][544] and the finest talents unfortunately require finance for fruition.[545]

I think that, by now, any of you who were[546] not aware before[,][547] of the importance of this Society's work must realise[,][548] now, not merely its importance,[549] but I would rather[550] say its absolute necessity.[551]

Before I sit down, I would like to say one word of Mr. Barzin. — — — I don't know if he indulges in what Shakespeare in the Midsummer Night's Dream so eloquently described as "a most obscene and courageous rehearsal", but having mentioned Shakespeare, I would venture to close these few remarks with a word from him which may well be a watchword

171

Glorious John

and inspiration for all those who work for music. Would[552] you might repeat to any who would question the vital necessity, especially in these troubled days,[553] that[554] music should take an ever increasing part in our lives, for Shakespeare[555] in his infinite wisdom has[556] said,

>"Preposterous Ass, that never read
>The cause why Music was ordained.
>Was it not to heal the mind of Man
>After his studies or his pain?"'[557]

'Statement to be used by the Little Symphony of Montreal'[558]

'I do want to congratulate the founders of The [*sic*] Little Symphony of Montreal on their courage and enterprise in starting a fine artistic venture at a time when we hear all too much of such things being given up. In these days we turn more than ever to Music [*sic*] for release and inspiration, and the continuance and fostering of all that is fine and beautiful in this world is needful for the sanity of us all now and in the aftermath of this terrible struggle. I wish the Little Symphony of Montreal the success it so thoroughly deserves and long may it flourish under the splendid musicianship of it[s] conductor Bernard Naylor.[559]

Signed: John Barbirolli'

A Tribute to Leslie Heward[560]

'To pay tribute to the genius of Leslie Heward[561] is a task which, though it should be simple, is in my case not quite the easy matter it appears on the surface.

To begin with, there is the danger of constant superlatives, which might be deemed insincere and, in my own particular case, the rather curious nature of our friendship. This, though warm and intimate to the fullest possible degree (so much so in fact that on looking back I find it hard to believe we had been together so little and so rarely), was in a sense limited.

I heard him conduct but twice, a performance of 'The Magic Flute' with the B.N.O.C. in 1927, and a rehearsal of his own Birmingham Orchestra a few years later – Sibelius's fifth [*sic*] Symphony, I remember. Yet even with so little personal contact, I was from the first made fully conscious of his quite

Part Four

extraordinary musical gifts and of his rare lovableness as a man: the more remarkable, this, since there never was a man who made less conscious effort to make one aware of the one or the other great quality. Smallness – musical or personal – was altogether out of his ken, but the bigness there was also an intimacy and tenderness too often lacking in people of that stature.

I should like, if I may, to recall two incidents which I am a little timid of recording, since they are in the nature of tributes paid to me. If, however, the reader will remember that they occurred at the very outset of my career as a conductor, and appeared at that time (and still do, for that matter) as acts of great encouragement from a man whose accomplishments were already legendary, they will be seen in their true perspective.

Soon after I joined the B.N.O.C. in 1926, Leslie came back from his South African engagement and, finding himself at a loose end, accepted the only position the company could offer him at the time: a position really unworthy of him, since it consisted mainly of répétiteur work and such conducting as might be needed. (Be it understood that this was nobody's fault in particular, it was just that other commitments had been made just before his rather unexpected return.) I can see him now, playing for some of my 'Falstaff' (Verdi) rehearsals; a miniature *full* score on the piano (and his achievements in the realm of score-reading bordered on the miraculous), playing exquisitely and happily, doing – in a favourite phrase of his – "a job of work," and thoroughly enjoying it. Imagine other conductors of repute in similar circumstances!! No, as I said earlier, Leslie was a rare musician and a rare being.

The other incident I have told to very few, since I do not think he would have liked it talked about: but as another example of his generosity I think it takes its place here. After a performance of 'Coq d'or,' which I conducted, he came to my room, gently took my face in his hands, and kissed me on the forehead. I had no words then, I have none now.

After this our paths drew apart: I went to Glasgow to the Scottish Orchestra and thence to New York, and he to Birmingham, so that for the last ten years we met but three or four times. Lovely it is to recall that we always seemed to begin again where we had left off, and I am grateful that it was granted me to spend two hours with him just after his operation in the summer of 1942, during my short visit to this country then. He seemed remarkably recovered and full of the future, and it was with high hopes that I left him. But before I was to return again, that enchanting (used in the sense of gifted, whimsical, beloved) spirit had left us.

Glorious John

It was a sad day for English music, for never was there a time when he could have been less spared than now. With the rising tide of orchestral activity, the larger public might have come to know him at his true stature and have received from the fount of his genius music pure and unstained from the commercialism and vulgarity of our day.

John Barbirolli'

'My First Season with the Hallé'[562]

'Now that I have reached the end of my first season with the Hallé Orchestra people ask me what my impressions have been and what my hopes for the future of the orchestra are. As far as the progress of the orchestra is concerned I am more than satisfied.

In fact I would not have thought it possible that in a few months an orchestra could have acquired such maturity of style and unity of expression, and it has been an immense gratification and reward for my labours to have such unstinted praise given to the orchestra by leading critics and composers of the calibre of Arnold Bax and Dyson. It is heartening to reflect that this is but the beginning.

I must, however, be enabled to produce and maintain the finest orchestra (after the war I want an orchestra of at least 90 players) able to play to the widest public, if need be at uneconomic prices. A grant of some sort seems inevitable, not necessarily to defray expenses but to remove the spectre of "having to make it pay".

This spectre leads to complete stultification of any adventurous ideas in programmes, overworking of orchestra and conductor, and the inevitable staleness arid "ordinariness" and mediocrity of our musical life, except for certain brilliant flashes.

Of course an orchestra can be made to pay. We have done it with the Hallé this year, but the task of making it pay and keeping up the standard, with present conditions of travel, feeding, and so on, is one I would not care to ask the orchestra to undertake again.

The orchestra has certainly played too much this season, and it is amazing vitality has stood the strain remarkably well, but this *must* not and *cannot* be repeated. Every concert must be an event, not a "routine" job.

During my six years with the New York Philharmonic Orchestra the general procedure was five rehearsals and four concerts a week; but there were never more than two programmes, and sometimes only one. The main

Part Four

thought was given to adequacy of preparation and quality of programme. This has been our guiding principle with the Hallé this past year, and it has, I believe, been the secret of our success.

After all, if you have an orchestra it should be the best. This is all the more important in view of the exceptional wave of enthusiasm for orchestral music which is now being revealed in this country. The masses have discovered music for what it really is, an emotional experience, the emotion being of varying shades, devotional, passionate, or gay.

Frankly, my stay in Manchester will depend on whether my ambitions for the orchestra as reciprocated – ambitions which are not personal to myself so much as to the interests of the city. One day I hope I shall see the city realise what a great and powerful advertising medium the Hallé has been, is, and will continue to be for Manchester the world over.

Politically, also, I feel it would be a move of great wisdom to show that the Mother Country has such great artistic traditions to hand on, and bestow on its family.

I am often asked what I think of women as orchestral players. My views are perfectly simple. When we held the auditions for the present Hallé the best players got the job, irrespective of sex, looks, or the clothes they wore. To the question are women as good as men, the answer is: There are shocking male players as well as good ones, and the same applies to the women.

It is obvious that but for the war I would have had more male applicants for positions, and when we enlarge the orchestra after the war first consideration will be given to men prevented from applying because of their service. But I cannot be expected to disturb the magnificent string ensemble laid down during the past year merely for sex reasons'.

Speech for the Inaugural Lecture of the Hallé Season, 1944-45[563]

'Last year I was recalled [from] the United States, and entrusted with a task of high honour and importance: namely, the reconstruction of your revered and beloved Hallé Orchestra. On my return to America in 1942, after my series of benefit concerts throughout England that summer when [having][564] witnessed the simple but steadfast courage with which the people of this country were bearing their heavy burdens, I am sure that my American friends will not misunderstood me when I confess to the nostalgia which overcame me to return to my native land.

175

Glorious John

When the first cables came with the offer that I should take charge of the Hallé, I, in my simplicity thought of it as an Act of God; but I have since been informed on the most unimpeachable authority that it was in reality an act of Godlee.

However, I came, and the last year's work has become musical history. With a courage and devotion to duty for which no praise can be too high, my young-old orchestra achieved what was seemingly the impossible. Financially and artistically results exceeded our wildest expectations. So far so good. Now comes the real test. We must not regard this success as an end in itself, but rather as the creation of a great opportunity. An opportunity which, if wisely handled, might have far-reaching effects, on the future musical life of this community.

Fortunately, there has come to us at this vital stage of our affairs, a brilliant young man (he is the same age as myself, so I like to think of him as young!) who has already given proof of exceptional gifts for his job, and of selfless devotion to it. I refer to my new colleague, Ernest Bean.[565]

Having made my decision to stay amongst you, I wanted some means of ascertaining whether, in addition to the grand and healthy new public which can easily be inveigled to come and listen to all the acknowledged masterpieces (in our case, even without the continuous bait of thunderous octaves from the piano) there existed also enough of a discriminating and healthily curious public ready to tread with me the "byways" as well as the "highways" of music; for without such a public at my back, there could be not serious future for a great orchestra.

So, from these thoughts was evolved the Albert Hall series.[566] The response has been overwhelming, and I would take this opportunity of saying to all those who wasted not a moment I giving practical proof of their confidence in me, a very big thank you from the bottom of my heart.

Two important new features stand out in contemplating these concerts. The generous collaboration of the University in giving this regular series of lectures, for which I am profoundly grateful; and the admission of the subscribers to the final rehearsal. This, as I pointed out in the preface written for our Prospectus, is not to be construed as a brilliant [piece][567] of salesmanship, but as sincere desire to help our listeners to come to grips with some of the more formidable items in the repertoire, so that these two features should help to increase your enjoyment of certain music and, with this preliminary study, enable you to share [the][568] more subtle delights [sometimes][569] hidden away in certain masterpieces.

We have tried to cover as much ground as possible in our programmes, and whilst it is impossible to please everyone, the [results] of my efforts in this direction seem to have met with pretty well universal approval.

The unifying thread is the performance, in chronological order of the [7][570] great symphonies of Sibelius (I think for the first time in this city) but since we have an expert to deal with these, in my old and valued friend Walter Legge,[571] I will deal very briefly and generally with some other of the music to be included.[572]

I am, fortunately for myself (and I might add, for you too) a musician of extraordinarily catholic tastes, and I feel about certain very self-righteous individuals who can only like one kind of music by hating another, that we should offer up for them the kind of prayer a little girl was once heard to utter, and which ran something like this. "Please make bad people good, and good people nice".

If you were to ask me which were particular favourites of mine, I would confess to being very happy could I witness a really enthusiastic success for such restrained masterpieces as the Pelleas and Melisande Entractes and Preludes, and the Delius Violin Concerto.

I was astonished to read one writer to the papers complain there was no [major][573] British work in the series: the inference to me being that if the Delius Violin Concerto and the Delius Piano Concerto are not major works, then the qualifying attributes of a major work must be length and loudness.

The Pelleas Entractes and Preludes I have specially arranged for concert performance, for they contain some of the greatest of Debussy's music, and conditions are such in the theatre that they are rarely heard, even when they are played there. Let me explain. They occur when the curtain is dropped for a change of scene, and the music is usually, especially in the more expensive parts of the house, immediately drowned by acidulous and none too whispered comments on the infidelities of dear Mrs So and So, and other talk of the same intellectual calibre.

It is a common fallacy that most French music consist mainly of wishy-washy pale impressionism. Nothing could be further from the truth. In one of these Preludes particularly there is a restrained power and greatness comparable to, and curiously resembling in structure, the Grail scene in Parsifal.

Music must be an emotional experience, the emotions of course being of varying kinds. They can be passionate, gay, sad, exalted, spiritual. You might ask me, is it necessary to study music in order to share emotion. The answer is an emphatic "No".

Glorious John

This is not to say that study will not add appreciation [to that which][574] has already stirred your emotions.

But unless you approach music through the emotions, study can be of no avail. The aim of these lectures will not be to usurp the function of the dissecting table. You cannot, or should not, dissect a living thing, and there is nothing more living, or of more enduring worth, than the beauty enshrined in the music you and I are going to share during the coming season'.

Notes for a speech given at an Edinburgh reception on 25 June 1946[575]

[I] wish I could convey [the] feelings of pleasure and delight [that] your gracious invitation to be your guests has given us. Edinboro['s] special place in our affections [enables us] make music in surroundings very different from those of our native Manchester, to put it mildly. [It] [c]annot be denied that [the] beauty of these surroundings, the lovely hall, the still lovelier city to roam about in, during our leisure, are a source of real inspiration to us. It might come to your ears Sir, that on Sat.[urday] [I] made an equally nice speech about Glasgow & you might think that I was merely doing what is in the elegant phrase of today know as "doing my stuff". But I assure you Sir [that] both speeches are equally sincere, stressing different qualities, tho[ugh] in these two cities where I spent so many happy years as the conductor of your S.[cottish] O.[rchestra], there is one quality that does not vary: the quality of your friendship. Not the least of the pleasures for me personally is the annual renewal of friendship formed then & still cherished. … [I am] indeed grateful for your kindness & proud of the honour conferred on me & the orchestra but assure you it will be a most happily treasured moment of our annual visit to you'.

Unidentified speech dated '4th July, 1946.'[576]

'In 1848 there came to Manchester one, Charles Halle, a German by birth, a Frenchman by adoption. He was a friend of a circle of musicians, including Berlioz, Chopin, Liszt, Cherubini, Paganini and Wagner, which made Paris their centre.

It surprised everyone (as it surprised everyone fifty years later when Hans Richter made a similar decision) that a man of such eminence should

Part Four

desert the cosmopolitan [attractions][577] of Paris for a cotton town in the grim north of England. But Halle knew what he was about. He knew that among the industrial surroundings of Manchester, perhaps because of the industrial surroundings – there was a potential love of good music which only needed fostering for it to develop its own traditions and culture.

So, in 1858, he started an orchestra – the Halle Orchestra, which from that day to this has enjoyed an unbroken existence and can, in fact, claim to be the third oldest orchestra in the world.

The outbreak of the second world war brought grave crises. Blackout conditions, the destruction by incendiary bombs of the Orchestra's concert hall, the enlisting of players in the forces, made it seem, for a time, as if the wisest course was to put the orchestra into 'cold storage' until the return of peace. Instead, the Committee of the Society took the bolder and more far-seeing course of establishing the orchestra on a full-time basis, to meet the increasing demands for good music.

I was invited from New York to take over the permanent conductorship and musical direction of the new orchestra, and very soon I found myself in the midst of one of the most remarkable musical renaissances ever known. With its concert hall destroyed, the orchestra was obliged to play in cinemas, mission halls, marquees, and ultimately in a large circus ring seating 6,000 people. Hardly a week passed without the hall being full to capacity.

At the beginning of the 1946 season, over 5,000 people bought season tickets for the entire season of concerts, and over 6,000 people voluntarily subscribed to the funds of the Society in addition to attending the concerts.

I have no time tonight to speak of the orchestra's associations outside Manchester. I wish I could tell you of the orchestra's adventures in taking music to towns and communities who, before the war, never heard a symphony concert from one year to another. This would be an exciting story of travels in all sorts of conditions, extending from Aberdeen in the far north of Scotland to Southampton on the South Coast of England, and of the memorable visit in December of 1944 to the battle fields of Western Europe.

What is the significance of this new musical awakening in the North of England? Is it only and escape from the miseries of the war years? Is it only a reaction against the conditions under which people in the industrial parts of England are obliged to live? Or is it, as I profoundly believe it to be, a symbol of a healthy determination on the part of the people of this

Glorious John

generation to create a new world of beauty and order out of the wreckage of the old?

I am proud to think that Manchester, which has always been noted for its liberal social principles, should be taking the lead in this remarkable renaissance'.

'Message of Greetings for the "Hallé" Magazine', dated '13th July, 1946'[578]

'These few words are in the nature of a welcome and greeting to our new [publication][579] "Halle". What magic and nostalgia the word conjures up. 89 years of vital music making interspersed with all the great musical figures that have appeared on this vast canvas during that time. Figures that have passed into history but whose power and magic have served to inspire those of us privileged to follow and carry on this fine, solid, supremely healthy tradition. I advisedly use the word "healthy" for it has never been an institution dependent on the erratic or (pace the Americans) erotic whim of man or woman, but on the love and loyalty of its own citizens of Manchester.

Knowing in whose hands this magazine is going to be, I prophesy for it a similar tradition.[580] Most musical magazines are either shop windows[581] for moribund or prematurely deceased anthems, or interminable analyses of works which in the main must live by their beauty or inward spiritual meaning and values rather than by a public dissection of their tissue and bone structure. Useful and admirable this may be, but don't try [to][582] teach an appreciation of classical sculpture by first holding forth in ecstasy on [the][583] perfect bowel and intestinal formation the Venus da Milo [must have possessed].[584] Rather I like to think [of][585] this new magazine as a link, a link forged to create new and firmer attachments between orchestra and concert-goer, also to strengthen our listeners' delight in old favourites and quicken interest in the new. So often the words "I know what I like" are apt to mean "I like what I know", and many are the tales I could tell of the enthusiastic reactions of audiences to works they would not have ventured to come [to][586] hear if not surrounded by some of their old friends.

Also [as a means by which][587] the needs and delights of our audience should reach the orchestra, and the audience know more of the life and difficulties of what is accurately termed even the "humblest member of the orchestra". There is no such thing: every member of the orchestra (in a really first-class orchestra) is of the most vital importance to the whole, and even the seating of a string section is an art, so that the needs, temperamental and otherwise, are satisfactorily adjusted.

Already I fear I have gone on longer than I intended and perhaps digressed from my original intent just to send my greetings and blessing. From time to time I hope (scant hope) I shall have a moment's leisure to talk to you a little regarding musical things I feel deeply about, but I could not bear [for][588] the first number to go out without my warmest greetings and good wishes to the Magazine, the Editorial Staff, and to you the faithful and gallant 6,600 who are the inspirers of our efforts to make the names of Hallé and Manchester ever more glorious in the musical annals of our land'.

'Observations by JB on Corporation Grant Issue', dated '28th September, 1946.'[589]

'Although we have managed to pay our way for the past few years, this was made possible, not only because the orchestra has attracted large and ever increasing numbers to our concerts, but also because JB,[590] due to special circumstances brought about by the war, etc., has been content to conduct an orchestra of at least 20 players short of what it should be. Had JB insisted on a full-sized orchestra from the beginning, the small surpluses which have been at our disposal each year so far would have amounted to a large deficit.

With the gradual return of normality the time is fast approaching when JB will very rightly refuse to remain at the head of the orchestra which is numerically inferior, not only to any comparable European orchestra of the Hallé's standing, but even the L.S.O., L.P.O., N.S.O., R.P.S.O., and the B.B.C.[591]

Furthermore, owing to the great demand for musicians in London, not only for symphonic work, but for the very highly paid film and gramophone and recording work, etc., the competition for first-class players is becoming desperately keen.

Another great difficulty the Halle [sic] has to face is it having no permanent home of its own. Forced to travel almost more than any other orchestra, this itself reduces the attraction of engagements. The time is soon coming when in order to retain our key players a drastic revision of the salaries at present being paid will have to be undertaken. Its seems obvious that if we seek to obtain the extra revenue needed for this by

181

considerable increases in the charges for admission, we would be taking the orchestra beyond the means of the vast numbers of ordinary people to whom it has come to mean so much.

If at any time we were forced to pay the same rates as are at present in operation for symphony concerts and opera in London, it is only too painfully obvious that, without adequate support either from the municipality or private munificence, the Hallé would have to close down'.

'Lord Mayor Reception after return from Austria Tour 1948'[592]

'Needn't be afraid ...not a long speech, but as you know etc. After much inforced [sic] idleness...

Last time in this building – most historic and moving occasion for this city – Mr Churchill – not the least moving part of the ceremony was the nobility and grace with which our Lord Mayor performed her almost insuperable task of worthily greeting our great and glorious guest on that occasion.

Not trying to draw [a] parallel between the occasions, but this, is in its own way, an historic and moving moment for us of the Halle [sic] for I believe it is the first time in almost a hundred years of Halle [sic] history that the Mayor and Corporation has had the opportunity of welcoming the orchestra after a great success abroad.

Worth waiting for, my Lord Mayor, to receive it at your gracious hands.

We live in stormy but enlightened days – for I must consider it a process of enlightenment that we have been asked here today. By your increasing material help you have made us feel you recognise the truly living part we play in the spiritual life of our fellow citizens.

[Remember when in America][593] American encyclopaedias – for H see M – for M see H[.]

So before we [are] properly joined together we might even have seemed to have been, may I put it, living in municipal sin, whereas now we can squarely face the world, and in time even boast of the splendid offspring I am sure will be ours.

Seriously, however ... Austria

Continent looks to us ... culture

[I] wish you could have seen the indescribable enthusiasm which greeted us [everywhere].[594] Few of us without tears in our eyes during the

Part Four

overwhelming ovation at the last Vienna concert.

And can you realise what it must have meant to our orchestra (I nearly said my orchestra) to have made music in the actual footsteps, so to speak, of the great masters we have revered and who have brought us so much strength and solace over the years. In Salzburg, Mozart[']s birthplace, where Mrs. Barbirolli and the orchestra gave the first performance of the newly discovered Mozart Oboe Concerto... In Vienna where I stood [with them all][595] on the platform where Brahms conducted and in the Theater am [sic] dem [sic] Wien where Mozart, Beethoven etc. [Magic Flute][596] ...Only Englishman...

They have returned home, I am sure you will find, enriched and mellowed by these great experiences and have now reached the stage when they should not be denied, at least once a year, a repetition of these vital and stirring contacts.

I am sure you will forgive me if I feel a little parental pride in my boys and girls and their achievements.

The season opening tomorrow will be my 5th year with you tho[ugh] no result of a five year plan, probably none the worse for that! Great encouragement to us that even when we hear, not without misgiving, that even [when][597] beer sales are dropping, our ticket sales continue to be normal, [& even in the presence of my meticulous manager, our T.E.B (T.E. Bean), I might say in present circumstances, abnormal.][598]

And now, my Lord Mayor, in thanking you for your hospitality may I particularly quote that part of your invitation "wanting to meet and talk individually" for there I think you have shown yourself truly sensitive to the true secret and spirit of this orchestra – a great family, happily if strenuously pursuing a fine ideal and spurred on in times of difficulty by the consciousness that in its hands is entrusted the keeping of a heritage and a tradition we hope will long endure'.

Speech for the '1949 Hallé Committee Dinner'[599]

'I hope you are not expecting an oration from me, & as you will observe (perhaps with relief) I have no notes which might betoken preparation of a speech worthy of the occasion, for since I am in a way the occasion, the whole proceeding might appear rather modest. I feel to-night a very proud, but very humble man. Proud that my sovereign, & you my friends have seen fit to do me so much honour.[600] [1st orchestral player to be so honoured.][601]

183

Glorious John

& humble when I realize how much still remains to be done. Found the following. "It is not the beginning, but the continuing of the same until it be thoroughly finished, which yieldeth the true glory". One of the finest things about this great organization the Hallé, is the unity which exists within it, the fact that we all love it, honour it, & want to serve it. This is no hypocritical half truth, but a plain statement of fact. So much so that the first time I spoke in public after the announcement of my honour, I spoke of it quite naturally as the honour which had been bestowed on me & the orchestra, for we are inseparable, & when I say the orchestra I mean also of course the Society. The inspiration we derive the feelings of loyalty to the ideal which has kept orchestral music going in M/C [Manchester] for close on a century, certainly helped sustain me during the first difficult & trying years when the responsibility of the organization was thrust upon me. I once in a speech at the close of an Albert Hall season when we had but recently returned from [the] B[ritish].L[iberation].A[rmy]. in 1944, took it upon myself to paraphrase our beloved Mr. Churchill & ventured to call that visit to the troops as perhaps the orchestra's "Finest hour", & now I feel I [could] almost go further and declare with him "We will play in the [illegible] & in the Chapels, until, in God's good time, the Free Trade Hall be restored to us". The company is so pleasant, the hospitality has been so gracious & generous, that I [would] not detain you longer from conversations with your neighbours probably far more interesting than what I have to say, but please[,] please believe dear Philip,[602] & all your colleagues on the Board of the Society that this evening will be enshrined in my heart, as long as I shall remain on this earth, & may I leave you with the word of Hans Sachs uttered after the Guild have paid him the kind of homage you have so, I like to think affectionately bestowed on me. "Words light to you, bow me to earth, Your praise is far beyond my worth"'.[603]

'Foreword' to *Sir Charles Hallé: a Portrait for Today*[604]

'On my desk at the Free Trade Hall is a small bust of Hallé, a gentle reminder to all who visit me there that I am conscious and proud of the spirit and integrity, continuity and tradition engendered by him. A spirit which I feel still hovers about us, and plays no small part in the resilience and remarkable revival of the great orchestra that bears his name.

"Of the making of books there is no end." It is well that it is so. Here is another story of human ashievement [*sic*], a revelation of the mind and

Part Four

works of a great man, a monument to a man who dedicated his life to the musical benefit of mankind. And it is fitting that to such a small degree as a Foreword to his biography I should pay tribute to Sir Charles Hallé, a man in whose footsteps I am happily privileged to tread.

Hallé had died four years before I was born. He was (as I am fast becoming) a Mancunian by adoption, and, for the last 45 years of his life he had been re-shaping a deeply founded musical tradition in the city and its neighbourhood – for 38 of them with his own orchestra. But it was not only Manchester that benefited – his line went out through the whole of the country. In London he stimulated the orchestral impulse; in Glasgow he laid the seeds of an orchestral growth; in Lancashire, Yorkshire and the North generally he brought the classics to the working man.

Then, as all men must, he died. Should his work die with him, and mankind be the richer for his coming, but the poorer for his going? The Hallé Orchestra had been his own private property, owned and sustained by him. Could a successful change be made to public ownership? The problem was solved by the altruism, imbued with Hallé's own spirit, of four men who forged an instrument to carry on the glorious work and handed it over to the Hallé Society. They brought a man who became the greatest conductor of his own day, Hans Richter, to care for their musical welfare.

All we know of Hallé's early life is taken from his autobiography. This published in 1896, stops short at the year 1860. Supplemented by fugitive extracts from his diary and some letters, it was woefully incomplete. Therefore this "Life" is all the more welcome and timely. I think we may deduce from Hallé's own early account that he had at first no influence to push him forward, a fact that interests me. Ability, integrity, and the capacity for hard work were his only mainstays.

He must also have been endowed with a streak of the adventurous spirit, that led him to Paris from the small German town of his birth. Paris was the Mecca of the artist, but there the brilliant young pianist achieved prominence even among much exceptional talent. Had it not been for the social cataclysm of 1848 he would not have been erupted to London. After some doubts, he found what he was seeking in Manchester.

I have not seen it suggested that Hallé knew much about practical conducting when he took over the band of the Gentlemen's Concerts in 1850, but he certainly was well established as a conductor when he formed his own orchestra. Looking for points of parallel in our work, one may be found in the fact that Hallé was proud, as I am, that "artisans" as well as what he called "starched shirts" people came to his concerts, a movement

Glorious John

carried even further this year with the establishment of the Hallé series of Industrial Concerts.

Again, I was much intrigued when reading his autobiography to find some pungent remarks on the question of conducting from memory, remarks almost *identical* with some of mine in a lecture on the history and art of conducting, delivered some years ago, and since republished in various magazines. I would like to quote the last two sentences of his pertinent words on this subject for the benefit of many of those impertinent people who practise this simple form of trickery to glorify their own self-esteem.

"The public who go into ecstasies over conducting by heart," said Hallé, "do not know how very easy it is, how much easier, for instance, than playing a concerto or sonata by heart, at which nobody wonders. Without the score, the conductor has only to be acquainted with the general outline of the composition and its salient features; then, the better the band, the easier the part of its chief."

Nearly 100 years have passed since the first "Hallé" concert was conducted by Sir Charles, and more than 50 since Richter opened his first momentous season. The inspiration, the memory, the tradition founded by Hallé, however, remain as vivid as ever, and has enabled the Concert Society to weather the storms of a changing world. During these years there have been great triumphs as well as moments of considerable anxiety, but all my brilliant predecessors have kept ever before them the ideal service and standard in music and performance. It is a worthy heritage and I greatly treasure it'.

'Chivalry lifted up her lance'[605]

'I – AT ST. ANN'S CHURCH
It is not going to be easy for me to talk of my friend P.G. [Philip Godlee, Hallé Chairman], as he was affectionately known in Hallé circles, for his sudden and untimely passing leaves a great gap in my heart, and in my musical life amongst you. For close on ten years now, he and I had worked unceasingly for the betterment, the honour and glory of the Hallé, and it is indeed sad that at a moment in which he himself felt Hallé fortunes were assuming a healthier, if not in deed healthy hue, he should be taken from us. In the last letter which I received from him, just after the Edinburgh Festival, he spoke of the "wonderful quality of the band, internal harmony, the discussion of plans for trips abroad" (happily he saw the negotiations for the Rhodesian

venture to their conclusion), and added, with his usual generosity, "all the world knows who has produced this miracle." But all the world does not know that, as I said in the *Manchester Guardian* on Monday, the miracle would not have been possible without him.

From that very rainy, dreary day in 1943 when I first arrived here, and he hustled me from the train to the Midland Hotel we seemed to find an affinity of spirit, identity of purpose, and source of mutual trust which, combined, have helped to give some of the happiest years of my life, and the memory of this gift, so generously bestowed, will remain graven on my heart for ever. But we who are gathered together this afternoon to pay loving and affectionate tribute to P.G. must not be wholly sad when we think of him, for I am sure he would not have wished it so. One of the most endearing qualities was his enchanting sense of humour, subtle and at times sardonic, but never, would I venture to say, unkindly. Who will ever forge having seen it, that magnificent monocle technique of his, when he loved to give the impression he was floundering though a speech, though in his heart I think he knew he was delivering a masterly one. For these, and many other happy thoughts of you which crowd on us, we are saying farewell to you with a smile, and feelings of deep and profound gratitude for the golden gift of your friendship.

We of the Hallé are rather prone to take him to ourselves and be unmindful of his many other activities and beneficences, for almost all he did was for others. But occasionally some others had the prescience to honour him and themselves at the same time. It was obvious to anyone close to him, how proud, and rightly so, he was of his *alma mater*, Marlborough, and I think few honours that ever came to him, pleased him more, than when last year, I think it was, he was made President of the Marlborough Club, in which office, I am sure, he most gracefully succeeded His Grace the Archbishop of Canterbury.

Of P.G. as a musician I hope to say a word later to-day at the Free Trade Hall during the concert, so now I would like to close these few random thoughts by dwelling for a moment on a word often chosen in churches of all denominations as a text or theme. The word is, in its simplicity, but pregnant possibilities, a very beautiful one – "service." To serve one's country, to serve the community, serve one's ideals, there can be little finer than this, and P.G. was a great servant who fulfilled all these. In the service of his country he sustained in the 1914-18 war severe wounds which cost him untold, but certainly very well disguised sufferings, to the end of his days. He served well the society he adorned, and all his fellow-workers in it, and through it and them, the cause of music he so much loved.

Glorious John

During the Festival of Britain and since, it has been our proud privilege to play in some of the noblest churches in the land. Visions rise before me of York, Gloucester, Chester, Wells, and not so well known, but magnificent memorial to the masons of Norman heritage, Southwell Minster. In all these places the presiding prelate, be he Bishop, Dean or Provost, has praised eloquently music as a servant of God, and rightly so, for much that is noblest in our art has been inspired by, and dedicated to the glory of God. So you too, my dear Philip, through your long and devoted service to music have served your God, in whose hands you have now found the blessedness of peace and well-earned repose. Those of us, closest to you, who have known how gallantly and bravely you concealed your physical sufferings on this earth, must not begrudge you the peace which has now descended upon you. In our love for you, rather than grieve we should find deep solace, and even sweet comfort in the blessedness of your rest.

II – AT THE FREE TRADE HALL

Little did I dream, barely a fortnight ago, as Philip Godlee and I toiled up the steep stairs to my dressing-room in this very hall, before the concert of the Bachad Society, that it would be my melancholy task after so short a period, to stand here and attempt to pay such tribute, as my emotion will permit, to that gay, courageous and noble spirit who is no longer with us. By some fateful, if fitting, coincidence, our season opens with a programme that would have been very near to his heart, beginning with the Froissart overture, inspired by those lines of Keats, lines so applicable to him, "When chivalry lifted up her lance on high," and which ends with the most fitting memorial to his life and work that I can conceive of, Elgar's Second Symphony. The second movement of this mighty work was written as a funeral elegy to the memory of King Edward VII, and I hope you will join me in consecrating to the memory of our beloved chief.

Earlier to-day when I spoke at the Memorial Service for him, in the lovely old church of St. Ann, I said two things: that we must not be wholly sad when we think of him, for he would not have wished it, and that I would reserve my references to him as a musician till this evening. His sense of humour was enchanting and unfailing, and I cannot forebear to think of that slightly sardonic little chuckle he would surely have emitted had he seen me in the pulpit on his behalf to-day.

To turn to his musicianship, one had to play chamber music with him to realise the full extent of it, and by what sure and sensitive instinct it was guided. His passion for it was unbounded, and I well remember an incident

Part Four

soon after I arrived here in 1943 when I first went to dine with him and that sweet and dear woman for so long his life's partner. All things were then in short supply, even chamber music players. We could not muster a quartet, but he soon found some Beethoven duets for violin and 'cello. He magnificently agreed to leave his large viola for its insignificant partner, the violin, and announced the following system of rationing: three Beethoven duets for one large Scotch, all duly delivered. I may say neither of us ever divulged which we enjoyed most. Intensely human and tolerant himself, he had the widest and most catholic tastes in music, a quality so essential to a just performance of the office he fulfilled with such unparalelled [sic] distinction, and to those who knew of his physical sufferings, unflinching courage and devotion.

He knew my love of tradition and of a certain pride in wearing rather out-moded clothes and silk hats on formal occasions, and on the last night I was with him in this hall, he showed me with a great gleam of satisfaction a black overcoat he was wearing, of truly Edwardian elegance, of which the *piece [sic] de resistance [*sic*]* was a large velvet collar, and said, "Look John, old boy, 1911. Almost as good as yours!"

1911 – fateful coincidence again, the date of the Symphony we are about to play. I have always been deeply moved when we reach the closing pages of this symphony, for there is a noble sadness in them that seems to foretell the time when, as Lord Grey said, "The lights went out in Europe and have never been lit again." Pages that seem to embody the close of an era, when grace, leisure, and tolerance still stalked the world. As we come to the final nostalgic cadences of this great work, it will also be the close of an era, this time in Hallé affairs; not an era followed, as that was, by constant conflict and chaos, but I hope an era that, fortified and inspired by Philip Godlee's noble and unselfish example, will form a worthy monument to the very dear chief and friend who has left us'.

'A Memorable Visit'[606]

'Some idea of the degree of interest and enthusiasm that was aroused amongst the people of Bulawayo by the Hallé's visit may be judged by the fact that the final figures of attendances showed that on average that every member of the population (white) had attended one concert. In various speeches made there, I referred to what I called "beautiful listening" of these audiences for they seemed to listen with reverence and understanding to all

Glorious John

types of music. Particularly gratifying to us was the enthusiasm with which Vaughan Williams' "Sinfonia Antartica" was received for we have come to regard this rather as a Hallé possession. All this becomes more than ever remarkable when it is realised that this was the first time a symphony orchestra had ever visited Bulawayo.

Naturally with 14 concerts and their attendant rehearsals in 14 days, social activities were somewhat restricted, but it was evident from the beginning that we were amongst an extremely hospitable people. The very first Sunday that we were there, the members of the Bulawayo Municipal Orchestra turned up in force with their cars to take us to the Matopos where lies the body of Cecil Rhodes, the founder of Rhodesia. Severe and massive of aspect and surmounted by huge boulders it gives an impression of solemnity and grandeur indelibly imprinted on all our minds. It seemed a stroke of genius to leave Rhodes' resting place unmarked by just a plain stone and his name. Everyone was profoundly moved by this unique experience.

In a lighter vein several cricket matches were played against extremely good and sporting sides who graciously dealt leniently with us. After a match with the Wanderers Cricket Club, Lady Barbirolli and I had the honour of being made life members, a gesture most warmly appreciated, but perhaps the most stirring event of this day was the *braavleis* which followed the match. This consisted of the cooking of succulent meats in deep embers, probably the most primitive form of cooking – and still the best.

Another function, more official in its nature but none the less appreciated, was the reception given us by the Mayor of Bulawayo and the Councillors. The Mayor and Mayoress, are both most attractive and delightful people and, it might amuse you to know, hail from Derby. Speeches were exchanged and the Mayor begged that we would see to it that the idea of the Bulawayans being a set of hard drinking, bush-barbarians should be dispelled. This we can certainly do with complete enthusiasm and truth.

Another particularly interesting, and to me personally, gratifying experience, was the occasion on which I had the honour of laying the foundation stone to the new buildings of the Rhodesian Academy of Music. Dr [Thomas] Fielden, of the Royal College of Music in London, has been appointed the new principal and under this musician of wide culture and sympathies this great pioneering effort should bear excellent fruit.

Our short season ended in a blaze of glory with the Gala Concert given in the presence of Her Majesty Queen Elizabeth The Queen Mother and

Part Four

Princess Margaret. The scene inside the theatre resembled more some great occasion in a great and ancient metropolis than anything that can possibly have been imagined in a comparatively new city.

The Royal Party was accompanied by the Governors of Southern Rhodesia, Nyasaland and Kenya and the Royal Box was a blaze of orders and flowers. In the hall the enormous audience which filled every inch of available space and were, please note, in evening dress, made the scene one of great vibrancy. The programme was All-British and showed how varied and entertaining such a programme can be.

Lady Barbirolli and I, in company with Mr. K[enneth]. Crickmore, Mr. Laurance Turner, and Mr. E. Edwards, had the honour of being received during the interval and Her Majesty and Princess Margaret, who are both extremely sensitive, knowledgeable and enthusiastic listeners, were graciously pleased to say how delighted they were that the Hallé's visit coincided with their own and how much they admired and enjoyed the choice of programme. I also happened to mention that the date of the Gala Performance coincided exactly with the 10th anniversary of the first concert of the reconstructed Hallé in 1943 and that I was using the identical baton of that evening, thoughtfully provided for me, without my having any inkling of it, by my faithful librarian Tom Cheetham, whereupon Her Majesty graciously wished us a further 10 happy years. We were also thrilled to hear from Her Majesty that she had watched the departure of the Orchestra from Blackbushe on television, and she remarked how happy they all looked.

Our greatest airlift so far has proved a memorable experience, and I must pay unstinted tribute to the Orchestra's playing during the whole period of our visit, sometimes under extremely difficult physical conditions.

From the host of letters I have received, and strangers who have spoken to me in streets and at airports (where, by the way, I discovered people had come thousands of miles to hear us), it is obvious that the visit of my great orchestra had been an inspiration that will live long in the minds of these people; and it is fitting that such an unusual inspiration for the Commonwealth should come from the homeland. Even more fitting, surely, that it should have been the task of the Hallé to provide it; so nurture and cherish our orchestra as never before, for it continues to write pages of glory in the grand old Society's history'.

Glorious John

'Kathleen... The Last Years'[607]

'There have been certain moments in my life when I have had to face tasks of the greatest difficulty. I doubt, however, if any of them compare with the difficulty of trying to write about Katie.[608]

Why should it be so difficult? To begin with, there is the grave danger of setting down a string of superlatives when writing or talking about her which in the end would tend to become meaningless. In her character was an almost startling simplicity which leaves little scope for elaborate analysis. Her sense of humour was of the broadest, and some of her comments on people and personalities in the musical world were edged with an almost Restoration sense of imagery and directness; bowdlerized for publication they would lose all that rich and salty tang which was their essence, so perforce they have to remain the treasured possession of such of us as had the good fortune to hear her utter them.

Hand in hand with this almost Rabelaisian trait in her was a sense of propriety of almost Victorian ferocity as far as her own personal behaviour was concerned.

It is possible that this great simplicity and directness of mind, fortified by a deep sense of duty and personal probity, was the foundation on which was built that sublimely heroic façade which she presented to the world when the inevitability of the final tragedy became daily more apparent. Apart from her sister Win, and the blessed Bernie who meant so much to her, I doubt if there is anyone more qualified than myself to speak of this; for during the last two years of her life a great deal of her work in this country was done with me, and, in addition, an ever-growing intimacy with Evelyn and the notorious Barbirolli 'family' brought us in almost constant contact. Of this period she would often say, 'These have been the happiest years of my life', invariably adding, 'What a lucky girl I am'. In view of what she knew of herself one cannot but marvel at the almost Olympian acceptance of her destiny.

It was when I first began to prepare a performance of *The Dream of Gerontius* in March 1948 that some of my players who had taken part in a few of her earliest broadcasts (early morning ones, with a kind of salon orchestra) came to me and begged me to have her sing the Angel. When I told her of this later she ruefully commented: 'I remember I got two guineas for the broadcast and someone charged me five quid for arranging the ruddy parts!'

Except for ten weeks in the summer of 1942, I had been in America

Part Four

since 1936, and of course did not yet know of the rise of this phenomenal singer. We were to do Elgar's *Sea Pictures* soon after, and I thought this a good opportunity to meet and hear her. Mercifully the superlatives can be dropped for a moment. Obviously not in great sympathy with these songs, she gave a competent and cold-blooded performance which greatly disappointed and even distressed me, though I admit I had been fascinated by this lovely, grave creature, who looked so sad, for she had sensed that all had not been well. Much later, when we laughingly recalled the incident, she confessed that she had been petrified at the thought of singing with me, a petrifaction which became almost panic when I flew into one of my rages (acoustics of the Sheffield City Hall being one of the main reasons) and threw a score at someone, which narrowly missed her. I was relieved to find that her orchestral friends had also been disappointed, but they begged me to postpone judgement till I had heard her in *Gerontius*. I heeded them, and on that memorable day when she sang her first *Gerontius* at a Hallé concert began an association that was to bring me some rare and deep musical personal experiences. There was a kind of disembodied warmth about her singing of this wondrous music that seemed to transcend all our feelings about it; posterity must surely accord her a place of the highest honour amongst the greatest interpreters of his part. Though I had been completely bowled over by the depth of understanding and the logic of phrasing she had shown here, I was not convinced that this was yet the best that could be made of her voice; and I felt there were ranges of nuance and colour yet unexplored. Frankly, I became a little terrified that owing to our local conditions and traditions she might degenerate into that queer and almost bovine monstrosity so beloved of our grandfathers and grandmothers – the 'Oratorio Contralto'. I persuaded her to take up some French music, and we started with Chausson's 'Poème de l'Amour et de la Mer'. In spite of her protests that it was too high for her, I nevertheless advertised it for performance, and she got down to hard work on it. As I had foreseen, the sensitivity of her musical nature soon became attuned to the more flowing and transparent texture of this kind of music, with a corresponding increase not only in the range of her voice but also in her resources of vocal colouring. Some time after she was giving a recital with Bruno Walter (who had not heard her recently), and I was delighted beyond words to hear him say: 'Barbirolli, what has Kathleen being doing? It is all so much freer and easier!'.

Talking of Chausson recalls an occasion when I found it almost impossible not to break down in front of her. It was not many weeks before she left us

193

Glorious John

and she was lying in her cot at the Westminster Hospital patiently enduring unspeakable agonies; she turned to me with a smile and said: 'Tita,[609] I sometimes pass the time trying to see how much I can remember of me words, and started going through the Chausson during the night, but always got stuck in the same place'. I told her I was always doing the same kind of thing, particularly in the Bach 'cello suites I had memorized as a boy. Then she began to sing to me the opening phrases of the Chausson in a voice with all the bloom and tender ache of spring in it; the ravages of the disease were destroying her body, but, as if in some act of divine defiance, the glory that was hers remained untouched.

Her visits to the Hallé concerts were always in the nature of a joyous family reunion, as happens when some particularly beloved member of it has been away awhile. It was an intensely Lancastrian 'do', with the place literally strewn with 'luvs'.

Here, too, we have poignant and imperishable memories of *Das Lied von der Erde* and *Kindertotenlieder*, but Bruno Walter will say all there is to be said about these.[610]

When, in December of 1950, Evelyn and I went off on an Australian tour, there was no hint of the blow that was so soon to fall. I arrived back in Manchester at the end of February 1951 far from well, the result of an attack of enteritis and, at that time, the so-far-undiagnosed appendix. I collapsed after my first rehearsal, and was told by my old friend and great Manchester surgeon Billy (W.R.) Douglas that I should have to be 'carved up'. I was not in the least perturbed at this, but greatly perturbed that I might not be able to conduct for Katie a concert performance of Gluck's *Orféo* which was due with the Hallé choir and orchestra in a fortnight's time. I had set my heart on this and had devoted a great deal of time to its preparation.

The understanding and resourceful Billy Douglas put me to bed for a few days and said that if I was a 'good boy' and obeyed instructions, he might be able to keep me going till then. Never was a patient more dutifully docile or obsequiously obedient than J.B. at that time. Every day I was 'vetted' before going to rehearsal, and all was well. The secret was well kept, and till the day of the last performance in Sheffield (for there were three all together: Manchester, Hanley and Sheffield) only my wife, my surgeon, and the general manager of the Hallé were aware of the fact. I confessed to Katie before the performance on the Saturday that I was to enter hospital on the Monday, and it was a being of exalted generous impulse that brought to the noble music that night an impassioned utterance which will remain graven on my heart for ever. We were to drive back to Manchester that evening, where

Part Four

she was as usual staying with us, but first we supped at the Grand Hotel, where, with her 'Eurydice' (Ena Mitchell), Marjorie Jegge, an old Lancashire 'buddy', and Kenneth Crickmore, the general manager of the Hallé, we had one of the most hilarious parties I can remember; so my appendix, though no longer with me, remains a thing of joy for ever. Little did I dream then that but a few weeks were to pass before she was to confide to me that she, too, was about to enter hospital. One of the first things I packed in my bag on going to the private patients' home (Manchester Royal Infirmary) was a score of *The Messiah* [*sic*]; at last the chance had come for some real leisure to study in detail and in historical perspective this wonderful work. I can never reach the chorus 'Lift up your heads' without feelings of apprehension, for I was trying to memorize it on the day of her operation, as a vain exercise in simulated calmness. One of her first outings after she left hospital was to come and hear a full rehearsal of the Verdi *Requiem* which we were giving at the Royal Festival Hall. I shall never forget how lovely she looked as she sat quietly there, completely absorbed and deeply moved. At the interval I went to her immediately, a little worried lest the emotional strain be too much for her. The typically modest remark she made to me was: 'I felt so proud when you came up to me'.

During her convalescence I was to have many a stimulating talk on various aspects of *The Messiah* [*sic*], and here it was that I discovered how her enquiring musical mind never ceased seeking illumination of the works which she never took for granted, no matter how many times she had sung them. She was in particular always worrying over the problem of bringing to 'O Thou that Tellest' the easy light phrasing the music demands, while the orchestration forced her to what she called graphically enough, 'Pump it out'. It suddenly occurred to me that, of course, Handel was in wise to blame for this touch of heaviness; for she had probably only sung the music in the Prout or Mozart version, and why not return to the original, which is for strings only? So I realized the figured bass and brought her a certain amount of vocal comfort in that piece at any rate.

Before leaving this subject I would much like to quote from a letter she sent before my first *Messiah*. She had been, of course, engaged for it, but one of her severe periods of treatment supervened, and I had to wait for her to till the next performance. The gift of letter-writing was yet another of her varied accomplishments, and I think this little quotation is a charming instance of its whimsical flavour. 'I am thinking of you so much today and wishing you well for your first ever *Messiah*. I only wish I could be there to share in your triumph, as I know it is sure to be – I think Mr

Glorious John

Handel will revolve in pride and peace tonight instead of whizzing round in bewilderment at the strange things done to his heart's outpouring!'.

While looking up this letter I came across another in which she makes illuminating reference to her feelings as to what the Chausson 'Poème' had done for her. It was after a performance at Nottingham, about the fourth or fifth she had sung. 'I think the old Chausson is growing a bit now, isn't it! I enjoyed it really for the first time last week, and now I feel I'm getting away from a *Messiah*-like sound!'.

It must have been about this time that the rebuilt Free Trade Hall was ready for its official opening by Her Majesty the Queen Mother (then Her Majesty the Queen). Knowing from past experience the intense and knowledgable [sic] musicality of Her Majesty, I wanted to make a programme that would be appropriate to the occasion and at the same time give her pleasure. In addition to Maurice Johnstone's coloured and spirited overture *Banners*, I chose the Handel-Harty *Water Music*, principally because I felt very keenly that my brilliant predecessor should be represented in some way; Vaughan Williams' *Serenade to Music*, so that the Hallé choir, and its incomparable chorus master, Herbert Bardgett, could also take its share in the proceedings; my own *Elizabethan Suite*, the suitability and significance of which I think are fairly obvious; and then came the question of the final item to make a fitting climax. After much thought I had what proved to be a real inspiration. Since this was a great Lancastrian occasion, what could be more fitting than to have the most exquisite and resplendent Rose of Lancaster, our Katie, as soloist in Elgar's 'Land of Hope and Glory'. By some alchemy of sincerity and inborn genius, she made the rather outmoded words seem not in the least incongruous, and lifted the whole thing to a noble climax which moved everyone, not least the conductor, to tears. I don't think I can do better than to quote a writer in the *Manchester Guardian*:

> And a grand climax of Miss Ferrier, the chorus, the orchestra, and a good many of the audience singing 'Land of Hope and Glory'. Here was a tribute in superb dimensions to many a great day in the old Free Trade Hall. A household tune of strong direct sentiment, wonderfully magnified. It was fine and it was right, but lovers of this tune will fear that never again can they hope to hear it in such glory. There were few dry eyes, as notices of such events used to say. And even those most heavily afflicted throats forgot during those rousing minutes to cough.

Part Four

Katie was at her most radiant during the time of the reopening festivities; she stayed on, and we even managed a drive into parts of Cheshire, the cool charm of which county completely captivated her. She was particularly enchanted by the villages of Gawsworth and Prestbury, and the little black-and-white timbered church at Marton. These few extracts from a letter written immediately after she left us that week-end show, I think, how much it had meant to her to be associated with the Hallé at that time. Referring to the week-end she said:

> It has been memorable and very moving one for me, and I have never been so proud to take a small part in your concert and triumph and to see, although I know it already, the love and respect Mancunians have for you – they BETTER HAD! [in large capitals][611] ...The run round Cheshire was an eye-opener and a delight on Sunday; and as for Sunday evening – what fun, what food, what *festa*...! It has been a memorable and most lovely few days, and I have saved some of the heather and rose petals of my posy to keep and gloat over in my old age!...

'What food' is a reference to some of Mémé's (the family name for my young-old mother) Festival efforts in the kitchen. From this time began a growing intimacy with my family, which I like to feel brought her much solace and quiet content.

I have said earlier that she often referred to these years as 'some of the happiest of my life'; and I want to emphasize that we, her friends, who loved her dearly, have brooded so long on the tragedy of it all that we are apt to forget this was, in a sense, really true. Quite often she would talk to me wistfully of the loneliness attaching to an artist who had reached the position she had attained in the musical world. On the one hand, the popular conception of glamour, adulation and endless entertainment; on the reverse side of the picture the constant travelling, memorizing in train, ship and plane, and the enervating, exhausting process of having to appear at your social best when body and soul cry out for peace and rest, the heart for the simple satisfactions of family life. The loss of the father she adored and had brought to London to live with her, and to whom she always very sweetly and amusingly referred to as 'Our Father which art in Hampstead', had been a severe blow, though she consoled herself with the thought that he had been spared the anxieties of her illness and operation. From this time to the end was a constant succession of periods of great activity and enforced rest and treatment; it will ever remain a physical and medical miracle that not only did she continue her career at this time but actually made an astonishing advance in her art, coming to an almost premature maturity, as if there were no time to lose. Writers and people have often speculated on what a Mozart or a Schubert would have achieved had they lived longer. Like them, Katie, I am convinced, had completely fulfilled herself as an artist, and, who knows, perhaps has even been divinely shielded from much of the harsh reality of our present-day world. It is in her flat at Frognal near the Heath she loved so well that I like to think of her best. There, with Win, and Bernie, and Evelyn, I can call on a host of memories; the times I used to go and cook for her, not forgetting the times she used to cook for me. She was an expert in that delectable but difficult art of fish and chips; but there was one revolting dish both she and Bernie adored which I was never, mercifully, even asked to sample. A strong, thick Scotch broth would be made, into which dumplings were introduced. So far, so good, but the climax of this – to me – extremely unsavoury culinary operation consisted of keeping back a dumpling or two well impregnated with onion and other vegetables, to be eaten with golden syrup! It is a heartening thought that even our Katie had her lapses from grace.

Apart from this one blot, however, innate taste in all things was hers; it is extraordinary how quickly this developed when she became aware of a world of lovely things denied her in her youth. It will come as a shock to many to know that she had been regarded as rather a plain child, and I confess that I would have found this difficult to believe but for the fun we had one afternoon looking though bundles of old photographs. Although she looked a buxom, handsome lass in her early twenties, there was still no hint of the grave beauty of loveliness which were so often to manifest themselves. The dormant beauty of her art which lay within her was to bring a physical transformation on its awakening, to culminate in a radiance that memory will never dim.

She had a passion for eighteenth-century furniture and glass, and my Evelyn, who is really an authority on the latter, was in this matter guide, philosopher (when you pick a wrong 'un), and friend. She had, too, a natural palate for wines; on her last two birthdays, when I was privileged to entertain her, these were selected with loving care. For those who might be curious to know where her tastes lay, here is the list, though it is fair to point out these were the wines 'de grandes occasions', not her staple diet. A Pouilly Fuissé '45, a Lafite '34, Bollinger '43; and as for port, one year it was a Taylor '27 and another a Cockburn '12. This last had been generously given me by Billy

Part Four

Douglas from a fast-dwindling pre-war cellar, and it was saved so that the occasion, the forty-first anniversary of the year which had produced a King of Wines and a Queen of Song, could be appropriately toasted.

It was rare for her iron self-control ever to falter, but on the occasion of the first birthday 'do', as she liked to call it, occurred a touching little episode. There were just the four of us, Katie, Bernie, Evelyn, and myself, and I had managed to get a musician-cum-baker friend to produce a rather nice cake. It was decorated with garlands and lyres and appropriate musical quotations from *Orpheus* and four candles, one for each decade. At a given moment the lights were put out; I entered with the lighted cake and she burst into tears. Smiling though them, she explained: 'Please forgive me, but, you see, this is the first birthday cake I have ever had!'

She had been our first guest when we moved into our new flat, and from now on was never allowed to go to an hotel when coming North for her engagements. She was very domesticated and happy and insistent on doing little chores about the place. We are the fortunate possessors of a treasure named 'Nelly' who come to help daily, and I shall always have a picture of our little kitchen with Nelly washing and a glamorously dressing-gowned Katie drying. At first this so overawed our Nelly that I feared the crockery bill would show ominous increase, but she came to love it all, and it is now for her a treasured memory, like the treasured memories Katie has left for millions the world over. As Liszt in music had the gift of releasing the genius of others, so did she have the gift of releasing all that was best in those with whom she came into contact. In the summer of '52 she spent some time with us all in Sussex and fell ever more deeply in love with the county of which Hilaire Belloc, in a poem of haunting wistfulness and charm, once wrote 'She blesses us with surprise'.

She had first gone there at my suggestion in the late spring of '51, after her operation, and spent some happy weeks painting and gently exploring the country round Alfriston. This time, with the car, we took her a little farther afield, and the truth of Belloc's words became ever more manifest. How her sense of beauty was stirred at the sight of Stopham Bridge, of which E. V. Lucas had written, 'It has the beauty not only of form but of gravity; a venerable grey in a world of green'. Amberley enchanted her with its sheer Sussexness (if I may coin such a word), all thatched roofs, whitewashed cottages, and flowery gardens; and a day of delights found its perfect cadence at the 'Dog and Duck' in Bury, where, if memory serves me aright, a remarkable cricket match between the single and married women of the hamlet was played some time in the eighteenth century. Yes, she was

Glorious John

happy then, and would regale us with anecdotes of her early days, such as her 'half-crown piano', an instrument she won in a competition for which the entrance fee was half a crown at the time she was in the local choral society. Talking of the local choral society, I wish I had enough literary ability to conjure up a picture of the lingual dexterity with which she pronounced the word 'Hallelujah'. It was a sight to be seen and savoured; and she would recount with perhaps unholy glee how she used this fascinating if slightly ribald accomplishment so that her friends could see where she was to be found in the choir. There was, too, the story of her as one of the finalists at the 'Golden Voice' trials, when she became so nervous owing to the momentousness of the occasion that posterity was deprived of the joy of hearing her saying 'At the third stroke, etc' owing to the 'popping in' of an extra aspirate. How we laughed, too, when she recalled 'putting me foot well in' at the Harewood wedding. It was soon after I had received my knighthood, and she was under the impression she had greeted me as *Mr* B. The reality was much worse, or, as I prefer to think, better. A large and distinguished gathering was waiting to assemble at the top of the church steps, and as I came within sight I beheld a gorgeously-gowned and magnificent-looking Katie, who greeted me in sonorous and broad Lancashire as 'Hello, luv!'. It made my day.

During this summer we had often talked of a project very near to my heart. I had begun conducting some opera again, and in the early autumn she often came to rehearsals, thoroughly enjoying the kind of leisure her previously intense activities had denied her. Seeing her there in the Royal Opera House at Covent Garden, it struck me as rather ludicrous that whilst we were attempting to give opera in English of the highest standards our greatest singer merely sat there listening. Also gnawing at me was the knowledge that, but for some unlikely miracle, time was short. Here I must pay unqualified tribute to David Webster, who, with infinite insight, kindness, courage, and understanding immediately agreed to put on an entirely new production of *Orpheus* in the New Year. I advisedly use the words courage and understanding; for with her final collapse after the second performance it became clear by how narrow a margin this final gift to the opera-going public was made possible.

During the next few months, a time when she had to cancel many engagements, she found a new interest in playing 'cello sonatas with me, whenever the Hallé and Covent Garden left me a moment; and sometimes Evelyn joined us in some trios for oboe, 'cello and piano, a most attractive combination, by the way. Of course there was her painting too; and the

Part Four

unforgettable hours spent with her as we practically re-translated the whole of *Orféo*. Whilst my 'cello playing, I am assured, retains some of its supposedly former distinction, my piano-playing is of the most dubious nature, but I could manage the recitatives, and I wish some young singers could have eavesdropped and learned with what infinite patience and degree of self-criticism her great results were obtained. Another thing which made work with her so absorbing and rewarding was that though I might make her repeat a phrase *ad nauseam*, there was never a hint of impatience or resentment if she knew that what we were both searching for was right. At Christmas she sang her last *Messiah* with us at Belle Vue,[612] before a vast audience of six thousand. It was difficult at the time to realize that this was to be so; for she was in fine fettle, not only vocally (though, as I mentioned earlier, it was extraordinary how her voice remained completely unaffected throughout this period), but physically too she seemed better. Movement which had become on occasion more difficult seemed freer, and that night, Evelyn having an important broadcast in London, she acted as hostess for me at a little dinner party I had for some particularly close friends of hers who had come for the performance. The Maitlands from Edinburgh, Ben Ormerod (Mr Justice Ormerod, who had played the timpani in the Blackburn Orchestra when she sang her first *Messiah* there), and Billy and Meg Douglas. The artist who had earlier in the day moved us all to tears by her nobly poignant utterance of 'He was despised' ended the evening by convulsing us with a supremely professional performance of a very naughty cabaret song.

May I recall just one more family remembrance before we pass on to the final triumph and tragedy. I was 'in the know' about her C.B.E., and I thought it would be nice to announce it at midnight on the 31st to the assembled Barbirollis (there are eleven of us at full muster), on this occasion reinforced by Win and Bernie. A New Year's Eve 'do' was accordingly arranged, and at twelve o'clock we toasted the new Companion [*sic*].[613]

Soon after began that saga of fortitude and courage that inspired us all during the final weeks of preparation for *Orpheus*. These rehearsals brought her much happiness, though she was already then beginning to suffer greatly, and movement was becoming difficult. Here her sense of humour shone at its resplendent best, and I shall never forget the impish glee with which she literally purred over one of the critic's comments that her movements were an object lesson even to the Sadler's Wells Ballet. The searing beauty of the only two performances which Destiny granted her I will not dwell on; they remain an imperishable memory to all who heard them. These were to prove her farewell to us as an artist; and no artist

Glorious John

ever said farewell with greater eloquence or dignity. As those of use near to her said on that memorable night in February, when at the close of the performance people threw their flowers to her from the auditorium. 'She was perfect to the end'. Those of us who had the sombre privilege of being near to her in her last days can repeat, 'She was perfect to the end'.

And so, beloved Katie, can I take my leave of you with these, I think, not oft-quoted words:

> 'Not without honour my days ran,
> Nor yet without a boast shall end,
> For I was Shakespeare's countryman
> And were you not my friend.'

'Her Last Festival Performances: a Tribute to Kathleen Ferrier'[614]

'To me, fate as accorded the sombre privilege of conducting nearly all Katie's last performances in various works which became her own, including her last performances at the Edinburgh Festival. These were (if memory serves me right) the Chausson "Poeme [*sic*] de l'amour et de la Mer," "The Dream of Gerontius" and "Messiah" – the last two with the Hallé Orchestra and Choir. It is, as the reader can understand, only with great diffidence and difficulty that one dares to commit any thoughts to paper on events of such sublime sadness. How glad I am now that I persuaded the Festival Authorities to include these works, and particularly "The Dream" and "Messiah," neither of which, through the incredible short sightedness of some very culpable person or persons, she ever recorded! (Another monstrous omission comes to mind in connection with an Artist as beloved as Katie, though fortunately still with us, when one realises there is no recording of the Elgar Concerto by Kreisler for whom it was written, and who, with our own Albert Sammons, remained the supreme interpreter.) I remember with vivid poignancy these particular performances, for she was not well, and her unflinching and unconquerable spirit, revealed itself in a mood of gentle resignation, which made her first words as the "Angel" – "My work is done, My task is o'er" almost unbearably prophetic. It will be difficult, if not impossible, to convey to future generations who never heard her sing the "Angel," just what made it what it was, for it was a compound of all her great gifts as a singer, an Artist, and above all – as a woman. A moment of ineffable tenderness comes to mind when she spoke almost, rather than sang, the words: "but thou knowest not, my child, what thou dost ask" – an utterance of such simple warmth, that yet seemed to literally embrace all humanity.

You had also to see her sitting there waiting to sing, her grave loveliness completely absorbed in every note that was being sung and played. I remember her saying to me once," Tita, it would be wonderful singing with you, if only I didn't have to sing" – which was her way of confessing what a struggle it was sometimes to control her emotion in music which was particularly close to her.

Of the "Messiah," two things linger in my memory. The Recit. "Then shall the eyes of the blind be opened," in which the miracles were made manifest; and the searing beauty of "He was despised" – for she, too, had known sorrows and was acquainted with grief. The Chausson brings to mind a moment I have described elsewhere how, when lying in her cot not long before the end, she told me, still smiling, of the way she used to try to while-away the long hours by trying to remember what she always called "me words." At that moment, she sang me the opening phrase; the body ravaged, the voice divinely shielded. I sometimes wonder, was I the last to hear that wondrous sound'.

'Sir John Barbirolli writes…'[615]

'WHEN I WROTE A SHORT MESSAGE for the first number of *Hallé* I ventured to prophesy for the magazine a similar tradition to that of the Orchestra: fine, solid, supremely healthy. I gave it as my view that "most musical magazines are either shop windows for moribund or prematurely deceased anthems, or interminable analyses of works which in the main must live by their beauty or inward spiritual meaning and values rather than by a public dissection of their tissue and bone structure. Useful and admirable this may be, but you don't try to teach an appreciation of classical sculpture by first holding forth in ecstasy on the perfect bowel and intestinal formation of the Venus da Milo. Rather I like to think of this new magazine as a link, a link forged to create new and firmer attachments between orchestra and concert-goer, also to strengthen our listeners' delight in old favourites and quicken interest in the new".

More than eleven eventful years have passed since I wrote those words, and now we have arrived at the centenary of this grand old Hallé Orchestra, and by a most happy and fitting coincidence at the hundredth issue of *Hallé*.

Looking back I am happy to say that my essay into the realms of prophesy was successful. The past ninety-nine issues have covered a field of musical writing surprising for its range and diversity; yet those in charge of the magazine's policy have skilfully avoided those dry-as-dust analyses without falling into the other traps of empty word-spinning or superficial gushings.

The magazine has gone through changes as the years have gone by, as any living thing must change, as any art must change if it is not to become a meaningless formality. But the idea of the link between orchestra and audience has been kept firmly in mind. The consciousness of that link has been an immense comfort to me during the trials and tribulations of the flesh which have beset me since I first wrote in these pages; and I feel sure that it has been strengthened by the regular publication of *Hallé*.

But I need not preach to the converted! Suffice it here for me to reiterate my warmest greetings and good wishes to the magazine, its Editor, and its readers as *Hallé* embarks on what I confidently hope will be another successful century'.

'The Centenary Season'[616]

'Those who have been close to me during the last fourteen years will know what it means to me to be at the head of my beloved Hallé in the year of its centenary. There must be many unaware that this is my second orchestral centenary, for I was the conductor of the New York Philharmonic when it celebrated its centenary in 1942; but let me put your minds at rest and say that my centennial ambitions cease here!

Historical and personal surveys of this great span covered by the Hallé Concerts, which might well be called the history of orchestral music in this country (for almost all the main orchestral series began after the middle of the nineteenth century), will be found elsewhere in this brochure; so I will confine myself to a few reflections on the task of preparing the programmes for this unique occasion.

If I may digress for a moment, I must confess to the feeling of shocked surprise that came over me when studying the programmes of the last hundred years (we fortunately possess them all) to find that the Golden Jubilee was allowed to pass with scant ceremony. The programme contained nothing of special significance, and the Orchestra's own conductor at the time, my great predecessor Richter, did not even think it worthwhile being present. This time, The Hallé Concerts Society Committee, the

Part Four

General Manager, and all concerned, have joined me in devising a worthy commemoration. In this connection I must not forget, too, the invaluable help afforded by Mr. Colin Mason of the *Manchester Guardian* and Mr. Michael Kennedy of the *Daily Telegraph*, who have shared with me hours of profitable and sometimes not unamusing discussion.

The programmes are fully dealt with elsewhere, but perhaps a brief word from me as to the *raison d'être* of certain items might help assuage your curiosity.

The opening of the Festival will be announced by the brass section of the Orchestra playing fanfares from the roof of the Free Trade Hall – an idea used most effectively at Bayreuth. The concerts proper then start inside the hall with a special piece written by my dear old friend Vaughan Williams, which he christened, unknown to me, *Flourish for Glorious John*. I am able to return the compliment, as the opening Sunday concert is devoted to some of the best-loved works by the Grand Old Man of British Music, in honour of his 85th birthday and performed, happily enough, in the composer's presence.

To return to the concerts on October 16th and 17th; they conclude with the lovely *Enigma Variations* of Elgar, written in the year I was born and first performed by Richter, though not with the Hallé. As will be seen, we have included a great deal of British music, for the Hallé is, after all, a British orchestra. Apart from Elgar and Vaughan Williams, we have works by Walton, Britten, Holst, Ireland, Delius, Arnold, Tippett (we shall give the first public performance after the première of his new symphony) and Lancashire-born Alan Rawsthorne, who has written a concert overture specially for our centenary and calls it simply, *Hallé*. There is also the charming *Romance* for Viola and Orchestra by Benjamin Dale, which was written for that master of the instrument, Tertis, who gave the first performance and will be the soloist here; and Finzi's *Fall of the Leaf*. Finzi had agreed to write the work for the occasion, but had not had time to do so before his tragic and untimely death.[617] Amongst his papers was found this lovely piece in piano duet form, but with the lay-out of the orchestration clearly marked, and the task of scoring it was undertaken by his friend Howard Ferguson. Mrs. Finzi offered me the work in place of the one he would have written – an offer which, needless to say, I accepted with profound gratitude.

When I was in Melbourne recently I was profoundly impressed by a symphony by Robert Hughes,[618] who is regarded as Australia's leading composer. Equally fine is the Sinfonietta he has written for the Hallé Centenary, which may be regarded as a tribute from the Commonwealth.

Glorious John

Again during my travels, this time in Norway, I heard music by Harald Saeverud and the playing of Hilda Waldeland. Both are now represented in the all-Norwegian first half of the concert on March 2nd; the former by the first performance in England of his *Ballad of Revolt*, which was inspired by the Norwegian resistance to the German occupation; and Miss Waldeland by her performance of the Grieg Concerto. We are thus able to hear the leading woman pianist of Norway in a most popular work by one of her countrymen.

The ranks of the Hallé itself have produced a fine piece of music in the form of the symphony by one of my trumpeters, Arthur Butterworth. This work was very well received when we gave it its première at the Cheltenham Festival this year, and makes a stirring conclusion to the concert on November 3rd.

The concerts in honour of the four permanent conductors of the Orchestra are mentioned elsewhere, and I should simply like to add how pleased and honoured we are that Lady Harty[619] has consented to be with us at the performance of some of her husband's music. This programme ends with Harty's favourite work, the Fantastic Symphony of Berlioz; which recalls the strange pattern of early Hallé Concerts. Hallé conducted the Waltz movement only at first, in 1866, and it was not until thirteen years had past and other part performances given that he felt the public would tolerate the whole symphony!

The regular concert series end with the great Second Symphony of Mahler, the *Resurrection*. The interval will come after the first movement in accordance with the instruction in the score, which reads "here there should be a break of least [sic] five minutes". Looking back with some pride to the course of events since those black days of 1943, and forward with hope to the start of this grand old Orchestra's second century, I feel that the choice of this work to close the season will not be considered inappropriate.

Turning to the concerts outside the series, I have included a special performance of the Verdi *Requiem* in memoriam to the founder of the Orchestra. Before this we will play the Overture *Ruy Blas*, which fate decreed to be the last piece played here by Charles Hallé. After a short interval the Requiem will be given without a break.

I am most gratified that Our Lady's Choral Society of Dublin will be able to join us for the performance of *The Dream of Gerontius*, for this great Catholic Irish Choir has sung the work with me on many occasions. One of the most memorable was the performance given to commemorate the 100th anniversary of the birth of Cardinal Newman; happily memorable as

Part Four

the occasion that I received the honorary degree of Doctor of Music of the University of Ireland in a room in Iveagh house which contained that day the manuscripts both of the poem and Elgar's exquisite setting, and poignantly memorable as the last time that beloved Kathleen Ferrier was to sing the Angel. The Hallé has collaborated with Our Lady's Choral Society many times, and I thought it a gesture of friendship and gratitude to invite them to share in our centenary celebrations.

Curiously enough the greatest programme problem which reared its ugly head was to find a worthy one for the actual centenary commemoration on January 30th. To reproduce the facsimile of the first programme was out of the question. To begin with it would have been far too long for such an occasion and even more important, musically unworthy; so a search began in my mind for what might prove both worthy and apposite. The *Freischutz* [*sic*] Overture, the first piece the Orchestra ever played, selected itself for it is at all times a magnificent opening to any programme. The great B flat Piano Concerto of Brahms suggested itself as an act of homage to Hallé the pianist, allied to the fact that he played its first performance here not long after it appeared. As soloist a British pianist was indicated since this a national occasion, and as Clifford Curzon is one of the supreme interpreters of this masterpiece at the present time, this guest presented no difficulty. For the crown of the concert, again owing to the unique occasion, a British composer of the right calibre seemed obvious; but not so obvious was the choice. It suddenly dawned on me lying in hospital (where most of these programmes originated) that Elgar's First Symphony was the piece. It can rightly be called the first great British Symphony; it was given its first performance by the Hallé under its then permanent conductor, Richter; and the venue was the Free Trade Hall. Surely then, no-one can dispute the fitness of this great work to express our feelings of solemnity, heavenly gratitude and exaltation on this evening of January 30th 1958!'

'Foreword' to *One Hundred Years of the Hallé*[620]

'It is customary for all foreword writers to begin by saying what pleasure the task gives them, and, in this particular case, the word pleasure is very much an understatement, for I bless the perspicacity and vision of whoever thought of inviting my old friend C. B. Rees to write this book. To lead the Hallé in the year of its centenary is an ambition I have cherished since I took the orchestra over in the critical days of 1943; an ambition that has

Glorious John

sustained me and my players through periods of great stress and strain. The following pages, however, will tell the story far better than I.

I pause and reflect sometimes to wonder how much the orchestra must have meant to the thousands who have been its devotedly loyal supporters over its long span – not only in Manchester, but since what I might call for want of a better appellation the Barbirolli-Hallé era, when it has become perhaps the most travelled orchestra in the world, to followers not only throughout the length and breadth of this island but abroad as well.

The true function of music as I see it is to bring joy and exultation in moments of elation, and solace and comfort when the spirit is wounded. C. B. Rees is perhaps unique amongst writers on musical matters, in that I know he can still go to concerts ready and willing to receive uninhibitedly the blessing that music can bring. His writing possesses at times a moving eloquence that springs from his poetic and Celtic heart; to which must be added a sensitive sense of imagery. At random I recall a phrase when he was describing Vaughan Williams interpreting a work of his own: 'conducting with a kind of shaggy grandeur'.

Shaggy or otherwise, I know he will not miss the grandeur of his subject, and to you, my dear C.B., I am content to leave the unfolding of the great story of the Hallé Band, its affectionate nickname in the North.

John Barbirolli'

'The Welfare State Calls the Tune'[621]

'The vast majority of British cultural activities have never paid their way, nor are they ever likely to do so. Although there are still some "by bread alone" men in political circles, it seems to be generally agreed these days that now that high taxation has virtually made private benefactions impossible, it is the duty of the State and the Local Authorities to become the Patron of the Arts

The State's chosen instrument for the allocation of subsidies is The Arts Council of Great Britain and the present government and its predecessors have been careful to give it freedom of action and particularly freedom from political control.

The present policy of the Arts Council is what the Council itself describes as "the basis of need." Under this policy the emphasis seems to be on guarantees against loss, or on grants which fluctuate from year to year (and which therefore over a period of time amount almost to the same thing).

Part Four

Nothing is easier than to prove "needs" of cultural organisations. A conductor can say he feels a "need" to present a large number of performances of works which it is known in advance will not only be unpopular with the public but will involve tremendous rehearsal costs. Another conductor might feel there is a "need" for his orchestral players to have more paid holidays than the players of other orchestras; yet another may feel there is a "need" to engage soloists whose fees are out of all proportion to their box-office potential – and so on.

In my view, the system of subsidising cultural institutions should be to try to see to it that there are two or more organisations in each category which can be regarded as comparable and then to allocate *outright grants for a fixed number of years ahead*. Guarantees against loss or grants which fluctuate from year to year are a sure road to inefficiency both artistically and financially. Under a system of equal grants the healthy competition so essential to art, as to other more practical matters, would be engendered. It is only natural that if similar institutions are given the same grants they will tend to vie with each other for prestige, both artistically and at the box-office. But a system based on the "larger the loss, the bigger the grant" is in my view the road to artistic as well as financial bankruptcy.

One group of cultural institutions which can be regarded as comparable is that of the five provincial orchestras. All these orchestras operate an identical contract for the employment of their musicians. All of them receive subsidies both from the Arts Council and their local authority. The following table taken from the recent Arts Council Report, published in October 1959, is an interesting one:

	From Arts Council £	%	From Local Authorities £	%	From the Public £	%
Hallé... ...	12,000	8	17,181	11	127,230	81
Bournemouth	20,000	22	16,177	18	55,761	60
Royal Liverpool	20,250	17	29,931	24	71,392	59
Birmingham...	17,000	17	30,000	30	54,128	53
Scottish National	24,500	25	37,415	37	37,632	38

In case it might be felt that, as Conductor-in-Chief of the Hallé Orchestra, I have quoted this table to demonstrate the success of the Hallé, I may say that I consider that the achievement of the Bournemouth Orchestra in securing from its concertgoers a higher percentage of support than the orchestras of the three largest cities in Great Britain is equally commendable, when one

Glorious John

considers that there are almost not concert halls of any size in the region which that orchestra serves.

Financial results are not all that matter and the principal aim of these orchestras is an artistic one. Nevertheless, they should not in my view receive subsidies from public funds unless a certain percentage of support comes from the concert-going public itself. What that percentage should be would be a very interesting question to be investigated by a Committee of Inquiry and this leads me to my main suggestion on my subject in general.

The present system of subsidising cultural organisations in this country undoubtedly leaves much to be desired. A committee of inquiry comprised of persons not engaged in the arts, but sympathetic to them, could do nothing but good, I for one would be glad to give up as much time as was required to give evidence and I am sure that the majority of my colleagues would feel similarly.

Britain – once *Das Land Ohne [sic] Musik* (The Country Without Music) – can be justly proud of the position it has taken up since the last war in the international field of music. It is without doubt a *leading* position and we have within these shores a great potential in artistic talent to justify our confidence in retaining it. Only one thing in my view can undo it – and that is the emergence of a welfare state of mediocre music. Great art is ruthless and cannot exist on an "I'm All Right Jack" basis'.

'George Weldon'[622]

'It is a saddening thought for all of us in the Hallé that this my 21st season should open with the shadow of the passing of that gay cavalier of music, George Weldon, hovering about us. For me, he was the perfect associate, musically and personally. A really fine musician of very wide range and sympathies; with an unsullied integrity, there was little he was not technically competent to tackle. I well remember when, having prepared the Stravinsky Symphony in 3 movements [sic], for performance at our mid-weeks, I was whisked off to a hospital for an operation two days before the performance, and he galantly [sic] stepped in and conducted a most accomplished reading. As a colleague he was helpfulness and loyalty personified, and his debonair personality (he had two great loves, music and very fast cars) had made the Manchester Proms quite an institution. He will be sadly missed and mourned by thousands of music lovers the country over.

Both the orchestra and I have given much thought regarding the musical tribute we want so much to pay to him, and have come to the conclusion that the most eloquent will be to play his own exquisite setting of Suo Gan.[623] This tribute will be played before the opening of tonight's concert. In addition, the Society and I have planned that the Carol Concert for the Poliomyelitis Fund, which was so near to his heart, shall for this year become the "George Weldon Memorial Concert"…'.

Congratulatory letter to the Vienna Philharmonic on the occasion of its 125th anniversary[624]

'It was not without a certain glow of pleasure that I received the request from Mr. Otto Strasser to write a few words for the commemoration programme celebrating your 125th season. I feel honoured indeed to send this message of heartfelt congratulations on this occasion of great historical and deeply important musical significance.

Every time I enter the beautiful Musikvereinsaal I sense some of the magic of its mighty past, with the names of legendary conductors and composers. Within these few words it is impossible to speak of many, but I feel I must mention: Hans Richter – who was your conductor from 1875-1897 and who then came to Manchester to be the most distinguished of my predecessors in the Halle [sic] Orchestra, which he conducted from 1897-1911; and Brahms, on the occasion when he conducted the first performance of his Variations on the St. Anthony Chorale, surely one of the loveliest of orchestral pieces.

The magic of it all persists to this day when your magnificent orchestra, with its own very personal qualities, remains one of the glories of the musical world. My own memories of music-making with you goes back 20 years or more now, and my recent re-union with some dear colleagues was a moment of great rejoicing for me.

In this way I feel I can send not only heartfelt but affectionate congratulations to you all, knowing that your greatness is not only of the past but will ever adorn the music-making of the future.

John Barbirolli[625]'

Glorious John

'Sir Malcolm Sargent'[626]

'For the last week or so every time on which music makers and music lovers have met together the occasion has been much saddened by the deeply felt sense of loss in the passing of my dear friend and greatly valued colleague, Malcolm Sargent.

It is particularly distressing to me that I will be abroad and cannot be with you, at this the first concert by the Hallé in the Free Trade Hall since this blow to our world of music, to pay a personal tribute, as I have already done in the Royal Festival Hall and at one of the Brighton Philharmonic Society Concerts.

To all of us in the Hallé when the news came our thoughts immediately turned to the magnificent services he rendered the Society in the early years of the war; services that this will be for ever remembered by us all, a debt we can only attempt to repay by holding him in treasured memory.

He had made for himself a niche in our music that was peculiarly and particularly his own and during the years of his stewardship of the Proms he achieved the almost impossible feat of aligning himself beside Henry J [Wood] in the affection and esteem of his public.

Loved by thousands, nay millions, through television and radio, he was to them the gay cavalier of music but we must not forget that if we dub him gay he was also in the manner of his passing, gallant. A loyal colleague, devoted friend, his place in the tapestry of our musical life is for ever assured'.

Draft of an entry for the Israel Philharmonic's Artists' House Guest Book[627]

'In Israel you find mystery, magic & miracles. I have during the years of my association with the great Israel Philharmonic known all three. The mystery of creating a fertile land from a desert, the magic imagination of Huberman allied to the genius of Toscanini,[628] which created the Israel Philharmonic & the loyal & devoted services of their followers which has made it almost a legend, & now the miracle, that in their greatest hour of trial,[629] has provided the most moving moment in their history. You may well ask what has this to do with the Artists [*sic*] House. Only this that, this haven of heavenly retreat, generosity & peace, springs from the same source of national pride[,] loyalty & devotion, & which under the leadership of our,

Part Four

"Carissima Edith" & her truly & enchanting staff, has given us musicians an atmosphere to work in, unique in the world.

With the affectionate devotion of an old friend, I am proud to be with you this[630] your 30th birthday, which destiny contrived to become a musical & martial glory'.

'A Message from Sir John Barbirolli'[631]

'I should not like to let the beginning of this season, which marks a quarter of a century of association between myself and the Hallé Orchestra, go by without sending a word of special greeting and really heartfelt thanks and gratitude to the Hallé Club for what it has done to help smooth what, at times, have been rather thorny paths for the Orchestra during its progress from its inception (I am now talking of what is sometimes called the "new Hallé" which began under enormous difficulties in 1943).

For 22 years now, from its foundation in 1945, the Hallé Club has been a devoted and loyal friend of the Orchestra and I am happy to have the privilege of being its first and only President so far.

The idea of forming the Club came from Ernest Bean, a dear and very valued friend and colleague, and I like to think that he must be very content at its development and progress. After about three years, it was an ordinary member, R. H. Parker, who suggested forming a branch in his own area, Altrincham, and from this stemmed all the other branches, of which I believe there are now nine.

The first Chairman was Professor Waller, at that time head of the Extra-mural Department of Manchester University. He was followed by J. L. Hodgkinson who, on his retirement in 1952, became the first Vice-President, and remains so. Our Chairman since 1952 has been W. A. Robinson, whose indefatigable efforts on behalf of the Orchestra have won my unstinted admiration and deeply felt gratitude.

For many years there have been student as well as full members and the Club now also has special rates of membership for Old Age Pensioners and a form of Associate Membership for out of town members, so it can be seen that no effort has been spared to bring in and develop new facets of membership.

I must also mention the Hallé Ball and, of course, the Hallé Magazine as these appear to be two of the most successful undertakings, on which, I gather, a profit has always been made, for which thanks are due to the hard

213

Glorious John

and ever willing work of a number of members.

Then there are the central activities in the form of various concerts of great distinction. I was glad to hear that my recommendation to have a visit last season of my friends of the Berlin Philharmonic Octet materialised, and a recital will be remembered a few years ago in which I took part with the members of the King's Lynn Ensemble.

Another facet of their activities for which I have been very grateful, and deeply touched, is the tremendously hard work they have done for the Trust Fund, founded in remembrance of my 21st Season, particularly with the sales of very practical things such as lapel pins, pens, Christmas cards, handkerchiefs, and what was, I gather, a very successful Spring Fair. So far there is the very remarkable figure of well over £2,000 which the Club has accumulated for the Fund and which is more than double their original target of £1,000. In fact the Club exceeded the first £1,000 in their first year. In this context I would particularly like to mention Miss Goonan and Miss Lea Axon and all their helpers who have done so much to contribute to this magnificent result.

The Club has also done much to help the Hallé with their donations to the Hallé Endowment Fund amounting to at least £100 a year. In the Centenary Year they made the Orchestra a splendid and most useful gift of a new travelling rostrum and stand, which are in regular use. The rostrum has, of course, been a constant companion during our visits abroad. If I may so put it, one of its proudest moments, if a rostrum can be said to have such moments, must have been when I had it brought out for the concert in the Helsinki University on the occasion of the annual Sibelius Festival, to which the Hallé had been invited for concerts.

I said at the beginning that this was a little and very personal tribute that I wanted to pay to the Members of the Club, because I am very deeply conscious of what I owe them. The only way I can hope to make a little repayment is to make this Silver Jubilee season worthy of all the devotion and affection I have received during the 25 years that it has been my privilege and honour to serve the great and venerable Society. In spite of all the difficulties which best us in these abnormal times of dissention and what seems at times the political perfidy in all parts of the world, the continued progress and strength of the Orchestra which, as my old friend Michael Kennedy said in an article in the "*Sunday Telegraph*" the other week, has managed to earn at the box office higher receipts than any other British orchestra, never ceases to be a great joy to me. So often one hears the phrase that all musicians are crazy, but I like to feel, and with a certain amount of truth, that perhaps we are the only sane people left in the world! Long may music flourish.

With my gratitude and affection,
John Barbirolli'

80th birthday greeting to the bassoonist, Archie Camden

'My regret at being unable to be present on this very special occasion – due to engagements in America – is really intense, for various reasons. Firstly, that Archie[632] and I have been friends and colleagues for so many years, secondly that he was a very famous member of my beloved Hallé Orchestra, and thirdly, because of my tremendous admiration for him as an instrumentalist and musician, and, of course, my personal affection for him.

It is, to me, quite unbelievable that you are celebrating today his 80th birthday; he looks exactly the same as when I first knew him, and that is quite a long time ago. He played a concerto with the Hallé three or four years ago, with that quite fantastic mastery of his instrument, and scrupulous musicianship.

Lady Barbirolli, with whom he plays regularly in a wind ensemble trio, with Wilfred Parry, is constantly coming home after concerts always saying "Really, Archie is a blinking marvel, he is playing now just as he has always done, in fact his tonguing (one of the most difficult aspects of certain wind instruments, particularly the oboe and bassoon) is, if anything, faster than ever."

To you, Archie, my old friend, I send you today, unfortunately not in person, my affectionate good wishes for many more years of music making, and for continued health and happiness.

John Barbirolli'[633]

Glorious John

Interview with Michael Kennedy[634]

'*M.K.*[:] Sir John, where did you and the Hallé go in your tour?
J.B.[:] Well, we started in Mexico – Mexico City and then we went on to Venezuela, where we played in Caracas; and then went to the West Indies; and from the West Indies on to Lima (lovely old town) and Santiago, Buenos Aires, Rio de Janeiro and other cities. I can never tell you whether it was Brazil or the Argentine, I am afraid I am too ignorant.

M.K.[:] How did you choose the music for a long tour of this nature?
J.B.[:] Well, naturally being sponsored largely by the British Council, they expected us quite rightly to play some British music, but I went on my old principle that I don't want to be a propagandist of British music. The finest British music doesn't need any propaganda, and I included the Elgar Second Symphony, *Sinphonia [sic] da Requiem* of Britten, which is one of his finest works, and the Rawsthorne piano concerto. And there was some Vaughan Williams, so that our music took its place amongst all the classics.

M.K.[:] How did the Latin-American audiences like Elgar, for instance?
J.B.[:] I was absolutely thrilled beyond words at the understanding, the perception and the enthusiasm – most extraordinary – and they'd never heard a note of an Elgar symphony (and an Elgar symphony takes an hour you know and they're very complex works, even though they sound euphonious) and it was really thrilling. And we played as an encore to that, the *Pomp and Circumstance No. 1* which they'd also never heard. Everywhere we played it, we had to play it twice. But can you imagine the thrill? You see, the connotation of "Land of Hope and Glory" means nothing at all to them except a great tune. It really was wonderful to feel the effect – the electrical effect – on a great audience. They were very sophisticated audiences some of them, and I'd like to remind our listeners in Manchester that we followed the Philadelphia and the Vienna Philharmonic, so we made a huge score against some of the best bowling in the world.

M.K.: A tour like this is very good for orchestral morale I suppose?
J.B.: The morale of the orchestra has never been higher, I must say the tour was beautifully administered, and I'd like to pay tribute to that. And they played absolutely superbly. It's a great uplift to see a great audience like at the Colon,[635] one of the most beautiful opera houses in the world; to see four thousand people nearly all in evening dress standing up and cheering for a

quarter of an hour. It does something to you.

M.K.[:] It's often said that, quite apart from the musical value of these tours, they have a tremendous extra value of publicising Britain abroad and thereby actually helping our balance of payments. Have you any concrete proof of this?
J.B.[:] Oh! well, I have concrete evidence. You know, relations with the Argentine over the foot and mouth and the Falkland Islands have not been the smoothest, and our Ambassador in Buenos Aires told me I did something that the Foreign Office had not been able to do. The President came to one of my concerts, and of course the British Ambassador sat in the box with the President in an atmosphere of great cordiality, and he said the image of Britain had changed overnight, though music.

M.K.[:] I believe you encountered a demonstration of student power?
J.B.: Yes, I think it was in Caracas, where we played in the Senate Hall of the University and I suppose they felt they had a right to get into their own university. The orchestra was on the stage – I was ready to go on when about 500 of them marched in singing and then making speeches. Then they started getting on to the platform and I got a bit nervous about the instruments. As you know, we've got some violins worth about £30,000 in the orchestra. It only takes one person to get a bit wild, so I took the orchestra off, but they were very orderly and nice. They were nearly all science students complaining about the lack of laboratory facilities and things like that. Then they sang a couple more songs and off they went – and then I came on with a beaming face, to great applause.

M.K.: Didn't any of them stay and listen to the concert?
J.B.: I don't know.

M.K.: It would be good for science students if they had! One of the things which took people's imagination, I think, in this country was that you took your own aeroplane on this tour. This must have made a tremendous difference.
J.B.: Indeed it did. We managed to take everybody but twelve. We travelled with all our instruments: had our own people to load and unload, always had the same staff on the aeroplane, the same crew and it ended up like a great family. The stewardesses were charming girls. I said in a final speech to them, that I already thought I had many daughters in the orchestra and I

Glorious John

found I had many more in the crew!

M.K.: So it made a wonderful climax to your 25th season?
J.B.: It really did. A season I shall never forget, which ended with two of my dearest wishes being fulfilled. First I conducted *Otello* for you all and the [*sic*] I took the orchestra to America at last.

Barbirolli's draft foreword to the autobiography of Rachel Morton[636]

'It is with the greatest pleasure[637] that I write this little forward to my dear old friend Rachel Morton's[638] autobiography, (or name of the book as you please) for I first met her at the time when I began my career as an opera conductor.[639] With the disarming candour, which, with other endearing qualities of warmth and affection, are so characteristic of her, I remember her first word when we met for our first rehearsal; Aida, in which she was to sing the name part. "You look very young to be a conductor". I was 26 & even then (as many orchestral players tell me now) probably looked younger than I really was! This was the prelude to many years of happy and satisfying years of work together in some of the greatest & dramatic works of the soprano repertoire, Aida, Tosca, Isolde etc. These were not without their storms & stresses; for with her very natural, & beautiful voice went a tremendous temperament, and I smiled, with a serenity I did not at times feel then, when she recalls in her book with charming simplicity & charm her frequent & distressing outburst of tears; in her very early years, a faculty she had not shed altogether when I first met her. But to return to her own story. I recommend it heavily to all young singers, and indeed anyone who is musically inclined for it speaks vividly & personally of many figures in the musical world of her youth which are now almost legendary. I have but to mention a few names to make the potential reader aware of this. Widor (great organist) Ravel, Reynaldo Hahn, Isadora Duncan, the Duke of Connaught (son of Queen Victoria), Count Sforza (distinguished Italian statesman) & above all that great man and artist who was her teacher Jean de Reszke.[640] She always used to say I c[ou]ld make her sing better than she really c[ou]ld. Well, as to that I will only comment, perhaps she had the fire well laid & I was able to ignite it. With many happy & moving memories of our work together, I say, Bless [*sic*] you and all good wishes to your charming & most interesting story.

J.B.'

Part Four

South Place Sunday Concerts[641]

'I did indeed feel honoured when Mr. George Hutchinson asked me if I could contribute a short preface to the book they propose to publish on the history of the concerts 1887-1969 during which time they will have given their 2000th concert. A unique and historic achievement; an achievement of much greater import than many may realise. I remember Fritz Kreisler saying to me on more than one occasion "No community, however flourishing their orchestral and opera situation may be, can call itself civilized unless its musical public has an interest in the world of chamber music". These simple words of this great musician and artist, can in a way be transcribed as a most eloquent tribute to Alfred Clements and his associates and the immense influsence [*sic*] with which their self sacrifice and devotion to one of the most noble aspects of our musical arts have enriched the lives of thousands of their fellow citizens.

The writing of these few inadequate words has naturally brought back nostalgic memories and I am agrateful [*sic*] that I took part in some concerts in the original Chapel, for even after 45 years I can still "smell" its unique atmosphere of tension and anticipation of the music to come. Recalling the generous attitude of Clements and his colleagues to the younger British composers, I can remember one concert with the Kutcher Quartet in which the programme included the Brahms A. Minor Quartet and a new Quartet by George Whittaker, the very gifted second violin of the Kutcher Quartet at that time. Looking back at the list of artists who were then the much more senior and distinguished of my colleagues I could write about them for hours (if I had the time) but I think particularly of the very distinguished John Saunders, who introduced the Beethoven Quartets to South Place and dear Albert (Sammons) perhaps the greatest of our violinists, giving us a most exciting half hour with Tommy Petre (second violin of the London String Quartet) playing some Spohr violin duets. From Spohr duets to a double cycle of all the Bartok Quartets between 1945-1953 is eloquent testimony to the vision and tradition of this great institution which is still being carried on and will endure to enrich the lives of generations as yet unborn'.

Glorious John

Ninetieth birthday greeting to Sir Robert Mayer in 1969[642]

'So the amazing Sir Robert Mayer[643] will be ninety on 5th June, on seeing him a few months ago he seemed almost exactly as I have ever known him which must be over 40 years now. The same zest, enthusiasm and drive were there, to pile achievement on achievement in the great crusade he has led with such distinction.

That a great deal of the healthy state of our musical public at the present, and in the near past, is the result of his magnificent pioneering work in the field of "Music for Young People" no one can gainsay. I played but a small part in all of this, but I do remember a very happy tour in the North with the now defunct Northern Philharmonic Orchestra based at that time in Leeds. We travelled together and talked over musical problems and personalities incessantly; the same Robert as he is today.

One of the most striking examples of the great benefits he has brought to the continuing life's blood flow to our audiences and music lovers he has helped to create is to be appreciated in Italy (where I often conduct). Here no such work for children and young people exists and the paucity of the numbers joining the splendid music conservatories (this was told to me by various directors of these institutions) and the lack of interest in music of young people generally, often causes me so much sadness.

But this is a joyous occasion in which the work of dear Dorothy (Lady Meyer [*sic*]) – a fine artist herself, whose great musical qualities I vividly remember – must not be forgotten, for this has been a truly perfectly balanced "Double Concerto".

With all my love and admiration,
John Barbirolli.'

Homily written on the death of the tenor, Giovanni Martinelli[644]

'It came as quite a distressing shock to hear of the death of my very dear old friend and that great artist, Martinelli.[645] We used to meet often, even in recent years in New York, as he sometimes lived in the same apartment house as I did.

As many may know, we had a very great bond in the fact that we were

Part Four

both Venetians (he by birth and myself through my father). Among the many operas I conducted for him, my greatest and most fervent remembrance of him was that he sang Calaf in *Turandot* for the first time in his long career under my direction, in what I can dare to call one of the great casts to ever adorn that opera – Eva Turner[646] as Turandot and Mafalda Favero[647] as Liù. That was at Covent Garden in 1937.

The magnificent sound he produced, aided by an aristocracy of feeling, and unfailing musicality, will never be forgotten by either those who worked with him (and what a magnificent professional colleague he was), or by those who were privileged to hear him.

May I be allowed to say 'goodbye' to him in Venetian: 'Ciao benedetto Giovanni e riposati bene'.

Interview in *Nihon Keizai Shimbun* (27 August 1969)[648]

'…It will be my first visit to Japan and I am looking forward to it very much. I've heard a lot about today's conditions in the big cities but I hope to travel around and see as many things as I possibly can – I feel a special interest in traditional Japanese architecture and I am fully aware of the depth of the… Japanese love of classical music.

The selection of works that I hope to conduct during my Japanese tour may possibly change sooner or later but I recently chose the following:- Of English composers I have chosen Benjamin Britten's Symphony du Requiem [*sic*] – I was the first to ever conduct this – and I hope to include other modern pieces such as chamber music by the composer Rawsthorne, as well as Brahms' Symphony No. 2[,] Beethoven's Eroica and works by Mahler.

If I were asked to choose my favourite composer I would say Debussey [*sic*], but my attitude to classical music being distinctly 'catholic', rather than making a distinction between classical and modern music, I distinguish between good music and music which is not up to the same standard. This being so I feel that the works chosen for my forthcoming visit to Japan make a very well balanced selection and I intend [to] perform them to the very utmost of my ability.

Music apart, I feel that EXPO 70 offers a wonderful opportunity for all countries to draw closer together and to promote an even greater understanding of each other'.

Glorious John

Barbirolli with Artur Rubinstein and his wife, Manchester, 1957

Barbirolli at Hallé's grave, Salford, Feburary 1958

Barbirolli – Umpire

Glorious John

Barbirolli and Lady Fermoy, Town Hall, Manchester, December 1961

After a performance of Mahler's *Ressurection Symphony*, Tel Aviv, June 1960

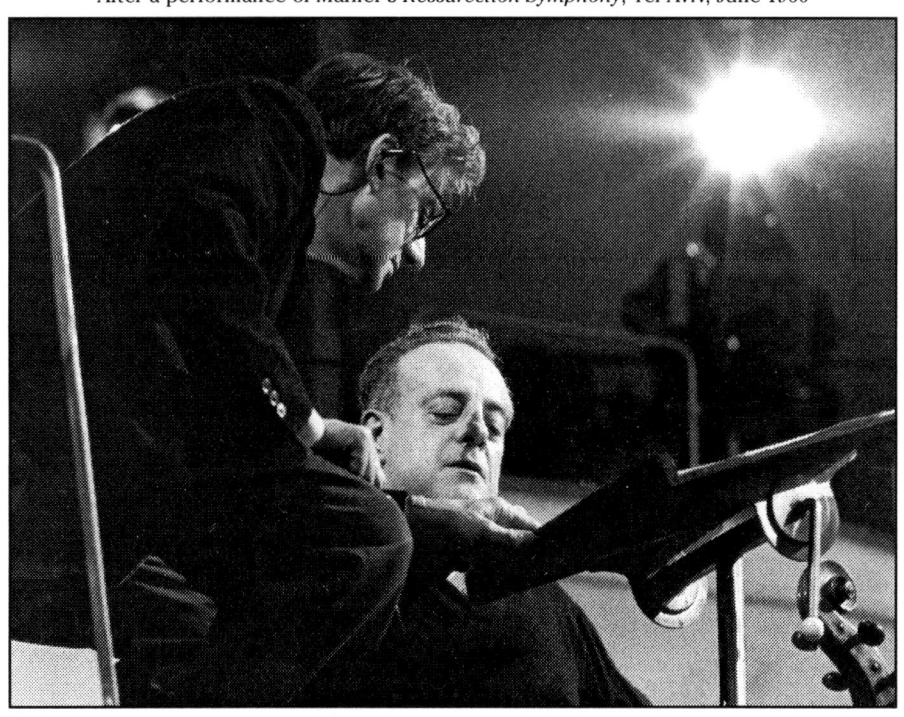

Barbirolli and André Navarra, 1961

225

Glorious John

Barbirolli with the production team of BBC Television's *Monitor* programme, 1964

Barbirolli looking at the plans for the Sydney Opera House, c. 1960s

Barbirolli conducting at Kenwood, August 1964

Glorious John

PART FIVE

On Programming and Audiences

'The Musical Highbrow Menace'[649]

'That highbrow is an ugly and much-abused word I admit. Yet experience suggests that the designation itself is no better and no worse than its namesakes in the musical world deserve.

For the highbrow should not be confused with the true music-lover, broadminded in tastes and outlook alike. On the contrary, he is a self-opinionated, disgruntled individual who adopts a patronisingly possessive attitude towards music, musicians, and the public that might be considered amusing were it not so often definitely harmful.

Personally, I have every sympathy with the ordinary man who enjoys such music as the "1812" *Overture*, Liszt's *Liebesträume Number Three*, and popular operas like *Faust* and *Butterfly*. But I have none whatever for the superior person who remarks with a sneer, "My dear fellow, you don't call *that* music!" For this attitude inclines the novice either to feel himself a hopelessly unmusical ignoramus or, alternatively, to determine to uphold his preferences in defiance of "all that highbrow stuff." And neither viewpoint will help or encourage him to increase his musical knowledge one iota.

Yet if these superior people could, or would, realise that, for us ordinary mortals, musical appreciation must begin with the works that can easily be understood – I well remember when to hear the "1812" was the thrill of my existence – there would be more chance of the general public's growing to love and appreciate the greatest things in music. In present circumstances, the vast majority, influenced by highbrow cant and criticism, imagine these to be the sacred preserve of a few chosen spirits.

One favourite highbrow grievance is that the average British audience actually prefers to hear the opera sung in its own language. Opera, the high-brow declares, should always be given in the original tongue. This is, of course, pure intellectual snobbery. That few of these people themselves possess more than a nodding acquaintance with German or Italian is amply proved by their fulminations against the banality of English libretti. Were they capable of following the originals, they would realise that no translation could be more futile than many of the foreign texts.

In addition, they ignore the fact that on the Continent, which they perpetually uphold as the paradise of operatic perfection. German operas are translated into Italian and Italian operas into German because even the musical foreigner likes to understand what is being sung!

A further destructive form of musical snobbery came under my notice recently – that of the type of critic who gibes at a *Falstaff* audience for obviously enjoying Falstaff's vulgar jokes on the stage, and equally obviously failing to appreciate the subtle humours of Verdi's scoring for bassoons. But why should the ordinary man be expected to understand the intricacies of orchestral scoring? He simply wants to enjoy *Falstaff* in his own way. Informed that his own way is beneath contempt, he will probably shrug his shoulders and decide that this opera stuff must be too deep for him and that, after all, musical comedy is more in his line.

Most of us have met the musical amateur who, having heard a dozen or so of the world's leading musicians, proceeds to belittle them in order to impress his less knowledgeable friends. "Chaliapine?" he will say, "Well, of course, his voice isn't what it was." Paderewski he dismisses for "thumping" and playing wrong notes, Heifitz' fiddling "expressionless," Kreisler's "sentimental," Sir Thomas Beecham conducts like a dancing dervish; and so on, and so on, until the distracted novice begins to wonder whether any of these supremely great artists can be worth hearing at all.

Indeed, I am inclined to believe that the musical highbrow is doing more to prejudice the future of music in this country than all the jazz bands, music halls, cheap radio sets, and inferior gramophones in existence. For his gospel of sickening superiority and intolerance inevitably influences the great mass of potential music-lovers – the average men and women whose opinions are formed largely by what they read and hear.

It is the highbrow who drives the ordinary man, in sheer self-defence, to avoid concerts and opera like the plague, laugh at the very idea of buying a "classical" record for his gramophone, and switch off the wireless set at the sound of the words "Symphony Concert." And to those of us who love music sincerely and would wish all the world to share our own intense joy in it, this is a saddening thought'.

Part Five

Untitled speech given during Barbirolli's tenure with the New York Philharmonic-Symphony Orchestra[650]

'Some years ago I made a tour of the English provinces conducting [, among other operas][651] Richard Strauss' lovely opera "Der Rosenkavalier." Several performances were given in each place so that some opera-lovers were enabled to hear the opera more than once.

Many of those who heard it twice came to me later and said they thought the second performance a great improvement over the first one.

The compliment may have been intended for me but those people were in fact flattering themselves without realizing it. The performance was not necessarily better. It was their understanding of it that had improved after they had shown enough interest in a new work to go back and hear it again.

I consider that a healthy demonstration. Music cannot come into existence unless it is accorded a tolerant, sympathetic, and understanding hearing. Centuries ago the public did not have the advantages it enjoys today in hearing music. Royalty ordered written the music royalty liked to hear. When it was completed the performance took place before a choice few at the imperial court. The public was thought too ignorant to take part in any such cultural activity.

Today music is the common property of all men, but I often wonder at the paradox that the modern music-lover is not always willing to listen tolerantly to a new piece of music, to go back and hear it again and again until he is sure he has understood it before forming a final opinion.

And what an enormous and magnificent opportunity the public has today to hear every conceivable kind of music played by splendid orchestras. The Montreal Orchestra, directed by its gifted conductor Dean Douglas Clarke, is a notable example of the growth of interest in local communities in symphony music in the last decade. Dean Clarke, in turning his attention periodically to the works of this day, is staying abreast of the twentieth century's creativeness and keeping faith with the artist who has something new to say and deserves to have a voice.

In so stressing the new music I do not wish to give the impression that the old occupies a smaller place in my affections. The treasures of the past that have been contributing to later generations by Purcell, Bach, Haydn, Mozart, Beethoven and the other great classic composers need not be dwelt upon. They have gained immortality. But they had to wait many generations for long-overdue recognition because understanding though repeated

231

Glorious John

hearing was slow in growing.

I also must mention my lack of patience with the modern snobbish tendency to look with derogatory scorn at the music of the Romantic composers, such as Tchaikovsky. Perhaps too close familiarity with some music that is played often as part of the standard concert repertory is just as unhealthy as deliberate refusal to give new, unfamiliar works an audience. That, however, is no reason for holding the nineteenth century in contempt. Perhaps such satiety might be offset by suspending attention to this music for a while and making a careful examination of what is being produced in the present generation. A later return to the Romantics might place them in a better light and the hearer meanwhile will have gained an insight into the masterworks of the present.

I often shudder to think of the loss this world would have suffered had not Sir Thomas Beecham so wisely and laboriously exerted his efforts toward bringing out the exquisite music of Frederick Delius, the great German-English composer who died in 1934. Early in this century Delius was not very warmly received. The bright hues of his complicated harmony were not understood and his unique way of developing his brief themes not recognized. [text removed]

Debussy is a better-known example of the frustration imposed on a great artist when he fails to win sympathetic listeners. Today the world does not even consider Debussy's harmonies extreme. We are used to them; we understand them.

Still, they are even today not given the listening attention they deserve. Because of my love for French music, and particularly for Debussy's "Pelleas et Melisande," I recently played in[652] a New York Philharmonic-Symphony [broadcast over the Columbia network and the Canadian stations of the CBC some][653] interludes and entr'actes from this great opera. I had another motive. Those interludes are rarely heard at the opera. When they are played the scenes are changing. When the scenes change the audience takes advantage of the respite to relax, adjust themselves in their seats, exchange comment with their neighbors [*sic*], and do anything but pay attention to the music. As a result I daresay many had never heard those portions of "Pelleas" before I played them at Carnegie Hall, even though they may have attended the opera several times.

After that performance I was visited by a prominent concert artist who told me that this concert had given him his introduction to "Pelleas et Melisande." Although he has spent many years on the concert platform he had never before heard one note of this opera, an established masterpiece for almost forty years.

Let us not treat the rising generation of composers like this. Let us always be willing to give them a fair and just hearing, and then a re-hearing, and another hearing. After that perhaps we shall be equipped to our own satisfaction to say either "That is poor; I dislike it," or "That is wonderful and rewarding music; I am glad I took the pains to find out about it."

'The Re-Opening of the Free Trade Hall, Manchester – 1951'[654]

'In penning these few words of introduction to the purely musical side of these Inaugural Concerts at our new home, the rebuilt Free Trade Hall, I should like, first of all, to congratulate the Manchester Corporation on their imagination and insight in planning the historic re-opening on these grand lines.

It's particularly fitting I think, that in Manchester, this great stronghold of liberal thought of generations, our celebrations should not have any parochial tinge. It is for this reason that we welcome so heartily our colleagues of other orchestras, not only the B.B.C. from our own land, but the great orchestras of Amsterdam and Hamburg under their permanent chiefs, Sir Malcolm Sargent, Eduard van Beinum and Hans Schmidt-Isserstedt.

The programmes have been planned with a view to the festive nature of the occasion, and of course utilising the resources of the great orchestras taking part. The opening concert for instance, at which the Hallé will have the honour of sounding the first notes in the new Hall, contains two works chosen for a very particular reason.

The Walton Viola Concerto, one of the first creations if the greatest of Lancashire composers, Sir William Walton, will make us feel proud that we have not only a fine concert hall and a great orchestra of our own, but, more important still, a great composer whose name will add lustre to local musical fame as long as music may survive.

The other large scale work of the evening, the Fantastic Symphony of Berlioz, has its particular and peculiar place in our local musical history, for it received its first performance in this city under the Hallé on Thursday, 9th January, 1879, on the very site of the present Hall.

And as for the opening item, the Meistersinger Overture, apart from its glories as pure music, what would be healthier and more propitious for our musical future in Manchester than that it should begin its new life with one of the grandest C major chords in music? Tippett, worthy representative of our younger school, and Elgar, mighty symbol of an era now closed, are the other two British composers represented.

Although I am only an adopted son, I have not lagged behind in sharing your local pride in your musical achievement in the past, and perhaps immodestly in the present; so may I be forgiven if these words end with a final boast that when we close this short Festival with the immortal 9th Symphony of Beethoven, the Choir will also be our own, and each of the four soloists native sons and daughters of Lancashire'.

Programming for the Trafalgar Day Concert, 1958[655]

'You may wonder why the Hallé and I should identify ourselves with this very particular occasion; the reason is twofold.

As this year's President of the Lord's Taverners I am anxious to further their splendid work in raising funds for the National Playing Fields Association. Naturally for my share I chose a concert; but what sort of concert?

Since childhood I have been a fervent admirer of that frail indomitable genius, Nelson. The other day whilst reading Oliver Warner's admirable book "A Portrait of Lord Nelson" the idea suddenly came to me. Here was a chance to help Playing Fields in a manner fitting our sea-loving "Twelfth Man", Prince Philip, and also to enrich the memory of our great Sailor. The link was formed, appropriate music welled to my mind.

On this "Trafalgar" evening let us feel pride and gratitude in our hearts for that man who showed such fortitude and calm assurance in moments of great national peril.

John Barbirolli'[656]

'Musings from the Maestro'[657]

'I have been asked: "What will the new hall [Jessie H. Jones Hall] mean to the Houston Symphony?"

Well, it will mean many things and good things, too – providing one factor. It will be the overriding factor: What will the acoustic properties of the hall be? This is in the laps of the gods: we shall know the answer as the

Part Five

orchestra actually plays in it.

First of all, the orchestra will have a "home" of its own. I have observed what this can mean when I have worked with orchestras such as those in Boston, Chicago, Philadelphia and New York. Apart from the physical comforts, there are great musical compensations in always rehearsing under the same conditions.

What are my plans for the opening season? They are disclosed in the programs, which I believe are both balanced and of widespread musical interest. Also, various members of the orchestra will be featured as soloists, substantiating my boast made before the performance of Strauss' "Bourgeois Gentilhomme" last season: "You may have heard of the 'Virtuosi di Roma' – you are now about to hear the 'Virtuosi di Houston'."

I would like to say something about the opening program. As may be imagined, a great deal of thought spread over a considerable period of time went into it. It was obvious, and my own wish, that the hall must be christened musically with a work by a contemporary American composer. I was very gratified when the very gifted Alan Hovhaness consented to submit some ideas to me – as is well known I am not in favour of commissioning works. I feel sure the finished product, "Ode to the Temple of Sound," will prove eminently suitable.

The greatly beloved Elgar's "Enigma Variations," which follow, appear as a tribute from my country. I also thought it would be appropriate to have a work from another generation of American composers and chose the beautiful "White Peacock" by Charles Griffes, which should prove an admirable prelude to the dazzling first and second suites of Ravel's "Daphnis and Chloe" in their original version with full chorus.

It has been a privilege for me to lead the orchestra to its present eminent position among the great orchestras of America and to say, "God bless and prosper you," to all my dear friends in the orchestra, the administration and to those wonderful people such as our beloved president, Gen. Maurice Hirsch, that great and gracious Lady [*sic*], Miss Ima Hogg, and all their co-workers who have been so faithful to the orchestra for so many years'.

Glorious John

Barbirolli conducting the Houston Symphony Orchestra, c. 1960s

Barbirolli on the steps of the Museum of Arts, Houston, c. 1960s

Glorious John

PART SIX

On the State of Music

Article for the *Daily Telegraph*, London[658]

'A good many years ago now, a young man who has since won distinction in England, W. H. Reed by name, was so moved on hearing one of Elgar's works for the first time that he waylaid him outside the artist's room of the Queen's Hall in London and egged Elgar for some lessons in composition. Elgar, characteristically, replied: "Well, I don't know much about that sort of thing, my boy, but come along and we'll have a little chat."

I felt rather the same way when the DAILY TELEGRAPH asked me to write an article on "Music in America" for English readers. Even after three seasons in New York I don't feel competent to cover so vast a field but I accepted the invitation, welcoming the opportunity for a "little chat" on a big subject.

America is a country of contrast and contradiction and it is not strange that in England, at a distance, it is not always understood. I came to the United States for the first time in October, 1936. I came with high hopes but also, I must say, with definite apprehensions. I had heard the usual rumors [*sic*]. In America the orchestras were marvelous but difficult to handle, the public restless and fickle, the country eager above all for sensation in art. I have found nothing to substantiate any of these charges. On the contrary, I have met everywhere audiences whose level of intelligence and understanding is only equalled by the quality of music consistently provided for them.

I have conducted not only my own Philharmonic-Symphony Orchestra but also the Ford Symphony which broadcasts weekly throughout most of the year. I have also personally heard many of the major orchestras of the country and have listened to others on the air. In each case, the orchestra represented a body of technically skilled, deeply sincere, disciplined men, united in the common cause of good music. The American audience in the concert hall takes real interest and delight in music, is courteous in

239

Glorious John

disapproval and generous with applause, listens with a combination of enthusiasm and discrimination that makes it one of the most stimulating audiences in the world.

As for "the great unseen public", I can best take the temperature of the country at large by its reaction to the Philharmonic-Symphony's Sunday afternoon broadcasts which have been on the air for the past eight seasons. The New York Philharmonic, as you may not know, is the second oldest symphonic organization in the world, predated only by London's own Royal Philharmonic. Its audience is among the most musical groups of listeners; its father and grandfathers have subscribed to the orchestra for almost a century. When I conduct the Philharmonic-Symphony in the Inaugural Concert of the World's Fair, it will be the 3525th concert in the history of the Society.

In view of this imposing record it is interesting to note that more people hear the Philharmonic-Symphony concerts every Sunday on the radio than have heard the concerts in person since the Philharmonic was founded. It is officially estimated that nine million people of the United States and Canada listen in to the Philharmonic broadcasts every week.

It is a staggering figure. What is this audience like, you ask? I think, in a general way, we know. Contrary to popular supposition, it is rarely stupid, in fact amazingly intelligent; traditional in its tastes rather than eager for novelty or sensation. We know all this through many sources. There are the 25,000 letters received each year by the Columbia Broadcasting System, literate letters combining praise and criticism, knowledge and sensitivity. There is my personal mail which pours in weekly from every state in the Union and from all over Canada, a mine of human and musical interest. There are reports forwarded by the Columbia network's member stations throughout the country, summarizing local problems and opinions. The sum total of all of this information would lead even the most skeptical [*sic*] to believe in the high intelligence of the average person and listening to a broadcast of good symphonic music.

The impression is confirmed from other workers in the same field. The Metropolitan Opera Saturday afternoon broadcasts are of incalculable musical value in a country of many orchestras, thousands of concert courses, but only one permanent opera house. Music lovers have also the choice of listening to other major orchestras which broadcast regularly, to symphonic hours paid for by such commercial sponsors as Henry Ford, to "music appreciation" hours and to chamber music, to concerts on the air offered by the great educational institutions such as the Curtis Institute of

Part Six

Music in Philadelphia.

The number of splendid orchestras in the United States is a great tribute to the public-spirited men and women who generously, in the interests of music, make up the inevitable annual deficit incurred in the giving of first-class performances of symphonic music. Every orchestra in America depends on its Board of Directors as well as its subscribers to cover the cost of producing its concerts.

I give you here a list, not complete, of the country's major orchestras and conductors, as an indication of the amount of symphonic music performed regularly in the [U]nited States. Each orchestra gives from twenty to one hundred subscription concerts a season, besides occasional series for children, and performances on tour:

Boston Symphony	Serge Koussevitzky, conductor
Philadelphia Orchestra	Eugene Ormandy, musical director and conductor
	Leopold Stokowski, conductor
Cincinnati Orchestra	Eugene Goossens, conductor
Los Angeles Philharmonic	Otto Klemperer, conductor
Chicago Symphony	Frederick Stock, conductor
San Francisco Symphony	Pierre Monteux, conductor
Minneapolis Symphony	Dimitri Mitropoulos, conductor
Cleveland Orchestra	Artur Rodzinski, conductor
Detroit Symphony	Franco Ghione, conductor
Indianapolis Symphony	Fabien Sevitzky, conductor
Rochester Philharmonic	Jose Iturbi, conductor
St. Louis Symphony	Vladimir Golschmann, conductor
Washington Symphony	Hans Kindler,[659] conductor
Pittsburgh Symphony	Fritz Reiner, conductor
and	
for broadcasting purposes only,	
the NBC Symphony Orchestra	Arturo Toscanini, director

This list of conductors is a concrete example of another factor which makes for fine music in America, the lack of chauvinism and the recognition that art is international, without the borders of country of nationality. Here you have, at the head of America's great orchestras, representatives of every country – Russia, Hungary, England, Germany, France, Greece, Poland, Italy, Spain, Holland, etc. They have achieved and held their posts on the basis of

241

Glorious John

one qualification – their musical merits. It is a healthy and heartening sign in a world of increasing frontiers. The universality of art still resolves – in America – all national differences.

It has been interesting to me, too, to see how music is intelligently exploited in the United States. It is curious how the old idea that art should not become involved with commerce still persists in the minds of some people – to the detriment of art. Music is an art which suffered particularly from this outworn idea. To many people, music is a rite, a form of devotion limited only to those who have some sort of inner consciousness. The suggestion that music is basically a form of entertainment is to many, at least, a very bad form.

In America the unintelligible mummery which has frightened so many away from art is, at last, being done away with. It is recognized that music is universal, not because it says the same thing to everyone, but because everyone can find in music a pleasure that is his own. One may love music, if technically versed, for its structure, but it is equally possible to enjoy and love music for the sake of beautiful sound, for mood, for emotional reasons.

This "universal pleasure" is recognized as a salable [sic] product by American "Big Business Men" like Mr. Ford who spends hundreds of thousands of dollars each year persuading the public to buy his automobiles through the medium of a weekly symphonic broadcast. Another example is the National Broadcasting Company which has found it worth a million dollars yearly in "good will" to establish the NBC Symphony and to persuade Toscanini to emerge from his retirement to head the orchestra. Music is an industry, and a profitable one, in the United States. And the greater the interest, the large [sic] the production, the higher the standard of program and performance.

There is still the difficulty here, as in England, of interesting the average lover in new works, of inducing him to make the effort to understand them. However, every year a certain amount of experimentation leaves its residue of new and good music to add to the standard repertoire, to be absorbed eventually into the national music consciousness.

As a whole, however, the American music public is receptive, fresh, and responsive. Most significant to me is the fact that music is important in the American life. I say "important" because art is perhaps all that remains as the saviour of our civilization in these troubled times. Shakespeare said it all in the "Taming of the Shrew" when he wrote: "Preposterous ass, that didst not read the cause why music was ordained. Was it not to ease the mind of man after his studies or his pain?"[660]

One word more might I be allowed, less eloquent I am afraid, than the preceding, but certainly not more heartfelt: my unceasing gratitude and affection for the members of my great Philharmonic-Symphony Orchestra for their magnificent loyalty, musical devotion and unstinted [sic] friendship, of which I confess I am inordinately proud'.

'Speech Given at the Re-opening of the Henry Watson Music Library'[661]

'I am not yet quite clear in my mind as to whether I am here to "open" a library, "transfer" one, or "carry it upstairs," and although the latter might prove a formidable task, even for one of my unbounded energies, I would almost undertake it, so that I could pay my heartfelt tribute to a great institution. I was at first somewhat diffident of accepting the Libraries Committee's invitation, for we are in a very busy season already, but as the one who is in charge of a great part of our "living" music in Manchester, I did feel it was perhaps not inappropriate that I should be in this way connected with the most living library I have ever had the good fortune to use. Accepting this invitation has made me delve a little into the history of this great library and the very remarkable man whose name it bears, Dr. Henry Watson, a man who made good and, incidentally, has never ceased doing good to musicians.

DR. WATSON
He never made a lot of money, he apparently even had the wisdom not to want to, but his love of music led him to success in his chosen profession – a man after my own heart. Watson must have been a personage, a man of genial sympathies, and kindly and helpful to all who went to him for advice, and it is very salutary and refreshing thought, in the selfish and material world in which we find ourselves today, that out of this kindliness of his, this Library sprang. He remembered his own early struggles to acquire knowledge and decided he would make things easier for struggling students of succeeding generations.

Henry Watson was born at Burnley just over a hundred years ago, in 1846, to be exact. I can but sketchily trace his career this evening, but we can think of him from about the age of ten when he had his first and, as it later proved, his only, piano lessons. Soon after, even at that tender age,

243

we find him with some local reputation as an accompanist. Then followed a brief period as an errand boy in a Blackburn music shop. This is perhaps not such a startling transition as appears at first sight, for some of the accompanists I have known and seen trailed about by the "world's greatest this or that" have been little more than errand boys! I would go even further and suggest that with the traditional opulent charms of the divas of that day, Watson's duties were probably lighter than those of his colleagues "at the piano" (why does nobody ever say "at the violin," "at the cello," or for that matter "at the vocal chords," though that does rather sound like a form of assault!)

When he was 14 or so he joined the music business of Messrs. Henry & Co., of Manchester, with whom he served a four years' apprenticeship in all branches of the trade. During this period he became well known as a pianist, and played for Henry Irving and Charles Calvert in connection with Shakespearean revivals. Thus it will be seen that gradually from business he may be said to have drifted into the profession. He was much sought after as a teacher and had in addition a good piano tuning and repairing connection.

His degrees were the result of advice from Dr. Fisher, who met him at Blackpool in 1880. Watson, who had up to then neglected the theoretical side of music, immediately set to work and four years later was successful in obtaining his Mus. Bac. at Cambridge, and three years after that, at the age of 41, he was successful with his doctorate – a remarkable effort of perseverance and concentration for such a busy man at that time of life. In 1893 the Royal Manchester College of Music was opened and Dr. Watson was appointed Professor of the Choral and Ear Training branches, an appointment which he held till his death in 1911.

He also had remarkable experience and success as a conductor of choral societies, having been conductor of at least a dozen of the most prominent in Manchester and district. But his chief claim to fame will ever rest in the Library which bears and will perpetuate his name.

Origin of Library
The collection began with a vocal score of Haydn's "Creation" which someone had discarded as useless. Remembering how handicapped had been his student days, through the difficulty of obtaining access to important and necessary works of reference, he formed the idea of presenting his Library to the Manchester Corporation, for the benefit of young people similarly handicapped. In 1899 he offered his collection numbering some 16,700

Part Six

volumes to the City, with the one condition that he should retain control until his death or retirement. How splendid the Libraries Committee have carried out their duties needs no further emphasis than the plain statement of fact that the Library now compromises over 72,000 volumes, 92,000 separate copies of sheet music, and 216,000 part songs and anthems. In fact, it has now become the biggest of its kind in the world.

It would take me all night if I began to talk to you of the singular beauty and interest of particular items, most of you probably know them for yourselves. I must not omit either to mention that this remarkable personage was also a collector of musical instruments. The main collection was presented to the Royal Manchester College of Music, but this indefatigable man commenced a duplication for the Library. This, although not large, contains one or two interesting specimens. Recently the collection has been greatly enriched through the generosity of Mr. J. C. Chapman, in memory of his father.

Living Library
And now before I stop, there are one or two things I very much want to say. Earlier on I talked of this as a "living library," and I want to make clear exactly what I mean by that. I have known libraries where they hand you books and music with about the same degree of alacrity with which you might obtain an order for exhumation. In fact, much better let the bodies, in this case the books and music, rest in peace rather than they should be disturbed. But here all is different; the books and music seem eager to come to you, and help you on your way. This is of course due to the inspiration of Mr. John Russell and his splendid staff, without whom a library of this sort would be useless. All is courtesy and helpfulness, and a great willingness to draw on the knowledge and experience they have acquired and to place it at the disposal of those who desire to use it.

Just imagine what the Library means to the musical life of the City. To all types and classes of music lovers, here is an opportunity to discover new treasures, renew acquaintance with beloved masterpieces, probe original editions, and keep a wary eye on the work, helpful and sometimes otherwise, of various editors. The great collection of orchestral scores, miniature and otherwise, have helped thousands, I would say, to a finer and keener perception of the miracles of orchestral colour, for people can take these home and listen to gramophone and wireless performances with a heightened pleasure and appreciation of this aid. And how greatly this habit has increased I can vouch for personally, for if there is any new work or little known classic to be performed, say in the excellent Third Programme of the B.B.C., a claim has to be staked pretty early to secure a copy. Only last week, forgetting I possessed a copy of Verdi's "Macbeth" of my own, I tried for one, and they were all out. A very healthy and encouraging sign. In short, here is a treasure of unburied gold, if I may use this expression without offence to my American friends. One more instance, an even more personal one this time, I would like to give you of the technical helpfulness to a practising musician of such an institution. Worried about a detail in the horn part in the slow movement of the Beethoven 4th Symphony, I happened to mention it to Mr. Russell one day, and I could immediately see from the small but shameless smile of triumph that illumines his features on these occasions that I was on to something. The Library contains the first edition of the full score and the band parts (published before the score) from which contemporary performances took place. Sure enough the tied note which had puzzled me and which is never shown in modern editions was there in the contemporary parts.

Permanent Quarters
This occasion marks the end of a pilgrimage shall we say? The transfer of the Library from its various temporary resting places to what might be regarded as it permanent quarters, changes dictated by ever growing demands and expansion of stock. Although the initial impulse and the nucleus – a very considerable nucleus it is true – came from Watson, the greater resources of the City and the vision of the Libraries Committee have led to a development that would have amazed and gratified him.

One thing more and I am finished. I do want to take this opportunity of saying a very personal word to my friend John Russell, for he is more to me than a very distinguished member of the staff of the Manchester Libraries. Through his unfailing kindness, courtesy, and help, (in addition to his programme notes), I feel he has become an integral part of the Hallé, and here in this Library has been cemented a friendship of loyalty and dependence on each other, which I fervently pray will one day find its counterpart, in the broadest sense, in the future relationship between musical and municipal Manchester'.

Barbirolli with Artur Rubinstein, Houston, 1960s

Glorious John

PART SEVEN

On Technology and Music

'The Lighter Side of Orchestral Accompaniments'[662]

'From the conductor's viewpoint, recording orchestral accompaniments is a nerve-racking business. Personally, I find making gramophone records a strain at the best of times. They must be so perfect. At a public performance, one has to forgive oneself mistakes that recorded would haunt their perpetrator to the end of his days. And to face a world-famous soloist and a large orchestra, knowing that one's slightest slip may impose an extra hour's work on sixty or seventy people, demands a degree of concentration both exhaustive and exhausting. To me, a whole week's rehearsing and conducting an opera daily and two on Saturday is little more tiring than a single afternoon in the H.M.V. studios.

Each side of each record is made in triplicate, so what with preliminary rehearsing and re-recordings due to unforeseen slips, everyone concerned has a pretty strenuous time. To infuse freshness and vitality into a tired orchestra toiling through a tricky passage on the sixth successive occasion is no light task, enthusiastic workers though our British instrumentalists are. And here I should like to mention that, despite the prevalent custom of disparaging native orchestras, every foreign artist I work with invariably comments upon our musician's splendid playing.

Another popular fallacy that needs exploding is the myth that great artists – and particularly great singers – are anything but pleasant to work with. My own impressions of such world-renowned stars as Chaliapine [sic], Melchior, Inghilleri,[663] Leider, Giannini, Olszewska, Suggia, Mischa Elman and Arthur Rubinstein have been that one and all are delightful people, far more concerned with helping us turn out successful records than with indulging in displays of temperament.

Even Chaliapine, autocrat of the opera house and concert hall, is like a great big child in the studio. I get quite used to his conducting with me, his arm round my shoulders – mounted on the conductor's dais I am just about

Glorious John

his height! – explaining with a wealth of gesticulation just what he wants and how he wants it. Yet, although I enjoy conducting for him in private, I would not undertake to pilot him through a public performance for a thousand pounds.

I remember one amusing scene when he was recording *Madamina* from *Don Giovanni*. After endless preliminaries, we had run through the aria to ensure that it was correctly timed within the limits of a ten-inch disc and were ready to begin the actual recording. But no sooner had this started then Chaliapine, oblivious of time and place, began to "spread himself" so lavishly that the record was overrun long before he had finished. With some trepidation, I broke the news to him, and during a lull in the ensuing storm of furious protestations, I hastily suggested that the record should be played back to us through the horn used for that purpose. Scowling ferociously, Chaliapine listened. Then, drawing himself up majestically, he declaimed with flashing eyes and magnificent Boris Godounovian gestures, "I sing with all my heart and with all my soul, and out of that horn comes..." Here followed a string of polyglot oaths which I dare not write down for fear some erudite reader might understand their meaning!

Most artists are thoroughly sporting over the slight contretemps that occasionally arise in the best-regulated studio. At all recording sessions, for instance, a distinctly rude little buzzer is used as a recoding room signal that something has gone wrong. I was conducting the Tchaikovsky Violin Concerto with the London Symphony Orchestra and Mischa Elman as soloist when Elman, giving a superb performance of the terribly difficult cadenza, was suddenly interrupted by the buzzer's loud "Brrrpp!" Unperturbed, this great little violinist turned to me with a broad grin. "That is a fine compliment!" he said.

My most hectic recording experience occurred when conducting the great *Fidelio* aria, *Abscheulicher, wo eilst du hin?* with Frida Leider an orchestra of sixty in Kingsway Hall. Starting work at two o'clock one afternoon, we slaved away for a couple of hours making what we all felt must be superb records. Suddenly, a wild-eyed messenger from the recording room burst in upon us with the glad tidings that none of the apparatus had been working! Speechless, we mopped our heated brows while Mr. Gaisberg of the Gramophone Company telephoned frantically to Queen's Hall, which, he learned, was available until five o'clock only. Forced to complete the recording that day, prima donna, conductor, orchestra and instruments were hustled helter-skelter into Kingsway, where we hailed every taxi in sight and drove furiously off to Langham Place. I shall never forget the priceless spectacle of little Gaisberg palpitating on Queen's Hall steps as he dived into his pockets, shovelling out fistful of shillings to pay off that army of taxis. By four-fifteen, however, we got our breathless and dishevelled performers to work again, and on the stroke of five I laid down my baton with a sigh of relief that the recording was safely completed at last.

A conductor grows used to various unconventional happenings during his day's work, but I have seldom been more taken aback than when Pertile, during the recording of excerpts from *Andrea Chénier*, flung his arms around my neck and kissed me on both cheeks. It happened like this. Pertile is a Venetian, and all Venetians, aristocrats and commoners alike, talk in a distinctive dialect used nowhere else in Italy. Now, although I was born and brought up in England, my people are really Venetians, and this particular patois, picked up from my grandmother, was the first language I spoke as a child.

Introduced to "John Something-or-other" in a British studio, Pertile naturally took me for a monoglot Englishman until, hearing his record played over, he broke into delighted exclamations in his native dialect and I laughingly replied in the same tongue. Thrilled and amazed to discover a fellow-Venetian in a foreign land, he enthusiastically embraced me, to the unconcealed joy of the onlookers.

Such unrehearsed incidents certainly add to the gaiety of nations, but one's best work is generally achieved under more or less humdrum conditions. The two finest records I have conducted, the *Brindisi* from *Otello* and the *Finale from Act One* of *La Tosca*, both with Inghilleri, Dua[664] and the Covent Garden Chorus and Orchestra – outstanding achievements vocally, orchestrally and atmospherically – were made without the slightest hitch. A tribute, I think, to the excellent organisation and methods of British recording in general and the Gramophone Company in particular.

John Barbirolli.'

Speech given at the Contemporary Club, Philadelphia[665]

'President Oakley, Ladies and Gentlemen:
Although my topic, "THE CONCERT HALL VERSUS THE RADIO," was not of my own choosing, I welcome the opportunity to arbitrate in a somewhat fantastic dispute. The argument which prompted our assigning me such a subject was no doubt that between the musicians who think radio is ruining

Glorious John

the concert business, and those other musicians who think that radio is a boon to all music.

I can't say that I agree wholly with either side. We all saw a falling off in concert attendance during the early days if high fidelity recordings and the early days of radio. We have also seen a rise in concert attendance, occasioned by the creation through radio of new audiences for music. That is old ground and I don't want to traverse it again. However, there still is a feeling in some quarters that radio and the concert hall are competitive media.

Well, I don't think I will be startling anyone when I say I believe that radio is here to stay, and of course you do too. Many people wonder what is to be done with radio in the future, what directions the medium will take. But nobody can conceive of life without this instrument of communication. We almost wonder how a coup was accomplished in the old days when a dictator could get on the air and tell everybody that he was the new boss.

You may note that radio has been referred to tonight as a medium. The concert hall, or auditorium, is a mechanism for permitting many people to gather and hear music or speech under comfortable conditions and with good acoustic effect. The radio is another mechanism which allows far more people to hear music or speech simultaneously under good acoustic conditions, but without its being necessary for the listeners to forgather under a single roof.

Now each of these mechanisms has its place, and each has its proponents and opponents. I am a proponent of both and an opponent of neither. The concert hall and the radio are supplementary devices for disseminating the auditory arts, music in particular, and I cannot see that we can serve any useful purpose in attempting to pit one against the other.

At first, many great performers were afraid to broadcast. They were not sure their tone and nuance would be done justice on the microphone, and I remember recently one violinist saying to me he did not like to be turned on and off like a tap. Today there are perhaps only a handful of world famous artists who have never done a broadcast. The two most notable ones are Rachmaninoff and Kreisler. However, both these gentlemen have made recordings which are in most respects indistinguishable from good radio reporduction [sic], so we must surmise their objections to arise from other causes than unfaithful reproduction.

Can you imagine a music student today asking himself, "Now, shall I become a concert artist, or a radio artist?" Practically every young musician plans to do both concerts and radio, if he is lucky enough to get either type of work. Every week, such schools as your Curtis Institute here in Philadelphia and the Cincinnati Conservatory broadcast on the Columbia Network. The teachers take it for granted that such work is part of every artist's essential experience.

For eight years the Columbia Network has been putting all the Sunday afternoon concerts by the Philharmonic-Symphony Orchestra on the air in full. Your great Philadelphia Orchestra is also a radio institution, admired in every corner of the land. If I may speak personally for a moment, let me say that radio conducting came somewhat naturally to me, as it has come to almost all young conductors of today. As you may or may not know, my father and grandfather were musicians, and I began playing the cello when I was seven. I was an orchestral musician for some time, and when I began conducting, radio was already part of every active musician's life.

From that point on I began an intimate association with the British Broadcasting Corporation in their radio concerts; and now I am in constant cooperation with the Columbia Broadcast System. I couldn't forget about radio even if I wanted to. My mail is constantly filled with letters from listeners to our Sunday afternoon broadcasts. They come from every state in the Union, from Canada and even from South America and Europe. And besides, my friends at Columbia are forever at me about the timing of numbers, balance of the orchestra, and the other myriad details that go into an international broadcast series!

All of that, of course, is in addition to our attention to the audience in the concert hall. Our Sunday audience at Carnegie Hall is a most inspiring, living thing, and I would even say their enthusiasm adds greatly to the quality of our broadcasts. This audience is one of the most intelligent groups of listeners in the world; and its members' fathers and grandfathers have been listening to the Philharmonic-Symphony Orchestra for almost a hundred years. Next Sunday afternoon will mark the 3,389th Philharmonic concert. That same day we shall have the 280th radio broadcast by the orchestra.

Mr. Deems Taylor, the Columbia Network's commentator for our broadcasts, has compiled some highly interesting figures about the audience we reach in the concert hall and that which hears us over the radio. According to these calculations, more people listen to the broadcast every Sunday afternoon than have heard the concerts in person during the entire history of the orchestra! The Sunday afternoon radio audience is composed of some nine million people! If it were possible to build an arena large enough to hold all our radio listeners, every Sunday afternoon during the concert season we should face an audience greater than the populations

Glorious John

of Greater New York and Philadelphia combined.

This figure of nine million is an estimate based upon various survey processes, such as telephoning a list of radio owners selected at random from the telephone directories of cities and towns all over the United States. We are not sure that there are fewer or more persons than that who hear the broadcasts at some time during the year. We should like very much to have accurate figures about the size of this enormous American audience for music, but so far we have not obtained them. I might tell you that next fall, we plan to ask the radio listeners to the Philharmonic-Symphony to write us cards and say how many persons listen in their homes. We are going to make the request for eight weeks and urge that everybody who listens to the broadcasts respond. You know, it is said that the audience for fine music on the air is inarticulate, and that it doesn't write fan letters. Well, we shall not ask for fan mail, but merely appeal in the strongest possible terms to this audience, which has heard the same program at the same time of day for eight years, to serve as a yardstick for measuring the American radio music public. I hope you will not fail to send you card, if you listen. I'll remind you to do so next fall when we return to the air. But according to all surveys, I repeat, we believe the audience to be huge.

What is this mammoth audience like? How does it differ from the audience in the concert hall? Well, contrary to popular supposition, it is a highly intelligent audience. We know that from the twenty-five thousand (25,000) letters we have received this year; from the reports that are forwarded to us from Columbia Network's member stations throughout the country; from the suggestions our listeners make and the criticism they offer.

It is a very discriminating audience for the most part. I receive innumerable letters discussing at length technically and musically the various works played on our programs.

So much for the quality of the radio audience. How else does it differ from those who come to the concert hall? It is a mass audience, but it does not respond as elements of a mass – because I doesn't listen in a single arena large enough to accommodate the combined populations of Greater New York and Philadelphia! It consists of isolated individuals, or of isolated small groups. And they listen under quiet, friendly, home-like circumstances.

It is also a blind audience. It cannot be interested in the clothes the artist wears – in the grace of his movements – or the cut of his hair.

It is an intimate audience. Nothing except the transmission mechanism comes between it and the music. It does not care about the color [*sic*] of Mrs. Jones' new dress or who is in the box with Mrs. Smith. It is not bothered

Part Seven

if someone in a house across the way is listening to the same music with his feet on the couch and a pipe in his mouth!

It is an impatient audience, and it feels no compunction about getting its money's worth. If the artist does not captivate it, off he goes with the simplest twist of the wrist. No amount of publicity will guarantee its fidelity; it makes it own decision quickly and irrevocably.

If this is a fair conception of the radio audience – and I believe it is – would one treat it any differently from the regular concert audience? I would not. It deserves and wants the best.

As many of your [*sic*] probably know, there are conflicting schools of thought about methods of broadcasting a symphony orchestra. The problem is that of the concert hall versus the radio studio. Is it better to broadcast a concert from a sound-proof studio or from a regular concert hall? Now here is a point where the radio companies and the concert hall owners have every reason to cooperate. It is my personal belief that building a concert hall these days without provision for radio equipment would be as anachronistic as building a home with one telephone line which would connect only to the kitchen and have no possible contact with the outside world. I share the opinion of Columbia Broadcasting System that a symphony orchestra can be broadcast best from a resonant hall. The tone of an orchestra is more than the sum of its parts. The mellow richness of the ensemble is produced in considerable measure by the resonance of the hall in which one plays. As much as I admire the men under my direction, I do not believe that they could make the same sound if the hall itself did not resound like a fine old musical instrument.

Proof that the technical men themselves are coming around to this point of view is evidenced by the latest tendency in recording. I have the privilege over a period of years of making a great many records in Europe and America. I can remember the days when a thoroughly "dead" – that is, non-resonating – studio was considered desirable for all recording purposes. I can remember, too, the complaints of musicians who said that they could not hear the tone of their own instruments as they sat in cramped quarters in heavily draped studios; in awkward and unnatural positions trying to accommodate themselves to the microphone. In these studios, the conductor himself found it difficult, if not impossible, to hear the balanced tone of the orchestra as he was used to hearing it in the concert hall.

But now, all this is changing. The recording engineers are coming more and more to simulate the conditions of the concert hall. Many of our best records in fact, are now made not in specially insulated studios, but actually in Carnegie Hall, in the Philadelphia Academy of Music or in "live" studios which reproduce the acoustic qualities of the concert hall.

The time when it was necessary for the artist to accommodate himself to the microphone is past. Today the microphone accommodates himself to the artist. The engineers tell me that they no longer balance the Philharmonic-Symphony Orchestra in the control room. The dynamic relations between instrument and instrument, and between choir and choir are left to the director. The engineers endeavour to reproduce with the highest possible fidelity the sound of the orchestra in the hall. In other words, they try to give a life-like photograph of the sound of the music rather than an abstract modern painting of what they think it should sound like.

I have heard the arguments of that second school of thought which champions the cause of broadcasting symphonic music from studios. One of the important points they make is that many people resent the presence of an ordinary audience. There is one man, for instance, who writes to Mr. Paley, President of Columbia Broadcasting System, regularly every year. He comments with heavy sarcasm upon Mr. Paley's engagement of his "star cougher" at Carnegie Hall. He knows that the man who coughs must be a professional, because no amateur could cough like that! However, such coughs can occur in studios too. The microphone picks up anything that is there to be heard.

I myself have to be warned every now and then not to sing too lustily with the orchestra in melodic passages. The microphone makes no distinctions – and the opinion that my voice adds little to the beauty of the orchestra seems to be unanimous! I might add in self-defense [sic], however, that I am not the only conductor suffering from this failing.

But we actually get letters thanking us for the human and non-musical sounds which accompany a broadcast from a concert hall. It is nothing unusual for a listener to praise us for carrying so much of the applause. It makes the listener feel that he is part of the spectacle which he can visualize.

You have heard the Detroit Orchestra, the Boston Orchestra, the Philadelphia Orchestra, and the Philharmonic-Symphony from resonant halls, and as nearly as we can judge, the result seems eminently satisfactory.

Well, we have compared audiences and have compared acoustics in radio and the concert hall. What about programs [sic]? One of the radio superstitions used to be that the radio public did not like long numbers. They were supposed to be able to endure enough short number to fill a whole day of broadcasting; indeed, they were expected to listen all day, and some of them did. But they were supposed to be fatigued by long pieces – symphonies, tone poems and operas. This theory has proved to be fallacious, because some of the broadcasts which make a point of presenting great music unabridged are among the most popular programs. I also believe that the idea that musically unsophisticated listeners dislike modern music is wrong. I have presented this season more than one contemporary work which seems to have met with a warmer reception on the air than it did in the auditorium. I am inclined to think that prejudice against a certain musical idiom is occasioned by having been brought up as a child on too restricted musical diet, and that the radio public knows it own tastes very well merely because it has been allowed to sample scores of all periods without undue emphasis on any one century.

A while ago I endorsed the platitude that radio is here to stay. I should like to add just here that I also think the concert hall will be with us indefinitely. People like to see music made, as well as to hear it made. They like to respond sometimes as parts of a crowd. It is exciting and it is social. This delight in sharing an artistic experience with hundreds or thousands of other listeners who are present and who applaud with you cannot be replaced by a private reaction detached from a gregarious occasion. I believe that there will be more concerts, not less, in the future, and that the best of these will be broadcast. Some broadcasts must necessarily not be concert music, or even music, and not all concerts are suitable for the air. But there is every reason to believe that the return to this country of my great predecessor at the Philharmonic-Symphony, Mr. Toscanini, to conduct a radio orchestra, is a healthful indication of this nation's interest in music'.

Glorious John

Barbirolli with Lionel Tertis, 1967

Kinloch Anderson (EMI Producer), John and Evelyn, Walton Lodge, 1969

Barbirolli with Lidia Arcuri, Genoa, 1967

Barbirolli with Fiorenzo Cossotto and Ivo Vinco, *Aida*, Rome, April 1969

Laurance Turner, Martin Milner, Barbirolli and Clive Smart, Manchester, 1967

Barbirolli and the RAI Symphony Orchestra, Turin, 1970

Glorious John

PART EIGHT

On Music, War and Politics

Easter statement from New York[666]

'I am always happy to have the opportunity of greeting the friends of the Philharmonic all over the country. I am particularly glad to do it today because it is Easter. Easter is the time of renewal, rebirth and hope. It is a day of promise and rejoicing.

It is a symbol of the light which must and will follow the darkness through which we are passing. Everyone of us must do our best to keep the torch kindled.

One of the best ways is through music. As a conductor I want more than ever to work all the time, to bring music to everybody, now when music is more important than ever before.

After my last concert next Sunday, I am going to England to conduct a series of benefit concerts in the provinces and London.[667] There against enormous odds and difficulties – all the younger musicians have been called; concert halls, instruments and music libraries destroyed – they have not only carried on but there is actually a music boom in England today. Bach, Mozart, Beethoven and all the other great masters have proven the barrier against depression, tiredness, and any lack of faith in the ultimate victory of our cause.

I shall tell them in England what America is doing and how despite all the calls made on everyone, music is being kept alive. I shall tell them particularly of our friends, the Radio Members of the Philharmonic, on whose support the Society is counting now more than ever.

The Philharmonic-Symphony Society is about to start on its second century, but it needs your help. I hope that everyone listening to me today will become a Radio Member. One dollar brings you a Centennial Medal and a Radio Membership Certificate. Five dollars makes you a Radio Program Member and gives you the medal and the weekly program notes. Just send your contribution to the Philharmonic-Symphony Society, New York City.

Glorious John

Thousands of you have at one time or another generously written me your love and appreciation of the Philharmonic-Symphony, so let tommorw's [*sic*] mail be full of dollar and five dollar bills. I want to tell English orchestras and English people how splendidly the banner of music is being kept flying here. A Blessed Easter to you all and thank you'.

Centennial Address to the New York Philharmonic-Symphony League[668]

'It is always with pleasure that I greet my friends, the Members of the New York Philharmonic-Symphony League, but today it is not without a certain emotion that I speak to you. It is an emotion springing from the thought that in this world of chaos and destruction there is one corner of the globe where at this moment is being celebrated not the destruction of an edifice of culture and beauty, but the survival of one which for a hundred years has stood as a monument to the love of music of the American people. I refer of course to the Centennial of the New York Philharmonic-Symphony Orchestra now being celebrated in this city.

The hundred years of its continued existence have not all been years of peace and ease; and yet through easy or difficult times, your forebears saw to it that they should not rob you of your inheritance. But to be the recipients of such an inheritance has its duties as well as privileges. Here in this country the obligation is to see that even through the darkness that may yet precede the light, this great institution will ever remain precious in your hearts.

There can never come a time when music will be a luxury. Of this I am forcibly reminded by letters from English musician friends. They write of the difficulties under which they must give concerts – blasted or damaged halls, depleted personnel, inadequate supplies of instruments, to mention only a few of the most obvious obstacles. However, they go on to say that their biggest problem of all is finding large enough halls to accommodate the thousands demanding music.

The circumstances in England are such that the flame of music is but a flicker, compared to its former glories; and in most of Europe it has died out altogether. All the more reason then that in this part of the world it should become a shining beacon to help and guide us one day to saner and better paths.

Part Eight

Draught article concerning Barbirolli's fourth season with the New York Philharmonic-Symphony Orchestra[669]

'Recently asked if under the circumstances of the present trying condition of his country, home and family he had found it particularly difficult to launch his fourth season as conductor of the New York Philharmonic-Symphony Orchestra, John Barbirolli replied, "It certainly has not been easy, but at the same time I think it has meant to all of us a magnificent challenge. Ordinarily none of us would suppose that we could draw any inspiration from the constant state of anxiety in which we find ourselves, especially we who have all our loved ones in England. Yet they are carrying on so magnificently, so determinedly that what can we do but follow their example?

Just as they in England are fighting the forces which threaten to uproot all that they revere, so must we redouble our efforts to preserve the priceless musical heritage over here. In times of stress music, like all the arts, is too often taken for granted, or resignedly looked upon as a source of solace. Even though the beloved institutions of the United States are not in such immediate danger as those abroad, they must nevertheless be conditioned to withstand the perils which threaten them, so that it is our duty to carry on with the same resolution of purpose as Britain. All must recognize the fact that the present state of affairs has increased our responsibilities to the things we hold dear, and I say it is from this conviction that artists and lovers of art must derive inspiration to consolidate and safeguard the standards that have been set up."

Waving a letter from his sister in London, the conductor said, "Just let me read you this bit: 'I must end this now, for soon we will be hearing a concert brought to us through the courtesy of Mr. Hitler. Really, my dear Tita, his crescendi put to shame any you have attained with your beautiful Philharmonic-Symphony Orchestra…'"[670]

Speech given at the Authors' Club, Hollywood[671]

'I accepted my friend, Dick Hagemann's invitation to come and speak to you, if not with reluctance, certainly with diffidence, for this little episode in my life of which he wishes me to speak to you was in reality an act of self indulgence on the part of an old Londoner, and please dismiss from your

265

Glorious John

minds any ideas or words of praise for my journey.

[*With her typical and gracious generosity Mrs. Frankel has allocated the time usually reserved for more practised speakers to me, so that I should tell you a little of my recent visit to England. This visit arose from a desire so intimate and personal, to be amongst my people just after one of the sternest hours of trial the little island has had to face, that I (would) not care to talk about it publically (sic), were it not that some of their problems may in a very modest way become your own*][672]

The story I have to tell you is a simple one, but it certainly contains some strong and beautiful facets of existence in England today. The will and determination to carry on as far as possible a normal artistic existence despite all obstacles, and the reward of such dogged determination. String Quartets [sic] and orchestras that have played on with bombs dropping all around, are perhaps obscure acts of courage, but since they are not concerned with the destruction, but with the preservation of beauty, may not be allotted the publicity accorded to bloodier deeds. Nevertheless they form an integral part in that intricate web of modern warfare, the section of that web which we call morale. In this connection I am more than happy that in that same spirit, the season of the Hollywood Bowl was not allowed to lapse here this last summer. In doing this they not only provided you with what I sure was an excellent series of concerts, but gave musical institutions in the whole country a lead of great spiritual value. And since we live on this earth and not in the clouds (which of the two is better or worse I leave to more scientific, adventurous, or more truthful minds than my own) I repeat since we live on this material earth, it is pleasant to record that the season was also a financial success.

[*In this instance I shouldn't think I am guilty of imparting information to the enemy, if I disclose that the main motive force in this admirable achievement was that stalwart soldier of symphony, your indomitable, Florence Irish*][673]

To return to my English journey, I must say that the trip filled me with happiness and has left me with a great inspiration, which I hope will not degenerate into boredom for you as I relate some of it. Before I start my tale I would console you with a little rhyme which I found in a book devoted to my favourite county of Sussex, which book provided part of my daily reading on the journey back here. These are the words of an old Parson of Lurgashall, (where Tennyson died by the way) who gave admiration advice to would-be public speakers.

Part Eight

"THOSE WHO WOULD CAPITIVATE THE WELL BRED THRONG SHOULD NOT TOO OFTEN SPEAK, NOR SPEAK TOO LONG"

HOW THE TRIP CAME ABOUT:
British Ministers of Information both here and in Britain both enthusiastic and so I left with the appreciation and the approbation of my Government. As soon as my New York season was over I sailed, and after just over three weeks from sailing, landed in Liverpool. As can be imagined my emotion on setting foot in the old country again after years of absence which included the whole of the war period, was great. As soon as we left the ship and entered the city streets, evidence of what a full scale attack can mean to a city were soon evident, but what struck me immediately, and it was an impression that was to be indelibly imprinted on my mind throughout my visits to about 20 of the largest towns and cities in England and Scotland, was the apparent normality of existence in this welter of destruction. As you probe deeper you find that all this has not been achieved without a great deal of self restraint and self sacrifice, and I venture to say that this newly found, I almost feel like using the word pleasure, in everything that is hardly [*sic*] come by, explains that sober cheerfulness and deeply moving appreciation of the finest things of live [*sic*], that is everywhere apparent.

[And here, I would like to pause for a moment and tell you how surprised I have been in casual conversation here, to find how only very dimly it is realised that air raid casualties, rationing, and other facets of war time existence really mean. How many of you realise, for instance, that in the first year of the big blitz civilian casualties, killed and wounded, amounted to something like 100,000. That for months after the great raid on Plymouth, a large number of the population slept in the open, and that a small inconvenience such as having to spend the winter in a house without windows and a minimum amount of fuel, as happened to my own mother and family, is not even mentioned. Many of the occupied nations fare even worse, so for God's sake don't let us begin to whimper about the trivial inconveniences which might assail us here.][674]

To return to the aspect of my visit with which I was more intimately concerned, I was astonished to find that the concert life of the community which normally died a natural death in March or April, was blazing alive. My offer to conduct a few concerts seemed naturally to interpret itself into a series of almost daily concerts, and in some cases twice daily.

This would happen when, in addition to the regular evening concert we would give a lunch hour concert of the lighter classics to the war workers of the particular city, or rather the workers who were off duty at the time;

Glorious John

and it was a fine and moving thing to feel the release from the strain and responsibility that our music seemed to bring to these men and women of all types and classes. This seemed to be the case too in the weightier programmes provided in the regular concerts, at which we were always greeted by a sold-out house and audiences of a living and unbounded enthusiasm. [*Even 350 years ago the wizard Shakespear (sic), with his infinite wisdom realized that music was one of the healing arts when he said in "The Taming of the Shrew" "Preposterous ass that never read so far to know the cause why music was ordained; was it not to refresh the mind of man after his studies for his pain"*[675]][676] You might almost say that the difficulties of attending a concert today (Transport, for there is no private motoring of any kind, complete blackout, finance, etc.) seems to intensify their pleasure in these things. Of course I have no time here to go into any analysis of average tastes and standards of performance prevailing at this time, but suffice it to say that they are quite remarkable considering the great and obvious difficulties (the younger men not already in the services leaving daily to join)[.] The one great thing that has been achieved is that music has not been allowed to lapse, and consequently, after all this mess is over, they will be spared the pangs and tribulations of bringing a new child into the world (and into a world in which most people would say it was an unnecessary extravagance) but just help to bring to maturity the one they have tenderly and lovingly cherished through almost insuperable difficulties.

As an extreme example of this continuity —— — tell the story of the Queens [sic] Hall[677]......

[*In this connection, I am going to be somewhat frank with you. Mrs. Irish tells me already many, far too many, subscribers have cancelled their Thursday subscriptions, even before they have confronted possible inconvenience from gas rationing. Being of an optimistic turn of mind I like to think I am preaching to the converted, but as a confirmed realist, propose to take no chances. Situated as you are in this metropolis of celluloid and seduction, might I not seduce you further to see whether an adventure in the dim-out (I can promise you a real black-out) may not have its thrills after all. Seriously though, please don't give in to any inconveniences our enemies might cause you quite so easily. Only a few days ago I had a very concrete example of what a real friend of fine music is prepared to do to help, no matter what personal inconveniences and labor (sic) might be involved. I approached a dear friend and great artist, and asked if he would care to come and take part in a programme to be dedicated to composers of the allied nations which I propose to give on December 3 and*

Part Eight

4th, the dates nearest to Pearl Habor (sic), of infamous but immortal memory. The piece I had in mind was Elgar's "Carillon" composed to words of the Belgian poet, Emil Cammerts, words which tell with heart-rending eloquence, but indomitable faith and unquenchable spirit, of that brave nation's deeds in the last great war. A new poem as noble in spirit, but perhaps more applicable to our present situation has been written by the English poet, Laurence Binyon, and adapted to Elgar's nobly inspired music. I had the privilege of giving this new setting the first performance with John Gilgud (sic) in London last June, and I know you will be thrilled to hear through the generosity of the great actor I have just referred to the first American performance of the work in its present setting will have the eloquent voice of the hero of "Mrs. Minniver" Walter Pigeon (sic), as its interpreter][678]

Another example of what Ellen Terry once called the thee [sic] great I's of Art, Intelligence, Industry and Imagination, came to flower in the splendid concerts which have been given daily since the big blitz first started, by another great Englishwoman artist, who I believe I am right in saying was much beloved here, Dame Myra Hess. — Tell Gallery incident — Probably Night Watchers — Music Schools

It strikes me here that I have forgotten the admonishment of my old friend the Parson of Lurgashall which I quoted you a little earlier, but I can but hope that you have found my little tale not too uninteresting. Just one more thing I would like to tell you which I like to think is symptomatic of the changed attitude in relation to music in certain English circles.

The British Government can never in the past have been accused of any excessive financial generosity or interest towards music — (quote one exception) — but this time it was my privilege and honour to [be] received at a private gathering before I left, the thanks of the Government on the success of my mission, charming [sic] expressed to me on their behalf by the First Lord of the Admiralty, Mr. A. V. Alexander. Mention of his name reminds me also of the revelation forced upon me during my six weeks at sea in convoy, of what we owe to those magnificent men and boys of The [*Allied*][679] Merchant Navy ... etc. ... [*It strikes me here that I have forgotten the admonishment of my old firned (sic) the parson of Lurgashall which I quoted to you a little earlier, but I can but hope that you have found my little tale not too uniteresting (sic). There is but one more think (sic) of which I feel I should speak, as to myself and the concerts I am to be privileged to conduct for you, it ill behooves (sic) me to speak well. But there surely (is) a time when it need not be taken a miss when a man speak(s) of his ideals. From earliest childhood I have been a passionate devotee and performer of music and such success as may have come to me is but, I like to think, the reward providence has seen fit to bestow on me for my disinterested but loving application to the art that it is my privilege to serve. Such is the talent in our midsts, fostered by such admirable institutions as the Meremblum Orchestra and the Brodetsky Ensemble, to name but two of the younger groups with which I have come in contact, it has been possible even with the depredations forced upon us by existing conditions to reform certain sections of our orchestra, and I venture to predict that those with enough fortitude to attend our concerts will hear one of the finest string sections we have been able to present to you for some time. The wind section of this orchestra, for those who have ears to hear, has long been regarded amongst connoisseurs as one of the most exquisite in the country. So you may take it from one who has conducted some of the most famous orchestras in Europe(,) England and America, that you needn't be ashamed to be proud of your own orchestra when you hear it. The programs (sic) which have been chosen, (and what time and thought this has taken few have any notion) will, I hope, prove of general interest to all. Suffice it to say that provided the people all put their backs to the wheel there is no reason why the finest music in America should not eventually be produced in this metropolis]* And now my last words to you, in brief, and I am afraid entirely unworthy of what I have in [my] heart to say to you. There are those destined to fight on the seas, in the air, and on the land; to some others of us for the time being is given another kind of fight to wage, for fight we all must if we are to survive. To those of us left behind, ours is the fight for the preservation, extension, and ultimate unification of spirit of the two great English speaking peoples, without whose mutual understanding and trust there can never be any rest for this tortured world'.

'Colonels and Privates Queued Together'[680]

[*'My journey was destined to be brimful of interest from the start for, on arrival at our point of departure, I found that the new Roman Catholic Archbishop of Westminster, Dr. Griffin, was to be of our party. He was on his way to Rome to visit the Pope, and to address our troops nearer the fighting line, and we flew together as far as Naples. It probably seems stale conventionalism to say that it was a privilege to have this opportunity of being with him, but anyone who has come into contact with him will realise that the simple courteous dignity, warm humanity and true Christian friendliness of this great English Churchman are things not easily forgotten. It was with an added interest then, that I listened to his splendid and statesmanlike address in the B.B.C. programme last Sunday, the King's Day of Prayer.*

Our first stop was Lisbon. It is a charming city and even now one might be in a pre-war Paris from the conditions there. There is still German propaganda to be seen with astronomical figures of Allied ships sunk in the invasion etc.

Our first sight of the East was Rabat in North Africa and after a brief stop there we flew on to Algiers & then to Naples...']681

'As soon as I arrived in Naples, I began to make arrangements for the first concerts.682 There existed only a very limited library of symphonic music with very few of the standard works. No Tchaikovsky symphonies at all, and the only Brahms Symphony (the Second, presented as a gesture of goodwill by an American woman) had been stolen almost immediately it was received. For the sake of maintaining smooth relationships in that part of the world, no hint was vouchsafed as to who the Brahms enthusiast might have been.

I lifted my baton for the first time in the land of my father at the historic San Carlo Theatre in Naples, where Nelson used to sit with Emma Hamilton in the royal box. The theatre is connected with the Royal Palace, where Nelson lived, which is now the Welfare Centre for 'other ranks' – probably the most magnificent of its kind in the world. It was opened by General Alexander, whose pet project it is, the day before the fall of Rome.

Naturally, it was not without emotion that I first conducted in the land where my father and grandfather had both taken part in the first performances of Verdi's *Otello* (under Franco Faccio, the greatest Italian conductor of his time and the first to conduct *Die Meistersinger* in Italy).

My reception by Italian musicians was overwhelming, and an incident repeated three times with each of the three orchestras I conducted touched me deeply, for I am sure it would have delighted my dear father. In Naples and Bari it happened at the close of my rehearsing the Preludes from *La Traviata*: in Rome after the rehearsal of *Semiramide* overture. In each case, the members of the orchestra spontaneously rose to their feet shouting: 'Bravo, maestro, bravo.'

Equally moving to me was the reaction of these Italian musicians to the music of Elgar and Delius, which I included in the twenty-five kilos of music I was allowed to take with me by air. Elgar's Enigma Variations meant as much to them as a Beethoven symphony.

Among the more amusing incidents was when the first violinist of the San Carlo Orchestra, in his enthusiasm at the first rehearsal, called out: 'Maestro, why don't you stay here?' And when I arrived at Taranto for a concert beginning with the *Semiramide* overture and including the Enigma Variations – both works with vitally important timpani parts – I found a very forlorn and miserable timpanist, *without* his timps! However, a telephone call and a jeep driven at great danger to the people of the district and all was well.

In Rome, it was for me, originally an opera conductor, somewhat of a thrill to find myself conducting my first Roman concert in the theatre at which the first performance of *The Barber of Seville* took place, the Argentina.

Of whatever size, large or small, what enchanting places these Italian opera houses are! The rows upon rows of boxes, white and gold with red plush, set an atmosphere that is very far removed from the chilly, forbidding, and stark interiors of many modern cinemas and theatres.

But the unforgettable impression of all was, and still is, the great need for fine music existing over there and the boundless enthusiasm with which the concerts were welcomed. My audiences were drawn entirely from members of the Services. No seats were reserved, and it was a grand sight, and truly indicative of the great natural discipline of our race, even in these of growing democracy, to see colonels queuing outside the theatre with privates long before the show was due to start in order to make sure of getting in.

In Naples I gave four concerts on four consecutive nights with audiences which packed the great San Carlo Theatre to suffocation. On the last two evenings the theatre had to be closed half-an-hour before the performance was due to begin because it was literally impossible to pack anyone else inside. The same thing happened in Bari, where by some magical means the theatre was made to hold fifty per cent more than it should. The same thing happened in Rome. I only wished that I could have stayed longer over there in order to prevent hundreds of men from being disappointed.

At each place I visited, the Italian musicians of the orchestras came and told me that they were impressed beyond all words by the wonderful behaviour of the audiences. Our men showed their appreciation not only by the shouting and cheering and clapping at the end of the performances, but by the sensitive silence in which they listened.

The warm feeling of the Italians for the British still exists, and everywhere I found Italian musicians wanting to know about music over here. I wish with all my heart that the original project suggested by E[ntertainments] N[ational] S[ervices] A[ssociation], which was to take the Hallé Orchestra of over seventy players with me, had materialised, but, understandably, the difficulties of transporting so large an orchestra and their valuable instruments could not be overcome.

Part Eight

I was away five weeks – five of the most unforgettable and inspiring weeks of my life – and I am grateful indeed that I was able to help fill the need of the troops for fine music for even a little time.

And, as an inveterate and incorrigible Londoner, may I end with an expression of humble pride which I felt on my return to my native city, the most war-scarred of any large city I saw on my trip, now happily ending her glorious martyrdom in the great cause of human freedom?'

Script for a broadcast on 'Music Magazine'[683]

'Many of you who are listening to me to-day will probably have read the article I have written about my trip to Italy in the Radio Times, where I have described my journey, my audiences, and my feelings on conducting for the first time in a country where my father and grandfather had such intimate personal contacts with the great musical events of that period.

For instance, they both took part in the first performances of Verdi's Otello, under Franco Faccio, great Italian conductor of his time who was also the first to conduct Meistersinger in Italy.

Another incident of that past I like to think about is the picture of a young violinist and cellist spending their spare time from opera rehearsals playing sonatas and duets together. The violinist was my father and the cellist none other than Arturo Toscanini, [who on these occasions played the piano].[684]

In the few moments at my disposal to-day it will be better I think, not to talk to you so much of the actual journey, but to try and convey a little idea of the orchestral conditions in Italy at the present time, in places where I had a chance to judge them.

I had hoped to have with me too, recordings taken at various concerts with the three different orchestras I conducted: the San Carlo Opera Orchestra, the Bari Symphony, and the Rome Radio Orchestra – the latter really a superb instrument. There was also a recording of a rehearsal in which the voluble imprecations, in flowing Italian, of this British conductor, caused a mild panic. As it happens the only recording available is of the Bari orch.[685] Following the incident I just told you about[686] the Italian orchestra decided that, though I might be British legally, my "sangue Italiano" betrayed itself in every bar of my conducting of their music. The work was hard, for excepting in Rome the orchestras I conducted were, by training and practice, mainly operatic orchestras, and almost everything we played had to be learned from scratch. But they tackled bravely such things as the Enigma [Variations] (by which work they were tremendously and visibly moved) and it was quite remarkable how quickly they sensed the atmosphere of a piece like the Delius' [On Hearing the First] Cuckoo [in Spring] which was their first acquaintance [with][687] his music.

[Perhaps this might be a good moment to let you hear a little of the Enigma played by the Bari orch (Start. Stop.)][688]

If there is such a thing as 101% co-operation, these people certainly gave it to me.

In Naples – where the San Carlo is run – and very efficiently too – by the British Military Authority, its director being Captain Grayson, they play 7 performances of opera a week, and of course all the rehearsals needed for these. Many times we had to begin rehearsing at 8.30 a.m. to fit everything in, so the Italian musician – in a place like Naples at least – is in great danger of being badly overworked. However, this is a situation on which for the moment they seem to prefer! In Bari, thanks to the enthusiastic efforts of Colonel Croom-Johnson, a series of three orchestral concerts a week are given by the Bari Symphony Orchestra (whose playing [you just heard][689]) under the aegis of the "Friends of Music" Society. A group of enthusiastic music lovers, English, American and Italian, whose splendid efforts have resulted in this regular series. This orchestra also plays for the local opera, in the exquisite 18th century Piccini Theatre. By the way, all these Italian towns possess the most enchanting theatres, and in Rome it was moving to be conducting in the theatre (the Argentina) where the first performance of the Barber of Seville took place. In Rome at the moment there are three orchestras functioning. The orchestra of the Teatro Reale, where performances of opera can be seen, with scenery and lighting which should make us hang our heads in shame when we think of our efforts in this direction: The Orchestra of Santa Cecilia, which was the old Augusteo Concerts Orchestra, and the Rome Radio Orchestra recently reconstructed under the permanent conductorship of Previtali, an excellent musician curiously enough hailing from the same province of Italy as my own ancestors, the Veneto. By the way, I wonder how many of you realise that Disraeli was also a Venetian only one generation further removed than I am.

[The Rome Radio Orch],[690] as I have said before, is really a first-rate body of players, and it is a lovely ending to my tour to have played the last concerts with them. They reminded me much of my own Halle, in their youth, eagerness and enthusiasm. Of the audiences little need be said, except that I shall never forget them.

The only sad thing is that we had to turn hundreds away at every performance – a fact that I hope the Powers that be will ponder. [And now to conclude here is the Bari S. O. playing part of the Semiramide ov(erture). [their own native music] Start. Stop.][691]

[I thought I (would) like to play you these recordings in case there are some listeners whose loved ones might have been at one of my concerts].[692] It may mean something to them to share in our experiences of that evening. To be listened to in the rapturous silence: to be greeted with an enthusiasm that even made the Italians sit up, and to be surrounded afterwards by smiling happy faces – faces that still bore traces of the joy the music had given them: these are things which will live with me for ever'.

On the death of President Roosevelt[693]

'To-morrow in Manch[ester], we are dedicating our perf[ormance] of the Requiem to the memory of the late P.[resident] R.[oosevelt][.] It has seemed to me that in this great city of yours, so intimately connected with the war effort, you might also like to join with us in paying musical tribute to the man who forged, to use his own words "The Arsenal of D[emocracy]."[694] [Although I am] Far from eloquent etc. [and it] ill befit[s] me [to] attempt [a] tribute but [I] may be permit[ted] [a] personal word. Apart from [the] pleasure & privilege of meeting him personally, the abiding memory of him I shall retain of him was of witnessing with what sublime courage he persuaded his people in the darkest days of 1940, to share his own unquenchable faith in our ultimate destiny. No Britisher in Ame[rica] at the time c[ou]ld have stood by & watched this spectacle unmoved. In a spirit of gratitude and thankfulness for this great soul then, let us join together in paying such humble tribute as lies within our power'.

'Impressions of Vienna: the Revival of Music'[695]

'During the ten days I spent in Vienna I had many opportunities, between rehearsals and concerts, of witnessing the life of the Viennese. What impressed me most, in the middle of the hardships of a winter far severer than our own and in spite of material impoverishment which is often terribly grim, was the extraordinary vitality of their artistic life. Out of a meagre

Glorious John

Budget the State still maintains the Vienna Philharmonic at 120 strong. There are two opera seasons running simultaneously, one in the Volksopera [*sic*] (a large theatre in which the more popular operas are given) and the other in the old Theater an der Wien.

I saw a very remarkable art exhibition, "The 950 Years Exhibition" which is a résumé of nine hundred and fifty years of Austrian art. It is composed of purely Austrian art treasures – paintings, sculpture, wood-carving, porcelain, glass – and is an attempt to recall to the consciousness of the people that Austria is Austria and not part of the artificially created Anschluss. The exhibition included a remarkable collection of Austria primitive paintings. One knows about the Dutch and Italian primitives and what they have contributed to the artistic consciousness of mankind. About the Austrian primitives little seems to be known. Yet their beauty is incredible. As against the pure formality and beautiful colouring of both the Dutch and Italian primitives one is struck by the extraordinary liveness [*sic*] of the Austrian pictures; their bright eyes and lively faces are an embodiment is what is meant by the "Viennese spirit." The Austrians are very proud of this exhibition; it is their first big attempt to reinstate themselves in the comity of nations.

I also visited the Hofburg, which used to be the Imperial Palace. I was a little disappointed yet agreeably surprised to find that the cream of its magnificent collection of pictures was at present on loan to Zurich. Apparently the Viennese concern for exports extends beyond manufactured commodities; they are proud to show to other countries the glories of the great Austrian collections.

REBUILDING THE OPERA HOUSE
The State Opera House was blitzed in 1945, but work on its reconstruction is already progressing at full swing. When I asked, with rueful memories of our own difficulties, about the "prior claims of housing" I was told that when the Staatsoper was burning the Viennese stood round in their thousands with tears pouring down their cheeks and that they regard the speedy rebuilding of this priceless common possession as essential to the morale of the community. Though I am proud to have been invited to conduct two gala performances of Verdi's "Requiem" in aid of the rebuilding of the Opera House, I should be prouder still to be conducting concerts in aid of an equally speedy rebuilding of Manchester's great concert-hall to meet the needs revealed by the war years.

But the Viennese are not allowing their pleasure in opera to languish for want of a home. I saw a performance of "Cosi fan tutte" in one of the halls in the Hofburg, called the Redoutensaal, which will remain as one of the most exquisite memories of my stay. The Redoutensaal was probably one of the great banqueting halls of the palace. It is a very large, long room, panelled in white and gold and lit by many magnificent chandeliers. At the end of the room is a raised platform with a double Renaissance staircase which is used as a permanent scene. In front of it are placed a few "props" and the "stage" is separated from the audience between acts by a simple red curtain. A pit has been made in the floor, in which the orchestra plays and in the rest of the hall sit the spectators. Thus by a little imagination and ingenuity and the expenditure of a few hundred pounds they have created a perfect opera theatre, resembling an eighteenth-century salon.

I was also taken over the Schonbrünn, the former summer residence of the Habsburgs and now the British Military Headquarters. The British are looking after it well and keeping it in fine repair. It is a beautiful schloss [sic] with a perfect little eighteenth-century theatre where Mozart often performed.[696] Concerts are given there regularly by a section of the Vienna Philharmonic Orchestra to the troops, perhaps as a sort of lend-lease in return for the re-education of the Nazis!

The gala performances of the Verdi "Requiem" already referred to are to take place in the Theater an der Wien – an eighteenth-century theatre quite unaltered inside, - which saw the first performance, among other works, of "The Magic Flute" and "Fidelio." To this day the drop curtain used at the first performance of the "Flute" is used. A musician cannot see these things without feeling deeply moved.

COMPARISONS WITH MANCHESTER

Another instance of their resourcefulness is that when the Opera House was destroyed in 1945 all the scenery and costumes were destroyed. We are now only in 1946, but already sixteen operas have been completely reset and re-costumed. And so, amidst all the poverty and shortage, there is still the glamour of the old musical life of Vienna and a determination not to allow the great traditions of the past to slip from them because of desperate circumstances. In this effort they have, of course, the inestimable advantage of being surrounded by living reminders of past greatness. There are the homes of the great musicians, the houses where Schubert and Mozart lived and died, the corner in the cemetery where their memory is perpetuated. Before conducting Beethoven's Seventh Symphony I was taken to see the house in which it was written. At the concert I stood on the platform from

Glorious John

which Brahms had conducted. And it was perhaps inevitable that I should ask myself to what heights the Hallé might rise if only it, too, could play in surroundings a little more worthy of the great art it serves.

I cannot end this account of my visit without a tribute to the splendid work being done in Vienna by the British Council. They have library which is always full of people, where books on British art and culture may be studied. There is a hall in which gramophone recitals of British music are given regularly. Through the interest so engendered the Viennese have arranged for a performance of "Belshazzar's Feast," which is to be conducted by Walton himself.

The benefits which would accrue if the funds of the British Council were made adequate to permit them to bring to Vienna and other capitals not gramophone records only but representative British orchestras to interpret British musical art would be incalculable'.

'Message for the British Council'[697]

'I most deeply regret that I have to forego the honour of opening the British Council Exhibition, but may I take the opportunity through my good friend Mr. Bean to send my warmest greetings and wishes for a worthy success. If I had been able to be present, one of the things I would like to have spoken about was the ignorant and narrow criticism sometimes levelled at the British Council, mainly by people who seem unaware that to many continental peoples (and I speak from personal experience during and immediately after the war), the British nation is still a country to which they would look for trustworthy moral leadership. Culture in the form of Literature, the Theatre, Music etc., being a much less inhibited part of their daily lives than is the case with us, is the one thing about us they are desperately keen to learn about, and whilst they have a traditional knowledge of our trading and manufacturing abilities, the arts, especially music, is one aspect of our great achievements of which they are profoundly ignorant, and ill- or mis-informed.

Here the British Council has a great work to do, and one in which it has made a splendid beginning. Our recent tour in Austria, greeted – even according to Austrian standards – with unparalelled [sic] enthusiasm, I will leave to Mr. [Ernest] Bean to tell you about, but there are two or three incidents I would like to quote to prove what I have said: -

(1) When I was thanking our Minister in Vienna – Sir Bertrand Jerome

– for the delightful party he gave to the members of the orchestra, he interrupted me with: "No, sir. It is I who have to thank you, for you have done more in five days than we could do in five years here."

(2) The second incident was the warm declaration of the Austrian Chancellor at the reception given to us by the C[ommander]-in-C[hief]. Austria, of the significance and value of our visit from all points of view.

(3) The third incident was a remark made to me here in Manchester by the head of the Santa Chechilia [sic] Academy in Rome, after reviewing our various artistic activities in England, and which were only just beginning to be known to the Italians: "If there had been a British Council in operation 25 years ago there could have been no war in England".

So, in the fervent hope that much more may be accomplished in the future by this splendid Institution, I extend my grateful congratulations on the much which has already been accomplished'.

'Speech to [a] Lanc[ashire] Trade Union at Belle Vue'[698]

'Now I have not come here to plead for any particular thing, but to tell you in a few simple words some facts which, I hope, will help you to judge this resolution solely on its merits but facts which I think you will find far more eloquent than any of the arts of oratory could possible [sic] make them. I would like if I may to put these facts to you in two sections. Firstly, let me tell you of the thousands who flock to this vast hall Sunday after Sunday – 6000 of them in the vilest of weathers (another heritage besides the Halle [sic] tradition, we have inherited here!) and during the war years with risky and inadequate transport, the 3,700 odd who come to the Albert Hall every fortnight, where, owing to the lack of a suitable hall, we have to repeat the programme two nights running to accommodate all who want to hear it (a fact I hope our fiery and imaginative Minister of Health will make a note of and sanction the start of the work on our wrecked Free Trade Hall, so that it will not have to go up with a plaque on the walls reading "John Barbirolli would have conducted here had he lived long enough") but I am getting away from what I came here to say. These vast crowds come here as I said before for one thing only – to seek solace for a few hours in communion with great music of all kinds – (grave and gay – imaginative and architectural) a few precious hours in which the burdens and the anxieties of our still tragically troubled times are forgotten. That is one side of the picture. Now we come to the purely material one, for ideals are but an aggravation and a disturbing factor without the will and means to supplement them.

We now come to the second section of what I have to say – the purely material side of the question. We have, since 1943 in the midst of almost insuperable difficulties, built a new Halle [sic] Orchestra, which I assured by the most responsible authorities, is second to none in the country. That judgment I am prepared to accept!! But to keep a great orchestra in constant being is a heavy financial responsibility and like many other things in these days of higher cost of living, the cost is always mounting whilst the revenue remains stationary. We of the Halle [sic] are particularly and peculiarly penalised because owing to the lack of a permanent hall which I so subtly referred to a few moments ago, we are forced to travel a great deal more than we want to. Just think what this means. Fares have gone up. As a result of the recent changes in the law regarding hotel and catering establishments prices of hotels have risen. One town I can think of, 100%. How does this affect us? The answer is supply. When the orchestra travels, a subsistence has to be paid and this of course had to be incurred to meet the greatly increased cost of living. But, and it is a mighty but, the revenue remains the same. Put the prices up some say. Let me tell you why we cannot do that. The great majority of our new audiences come from what I think can be termed the "middle classes" and young people just beginning work so that if we put the lowest prices beyond their reach we take the music away from those who want and need it most and it becomes again the prerogative of the privileged few. Giving to those who want is an accepted creed of humanity to-day but to give only material things is to destroy the ultimate fruits of that leisure which our people rightly feel is their due.

I have told you why prices cannot go up. There is another field of economy – don't have such a big or such a good orchestra if you can't afford it. I can only call such a though[t] degrading. Take two public services, libraries and picture galleries. Has it ever occurred to a public authority to stock the shelves with third class literature or a gallery with cheap pictures! Of course not. These are considered essential public services, even though sometimes the only occupants of a picture [gallery] I have seen were an obviously devoted young couple who found there the highest privacy at the lowest cost. I will not for a moment admit that a society like ours which provides the finest music at prices which have changed little for over a century. When Halle [sic] was engaged [to] conduct an orchestra of 100 players at the Great Art Treasures Exhibition in Manchester in 1857 it was considered wonderful that some tickets were available at 1/-[.] That to-day you can attend a Halle [sic] concert here in Belle Vue or at the Albert Hall for 1/6d well then, if you will permit me some Shawian phraseology 'that's a b... miracle'.

All that is needed therefore is something that will bridge the gap between the provision of a first-class assett [sic] which the community badly wants and needs as has been abundantly proved here and what that community is able to pay for it. Manchester without the Halle [sic] would be unthinkable and rightly so, because, for nearly a century now, this great Society has, without financial reward of any kind, rendered a public service to this city, which has but added lustre and distiction [sic] to its fame.

February 24th. 1949.'

Glorious John

NOTES

[1] A remark by Sir Adrian Boult reported to the author by the violinist, Marie Wilson.

[2] Barbirolli was named Giovanni Battista Barbirolli at birth.

[3] Frederick Austin (1872-1953). English singer, composer and impresario.

[4] At the concert with the London Symphony Orchestra, Barbirolli conducted Haydn's Symphony No. 104 ('London'), Haydn's 'Cello Concerto in D major (Pablo Casals, 'cello) and Elgar's Symphony No. 2. For his concert for the Royal Philharmonic Society, he conducted Vivaldi's Concerto for Strings in E minor, Delius' 'Cello Concerto (Alexandre Barjansky, 'cello), Haydn's Symphony No. 92 ('Oxford') and Debussy's *La Mer*.

[5] During Barbirolli's tenure with the Scottish Orchestra, the Lord Provosts of Glasgow were Sir Alexander B. Swan (1932-5) and Sir John Stewart (1935-8).

[6] Wolfgang Stresemann, 'Sir John Barbirolli zum Gedenken', ... *und abends in die Philharmonie* (Frankfurt, Berlin and Vienna, 1981), pp. 231-7.

[7] Text taken from *Glorious John: 25th Anniversary of the Society Journal*, The Barbirolli Society, February 1997, pp. 30-31. The article appeared originally in the October 1936 issue of *Gramophone*.

[8] Although Barbirolli made his debut at the Queen's Hall with the Trinity College of Music's Orchestra playing the Cantilena from Goltermann's 'Cello Concerto on 16 December 1911, his first performance of a complete concerto was that of Saint-Saën's 'Cello Concerto at the same venue with the same orchestra on 11 July 1912.

[9] Here Barbirolli is referring to Haydn's 'Cello Concerto No. 1 in C major. Haydn's 'Cello Concerto No. 2 in D major was not verified as a work by the composer until 1951.

[10] Text taken from Barbirolli's handwritten manuscript which is held at the Royal Academy of Music. The text is dated by another hand '2nd December 1949'.

[11] Before the words, '50 NOT OUT', Barbirolli noted 'Churchill. tears. Great warrior. humble [illegible]. Under circs. feeble thanks for lovely gifts. Listeners['] Club. Too kind to your President. Chorus Members. Already in your debt, now, unless Cripps helps me out can never repay it. Kids on the Platform. To me one of the most touching & memorable gifts I am ever likely to receive. Bill Edrich. Always knew w[ou]ld be fruitful result, not in Shantto, very sweet of him etc. & such a brilliant exponent. Pianists, [illegible], composer'.

[12] Here, Barbirolli is referring to the legendary cricket matches between the county sides of Lancashire and Yorkshire.

[13] Laurance Turner was leader of the Hallé Orchestra until 1958.

[14] After 'who', Barbirolli excised 'of the memorable [illegible]'.

[15] Wilfred Rhodes (1877-1973). Cricketer for England and Yorkshire.

[16] Barbirolli is referring here to the cricketing test series between Australia and England that took place in 1926 at which Rhodes was the leading bowler.

[17] Text found in *Hallé*, January 1951, pp. 26-7.

[18] At the Gold Medal concert, Barbirolli conducted Vaughan Williams' Symphony No. 6 and Sibelius' Symphony No. 2.

[19] Text taken from Barbirolli's handwritten manuscript which is held at the Royal Academy of Music.

[20] Before this sentence, Barbirolli wrote 'Preamble. Perhaps keep Mackenzie, Levien (Walenn) Norman O'Neill till near close./ Quote W.[inston] C[hurchill]./ Some of what I have got already c[ou]ld be put in better order and conciser [*sic*] –might do. Now talk a little of some special progr[ammes] in my period as a cellist in the orch[estra]. (last desk) (Somehow got to first

Notes

desk for Sacre du Printemps, with E[ugene]. G[oossens]. I did not crawl up me crotches then, crawled down some steps; for this special embrace)'.

[21] After 'intent', Barbirolli excised 'In another programme I see the name of Balfour which reminds me of a story that Fred Austin used to love to tell. Gardiner, Fred, Grainger & Bax'. Above 'Fred Austin' Barbirolli inserted 'Bax'.

[22] Landon Ronald (1873-1938). English conductor, composer, pianist, author and administrator.

[23] Frank Mullings (1881-1953), Norman Allin (1884-1973) & Edna Thornton (dates unknown). British singers.

[24] Albert Sammons (1886-1957). English violinist.

[25] Robert Radford (1874-1933). British singer.

[26] Bracketed text excised by Barbirolli.

[27] After 'Ysaye', Barbirolli excised 'Then another singer Murray Davey. Only two short arias Berlioz, [illegible] which somehow created an impression of style & delicious humour that I still retain'.

[28] Here, Barbirolli is referring to the English 'cellist, Jacqueline du Pre (1945-87), who won the Suggia Prize at the Royal Academy of Music.

[29] After 'dash', Barbirolli excised 'for'.

[30] Frederick Lamond (1868-1948). Scottish pianist.

[31] After 'way', Barbirolli excised 'And finally'.

[32] Barbirolli is referring to Bax's *Phantasy* for viola and orchestra.

[33] Bracketed text excised by Barbirolli.

[34] Herbert Walenn (dates unknown). English 'cellist and Barbirolli's principal 'cello teacher.

[35] Bracketed text replaced 'having me in the orchestra'.

[36] After 'artists', Barbirolli excised 'is incalculable, as a young man my debt is incalculable & undying'.

[37] After 'music', Barbirolli excised 'my debt as a young man my debt [sic] is incalculable & undying'.

[38] Bracketed text replaced 'earlier'.

[39] After 'conductor', Barbirolli excised 'as an earlier generation might say "not done old boy".

[40] Bracketed text replaced 'me'.

[41] After 'them', Barbirolli excised 'In those days 2 reh[earsal]s was the maximum we played a Vivaldi string concerto a Haydn Symphony & they were (& so was I) anxious to do the Delius cello concerto and Delius himself had recommended a Russian cellist named Barjansky who played the original version (almost unplayable) & was a very fine cellist and revered artist but for the fastest vibrato I think I have ever heard. For years etc La Mer story. With my dear friend Willie Reid leading the orchestra did a wonderful job for me'.

[42] After 'accompanying', Barbirolli excised 'Elena'.

[43] a. Bracketed text replaced 'her death'.
b. Elena Gerhardt (1883-1961). German singer and protégée of the renowned Hungarian-born conductor Arthur Nikisch (1855-1922).

[44] Bracketed text replaced 'Gerhardt'.

[45] After 'am', Barbirolli excised 'grateful'.

[46] Barbirolli conducted Mahler's Symphony No. 9 at the Royal Festival Hall, London, on 22 March 1955.

[47] Mémé was Barbirolli's mother.

Glorious John

[48] After 'great', Barbirolli excised 'English'.

[49] Here, Barbirolli is referring to Ralph Vaughan Williams.

[50] After 'the', Barbirolli excised 'great'.

[51] After 'wit', Barbirolli excised 'I can remember the chuckles'. After the excised material, Barbirolli wrote 'Coda', 'with Gold Medal as climax' and 'Katie's [Ferrier] Gold Medal'.

[52] Richard Wagner discusses the importance of 'Melos' in his influential treatise, *Über das Dirigiren* (*On Conducting*).

[53] After 'thank', Barbirolli excised 'you adequately for all'.

[54] After '&', Barbirolli excised 'the maintenance of them'.

[55] Here, Barbirolli is quoting freely from Abraham Lincoln's 'Lyceum Address' of 27 January 1838.

[56] Text taken from *The Barbirolli Journal*, June 1996, page unidentified. The article appeared originally in the Hallé Proms prospectus for 1952.

[57] 'Foreword', as found in *Gods or Flannelled Fools?*, Keith Miller and R.S. Whitington (London, 1954), pp. v-vii.

[58] 'John Barbirolli' is written as a signature'.

[59] Text taken from *Hallé*, October 1956, pp. 5-6. Text was part of an interview with Barbirolli recorded after an operation in 1956.

[60] Barbirolli received his knighthood in 1949, the year of his fiftieth birthday.

[61] The Al-Azhar University in Cairo is considered the world's oldest university: the first lecture was delivered there in 975 AD. The oldest university in Europe is that of Bologna, which was founded in 1088.

[62] In Barbirolli's engagement book for 1956, he indicates that he gave a concert with 'Rome Radio' on 5 November. The programme apparently included '[his] Elizabethan [Suite,] Hindmith['s] Viola [Concerto and] Bartok['s] Concerto for Orch[estra]'. He also inserts on 8 December 'Sheffield Messiah' and, on 9 December, 'B[elle]. V[ue]. Messiah'. Information taken from Barbirolli's unpublished engagement books.

[63] Text taken from *The Boundary Book*, ed. Leslie Frewin, (London, 1962), pp. 177-9.

[64] In 'J.B.', the 1964 *Monitor* documentary for the BBC, Barbirolli recalled that during his time in the army 'an old Indian Army regular, a drunken old Irishman, but the most enchanting person you ever met, ...christened me "Bob O'Reilly"'.

[65] The photograph referred to by Barbirolli has not been reproduced in this book.

[66] Text taken from *The Barbirolli Society Journal*, date unidentified. The article appeared first in the programme of the St Martins-in-the-Fields Christmas Matinee at the Theatre Royal, Drury Lane, on 20 December 1962.

[67] Text published in *Hallé*, 1963-4, pp. 5-11. A shortened version of the text appeared in *The Sunday Telegraph* on 30 June 1963.

[68] Ibbs and Tillett was one of the most powerful London concert agencies during much of the twentieth century. Emmy Tillett was one of the directors of the agency.

[69] Musica Viva was pioneered by Sir John Pritchard, then simply John Pritchard, at concerts with the Royal Liverpool Philharmonic Orchestra in the 1950s. This approach to programming, with its emphasis on new music, was based on a model first developed in Munich. Conversation between the Editor and Iain Hamilton at Covent Garden in the 1980s.

[70] Barbirolli gave the premières of Fricker's Symphony No. 1 in 1950 and the symphonies of Gardiner and Benjamin in 1951 and 1948 respectively at the Cheltenham Festival.

[71] Extracts from an unidentified newspaper interview with Ray Purcell.

Notes

[72] Barbirolli conducted Bach's Piano Concerto in A major (Daniel Wayenberg, piano), Mozart's Piano Concerto in C minor (Daniel Wayenberg, piano) and Elgar's Symphony No. 1 on 2 and 3 December 1964 with the Hallé Orchestra at the Free Trade Hall. He repeated the programme at St. George's Hall, Bradford, on 4 December. Information taken from Barbirolli's unpublished engagement books.

[73] 'The Maestro Remembers...' was published in *Cheshire Life* (date unknown). As Barbirolli conducted in Belgrade in December 1963, it is likely that this article appeared in 1964. *see* Note .

[74] Lionel Monckton (1861-1924). English composer.

[75] Barbirolli recorded in his engagement book for 1963-4, that he flew to Belgrade on 'Dec[ember] 23' and that he had a concert there on 'Dec[ember] 27'. The programme was 'Overture Oberon Weber/ L'Apres Midi Debussy/ P[iano]. Concerto in D minor Mozart (K.466)/ 7th Symphony Beethoven'. Information taken from Barbirolli's unpublished engagement books.

[76] Pope Pius XII (1876-1958). Pius XII was the 260th pope.

[77] Text taken from Barbirolli's typewritten manuscript which is held at the Royal Academy of Music. A part handwritten and part typewritten draft copy of the speech is also housed at the Royal Academy of Music. Barbirolli was made a Companion of Honour in 1969.

[78] Charles Wheeler (1892-1974). English sculptor.

[79] Evelyn Laye (1900-1996). English actress and singer.

[80] Text in brackets is missing from Barbirolli's typewritten manuscript but is found in his draft copy.

[81] Here, Barbirolli is referring to his period in the army during World War One. It was as a soldier that he conducted for the first time.

[82] Arthur Catterall (1893-1943). English violinist.

[83] Barbirolli misquotes Shakespeare, who wrote 'You have witchcraft in your lips, Kate'.

[84] Speech dated on the last page 'Milano 12/10/69'. Text taken from Barbirolli's typewritten manuscript which is held at the Royal Academy of Music. An annotated typewritten copy and a handwritten draft in pencil are also housed at the Royal Academy of Music.

[85] In the typed manuscript, the bracketed text was written twice by error.

[86] Text taken from an article that was to be published in *Colour Magazine* marking the seventieth birthday of Barbirolli in 1969.

[87] Frank Woolley (1887-1978). English cricketer.

[88] This article was published in *The Gramophone* in April, 1928

[89] Text taken from Barbirolli's undated handwritten and typewritten manuscripts which are held at the Royal Academy of Music. *see* Note 90 .

[90] Barbirolli conducted Wagner's *Tristan und Isolde* at the Theatre Royal, Glasgow, for the Covent Garden Opera Company on 31 October 1932. It is possible, therefore, that this lecture was given on 1 November 1932. Information kindly provided by David Lloyd Jones.

[91] Bracketed text in italics was written in pencil on a separate sheet from the main text by Barbirolli. Notes for this text were made by him on the first page of the typewritten text.

[92] Bracketed text replaced 'would'.

[93] Bracketed text replaced 'British'.

[94] Bracketed text replaced 'nothing better than'.

[95] *The Geisha* was composed by Sidney Jones to a libretto by Owen Hall. Extra musical numbers were written by Lionel Monckton; it was given its first performance on 25 April 1896.

[96] *Véronique* was written by André Messager to a libretto by Georges Duval; it was given its first

Glorious John

performance on 10 December 1898.
[97] Bracketed text added later by Barbirolli in pencil.
[98] Bracketed text added later by Barbirolli in pen.
[99] Bracketed text replaced 'our'.
[100] 'G&S' refers to Gilbert and Sullivan.
[101] 'D.C.' refers to the Doyle Carte Company.
[102] Bracketed text added later by Barbirolli in the margin in pencil.
[103] Bracketed text replaced 'Why is it, for example, we'.
[104] Bracketed text replaced 'except by way of a performance recently broadcast by the B.B.C. from a London studio? When are we to hear the most successful of the recent comic operas'.
[105] Bracketed text replaced 'There are'.
[106] After 'shall have.', Barbirolli removed 'If it really is comic opera they most wish to see we are more than willing to be told so'.
[107] Bracketed text replaced 'British public'.
[108] Bracketed text added later by Barbirolli.
[109] Bracketed text replaced 'amateur'.
[110] Bracketed text replaced 'and I am assuming each of you has furnished yourself with a copy'.
[111] Bracketed text added later by Barbirolli.
[112] Bracketed text added later by Barbirolli.
[113] Bracketed text replaced 'by'.
[114] Bracketed text added later by Barbirolli.
[115] Barbirolli later added in the margin 'and of great charm. Play record'.
[116] Bracketed text replaced 'while'.
[117] Barbirolli adds above the text at this point 'elbow lifter: glutton, no racing, story teller, in fact describes as what I should think a most dangerous kind of husband'.
[118] Beside this section of the text, Barbirolli later added 'Here speak of possible objection & own case'.
[119] Beside this section of the text, Barbirolli later added 'duet speak about [illegible]'.
[120] Bracketed text later removed by Barbirolli.
[121] Bracketed text replaced 'to the'.
[122] Bracketed text replaced 'In the third act there is a diversion'.
[123] Bracketed text added later by Barbirolli to replace 'some dances, and a little duet as pretty as a pearl and as dainty as lace. It would be a cold audience that would not plead for an encore.'
[124] At this point, Barbirolli removes 'a jewel in a golden setting' and adds in pencil 'difficult to perform as if it is for 2 contralti[.] Strange loveliness probably comes from this. 2 baritones & bass (illegible)'.
[125] At the beginning of this sentence, Barbirolli adds in pencil 'solo or Marie'.
[126] Under 'this time a kind of bickering match', Barbirolli later added 'premature one w[ou]ld have thought'.
[127] Bracketed text removed later by Barbirolli.
[128] Bracketed text replaced 'daintier'.
[129] At this point, Barbirolli inserts '(illegible. Record.)'.
[130] At this point Barbirolli added later by hand 'Difficulty of performing comic works. Weeks of rehearsal. Acting resources required, people cannot stand still for half an hour at a time groan

Notes

away as in serous works, also figures of people. Cast & costumes from Prague. Production ballet master from Metropolitan. Jubilee 1906. Producer'.

[131] Text taken from Barbirolli's typewritten manuscript which is held at the Royal Academy of Music. The lecture was delivered to the Halifax Music Society on 11 February 1932; admission to the talk cost 6 schillings. Two further copies of the lecture – one published and one manuscript – are also housed at the Royal Academy of Music.

[132] Above and intermingled with this text, Barbirolli wrote enigmatically 'as is the way with children jager with a kind of inhuman pleasure at the depth of the scaffold, and mused on what must have been the feelings of people when they were led there. M & M has gratified that amnesty etc. Master –novice'.

[133] Above 'many' Barbirolli later inserted 'most'.

[134] After 'Mozart', Barbirolli later inserted 'stop.' in the margin.

[135] Here, Barbirolli is wrong. Bülow engaged Strauss as his assistant, with the title, Hofmusikdirektor. When Bülow resigned from the Meininger Hofkapelle in 1885, Strauss was offered his mentor's former post but decided to accept the position of Musikdirektor (Third Conductor) at the Munich Hofoper instead.

[136] After 'Berlin', Barbirolli later inserted 'don't stop'.

[137] After 'music', Barbirolli later added 'go on'.

[138] Here, Barbirolli is mistaken. The first of the one-movement tone poems written by Strauss was *Macbeth*. This was composed in 1886-8 and later revised in 1889-90. *Don Juan* was composed in 1888-9.

[139] Above 'Nietzsche's', Barbirolli writes phonetically 'Neechers'.

[140] After 'windmill', Barbirolli later inserted 'go on'.

[141] Below "A hero's life" Barbirolli later added "Ein Heldenleben".

[142] Above 'excerpts', Barbirolli later added 'pieces'.

[143] The next sentence – 'Libretto, you know, is what you buy at the Box Office, or from a collarless man outside the Theatre, who calls it "the book of words" – was later excised by Barbirolli.

[144] Richard Strauss married Pauline de Ahna on 10 September 1894.

[145] Above 'to rebuke' Barbirolli later wrote 'don't stop'.

[146] After 'opera', Barbirolli excised 'and he is called, you will always remember, the Librettist'.

[147] Bracketed text replaced 'when'.

[148] Bracketed text replaced 'willy-nilly'.

[149] Above 'composers', Barbirolli later inserted 'short sentence'.

[150] Above 'Massenet, Verdi' Barbirolli later inserted 'short sentence'.

[151] Above 'irradiate' Barbirolli later added 'illumine'.

[152] Barbirolli later added in the margin 'Since writing thought of Forzano [*sic*] and Gianni'.

[153] Bracketed text added later by Barbirolli.

[154] Here, Barbirolli is mistaken. Strauss, after marrying his wife, Pauline, in 1894, composed at her family home at Marquartstein. But, with the popular success of *Salome*, Strauss built a villa in Garmisch, where he composed much of *Der Rosenkavalier*.

[155] Bracketed text added later by Barbirolli.

[156] Sir Thomas Beecham gave the first British performance of *Der Rosenkavalier* on 29 January 1913 at the Royal Opera House, Covent Garden.

[157] Bracketed text replaced 'predeliction' [*sic*].

[158] a. Bracketed text replaced 'Pray do not jump in your seats, or look at me only through

287

Glorious John

scandalised lattice-work of raised fingers, to hide your blushes! If you go to see one of Mr. Cochran's Reviews, you will find it plentifully sprinkled with characters clad in the most transparent of pyjamas and feminine what-nots; scenes in bedrooms, and – for all I know – bathrooms too, form part of the usual stock-in-trade of these kind of theatrical enterprises'.
b. Charles B. Cochran (1872-1951) was an English impresario who specialized in mounting popular theatrical productions London's West End.

[159] Bracketed text replaced 'Will those whom this announcement perturbs so keenly that they have already decided to manifest their disappointment by staying away from our performance, kindly hold up their hands? ...Thank you!'.

[160] In the margin, Barbirolli later added 'Tell about Mariandel, to avoid confusion'.

[161] After 'bird-song', Barbirolli later excised '"the early pipe of half-awakened birds", as Tennyson has it'.

[162] Bracketed text added later by Barbirolli.

[163] Bracketed text added later by Barbirolli.

[164] After 'maids', Barbirolli later inserted 'Record not there'.

[165] Above 'baggage' Barbirolli later inserted 'stop'.

[166] Bracketed text added later by Barbirolli.

[167] Bracketed text added later by Barbirolli.

[168] After 'health', Barbirolli excised 'He is quite frank, you see'.

[169] Bracketed text inserted later by Barbirolli.

[170] Above 'a dealer in pet animals', Barbirolli later added 'story of the dog [illegible] 1st violin'.

[171] Bracketed text inserted later by Barbirolli.

[172] Bracketed text replaced 'as is still the unfortunate way of most singers to this day!'.

[173] After 'beauty', Barbirolli excised 'Gramophone record here'.

[174] Under 'besides', Barbirolli later added '(straight on) the prospect of a dainty'.

[175] After 'settlement', Barbirolli later added 'stop'.

[176] Bracketed text added later by Barbirolli.

[177] Bracketed text added later by Barbirolli.

[178] Bracketed text added later by Barbirolli.

[179] After 'falls', Barbirolli later inserted 'Record'.

[180] Bracketed text later removed by Barbirolli.

[181] Throughout the printed text, Barbirolli refers to 'Sophie' as 'Sophy'. It is unclear why he chose this spelling, but the translation of the opera from which he was working might be the reason.

[182] Above 'visualization', Barbirolli later added 'effect'.

[183] Bracketed text replaced 'The whole makes us realize the truth of Marlowe's saying:'.

[184] *Who ever loved, that loved not at first sight* is a poem by Christopher Marlowe (1564-1593).

[185] At this point, Barbirolli later added 'Yes'.

[186] Above 'nurtured', Barbirolli later inserted 'brought up'.

[187] Above 'wretch', Barbirolli later inserted 'rake'.

[188] Bracketed text added later by Barbirolli.

[189] Above 'curmudgeon', Barbirolli later added 'scoundrel'.

[190] After 'meanness', Barbirolli later added in the margin 'stop'.

[191] After 'waltz-time', Barbirolli later added 'Record'.

[192] Above 'a', Barbirolli later added 'another'.

[193] After 'laughter', Barbirolli later excised 'I will merely leave it at that!'.

Notes

[194] Bracketed text added later by Barbirolli.

[195] Bracketed text added later by Barbirolli. The bracketed text was followed by '(continua)'.

[196] Bracketed text replaced 'The Baron'.

[197] Bracketed text replaced 'evening'.

[198] Above 'apparitions of intruding', Barbirolli later added 'long sentence'.

[199] Bracketed text added later by Barbirolli.

[200] Bracketed text later excised by Barbirolli.

[201] Above 'sorry pickle', Barbirolli later added '(mess)'.

[202] Beside this part of the text, Barbirolli later added 'The Komissar knowing goes to help furious Oct.[avian]'.

[203] Bracketed text replaced 'conceive'.

[204] After 'no more', Barbirolli later inserted 'Here record'.

[205] After 'feared', Barbirolli later inserted 'Here record'.

[206] Bracketed text replaced 'claps'.

[207] After 'song', Barbirolli later inserted '(Tell them about Wiegenlied Schubert, & [illegible] of when duet theme returns.)'. Barbirolli then excises 'I am glad to be able to let you hear this on the Gramophone. (Put on record of Final Duet)'.

[208] Beside 'resumed', Barbirolli later added in the margin 'Mixture of themes here'.

[209] After 'contains!', Barbirolli later added '(Tell of great difficulties, and Norman & part [illegible] Ochs'.

[210] Text taken from Barbirolli's typewritten manuscript with handwritten notes, dated 'Harrogate London Pullman 12. 3. 33.', which is held at the Royal Academy of Music. A second, unannotated, typewritten copy is also housed at the Royal Academy of Music. The lecture was illustrated with sound recordings and live music examples.

[211] Throughout much of the typed text, Barbirolli writes 'Don Carlos' rather than 'Don Carlo'. This, however, seems to have been a typist's error, because Barbirolli later removed the 's' from the name.

[212] Bracketed text added later by Barbirolli.

[213] Bracketed text added later by Barbirolli.

[214] Bracketed text replaced 'curve'.

[215] Bracketed text added later by Barbirolli.

[216] Bracketed text replaced 'some'.

[217] Bracketed text replaced 'her'.

[218] Bracketed text added later by Barbirolli.

[219] Bracketed text added later by Barbirolli.

[220] Bracketed text added later by Barbirolli.

[221] Bracketed text replaced 'might be called'.

[222] Bracketed text added later by Barbirolli.

[223] Bracketed text added later by Barbirolli.

[224] Bracketed text underlined later by Barbirolli.

[225] Bracketed text added later by Barbirolli.

[226] Bracketed text added later by Barbirolli.

[227] Bracketed text added later by Barbirolli.

[228] Bracketed text replaced 'will'.

[229] Bracketed text added later by Barbirolli.

[230] Bracketed text replaced 'the'.

[231] Bracketed text added later by Barbirolli.
[232] Bracketed text added later by Barbirolli.
[233] The portion of text from *Don Carlo* should read 'Perduto ben, mio sol tesor'.
[234] Bracketed text replaced 'vile' after which Barbirolli later added 'Joke? after duet'.
[235] After 'part', Barbirolli later added 'Aria Licette'.
[236] After 'driven', the original text read 'Flanders, the'.
[237] Bracketed text added later by Barbirolli.
[238] Bracketed text added later by Barbirolli.
[239] Bracketed text added later by Barbirolli.
[240] After 'ACT III', Barbirolli added later 'Better have Prelude here P.T.O.'. The playing of the Prelude to Act III was originally to be heard part way through page five of the original text.
[241] Bracketed text replaced 'love'.
[242] Bracketed text replaced 'would'.
[243] Bracketed text added later by Barbirolli.
[244] After 'Othello', Barbirolli excised 'PRELUDE' but added later 'Back to Act III. Scene I.'.
[245] Bracketed text replaced 'a'.
[246] Bracketed text added later by Barbirolli.
[247] Bracketed text added later by Barbirolli.
[248] Bracketed text replaced 'continuing'.
[249] Bracketed text replaced 'victorious'.
[250] Bracketed text added later by Barbirolli and presumably refers to a sound example.
[251] Bracketed text replaced 'grammai'.
[252] After 'm'amò', Barbirolli added 'one might'.
[253] 'RECORD' is circled by Barbirolli.
[254] Bracketed text added later by Barbirolli.
[255] *see* Note 211.
[256] Bracketed text replaced 'He'.
[257] The title if the aria from *Don Carlo* should read 'O don fatale'.
[258] Bracketed text replaced 'writing'.
[259] After 'die', Barbirolli excised 'he'.
[260] After 'man', Barbirolli excised 'unseen'.
[261] Bracketed text added later by Barbirolli.
[262] After 'him', Barbirolli excised 'the'.
[263] Bracketed text added later by Barbirolli.
[264] Bracketed text added later by Barbirolli.
[265] Bracketed text replaced 'quoted. When'.
[266] Bracketed text replaced 'of'.
[267] Bracketed text added later by Barbirolli.
[268] Bracketed text added 'the'.
[269] *see* Note 233.
[270] Bracketed text replaced 'service'.
[271] Bracketed text replaced 'beautifullest' [sic].
[272] Bracketed text replaced 'lot'.
[273] Barbirolli circled 'DUET'.
[274] Barbirolli underlined 'any' twice.
[275] Bracketed text added later by Barbirolli.

Notes

[276] This pre-concert talk was to be 'Read at [a] concert [on] 1/11/44 [at] Manchester'. The text is taken from Barbirolli's typewritten manuscript which is held at the Royal Academy of Music.

[277] Christopher Morley (1890-1957). American writer.

[278] Text taken from Barbirolli's typewritten manuscript which is held at the Royal Academy of Music. Barbirolli's handwritten draft of this article is also housed at the Royal Academy of Music.

[279] This article was written before Barbirolli was involved closely with Mahler's works.

[280] At the end of Barbirolli's handwritten draft of this article, he signs and dates the draft '21-X/49.'

[281] As found in *Edward Elgar Centenary Sketches*, ed. Herbert Arthur Chambers, Novello & Co. (London, 1957), pp. 3-4.

[282] Felix Salmond (1888-1952). English 'cellist. Salmond gave the first performance of Elgar's 'Cello Concerto, with the composer conducting the London Symphony Orchestra, at the Queen's Hall on 27 October 1919.

[283] Sir Dan[iel] Godfrey (1868-1939). English conductor. Godfrey founded a band for the Winter Gardens, Bournemouth in 1893. This group was the basis for the Bournemouth Municipal Orchestra (now Bournemouth Orchestra), which he conducted until 1934.

[284] Text published in *Hallé*, Number 96, May 1957, pp.1-3. Following Barbirolli's article, *Hallé* reported (p. 3) that *'It is fitting, in view of the Hallé's close association with Elgar, that Sir John should have arranged several tributes to mark the centenary of the great composer's birth. On May 1st and 2nd an all-Elgar programme at the Free Trade Hall includes the Cello Concerto, with André Navarra ...as soloist. Sir John will play the cello, with Laurance Turner, Sydney Partington, Rachel Godlee, Carmel Hakendorf and Wilfred Parry at the concert of Elgar's Chamber Music at the Lesser Free Trade Hall on May 7th... Finally, on the actual birthday (June 2nd) there will be the performance [of] the "Dream of Gerontius" referred to above, with Constance Schacklock, Ronald Dowd and Nowakowski'*. [Italics used in the original text. Square-bracketed text not found in the original text]

[285] Text published in *Hallé*, November 1957, p.15.

[286] Text taken from *Glorious John: 25th Anniversary of the Society Journal*, The Barbirolli Society, February 1997, p. 13. The article appeared originally in the 1958 issue of *Hallé*.

[287] Text published in *The Musical Times*, October 1958.

[288] Interview given at Boston for the *Sunday Times*.

[289] Vaughan Williams wrote his *Romance* for harmonic in 1951 for Larry Adler.

[290] Text found in *Music & Musicians*, December 1958.

[291] I Zingari is an amateur cricket club that was formed by former Harrovians on 4 July 1845.

[292] Text taken from *Glorious John; 25th Anniversary of the Society Journal*, The Barbirolli Society, February 1997, p. 24.

[293] As found in *Record Times*, date unknown, p. 7.

[294] W[illiam]. H[enry]. Reed (1876-1942). English violinist. Reed was leader of the London Symphony Orchestra between 1912 and 1935.

[295] Text published in the accompanying booklet to Barbirolli's 1964 commercial recording of Elgar's *The Dream of Gerontius* for EMI.

[296] *see* Note 76.

[297] Gervase Elwes (1866-1921). English tenor.

[298] As found in *Record Times*, September 1964, p. 7.

[299] Here, Barbirolli is mistaken. He conducted Mahler's Symphony No. 9 first at St George's

Glorious John

Hall, Bradford, on 19 February 1954 and then at the Free Trade Hall, Manchester, on 24 and 25 February 1954.

[300] Taken from an unidentified extract of an interview given by Barbirolli to *Die Welt*.

[301] Barbirolli also performed Mahler's Symphony No. 9 with the Turin Radio Orchestra. A recording of that performance was released on LP by Fonit Cetra in 1981.

[302] Here Barbirolli is mistaken. He conducted Mahler's Symphony No. 6 at the Proms on 26 July 1965 not in 1968. At the Proms on 9 August 1968, Barbirolli conducted a programme of works by Schubert, Elgar, Bax and Sibelius and, on 10 August 1968, he conducted a programme of works by Mozart, Johann Strauss and Richard Strauss.

[303] Text published by Barbirolli in his 1968 recording of Verdi's *Otello* for EMI.

[304] Franco Faccio (1840-1891). Italian conductor and composer.

[305] Victor Maurel (1848-1923). French baritone.

[306] Text taken from Barbirolli's undated typewritten manuscript which is held at the Royal Academy of Music.

[307] Text taken from a typewritten manuscript which is held at the Royal Academy of Music and which was the basis for an article in *The Etude* by Verna Arvey. Verna Arvey (1910-87) was a pianist and a music journalist and was married to the American composer, William Grant Still. *The Etude* was published in Philadelphia between 1883 and 1957.

[308] In 1928, Barbirolli conducted Puccini's *La Bohème*, and *Madama Butterfly* at the Royal Opera House, Covent Garden.

[309] Lecture typed on A3 paper and scheduled 'For Release – Wednesday, November 2, 1938'. Barbirolli first wrote the lecture in longhand. That version was written 'On board [the] Normandie. 10/10/38'. The speech was the first of a series of lectures under the auspices of the New York Philharmonic-Symphony League and was delivered on 'Tuesday Evening, November 1 [1938] - - Barbizon-Plaza Concert Hall'. Barbirolli used this piece as the basis for similar articles and lectures in and for: 'A Few Words on Conducting', *La Rivista Commerciale Italo-Americana*; 'Conducting', *The Dane* (June 1944); 'A Brief History of Conducting', *Texas String News* (Summer 1951); 'A Few Words on Conducting', *Forum* (date unknown); C. B. Rees, *100 Years of the Hallé* (London, 1957), and a speech for the 'Philharmonic Symphony League Luncheon' at the 'Hotel Plaza' on '4/18/39'.

[310] Remarks in square brackets superimposed on the first sentence in pencil by Barbirolli.

[311] Remarks in square brackets inserted in pencil below the last line of the first page by Barbirolli.

[312] Round brackets inserted by Barbirolli in pencil.

[313] Text in brackets inserted by Barbirolli in pencil.

[314] 'Art' was inserted in pencil above the original typewritten 'job' by Barbirolli.

[315] After 'own', Barbirolli inserted 'De Falla and' in pencil.

[316] After 'other', Barbirolli inserts in pencil 'Tchaikovsky slow'.

[317] 'Has it ever occurred to you', which was inserted by Barbirolli in pencil, replaced the typewritten 'Has it often been thought'.

[318] Text in brackets added later by Barbirolli in pencil. The conductor to whom Barbirolli is referring is probably Leopold Stokowski.

[319] Text in brackets added later by Barbirolli in pencil.

[320] Text in brackets added later by Barbirolli in pencil. Original typewritten text read 'it must not start on a Friday'.

[321] Text in brackets added later by Barbirolli in pencil.

Notes

[322] Original typed text read 'performances of singers'.

[323] Text in brackets added later by Barbirolli in pencil.

[324] Text in brackets added later by Barbirolli in pencil.

[325] Text in brackets added later by Barbirolli in pencil. Original typed text read 'make his watchwords'.

[326] Text taken from Barbirolli's handwritten manuscript which is held at the Royal Academy of Music. The lecture was given at the Hallé Club's annual general meeting on 13 May 1947.

[327] Text in brackets were inserted Barbirolli to replace 'my craft'.

[328] Text taken from Barbirolli's typewritten, and partly handwritten, manuscript which is held at the Royal Academy of Music. The speech was given after his first season (1933-4) with the Scottish Orchestra to an unidentified organization.

[329] Bracketed text added later by Barbirolli. Beside the bracketed text in the margin, Barbirolli wrote, and later excised, 'In talking of the [illegible].

[330] Bracketed text replaced 'in'.

[331] Above the first sentence, Barbirolli later added 'Also I am rather at a loss as to what to address you about, but as I am at the moment so intimately connected with the Scottish Orchestra, and regarding it as I do, not as a local, but rather as a National Institution, I propose without discourtesy to other organizations to confine my few words to them'.

[332] Bracketed text added later by Barbirolli.

[333] Bracketed text replaced 'audience has seemed'.

[334] Bracketed text replaced 'tribute that has'.

[335] a. Bracketed text replaced 'has given me the greatest delight coming as it does from a great Musician and one of the greatest English conductors of our time, is the letter I received from Sir Landon Ronald after his Concert here a few weeks ago. If you will allow me, I should like to read it to you. …Read letter… I value this testimony all the more in that, though I know Sir Landon Ronald to be a kind man, I know also the pleasure of paying a compliment will not lead him from the path of strict veracity. You will notice that he talks of the hard work that has gone to the making of the ensemble of your Orchestra. In that he certainly speaks truth, and it will perhaps interest you to know some of our working conditions'. After the newly inserted text, Barbirolli continued with 'Sir L[andon]. R[onald]. conducted etc., and afterward sent me etc. The tribute of Tovey unfinished. Tell them about Busch-Tovey Brahms No. 2'.

b. Donald Tovey (1875-1940). English scholar, composer and pianist.

[336] Bracketed text added later by Barbirolli.

[337] Bracketed text added later by Barbirolli.

[338] Here, Barbirolli is referring to Tommy Cheetham, who also acted as Barbirolli's librarian with the Hallé Orchestra.

[339] Bracketed text added later by Barbirolli.

[340] Beside this sentence in the margin, Barbirolli wrote 'Mention Petrushka'.

[341] Bracketed text added later by Barbirolli.

[342] Bracketed text added later by Barbirolli.

[343] Bracketed text added later by Barbirolli.

[344] Bracketed text added later by Barbirolli.

[345] Bracketed text added later by Barbirolli.

[346] Bracketed text replaced 'Edinburgh'.

[347] Bracketed text replaced 'your'.

[348] Bracketed text replaced 'already set'.

Glorious John

[349] Bracketed text added later by Barbirolli.

[350] Bracketed text replaced 'and flash the name of your great city rough [sic] these Islands as one of the first to have restored the great Art of Music to its rightful place in the cultural life of the land'.

[351] Beside the square-bracketed text, Barbirolli later added 'Here if you would allow me to use a word which tho', of sanguinary derivation found a place in the classics of our literature I could tell you a story which saved us (illegible) 6hrs etc.'.

[352] Text taken from Barbirolli's undated, handwritten manuscript which is held at the Royal Academy of Music.

[353] After 'that', Barbirolli excised 'question of what'.

[354] After 'among', Barbirolli excised 'a certain class of'.

[355] After 'incidentally', Barbirolli excised 'apart from'.

[356] After 'I', Barbirolli excised 'suggest'.

[357] Text taken from Barbirolli's typewritten manuscript which is held at the Royal Academy of Music.

[358] Bracketed text added later by Barbirolli.

[359] Bracketed text added later by Barbirolli.

[360] After 'B.B.C.', Barbirolli excised 'will'.

[361] After 'sure,', Barbirolli excised [not].

[362] Text taken from Barbirolli's typewritten manuscript which is held at the Royal Academy of Music. A handwritten manuscript of the speech is also housed at the Royal Academy of Music.

[363] Bracketed text replaced 'these'.

[364] Bracketed text replaced 'rooms'.

[365] Bracketed text replaced 'might'.

[366] Bracketed text replaced 'I'.

[367] Bracketed text added later by Barbirolli.

[368] Bracketed text replaced '1st'.

[369] Bracketed text added later by Barbirolli.

[370] After 'instance', Barbirolli added the musical symbol for a fermata: ⌢.

[371] Bracketed text added later by Barbirolli.

[372] Bracketed text replaced 'of'.

[373] Bracketed text replaced 'supported'.

[374] Bracketed text added later by Barbirolli.

[375] Bracketed text added later by Barbirolli.

[376] Around 'out of profits', Barbirolli added the musical symbols for repeat.

[377] 'MUST' underlined thrice by Barbirolli.

[378] After 'again', Barbirolli later inserted '(Here I am reminded [of] Sir Dan's Christmas Card present'.

[379] Bracketed text replaced 'contain'.

[380] Bracketed text replaced 'Thus you have the rough outline of the career of the oldest established institution of its kind in the country'.

[381] Bracketed text replaced 'The next thing I would remind you of is the'.

[382] After 'musicians', Barbirolli excised 'who'.

[383] Bracketed text added later by Barbirolli.

[384] Bracketed text added later by Barbirolli.

Notes

[385] Bracketed text added later by Barbirolli.
[386] Bracketed text added later by Barbirolli.
[387] Bracketed text added later by Barbirolli.
[388] Bracketed text added later by Barbirolli.
[389] Below this sentence, Barbirolli also added later 'Mlynarski, Sir Fred[erick]. Cowen'.
[390] Bracketed text added later by Barbirolli. After 'season', Barbirolli excised 'Now'.
[391] Bracketed text replaced 'I.'.
[392] Bracketed text replaced 'Guarantor'.
[393] Bracketed text added later by Barbirolli.
[394] Bracketed text replaced 'II.'.
[395] Bracketed text added later by Barbirolli.
[396] Bracketed text added later by Barbirolli.
[397] Barbirolli underlined 'most' twice.
[398] Bracketed text added later by Barbirolli.
[399] After 'stand', Barbirolli excised 'will be of interest here'.
[400] Bracketed text replaced 'Guarantor'.
[401] Bracketed text added later. After 'Corporation', Barbirolli excised 'of Glasgow'.
[402] Bracketed text added later by Barbirolli.
[403] Bracketed text replaced 'to her'.
[404] Bracketed text replaced 'this'
[405] Bracketed text added later by Barbirolli. After 'time', Barbirolli excised 'the'
[406] Bracketed text added later by Barbirolli.
[407] Bracketed text added later by Barbirolli.
[408] Bracketed text added later by Barbirolli.
[409] Bracketed text added later by Barbirolli.
[410] Bracketed text replaced 'We have'.
[411] Bracketed text added later by Barbirolli.
[412] Bracketed text added later by Barbirolli.
[413] Bracketed text replaced 'I know'.
[414] Bracketed text replaced 'their'.
[415] Barbirolli underlined 'apathy' twice.
[416] Bracketed text added later by Barbirolli.
[417] Bracketed text replaced 'are'.
[418] Square-bracketed text added later by Barbirolli.
[419] Above 'Blazes', Barbirolli later inserted some illegible text.
[420] Bracketed text replaced 'now'.
[421] Bracketed text added later by Barbirolli.
[422] Bracketed text replaced 'to'.
[423] Bracketed text replaced 'It is a'.
[424] Bracketed text added later by Barbirolli.
[425] Bracketed text added later by Barbirolli.
[426] Bracketed text replaced 'Two especial favourites of Toscanini (?)'.
[427] Bracketed text added later by Barbirolli. After 'Gerhard [sic]', Barbirolli later excised 'are to appear'.
[428] Bracketed text replaced 'who'.
[429] Bracketed text added later by Barbirolli.

Glorious John

[430] Bracketed text added later by Barbirolli.
[431] The artists named by Barbirolli played in the Scottish Orchestra's 1933-4 season.
[432] Bracketed text replaced 'Secondly'.
[433] After 'country', Barbirolli added the musical symbol for a fermata: ⌒.
[434] Beside 'no inferiority complex' in the margin, Barbirolli later added enigmatically '3X'.
[435] Bracketed text replaced 'overhauled'.
[436] Bracketed text replaced 'and some of our new'.
[437] Bracketed text replaced 'Covent Garden'
[438] Bracketed text added later by Barbirolli.
[439] Bracketed text added later by Barbirolli. After 'losses', Barbirolli excised 'of'.
[440] Bracketed text replaced 'to'.
[441] Bracketed text added later by Barbirolli.
[442] Bracketed text added later by Barbirolli.
[443] Bracketed text added later by Barbirolli.
[444] Above 'set it alight', Barbirolli added later 'I have been told that in the "good old days" there was a lot of "family concert going". An enchanting custom I would be very happy to see revived'.
[445] Bracketed text added later by Barbirolli.
[446] Bracketed text replaced 'is 100% cheaper than'.
[447] Bracketed text added later by Barbirolli.
[448] Above 'most', Barbirolli later added 'twice'.
[449] Bracketed text added later by Barbirolli.
[450] Bracketed text added later by Barbirolli.
[451] Bracketed text replaced 'to all'.
[452] Bracketed text added later by Barbirolli.
[453] Bracketed text replaced 'Guarantor'.
[454] Square-bracketed text added later by Barbirolli.
[455] Bracketed text added later by Barbirolli.
[456] Bracketed text added later by Barbirolli.
[457] Square-bracketed text added later by Barbirolli.
[458] Bracketed text added later by Barbirolli.
[459] Bracketed text replaced 'not wandered far'.
[460] Text taken from Barbirolli's incomplete handwritten manuscript which is held at the Royal Academy of Music.
[461] After 'you', Barbirolli excised 'once again'.
[462] After 'Halls', Barbirolli excised 'To the Lord Provost and the Corporation of Glasgow I would like immediately'.
[463] Square-bracketed text added later by Barbirolli.
[464] Bracketed text replaced 'one cannot'.
[465] Bracketed text replaced 'year'.
[466] After 'quality', Barbirolli excised 'tho' I shall still have one or two things to say to you'.
[467] After 'concert', Barbirolli added but later excised 'last year'.
[468] Bracketed text replaced 'that the younger older and younger sought to' [sic].
[469] Square-bracketed text added later by Barbirolli.
[470] After 'long', Barbirolli excised 'masqueraded as music'.
[471] After 'one', Barbirolli excised 'day encounter a gentleman'.

Notes

[472] Bracketed text replaced 'fragrance'.
[473] Bracketed text replaced 'and in this connection I would venture to say'.
[474] After 'to-day', Barbirolli excised 'has'.
[475] The artists mentioned in the following sentence in the main text all performed in the Scottish Orchestra's 1934-5 season.
[476] After 'pianists', Barbirolli excised 'of to-day'.
[477] After 'Thibaud', Barbirolli excised 'are certainly among the first six'.
[478] Bracketed text replaced 'the world'.
[479] After 'epoch', Barbirolli excised 'this is not to belittle others'.
[480] Bracketed text replaced 'In this connection we'.
[481] After 'Huberman', Barbirolli excised 'and'.
[482] After 'interest', Barbirolli excised 'and pleasure'.
[483] Georg Schnéevoigt (1872-1947). Finnish conductor and 'cellist.
[484] Bracketed text replaced 'his countryman's music & Sibelius'.
[485] Bracketed text added later by Barbirolli.
[486] Bracketed text replaced 'the most important and vital portion of business of the evening'.
[487] Bracketed text replaced 'are'.
[488] Final page/s missing from the Barbirolli papers at the Royal Academy of Music.
[489] Text taken from Barbirolli's typewritten manuscript which is held at the Royal Academy of Music. A handwritten draft of the speech is also housed at the Royal Academy of Music.
[490] Bracketed text added later by Barbirolli.
[491] After 'and', 'the' was later excised by Barbirolli.
[492] Bracketed text replaced 'faity'.
[493] After 'to', Barbirolli later added 'not necessary to repeat here'.
[494] David McCallum, David Nichols, Charles Meert, George Maxted, Evelyn Rothwell (later Lady Evelyn Barbirolli) and Eileen Grainger played respectively violin, 'cello, viola, trombone, oboe and viola in the Scottish Orchestra.
[495] Bracketed text added later by Barbirolli.
[496] Bracketed text added later by Barbirolli.
[497] Bracketed text replaced 'with'.
[498] Bracketed text added later by Barbirolli. Above the bracketed text, Barbirolli also added later "Who in this that darkeneth counsel by words without knowledge'.
[499] Bracketed text added later by Barbirolli.
[500] After 'Strauss', Barbirolli excised 'works' from the text.
[501] Bracketed text added later by Barbirolli.
[502] Bracketed text replaced 'increasing'.
[503] Bracketed text added later by Barbirolli.
[504] Above '2/6 equals 1/10', Barbirolli later inserted 'saves [illegible] or 4 free concerts'.
[505] Central digit missing from the typed text.
[506] Originally, Barbirolli wrote '£1.1' but later crossed out '£1'.
[507] Under 'B.B.C.', Barbirolli later added 'supposedly [illegible]'.
[508] Bracketed text added later by Barbirolli.
[509] Bracketed text replaced 'they'.
[510] Bracketed text added later by Barbirolli.
[511] After '(Charles II tale)', Barbirolli later added 'I am not going to be so ungallant as to suggest there is now an excess in the [illegible] of women to talk to but certainly matters have

Glorious John

improved in that respect. Society Musicians etc.'.
[512] Bracketed text replaced 'them'.
[513] Under this sentence, Barbirolli later added '(if they survive already 84 concerts booked for them)'.
[514] Bracketed text added later by Barbirolli.
[515] Bracketed text added later by Barbirolli.
[516] Text taken from Barbirolli's typewritten manuscript which is held at the Royal Academy of Music. The text is dated 18 April 1939.
[517] The original typed 'to foster and' replaced later in pencil by Barbirolli with 'to'.
[518] The original typed 'your' replaced later in pencil by Barbirolli with 'any'.
[519] Handwritten speech written on 'The St Moritz on the Park New York' headed notepaper.
[520] Barbirolli is quoting from Act 3, Scene 1 of Shakespeare's *The Taming of the Shrew*.
[521] Text taken from Barbirolli's undated, typewritten manuscript which is held at the Royal Academy of Music.
[522] Barbirolli circled 'causes' in the typewritten text.
[523] Barbirolli circled 'undeserved' and 'unimaginable' and underlined 'worthy of a better fate' in the typewritten text.
[524] Barbirolli underlined 'in their time rendered long and honourable service to music' in the typewritten text.
[525] Barbirolli underlined 'gratitude rather than in charity' in the typewritten text.
[526] Barbirolli added the comma after the typewritten text was complete.
[527] Text taken from Barbirolli's undated, typewritten manuscript which is held at the Royal Academy of Music. A second, annotated copy of the speech is also held at the Royal Academy of Music.
[528] In Barbirolli's second typewritten copy of the speech, the comma is added.
[529] In Barbirolli's second typewritten copy of the speech, the comma is added.
[530] 'By training and equipping your young' is underlined in Barbirolli's second copy of the typewritten script.
[531] 'I wonder how many people realise' is underlined in Barbirolli's second typewritten copy of the speech.
[532] In Barbirolli's second typewritten copy of the speech, 'orchestral' is underlined.
[533] In Barbirolli's second typewritten copy of the speech, this sentence has been corrected in pencil to read 'Let us take for instance the string ensemble. A violinist or cellist playing a solo in a large hall, knows from experience that even in a pp. he must produce a tone which, though soft, must be of fairly full quality to carry well'.
[534] In Barbirolli's second typewritten copy of the speech, 'wind players' is underlined.
[535] In Barbirolli's second typewritten copy of the speech, 'best' is crossed out, 'orchestral literature' is underlined and '(Burney & Meiningen orchestra.)' is inserted above the first line of the paragraph.
[536] At the beginning of this sentence, Barbirolli inserts in his second typewritten copy 'Through their grounding in the classics' and, towards the end, crosses out 'classical'.
[537] In Barbirolli's second typewritten copy of the speech, 'modern music' is underlined.
[538] In Barbirolli's second typewritten copy of the speech, 'opportunity of cultivating' and 'extending their reading powers' are underlined.
[539] In Barbirolli's second typewritten copy of the speech, 'young composers' is underlined.
[540] In Barbirolli's second typewritten copy of the speech, 'direction' is crossed out and replaced

Notes

by 'direct tuition'.

[541] In Barbirolli's second typewritten copy of the speech, 'Orchestra' is crossed out and replaced by 'Philharmonic'.

[542] In Barbirolli's second typewritten copy of the speech, 'This is an achievement of which' is underlined.

[543] In Barbirolli's second typewritten copy of the speech, 'slacking' is crossed out and replaced with 'slackening'.

[544] In Barbirolli's second typewritten copy of the speech, the comma is added.

[545] In Barbirolli's second typewritten copy of the speech, 'talents unfortunately require finance for fruition' is underlined.

[546] In Barbirolli's second typewritten copy of the speech, 'by now, any of you who were' is underlined.

[547] In Barbirolli's second typewritten copy of the speech, the comma is added.

[548] In Barbirolli's second typewritten copy of the speech, the comma is added.

[549] In Barbirolli's second typewritten copy of the speech, the comma after 'realise' is added, 'now' is removed, 'the importance' is changed to 'its importance' and 'its importance' is underlined.

[550] In Barbirolli's second typewritten copy of the speech, 'rather' is crossed out and replaced with an illegible word.

[551] In Barbirolli's second typewritten copy of the speech, 'absolute necessity' is underlined.

[552] In Barbirolli's second typewritten copy of the speech, 'Would' is replaced by 'Words'.

[553] In Barbirolli's second typewritten copy of the speech, 'especially' is underlined and 'the' is replaced with 'these'.

[554] In Barbirolli's second typewritten copy of the speech, 'that' is preceded by 'of seeing'.

[555] In Barbirolli's second typewritten copy of the speech, 'has not' is inserted between 'for' and 'Shakespeare'.

[556] In Barbirolli's second typewritten copy of the speech, 'has' is removed.

[557] Here, Barbirolli slightly misquotes Shakespeare. *see* Note 520.

[558] The date of writing is not specified in the text, but was probably penned in the 1940s. *see* Note 559.

[559] Bernard Naylor (1907-1986). English composer, conductor and organist. Naylor founded the Little Symphony of Montreal in 1942.

[560] As found in *Leslie Heward, 1897-1943. A Memorial Volume*, ed Eric Blom, J. M. Dent & Sons (London, 1944), pp. 55-6.

[561] Leslie Heward (1897-1943). English composer and conductor.

[562] Text taken from an unidentified newspaper found in *The Barbirolli Society Journal*, Winter 2006, pp. 56-7.

[563] Text taken from Barbirolli's typewritten manuscript which is held at the Royal Academy of Music.

[564] Barbirolli inserted the text in brackets later in pencil.

[565] Ernest Bean (1900-1983). English music administrator.

[566] After the Free Trade Hall was destroyed during World War Two, and before it was reopened in 1951, the Hallé Orchestra performed regularly at the Albert Hall, Manchester.

[567] Text in brackets added later by Barbirolli, replacing 'act'.

[568] Text in brackets added later by Barbirolli, replacing 'some'.

[569] Text in brackets added later by Barbirolli.

Glorious John

[570] Numeral in brackets added later by Barbirolli.

[571] Walter Legge (1906-1979). English music administrator, writer and record producer.

[572] Beside this paragraph in the margin, Barbirolli added 'whose writing & unflagging efforts to encourage & propagate all that is best in our music are deserving of the highest praise'. This addition refers presumably to Walter Legge.

[573] The bracketed word was added later by Barbirolli, replacing an illegible original.

[574] Text in brackets was added later by Barbirolli, replacing 'that'.

[575] Text taken from Barbirolli's handwritten manuscript which is held at the Royal Academy of Music.

[576] Text taken from Barbirolli's typewritten manuscript which is held at the Royal Academy of Music.

[577] Text in brackets added later by Barbirolli in ink, replacing the typewritten 'appeals'.

[578] Text taken from Barbirolli's typewritten manuscript which is held at the Royal Academy of Music.

[579] Bracketed text added later by Barbirolli, replacing first 'musical magazine' and then 'journal'.

[580] After 'tradition', Barbirolli removed 'for our new musical journal quarterly (or whatever it is going to be)'.

[581] Barbirolli's original read 'a shop window'.

[582] Text in brackets added later by Barbirolli, replacing 'and'.

[583] Text in brackets added later by Barbirolli, replacing 'what'.

[584] Text in Brackets later crossed through twice by Barbirolli.

[585] Text in brackets added later by Barbirolli.

[586] Text in brackets added later by Barbirolli, replacing 'and'.

[587] Text in brackets added later by Barbirolli, replacing 'that'.

[588] Text in brackets later crossed through twice by Barbirolli.

[589] Text taken from Barbirolli's typewritten manuscript which is held at the Royal Academy of Music.

[590] 'JB' refers to John Barbirolli.

[591] The orchestras to which Barbirolli is referring by initials are the London Symphony Orchestra, the London Philharmonic Orchestra, the New Symphony Orchestra [of London], the Royal Philharmonic Society Orchestra and the BBC Symphony Orchestra.

[592] Text taken from Barbirolli's typewritten manuscript which is held at the Royal Academy of Music. A draft, handwritten manuscript of the talk is also housed at the Royal Academy of Music.

[593] Text in brackets inserted later by Barbirolli in pencil.

[594] Text in brackets added later by Barbirolli in pencil.

[595] Text in brackets added later by Barbirolli in pencil.

[596] Text in brackets added later by Barbirolli in pencil.

[597] Text in brackets added later by Barbirolli.

[598] Text in brackets added later by Barbirolli.

[599] Text taken from Barbirolli's handwritten manuscript which is held at the Royal Academy of Music.

[600] Barbirolli was knighted in 1949.

[601] Text in brackets added later by Barbirolli.

[602] Here, Barbirolli is referring to Philip Godlee.

Notes

[603] Here, Barbirolli is quoting from Act 3, Scene 5 of Wagner's *Die Meistersinger von Nürnberg*.

[604] As found in *Sir Charles Hallé: a Portrait for Today*, Charles Rigby, Dolphin Press (Manchester, 1952).

[605] As found in *Philip Godlee by His Friends*, ed. Charles Rigby (Manchester, 1954), pp. 14-18.

[606] Text published in *Hallé*, Number 61, Summer 1953, pp. 1-4.

[607] 'Kathleen... The Last Years', as found in *Kathleen Ferrier: a Memoir*, ed. Neville Cardus, Hamish Hamilton (London, 1954), pp. 36-53

[608] After 'Katie', Barbirolli inserted a footnote which reads 'I shall always refer to her as Katie, the name Evelyn and I always called her by'.

[609] After 'Tita', Barbirolli inserted a footnote that reads 'The name she always called me, and which is the Italian diminutive of Giovanni Battista'.

[610] Bruno Walter devotes most of his chapter, 'Farewell', to his memories of working with Ferrier on Mahler's *Das Lied von der Erde*. Cf. *Kathleen Ferrier: a Memoir*, pp. 109-114

[611] Square-bracketed text written in that format in Barbirolli's original text.

[612] Belle Vue was also a venue for circuses in Manchester.

[613] Here, Barbirolli must have meant 'Commander' rather than 'Companion'.

[614] Text taken from *Glorious John: 25th Anniversary of the Society*, The Barbirolli Society, February 1997, p. 17.

[615] Text taken from *Hallé*, December 1957, p. 2.

[616] As found in the Hallé Orchestra's Centenary Programme, pp. 31-2.

[617] Gerald Finzi (1901-1956). English composer.

[618] Robert Hughes (b. 1912). Scottish-born Australian composer

[619] Agnes Nicholls (1877-1959). English soprano. Nicholls married Hamilton Harty in 1904. She was his first wife. His second wife was his former secretary, Olive Elfreda Baguley, whom he married after the death of Nicholls.

[620] As found in *One Hundred Years of the Hallé*, C. B. Rees, Macgibbon & Kee, (London, 1957), pp. 9-10

[621] First published in Grant's *Focus* and reproduced later in *Hallé*, 1960/61, pp. 5-6.

[622] Text taken from *The Barbirolli Society Journal*, December 1996, page unidentified. The tribute appeared first in a Hallé Orchestra concert programme in October 1963.

[623] *Suo Gan* was a Welsh melody that was arranged for orchestra by George Weldon.

[624] This tribute was published in *125 Jahre Wiener Philharmoniker*.

[625] 'John Barbirolli' written as a signature in the published copy.

[626] Text taken from *Hallé*, 1967-8, p. 23. The tribute was first published in the Hallé Orchestra's programme of 12 October 1967.

[627] Text taken from Barbirolli's handwritten draft which is held at the Royal Academy of Music. The text is dated 'July 4 1967'.

[628] After 'Toscanini', Barbirolli excised 'which has become almost a legend, by the'.

[629] After 'trial', Barbirolli excised 'have given their greatest'.

[630] After 'this', Barbirolli excised '30th bi'.

[631] Text taken from *Hallé*, 1967-8, pp. 2-3. A typewritten draft of this article is housed at the Royal Academy of Music.

[632] Archie Camden (1888-1979). English bassoonist.

[633] 'John Barbirolli' signed in the printed copy.

[634] Text published in *Hallé*, 1968-9, pp. 11-13. Text is an edited transcript of a Radio 3 broadcast, transmitted on 18 August 1968. The interview followed the Hallé Orchestra's 1968 tour of Latin

Glorious John

America.

[635] Here, Barbirolli is referring to the Teatro de Colón in Buenos Aires.

[636] Text taken from Barbirolli's handwritten manuscript which is held at the Royal Academy of Music.

[637] After 'pleasure', Barbirolli excised both 'and warmth of feeling' and 'feelings of affection'.

[638] Rachel Morton (1888-1982). English singer.

[639] Before the main text, Barbirolli added 'My dear Rachel. Forgive the tardy arrival of the forward, but I have not had a moment to myself since I last saw you. Not only with my own Hallé Orchestra here, but in Berlin, Russia, Prague, Poland, Italy etc. I do hope my few words will please you & help you get the book published. Do let me know. With love to you, Your affectionate & devoted [illegible] Maestro'.

[640] For clarity, under 'Reszke' Barbirolli wrote '(RESZKE)'.

[641] Article taken from Barbirolli's typewritten manuscript which is held at the Royal Academy of Music. The article was written at the request of George Hutchinson and was to be included in a book celebrating the history of the South Place Concerts, 1887-1969. A handwritten copy of the manuscript and accompanying correspondence is also housed at the Royal Academy of Music.

[642] This tribute was intended for publication in *Double Concerto*. Text taken from the Barbirolli's typewritten manuscript which is held at the Royal Academy of Music. A handwritten copy and accompanying correspondence is also housed at the Royal Academy of Music.

[643] Robert Mayer (1897-1985). German-born English music patron.

[644] Barbirolli's text was published in *Opera* in April 1969.

[645] Giovanni Martinelli (1885-1969). Italian tenor.

[646] Eva Turner (1892-1990). English soprano.

[647] Mafalda Favero (1903-1981). Italian soprano.

[648] Interview published in Japan's *Nihon Keizai Shimbun* on 27 August 1969 concerning Barbirolli's planned visit to Japan and the World Exposition in 1970. Text taken from a translation sent by Pauline Bush, Secretary to the British Commissioner General to the Japan World Exposition at Osaka in 1970. The text is held at the Royal Academy of Music. The interview was conducted by the London correspondent of *Nihon Keizai Shimbun*, Soschichi Miyachi. Barbirolli died before performing in Japan in 1970; the concerts were conducted by Sir John Pritchard (then, John Pritchard). A copy of the interview in Japanese is also held at the Royal Academy of Music.

[649] Text published in *The Gramophone*, March 1931, p. 480.

[650] Text taken from Barbirolli's typewritten manuscript which is held at the Royal Academy of Music.

[651] Text in brackets added in hand by Barbirolli later.

[652] Barbirolli replaced the original typed 'at' with 'in'.

[653] Text in brackets added later by Barbirolli.

[654] Text taken from *The Barbirolli Society Journal*, June 1996, page unidentified. The article was published first in *Manchester Free Trade Hall*, a booklet issued for the re-opening of the reconstructed Free Trade Hall, November 1951.

[655] Text taken from an unidentified printed source, which is held at the Royal Academy of Music.

[656] 'John Barbirolli' appears as a signature at the end of the text.

[657] Text taken from *The Barbirolli Society Journal*, July 1999, p. 9. The article appeared first in

Notes

the *Houston Chronicle* on 2 October 1966.

[658] Text taken from Barbirolli's typewritten manuscript which is held at the Royal Academy of Music.

[659] Hans Kindler (1892-1949). Dutch-born American conductor and 'cellist.

[660] *see* Note 520.

[661] Text taken from the transcription of the speech that was published in the *Manchester Review*. Two typewritten manuscript drafts, both of which are dated '16th. September, 1947.', are housed at the Royal Academy of Music. One of the drafts contains additional annotations by Barbirolli. 16 September 1947 was the day on which the Henry Watson Music Library was moved to the Second Floor of Manchester's Central Library. Barbirolli made this speech at the request of the Manchester Libraries Committee.

[662] Text published in *The Gramophone*, August 1931, pp. 79-80.

[663] Giovanni Inghilleri (1894-1959). Italian baritone.

[664] Octave Dua (1882-1952) Belgian tenor.

[665] Text taken from Barbirolli's typewritten manuscript which is held at the Royal Academy of Music.

[666] Text taken from Barbirolli's typewritten manuscript which is held at the Royal Academy of Music.

[667] As the journey to which Barbirolli is referring took place in 1942, it can be assumed that this talk was also given that year.

[668] Text taken from Barbirolli's typewritten manuscript which is held at the Royal Academy of Music. The address was delivered on the 100th anniversary of the New York Philharmonic-Symphony Orchestra in 1942.

[669] Text taken from Barbirolli's typewritten manuscript which is held at the Royal Academy of Music. The text appears on the New York Philharmonic-Symphony Orchestra's headed notepaper.

[670] The remainder of document is missing.

[671] Text taken from Barbirolli's typewritten manuscript which is held at the Royal Academy of Music. The manuscript is dated 'September 16, 1942'. A second version of the speech is also held at the Royal Academy of Music. That version was delivered at the Ambassador Hotel, Los Angeles, on 17 November 1942.

[672] Bracketed text inserted as a replacement for paragraph one when the speech was repeated at the Ambassador Hotel, Los Angeles, on 17 November 1942.

[673] Bracketed text inserted as a replacement for 'And since' in paragraph two to 'financial success' at the end of paragraph two when the speech was repeated at the Ambassador Hotel, Los Angeles, on 17 November 1942.

[674] Bracketed text inserted between the second and third paragraphs when the speech was repeated at the Ambassador Hotel, Los Angeles, on 17 November 1942.

[675] *see* Note 520.

[676] Bracketed text inserted when the speech was repeated at the Ambassador Hotel, Los Angeles, on 17 November 1942.

[677] The Queen's Hall was destroyed by German bombing on the night of 10-11 May 1941.

[678] Bracketed text inserted when the speech was repeated at the Ambassador Hotel, Los Angeles, on 17 November 1942.

[679] Bracketed text inserted when the speech was repeated at the Ambassador Hotel, Los Angeles, on 17 November 1942.

Glorious John

[680] Text published in the *Radio Times*, 22 September 1944. A typewritten, manuscript copy of the text is held at the Royal Academy of Music.

[681] Text in brackets found in Barbirolli's typewritten manuscript but omitted from the published article.

[682] Barbirolli conducted in Italy for five weeks during the summer of 1944. He conducted Italian orchestras for the men of the First and Fifth Armies. *Radio Times*, 22 September 1944, p. 5.

[683] Text taken from Barbirolli's typed manuscript, dated 'September 24th 1944'. Two versions of this text are held at the Royal Academy of Music.

[684] Text in brackets added later by Barbirolli in pencil.

[685] 'As it happens the only recording available is of the Bari orch.' was inserted later by Barbirolli in pencil replacing the original typewritten 'Unfortunately this also has not materialised'.

[686] Barbirolli inserted 'the incident I just told you about' in pencil, replacing the original typewritten 'that incident'.

[687] Text in brackets added later by Barbirolli in pencil.

[688] Text in brackets added later by Barbirolli in pencil.

[689] Text in brackets added later by Barbirolli in pencil, replacing the typewritten 'you will hear in a moment'.

[690] Text in brackets added later by Barbirolli in pencil, replacing the typewritten 'This orchestra'.

[691] Text in brackets added later by Barbirolli in pencil.

[692] Text in brackets added later by Barbirolli in pencil, replacing 'I would now like to play you a few excerpts from recordings I brought back with me of the actual concerts in Bari. I thought there might be some listening in who had a loved one at one of my concerts'.

[693] Text taken from Barbirolli's handwritten manuscript which is held at the Royal Academy of Music.

[694] Barbirolli is referring to the radio address delivered by President Roosevelt from Washington on 29 December 1940 known commonly as the 'Arsenal of Democracy Speech'.

[695] Text taken from Barbirolli's unidentified published article which is held at the Royal Academy of Music.

[696] Mozart's *Der Schauspieldirektor* was given its première at Schonbrünn on 7 February 1786.

[697] Text taken from Barbirolli's typewritten manuscript which is held at the Royal Academy of Music. The manuscript is dated 'October 4th 1948'.

[698] Text taken from Barbirolli's typewritten manuscript which is held at the Royal Academy of Music. The text is dated 'Feb 26 1949'. A handwritten draft of this lecture on paper with Barbirolli's letterhead is also housed at the Royal Academy of Music.

Illustrations

Cover painting by Brian Denington	
EMI recording session for Schubert's Symphony No. 9 †	Frontispiece
Sir John, c. 1950	20
Giovanni at three-and-a-half years old	56
Giovanni with his sister Rosa, 1907	57
Barbirolli in 1924	58
Liverpool 1930	59
Covent Garden Opera Football Team, c. 1930	59
Percy Heming and Barbirolli, Cologne 1930	60
Evelyn, Paul Kilburn (viola player, Scottish Orchestra) and Barbirolli, 1937	60
Barbirolli and the New York Philharmonic-Symphony Orchestra, 1937	61
Barbirolli conducting the Vienna Philharmonic, Musikvereinsaal, 1948	61
Barbirolli at Loch Lomond, c.1930	62
Barbirolli – New York, 1942	119
Barbirolli at Niagara Falls, c. 1940	120
John and Evelyn, Hollywood, 1941	120
Celebrating the Centenary of the New York Philharmonic Symphony Orchestra, 1942	121
John and Evelyn visiting a steel mill, NYPSO tour, 1941	121
Barbirolli rehearsing the New York Philharmonic-Symphony Orchestra	122
Barbirolli conducting the New York Philharmonic-Symphony Orchestra	123
Barbirolli, Royal Albert Hall, London, 1950	124
Recording at Abbey Road Studios, London †	143
Belle Vue, Manchester, 1949 ‡	144
Recording session for the BBC's *International Concert Hall*, Free Trade Hall	144
Barbirolli conducting the National Anthem, Belle Vue, Manchester, 1949 ‡	145
Passport control – on tour with the Hallé, c. 1950	146
Mémé and Barbirolli, Sussex 1951	146
Barbirolli – from the family photo album – date unknown	147
Barbirolli and Kathleen Ferrier, Sussex, 1951	148
Associated-Rediffusion studios, 1957	149
Barbirolli and Vaughan Williams, 2 May, 1956	149
Barbirolli conducting in Sheffield – date unknown	150
Barbirolli with Artur Rubinstein and his wife, Manchester, 1957	222

Glorious John

Illustrations

Barbirolli at Hallé's grave, Salford, Feburary 1958	222
Barbirolli – Umpire	223
Barbirolli and Lady Fermoy, Town Hall, Manchester, December 1961	224
After a performance of Mahler's *Ressurection Symphony*, Tel Aviv, June 1960	225
Barbirolli and André Navarra, 1961	225
Barbirolli with the production team of BBC Television's *Monitor* programme, 1964	226
Barbirolli looking at the plans for the Sydney Opera House, c. 1960s	226
Barbirolli conducting at Kenwood, August 1964	227
Barbirolli rehearsing – Free Trade Hall, Manchester, 1957	228
Barbirolli conducting the Houston Symphony Orchestra, c. 1960s	236
Barbirolli on the steps of the Museum of Arts, Houston, c. 1960s	237
Barbirolli conducting the Houston Symphony Orchestra, c. 1960s	238
Barbirolli with Artur Rubinstein, Houston, 1960s	247
Barbirolli conducting the Budapest Radio Symphony Orchestra, September 1961	248
Barbirolli with Lionel Tertis, 1967	258
Kinloch Anderson (EMI Producer), John and Evelyn, Walton Lodge, 1969	258
Barbirolli with Lidia Arcuri, Genoa, 1967	259
Barbirolli with Fiorenzo Cossotto and Ivo Vinco, *Aida*, Rome, April 1969	260
Laurance Turner, Martin Milner, Barbirolli and Clive Smart, Manchester, 1967	261
Barbirolli and the RAI Symphony Orchestra, Turin, 1970	261
Barbirolli recording the Brahms Symphonies with the Vienna Philharmonic Orchestra †	262
Barbirolli recording Mahler's Symphony No.9 with the Berlin Philharmonic Orchestra †	306

Photographs courtesy of Lady Barbirolli, except
† EMI Records and ‡ The Barbirolli Society

Glorious John

Index

Academy of Music, Philadelphia, 256
Accademia Nazionale di Santa Cecilia (Academy of Saint Cecilia), Rome, 279
Aeolian Hall, London, 15
Albert Hall, Manchester, 176, 184, 279, 281
Adler, Larry, 102
Alexander, A. V., 269
Alexander, General Harold, 271
Allin, Norman, 26
Anderson, Ronald Kinloch, 108-110, 113-4
Ansermet, Ernest, 51
Argentina Theatre, Rome, 272, 274
Arnaud, Yvonne, 160
Arnold, Sir Malcolm, 205
Art of Musical Russia Opera Company, The, 169
Arts Council of Great Britain, The, 208-10
Astor, Brooke, 168
Asquith, Lord (Herbert), 152
Austin, Frederick, 15, 23, 26, 131
Austral, Florence, 17, 160
Authors' Club, Hollywood, 265-70
Axon, Lea, 214
Bach Gesellschaft, 31
Bach, Johann Sebastian, 16, 71, 91, 107-8, 130, 134, 231, 263; *St Matthew Passion*, 31, 40, 41, 107-8; Mass in B minor, 132; 'Cello Suites, 194
Bachad Society, 188
Baker, George, 26
Balfour, Lord (Arthur), 26, 51, 154
Barbirolli, Antonio (grandfather of Barbirolli), 14, 18, 32, 45, 48, 49, 116, 117, 129-30, 253, 271, 273
Barbirolli, Evelyn (Lady Barbirolli) (wife of Barbirolli), 31, 35, 37, 41, 48, 54, 97, 103, 106, 165, 183, 190, 191, 192, 194, 198, 199, 200, 201, 215
Barbirolli, Sir John, Birth, 14; 'Cellist, 14-15, 21-2, 29, 47, 49, 50, 51-2, 64, 96, 98-9, 102, 103, 104, 108, 111, 116, 129, 130, 131, 153, 194, 200, 201, 214, 219, 253; Army, 15, 22, 111, 131; Becoming a conductor, 22, 128-33; John Barbirolli Chamber Orchestra, 15, 109-110, 131; Chenil String Orchestra, 64; British National Opera Company (B.N.O.C.), 15, 23, 26, 42, 63, 131, 140; Covent Garden Opera Company, 66, 67, 68, 70; Opera conductor, 15, 32, 42, 50, 65-93, 132, 141-2, 200, 201, 218, 221, 272; Scottish Orchestra, 16-17, 35, 97, 151-67, 173, 178; New York Philharmonic-Symphony Orchestra, 17-18, 21, 33, 35, 125-7, 128, 141, 167-9, 170-1, 174, 204, 231-3, 239-40, 243, 253, 254, 256, 263-5; Hallé Orchestra, 18-19, 33, 35-43, 52, 95, 97, 98, 99, 102, 110, 111, 142, 174-8, 178-84, 184-6, 186-7, 189-91, 193, 194, 197, 200, 202, 203-4, 204-8, 208-10, 211, 213-15, 216-18, 233-4, 246, 272-3, 274, 278, 279, 280-1; Houston Symphony Orchestra, 19, 40-2, 234-5; Approach to score analysis, 14, 115-6; Conducting style and technique, 15, 22, 129, 133-42; Wagner's thoughts on conducting, 28, 95, 136; Conducting from memory, 129, 139-40; Batons, 139; Conducting concertos, 139; Touring, 18; Psychology of conducting, 22, 128, 136-7; String technique and orchestral sound ('Barbirolli sound'), 39-40, 100-1, 114, 151-2; Playing and conducting from memory, 22-3, 186; Relationships, training and welfare of and with musicians and singers, 17-18, 23, 26-7, 52, 54, 125-7, 128, 137, 152, 160, 168-70, 170-2, 172, 174, 180-1, 183, 192-203, 209, 210-13, 215, 218, 220-1; Young players, 30; Women in orchestras, 175; Funding, 36, 37-8, 42, 155, 157-60, 161, 163, 166, 169-70, 174, 181-2, 208-10, 214, 263-4, 276, 280-1; Programming, 37, 38, 39, 42, 126, 137-8, 155-6, 160-1, 162, 164-5, 174-5, 176, 177, 204-7, 209, 229-35, 256-7, 270, 279; Halls and theatres, 42, 114; Orchestral seating, 138-9, 181; Arranger, 63-4, 132, 196; Accessibility to music, 16, 28-9, 165, 168, 170, 176, 179, 180-1, 182, 185-6, 203-4, 208, 213-

309

Glorious John

15, 220, 229-30, 239-43, 243-6, 249-57, 263-4, 278, 279-81; Recording and broadcasting, 16, 17, 19, 21, 23, 48, 63-5, 128, 155-6, 159, 161-2, 163, 165, 166-7, 169, 181, 212, 232, 239-43, 245-6, 249-57, 263-4, 273-5, 278; Tradition and history, 19, 21, 24-5, 34-5, 43, 43-7, 47-52, 52-3, 97-8, 127, 132, 133-4, 157-8, 178-80, 183-4, 184-6, 189, 203-4, 204-8, 211, 212-13, 218, 219, 220, 233-4, 253, 263-4; Gold Medal of the Royal Philharmonic Society, 24-5, 27-8, 48; Freeman of the City of Manchester, 41; Companion of Honour, 47-52; Knighthood and honorary degrees, 31, 49, 55, 200, 207; Freeman of King's Lynn, 52-3; Freeman of the City of London, 53; Honorary Liveryman of the Worshipful Company of Dyers, 53, School, 45, 49; Family life, 54-5; Christmas, 34-5, 43-7; Fiftieth birthday, 24; Marriage, 37, 54; Religion, 44-6, 54, 188, 263-4; Cricket, 24, 29-30, 32-4, 190; Politics and war, 18, 127, 162, 167-8, 169, 172, 174-5, 181, 185, 187, 212, 214, 217, 242, 263-81;
Barbirolli, Lorenzo (father of Barbirolli), 14, 18, 28, 29, 31, 32, 34, 44, 45, 48, 49, 51, 97, 109, 116, 117, 118, 129-30, 131, 221, 253, 271, 273
Barbirolli, Louise Marie (Mémé) (mother of Barbirolli), 14, 27, 34, 44, 48, 49, 50, 55, 131, 197, 267
Barbirolli, Rosa (sister of Barbirolli), 45, 48, 50, 265
Barbirolli, Rosina (grandmother of Barbirolli), 50, 141, 251
Bardgett, Herbert, 196
Bari Symphony Orchestra, 273, 274, 275
Bartlett, Ethel, 22, 23, 160
Bartók, Béla, 219
Barzin, Leon, 171
Bauer, Harold, 26
Bavagnoli, Gaetano, 104
Bax, Sir Arnold, 26, 27, 129, 174; *Phantasy for viola and orchestra*, 26; Overture, Elegy and Rondo, 27; Symphony No. 2, 165; Symphony No. 3, 165; Symphony No. 4, 165; *The Tale Pine Trees Knew*, 165
Bayreuth Festival Theatre, 42, 94, 111, 205
BBC Northern Orchestra, 36
BBC Symphony Orchestra, 40, 72, 181, 233
Bean, Ernest, 176, 183, 213, 278
Beardsley, Aubrey, 76
Beck, Harold, 52
Beck, Richard, 52
Beecham Opera Company, 22, 131, 140
Beecham, Sir Thomas, 15, 16, 23, 25-6, 48, 63, 74, 77, 108, 109, 230, 232
Beethoven, Ludwig van, 16, 25, 26, 47, 71, 72, 97, 98, 130, 139, 152, 183, 189, 219, 231, 263, 271; Piano Concerto No. 4, 26; Symphony No. 5, 34; Piano Concerto No. 5 ('Emperor'), 37; Violin Concerto, 40; Symphony No. 9 ('Choral'), 41, 234; *Fidelio*, 51, 250, 277; Symphony No. 2, 95; Symphony No. 3 ('Eroica'), 95, 221; Symphony No. 4, 246; Symphony No. 7, 277
Beinum, Eduard van, 233
Belle Vue, Manchester, 41, 42, 46-7, 201, 279, 281
Belloc, Hilaire, 199
Benjamin, Arthur, 40
Berg, Alban, 40; Violin Concerto, 38
Berlin Philharmonic, 18, 19, 39, 113-4, 114
Berlin Philharmonic Octet, 214
Berlioz, Hector, 47, 72, 178; *Symphonie fantastique*, 206, 233
Binyon, Laurence, 269
Birmingham Festival, 95, 112
Blackburn Orchestra, 201
Boito, Arrigo, 106
Boston Symphony Orchestra, 235, 241, 256
Boult, Sir Adrian, 162, 163
Bournemouth Symphony Orchestra, 15, 209
Brahms, Johannes, 16, 71, 72, 97, 98, 130, 139, 165, 183, 211, 271, 278; Piano Concerto No. 2, 207; Variations on a Theme of Haydn (St. Anthony Chorale), 211; String Quartet No. 2, 219; Symphony No. 2, 221
Brighton Philharmonic Society, 212
British Broadcasting Corporation (B.B.C.), 16, 35, 36, 71, 155-6, 159, 161-2, 165, 166-7, 245-6, 253, 271
British Council, 216, 278-9
British Council Exhibition, 278

310

Index

British Liberation Army, 184
British National Opera Company (B.N.O.C.), 15, 23, 26, 42, 63, 131, 140, 172, 173
Britten, Lord (Benjamin), 205; *Sinfonia da Requiem*, 38, 40, 216, 221; Violin Concerto, 40
Brodetsky Ensemble, 270
Bruckner, Anton, 40, 98, 114
Buckingham Palace, 110
Bulawayo Municipal Orchestra, 190
Bull, John, 132
Bülow, Hans von, 71, 72, 135, 158
Burney, Charles, 52
Burney, Fanny, 52
Busch, Adolf, 17, 160
Butterworth, Arthur, 206
Byrd, William, 132, 154
Calvert, Charles, 244
Cambell, Mrs. Patrick, 125
Cambridge, University of, 244
Camden, Archie, 215
Cammerts, Emil, 269
Canadian Broadcasting Corporation (C.B.C), 232
Caracas, University of, 217
Cardus, Sir Neville, 27, 51, 98, 113, 115
Carl Rosa Opera Company, 106
Carl Rosa Opera Company Orchestra, 22
Carnegie Hall, New York, 232, 253, 256
Carnegie United Kingdom Fund 155
Carpenter, Scott, 43
Caruso, Enrico, 86, 105
Casals, Pablo, 23, 27, 47, 48, 51, 109
Cassidy, Claudia, 17
Castel Gandolfo, 46, 110
Catterall, Arthur, 51
Chaliapin, Fyodor, 51, 230, 249-50
Chapman, J. C., 245
Charles II, King, 63, 166
Chausson, Ernest, *Poème de l'amour et de le mer*, 42, 193, 194, 196, 202, 203
Cheetham, Tommy, 152, 191
Cheltenham Festival, 100, 101, 103, 206
Chenil Galleries, 23
Chenil String Orchestra, 64
Cherubini, Luigi, 178
Chicago Symphony Orchestra, 17, 235, 241
Chicago Tribune, 17
Chopin, Fryderyk, 178

Churchill, Sir Winston, 24, 50, 182, 184
Cincinnati Symphony Orchestra, 241
City of Birmingham Symphony Orchestra, 172, 209
Clarke, Sir Ashley, 111
Clarke, Dean Douglas, 231
Clements, Alfred, 219
Cleveland Orchestra, The, 18, 241
Cochran, Charles B., 78
College-Conservatory of Music, Cincinnati, 253
Collier, Charles, 40
Columbia Broadcasting System (C.B.S.), 232, 253, 254, 255
Concertgebouw Orchestra, Amsterdam, 163, 233
Connaught, Duke of, 218
Contemporary Club, Philadelphia, 251-7
Corelli, Arcangelo, 50
Cortot, Alfred, 26
Covent Garden Opera Company, 66, 67, 68, 70, 154
Covent Garden Opera Syndicate, 15
Crickmore, Kenneth, 24, 191, 194, 195, 204
Croom-Johnson, Colonel, 274
Cunard, Lady, 50
Curtis Institute of Music, Philadelphia, 240-1, 253
Curzon, Sir Clifford, 37, 207
Czech National Theatre (Národní Divaldo), Prague, 67
Daily Telegraph, 205, 239
Dale, Benjamin, Romance for Viola and Orchestra, 205
Dawson, Herbert, 63
Debussy, Claude, 114, 130, 152, 154, 221, 232; *La Mer*, 38, 165; *Pelléas et Mélisande*, 91-5, 177, 232-3
Delius, Frederick, 22, 26, 132, 152, 155, 165, 205, 232, 271; Violin Concerto, 26, 165, 177; Requiem, 27; Dance Rhapsody No. 1, 29, 130; *North Country Sketches*, 165; *Eventyr*, 165; Piano Concerto, 177; *On Hearing the First Cuckoo in Spring*, 274
Detroit Symphony Orchestra, 241, 256
Diaghilev, Sergey, 51
Dickens, Charles, 39
Dieren, Bernard van, 23
Dinwiddie, Mr., 155, 163

Glorious John

Disraeli, Lord (Benjamin), 274
Douglas, Meg, 201
Douglas, W. R. (Billy), 194, 198-9, 201
Downes, Olin, 17
Dowson, Ernst, 76
Doyle Carte Company, 66
Drury Lane Theatre, 22, 49
Dua, Octave, 251
Duleepsinjhi, Kumar Shri, 29
Duncan, Isadora, 218
Du Pré, Jacqueline, 26
Düsseldorf Festival, 95
Dvořák, Antonin, 39, 68; Symphony No. 7, 39; Symphony No. 9 ('New World'), 39
Dyson, Sir George, 174
Edinburgh, Corporation of, 156
Edinburgh Concert Society, 156
Edinburgh Festival, 19, 111, 186, 202
Educational Institute of Scotland, 156, 166
Edward VII, King, 48, 188
Edwards, Mr. E., 191
Elgar, Sir Edward, 16, 35, 38, 40, 46, 51, 64, 65, 71, 95, 96, 97-8, 99, 107, 108-110, 110-12, 133-4, 154, 205, 207, 216, 234, 239, 269, 271; 'Cello Concerto, 15, 96, 98-9; Symphony No. 2, 23, 42, 48, 96, 97, 108-110, 188, 189, 216; *Falstaff*, 26; *The Dream of Gerontius*, 40, 42, 46, 51, 95, 96, 99, 110-12, 116, 192, 193, 202, 206; Introduction and Allegro for Strings, 64-5, 109-110; Quartet, 96; Quintet, 96; Variations on an Original Theme ('Enigma'), 97, 205, 235, 271, 272, 274; Symphony No. 1, 43, 108, 157, 207; 'Froissart' Overture, 188; *Sea Pictures*, 193; *Land of Hope and Glory*, 196, 216; Violin Concerto, 202; 'Pomp and Circumstance' March No. 1, 216; *Memorial Chimes (Carillon)*, 269
Elizabeth I, Queen, 154
Elizabeth, Queen (later The Queen Mother), 24, 27-8, 48, 49, 52, 55, 98, 190, 191, 196
Ellington, Duke, 54
Elman, Mischa, 17, 249, 250
Elsie, Lily, 49
Elwes, Gervase, 51, 111
E.M.I., 109, 112, 116
Empire Theatre, Leicester Square, 45, 49
Entertainments National Services Association (E.N.S.A.), 272-3
EXPO 70, Osaka, 221
Faccio, Franco, 117, 271, 273
Farnaby, Giles, 132
Favero, Mafalda, 221
Federation of Music Societies, 155
Ferguson, Howard, 205
Fermoy, Lady (Ruth), 26, 52
Ferrier, Kathleen, 19, 42, 51, 111, 192-203, 207
Ferrier, Win, 192, 198, 201
Ferrier, William, 197
Feuermann, Emmanuel, 17
Fielden, Thomas, 190
Finzi, Gerald, *Fall of the Leaf*, 205
Finzi, Joy, 205
Fisher, Alice, 52
Fisher, Dr., 244
Fitzwilliam Virginal Book, 132
Flesch, Carl, 162
Forbes, R.J., 36, 37
Ford, Henry, 240, 242
Ford Symphony Orchestra, 239
Foreign Office, 217
Franck, César, 47, 154; *Variations symphoniques*, 26; Quintette, 26, 50
Frankel, Mrs., 266
Free Trade Hall, Manchester, 28, 99, 184, 187, 188, 196, 205, 207, 212, 233-4, 279
Fricker, Peter Racine, Symphony No. 1, 40
Fry, C.B., 51
Furtwängler, Wilhelm, 16
Gaisberg, Fred, 23, 48, 109, 250, 251
Galilei, Galileo, *Dialogo*, 134
Galsworthy, John, 39, 94
Gardiner, John, Symphony, 40
Genée, Adline, 49
Gentlemen's Concerts, Manchester, **185**
George V, King, 48
George Weldon Memorial Concert, 211
Gerhardt, Elena, 27, 160
Gershwin, George, 16
Gewandhaus Concerts, Leipzig, 135
Ghione, Franco, 241
Giacchetti, Rina, 50
Giannini, Dusolina, 249
Gibbons, Orlando, 154
Gielgud, Sir John, 269
Gieseking, Walter, 17
Gigli, Benjamin, 51, 105

Index

Gilbert, Sir W(illiam). S(chwenck)., 66, 76
Ginster, Ria, 160
Giordano, Umberto, *Andrea Chénier*, 251
Glasgow, Corporation of, 155, 156, 158, 161, 166
Glasgow Choral Union, 152, 155, 157, 164
Glasgow Choral and Orchestral Union, 155, 158, 163
Gluck, Christoph Willibald, 52; *Orfeo ed Euridice*, 194, 199, 200, 201
Godfrey, Sir Dan, 96, 98
Godlee, Philip, 19, 36, 37, 42, 176, 184, 186-9
Goltermann, Julius, 'Cello Concerto Op. 14 (Cantilena), 14
Golschmann, Vladimir, 241
Goodwin, Felix, 68
Goonan, Miss, 214
Goossens, Eugene, 241
Goss, John, 23
Gounod, Charles-François, 75; *Roméo et Juliette*, 131, 140; *Faust*, 229
Grace, W.G., 25
Grainger, Eileen, 165
Gramophone, The, 15, 21
Gramophone Company, 250, 251
Grand Hotel, Sheffield, 195
Grayson, Captain, 274
Great Art Treasures Exhibition, Manchester, 281
Grey, Lord (Edward), 189
Grieg, Edvard, Piano Concerto, 37, 206
Griffes, Charles, *White Peacock*, 235
Griffin, Archbishop (Bernard William), 270
Guardian, The, 35, 187, 196, 205
Guild of Singers and Players, 22
Guilini, Carlo Maria, 41
Habsburg Family, Austria, 277
Hagemann, Dick, 265
Hahn, Reynaldo, 218
Hallé, Sir Charles, 38, 178, 179, 184-6, 206, 280
Hallé Ball, 213
Hallé Choir, 46, 111, 194, 196, 202, 234
Hallé Club, 142, 213-15
Hallé Concerts Society, 36, 38, 179, 184, 185, 186, 191, 204
Hallé Endowment Fund, 214
Hallé Magazine, 94, 180-1, 203-4, 213
Hallé Orchestra, 14, 18-19, 25, 28, 29, 30, 31, 33, 35-43, 51, 52, 95, 97, 98, 99, 102, 110, 111, 112, 142, 160, 174-8, 178-84, 184-6, 186-7, 189-91, 193, 194, 195, 197, 200, 202, 203-4, 204-8, 208-10, 210-11, 212, 213-15, 216-18, 233-4, 246, 272-3, 274, 278, 279, 280-1
Hallé Orchestra Promenade Concerts, 28-9, 210
Hamburg Philharmonic, 233
Hamilton, Lady (Emma), 271
Handel, George Frideric, 40, 51, 52, 130, 196; *Messiah*, 31, 41, 46, 47, 112, 195, 196, 201, 202, 203; *Water Music* (arr. Harty), 196
Harty, Sir Hamilton, 35, 36, 206
Harty, Lady (Agnes), *see* Nicholls, Agnes
Haydn, Joseph, 52, 72, 231; 'Cello Concerto No. 1 in D major, 23, 109; Symphony No. 104 ('London'), 63, 109; String Quartet No. 62 ('Emperor'), 95; *Die Schöpfung (The Creation)*, 24
Heifitz, Jascha, 17, 230
Helsinki University, 214
Henry VIII, King, 154
Henry & Co., Manchester, 244
Henry Watson Music Library, 243-6
Henry Wood Promenade Concerts, 28-9, 96, 97, 115, 160, 212
Henschel, Sir George, 158
Hess, Dame Myra, 37, 269
Heward, Leslie, 172-4
Hirsch, Maurice, 235
His Master's Voice (HMV), 17, 23, 48, 100, 249
Hitler, Adolf, 53, 265
Hobbs, John ('Jack'), 32
Hodgkinson, J. L., 213
Hofburg (Imperial Palace), Vienna, 276
Hofmannsthal, Hugo von, 74-7, 80; *Elektra*, 76; *Ödipus und die Sphinx*, 76; *Jedermann*, 76
Hogg, Ima, 235
Hollywood Bowl, Los Angeles, 266
Holst, Gustav, 205; *Perfect Fool*, 27
Horowitz, Vladimir, 17, 162
Houston Symphony Orchestra, 19, 42, 234-5
Hovhaness, Alan, 235; *Ode to the Temple of Sound*, 235
Huberman, Bronislaw, 17, 162, 163, 212

Glorious John

Hughes, Robert, 205, *Sinfonietta*, 205
Hutchinson, George, 219
Ibbs and Tillett, 37
Indianapolis Symphony Orchestra, 241
Inghilleri, Giovanni, 249, 251
International String Quartet, 100
Ireland, John, 205
Irish, Florence, 266, 268
Israel Philharmonic, 212-13
Israel Philharmonic's Artists' House, 212-13
Irving, Sir Henry, 244
Iturbi, José, 241
Jegge, Marjorie, 195
Jerome, Sir Bertrand, 279
Jesse H. Jones Hall, Houston, 234
Joachim, Joseph, 72
Joachim Quartet, 138
John Barbirolli Chamber Orchestra, 15, 109-110, 131
Johnson, Samuel, 52
Johnstone, Arthur, 112
Johnstone, Maurice, 'Banners' Overture, 196
Jones, Sydney, *The Geisha*, 66
Judson, Arthur, 17
Kabalevsky, Dmitry, 47
Keats, John, *When chivalry lifted up her lance on high*, 188
Kennedy, Eslyn, 103
Kennedy, Michael, 35-43, 103, 104, 205, 214, 216-18
Kern, Jerome, 54
Kindler, Hans, 241
King's Lynn Ensemble, 214
Kingsway Hall, London, 250
Kipnis, Alexander, 17
Klemperer, Otto, 241
Kodály, Zoltán, 47
Koussevitzky, Serge, 158, 241
Kreisler, Fritz, 17, 23, 51, 54, 103, 202, 219, 230, 252
Kubelik, Rafael, 17
Kutcher Quartet, 15, 219
Lamond, Frederick, 26
Lang, Archbishop (William), 48
Lark, Mr., 85, 86
Lawton, Frank, 49
Laye, Evelyn, 49
Legge, Walter, 177

Lehàr, Franz, *Die lustige Witwe* (*The Merry Widow*), 49, 66
Lehmann, Lotte, 140
Leider, Frida, 17, 249, 250
Levi, Hermann, 135
Licette, Miriam, 90
Lincoln, Abraham, 28
Lincoln Cathedral, 112
Lister, Joseph, 54
Liszt, Franz, 72, 178, 199; *Liebesträume* (No. 3), 229
Little Symphony of Montreal, 172
London Philharmonic Orchestra, 181
London School of Economics, 49
London String Quartet, 219
London Symphony Orchestra, 16, 23, 48, 63, 108, 109, 111, 132, 160, 181, 250
London Violoncello School, 15
Los Angeles Philharmonic, 241
Lucas, E. V., 199
Mackenzie, Sir Alexander, 158
Maggio Musicale Orchestra (Florence), 112
Mahler, Gustav, 27, 40, 51, 113-4, 114-6, 221; *Kindertotenlieder*, 27, 194; Symphony No. 9, 27, 113-4, 115; Symphony No. 4, 113, 115; Symphony No. 6, 115; *Das Lied von der Erde*, 194; Symphony No. 2 ('Resurrection'), 206
Manchester, Corporation of, 233, 244
Manchester, University of, 213
Manchester Guardian, The, see *Guardian, The*
Manchester Libraries, 246
Manchester Royal Infirmary, 195
Manchester Town Hall, 24
Manns, Sir Augustus, 158
Marcello, Benedetto, Allegretto, 64
Margaret, Princess, 191
Maria Theresa, Empress, 77
Marie (of Rumania), Queen, 154
Marlborough Club, 187
Marlborough School, 187
Martinelli, Giovanni, 220-1
Mascagni, Pietro, 47
Mason, Colin, 205
Massenet, Jules, 75
Maurel, Victor, 118
Maxted, George, 165
Mayer, Dorothy [Lady], 220
Mayer, Sir Robert, 220

Index

McCallum, David, 165
McCloud, Mrs., 158
Meert, Charles, 165
Meiningen Court Orchestra, 72
Melchior, Lauritz, 249
Mendelssohn(-Bartholdy), Felix, 71, 72, 135; 'Ruy Blas' Overture, 206
Menzies, Sir Robert, 29
Meremblum Orchestra, 270
Messager, André, *Véronique*, 66
Metropolitan Opera, New York, 135, 240
Midland Hotel, Manchester, 37, 187
Miller, Keith, 29, 30
Minneapolis Symphony Orchestra, 241
Mitchell, Ena, 195
Mitropoulos, Dimitri, 241
Moiseiwitsch, Benno, 37
Monckton, Lionel, 44, 49; *The Quaker Girl*, 44; *The Geisha*, 66
Monteux, Pierre, 241
Montreal Symphony Orchestra, 231
Morlacchi Theatre, Perugia, 112
Morley, Christopher, 91
Morton, Rachel, 218
Mottl, Felix, 135
Mozart, Wolfgang Amadeus, 52, 69, 70, 71, 72, 77, 80, 95, 130, 139, 152, 154, 183, 195, 198, 231, 263, 277; Sinfonia Concertante K. 364, 26; *Le nozze di Figaro*, 66, 69, 77; overture to *Le nozze di Figaro*, 68; Clarinet Quintet, 95; *Die Zauberflöte*, 172, 183, 277; Oboe concerto, 183; *Don Giovanni*, 250; *Così fan tutte*, 277
Mullings, Frank, 26
Music for Young People, 220
Music Hall, Houston, 42
Musica Viva, Liverpool, 39
Musicians' Emergency Fund (USA), 17, 169-170
Musikvereinsaal, Vienna, 211
National Broadcasting Company (N.B.C.), 242
National Gramophonic Society, 21, 22, 63
National Finnish Orchestra, 163
National Orchestral Association (USA), 17, 170-2
National Playing Fields Association, 234
Naylor, Bernard, 172
Nazi Party, 277

N.B.C. Symphony Orchestra, 241, 242
Nelson, Lord Horatio, 54, 234, 271
Neveu, Ginette, 42
Newman, Cardinal (John Henry), 46, 110-11, 206
Newman, Ernest, 39, 94
New Symphony Orchestra of London, 181
New York Philharmonic Orchestra, *see* New York Philharmonic-Symphony Orchestra
New York Philharmonic Society, 21
New York Philharmonic-Symphony League, 125-7, 133, 167-9, 264
New York Philharmonic-Symphony Orchestra, 17-18, 21, 33, 35, 125-7, 128, 141, 167-9, 170-1, 174, 204, 231-3, 235, 239-40, 243, 253, 254, 256, 257, 263-5
New York Times, The, 17
Nicholls, Agnes, 206
Nichols, David, 165
Nihon Keizai Shimbun, 221
Nikisch, Arthur, 27, 108, 130
Northern Philharmonic Orchestra, 220
Oakley, President (of the Contemporary Club, Philadelphia), 251
Offenbach, Jacques, 66
Olszewska, Maria, 160, 249
Opéra Comique, Paris, 68
Opera House, Manchester, 42
Orchestra of the Academy of Saint Cecilia, Rome, 274
Ormandy, Eugene, 241
Ormerod, Ben, 201
Our Lady's Choral Society, Dublin, 46, 110, 112, 206, 207
Paderewski, Ignaz, 230
Paganini, Nicolai, 178
Palace Theatre, Manchester, 42
Paley, Mr. (President of C.B.S.), 256
Paris Opéra, 134
Parker, R. H., 213
Parry, Hubert, 31
Parry, Wilfred, 215
Paterson, Messrs., 158
Pertile, Aureliano, 251
Petre, Tommy, 219
Philadelphia Orchestra, The, 216, 235, 241, 253, 256
Philharmonic Society of London, *see* Royal

Glorious John

Philharmonic Society of London
Philharmonie, Berlin, 113, 114
Philip, Prince (Duke of Edinburgh), 234
Piccini Theatre, Bari, 274
Pidgeon, Walter, 269
Pinza, Ezio, 89
Pittsburgh Symphony Orchestra, 241
Pius XII, Pope, 46, 110-11, 270
Poliomyelitis Fund, 211
Potter, Stephen, 33
Pratt, Mrs., 127
Previtali, Fernando, 274
Pritchard, Sir John, 14
Prout, Ebenezer, 195
Puccini, Giacomo, 32, 47, 75, 94, 104-7; *Madama Butterfly*, 50, 131, 140, 229; *Gianni Schicchi*, 66, 104, 105, 106; *Il Tabarro*, 104, 105; *Suor Angelico*, 104; *La Bohème*, 105, 106; *Tosca*, 105-6, 140, 218, 251; *Manon Lescaut*, 106; *Il Trittico*, 104-6; *Turandot*, 221
Purcell, Henry, 22, 231; Suite for Strings (arr. Barbirolli), 63, 65; *The Married Beau*, 64
Queen's Hall, London, 15, 16, 21, 23, 47, 96, 99, 108, 130, 133, 239, 250, 251, 268
Queen's Hall Orchestra, 15, 22, 28
Queen's Hotel, Leicester Square, 28, 45
Rachmaninov, Sergei, 51, 252; Piano Concerto No. 2, 37
Radford, Robert, 26, 152, 155
Radio Times, 273
Raff, Joachim, *Cavatina*, 100-1
R.A.I. Chorus (Rome), 111
R.A.I. Orchestra (Rome), 111, 273, 274
Rawsthorne, Alan, 205, 221; 'Hallé' Overture, 205; Piano Concerto, 216
Ravel, Maurice, 130, 218; *Daphnis et Chloë*, 38; *Daphnis et Chloë* Suites Nos. 1 and 2, 235
Redoutensaal (Hofburg), Vienna, 277
Reed, W[illiam]. H[enry]., 109, 110, 112, 133, 239
Rees, C. B., 207-8
Reid Orchestra, 156
Reiner, Fritz, 241
Reszke, Jean de, 218
Rhodes, Cecil, 190
Rhodes, Wilfred, 24, 32, 33
Rhodesian Academy of Music, 190

Richter, Hans, 51, 112, 135, 178, 185, 186, 204, 205, 207, 211
Rimsky-Korsakov, Nikolay, *Le Coq d'Or*, 173
Ritter, Alexander, 72-3
Roberts, Lord (Frederick Sleigh), 50
Robertson, Rae, 23, 160
Robinson, W. A., 213
Rochester Philharmonic Orchestra, 241
Rodzinski, Artur, 241
Ronald, Sir Landon, 26, 151, 158
Roosevelt, Franklin D., 275
Roper, Dr., 63
Rossini, Gioachino, *Il barbiere di Siviglia*, 66, 272, 274; Overture to *Semiramide*, 271, 272, 275
Rothwell, Evelyn, *see* Barbirolli, Evelyn (Lady Barbirolli) (wife of Barbirolli)
Royal Academy of Music, London, 15, 50, 130
Royal Albert Hall, London, 98
Royal College of Music, London, 190
Royal Festival Hall, London, 195, 212
Royal Liverpool Philharmonic Orchestra, 209
Royal Manchester College of Music, 36, 244, 245
Royal Opera House, Covent Garden, 23, 26, 42, 49, 50, 55, 68, 91, 104, 108, 131, 132, 140, 200, 221
Royal Opera House, Covent Garden, Chorus, 251
Royal Opera House, Covent Garden, Orchestra, 104, 160, 251
Royal Philharmonic Society of London, 16, 24-8, 48, 129, 135
Royal Philharmonic Society Orchestra, 132, 181, 240
Rubbra, Edmund, 40
Rubinstein, Artur, 17, 160, 162, 249
Russell, John, 245, 246
St. Andrew's Hall, Glasgow, 165
St. Ann's Church, Manchester, 186, 188
St. Louis Symphony Orchestra, 241
Sabina, Karel, 68
Sacred Music Festival (*Sagra Umbria*), Umbria, 46, 112
Sadler's Wells Ballet, 201
Saeverud, Harald, 206; *Ballad of Revolt*, 206
Saint-Saëns, Camille, 'Cello Concerto, 21
Salmond, Felix, 96

Index

Sammons, Albert, 26, 202, 219
San Carlo Opera Orchestra, Naples, 271, 273
San Carlo Theatre, Naples, 271, 272
San Francisco Symphony Orchestra, 241
Sanzogno, Nino, 41
Sarasate, Pablo, 40
Sargent, Sir Malcolm, 212, 233
Saunders, John, 219
Scala, La, Milan, 14, 115, 116
Scarlatti, Domenico, 47
Schmidt-Isserstedt, Hans, 233
Schnabel, Arthur, 17, 162
Schnéevoigt, Georg, 163
Schonbrünn Palace, Vienna, 277
Schubert, Franz, 198, 277
Schumann, Robert, 71, 130; 'Cello Concerto, 27; Piano Concerto, 37
Schweitzer, Albert, 31, 107, 108
Scott, Robert Falcon, 48
Scotti, Antonio, 86
Scottish (National) Orchestra, 16-17, 35, 97, 151-67, 173, 178, 209
Sevitzky, Fabien, 241
Sforza, Count (Carlo), 218
Shakespeare, William, 51, 127, 134, 169, 171, 242, 244, 268; *Titus Andronicus*, 39; *King Henry V*, 51; *Julius Caesar*, 77; *The Taming of the Shrew*, 127, 169, 172, 242, 268; *A Midsummer Night's Dream*, 171
Shaw, George Bernard, 35, 281
Sheffield City Hall, 193
Sheffield Philharmonic Chorus, 46
Sibelius, Jean, 47, 97, 99, 110, 152, 163; Symphonies Nos. 1-7 (complete cycle), 39, 177; Symphony No. 1, 165; Symphony No. 2, 165; Symphony No. 5, 165, 172; Symphony No. 7, 165; *Pohjola's Daughter*, 165
Sibelius Festival, Helsinki, 214
Siloti, Alexander, *Cavatina*, Op. 13, 26
Sistine Chapel, 134
Smetana, Bedřich, *The Bartered Bride*, 65-71
Smyth, Dame Ethyl, 26; *The Wreckers*, 26
Snowden, Lord, 154
Solomon, (Cutner, Solomon), 17, 160
South Place Sunday Concerts, 219
Southwell Minster, 188

Spohr, Louis, 135, 219
Stock, Frederick, 241
Stokowski, Leopold, 19, 40, 241
Strasser, Otto, 211
Strauss, Franz, 71
Strauss, Johann, *Die Fledermaus*, 66; *Der Zigeunerbaron* (*The Gypsy Baron*), 66
Strauss, Richard, 15, 39, 42, 71-85, 94-5, 152, 165; *Der Rosenkavalier*, 66, 71-85, 154, 231; Serenade for Thirteen Wind Instruments, Op. 7, 71-2; Symphony in F minor, Op. 12, 72; *Don Juan*, 73; *Tod und Verklärung* (*Death and Transfiguration*), 73; *Till Eulenspiegel*, 73; *Also Sprach Zarathustra*, 73; *Don Quixote*, 73; *Ein Heldenleben*, 73; *Guntram*, 73, 74; *Feuersnot*, 74; *Salome*, 74, 77; *Elektra*, 74, 77, *Die Frau ohne Schatten*, 74; *Die ägyptische Helena*, 74; *Metamorphosen*, 95; *Le bourgeois gentilhomme*, 235
Stravinsky, Igor, 152; *Pulcinella*, 165; *Petrouchka*, 165; Symphony in Three Movements, 210
Stresemann, Wolfgang, 19, 113
Suffolk Regiment, 22
Suggia, Guilhermina, 26, 249
Sullivan, Sir Arthur, 66, 76, 158
Sunday Symphony Concerts (Queen's Hall), 96
Sunday Telegraph, 214
Sunday Times, 94
Sutcliffe, Herbert, 32
Swan, Mrs., 161
Tamagno, Francesco, 117
Taylor, Deems, 253
Tchaikovsky, Peter, 232, 271; '1812' Festival Overture, 28, 29, 40, 229; Piano Concerto No. 1, 37; Violin Concerto, 250
Teatro de Colón, 216
Teatro Reale, Rome, 274
Tennyson, Lord (Alfred), 266
Terry, Charles Sanford, 31, 107
Terry, Dame Ellen, 269
Tertis, Lionel, 26, 47, 205
Theatre an der Wien, Vienna, 183, 276, 277
Thibaud, Jacques, 17, 26, 51, 162
Thornton, Edna, 26
Three Choirs Festival, 103, 111

Glorious John

Tillett, Emmy, 37
Tippett, Sir Michael, 205, 234
Toscanini, Arturo, 14, 17, 21, 106, 128, 130, 212, 241, 242, 257, 273
Tovey, Sir Donald Francis, 151, 156
Trinity College of Music, 14
Turner, Dame Eva, 221
Turner, Laurance, 24, 191
Vaughan Williams, Ralph, 24-5, 27-8, 48, 100-4, 110, 111, 132, 205, 208, 216; Symphony No. 6, 24-5, 28, 100-1, 208; Symphony No. 3 ('Pastoral'), 27; Fantasia on Sussex Folk Tunes, 27; Symphonies 1-9 (complete cycle), 39; Symphony No. 5, 39, 100; *Sinfonia antarctica* (Symphony No. 7), 100, 102, 190; Symphony No. 8, 100, 101, 102; *A London Symphony* (Symphony No. 2), 100, 103; Symphony No. 4, 102; *Linden Lea*, 102; *A Sea Symphony* (Symphony No. 1), 102-3; Fantasia on a Theme by Thomas Tallis, 165; *Job*, 165; *Serenade to Music*, 196; *Flourish for Glorious John*, 205
Vaughan Williams, Ursula, 102, 103, 104
Verdi, Guiseppe, 15, 75-6, 96, 98, 106, 116-8; *Otello*, 14, 88, 91, 116-8, 129-30, 218, 251, 271, 273; *Aïda*, 26, 75-6, 87, 88, 91, 117, 131, 140, 218; Requiem, 42, 195, 206, 276, 277; *Falstaff*, 50, 77, 91, 106, 154, 173, 230; *Rigoletto*, 70; *Don Carlo*, 86-91; *Macbeth*, 246; Preludes to *La Traviata*, 271
Verne, Jules, 159
Victoria, Queen, 48, 218
Vienna Philharmonic, 211, 216, 276, 277
Vienna State Opera, 276, 277
Virtuosi di Roma, 235
Volksoper, Vienna, 276
Wagner, Richard, 15, 28, 42, 65, 71, 72, 73, 74, 84, 94, 95, 96, 98, 117, 135, 136, 138-9, 178; *Die Meistersinger von Nürnberg*, 25, 66, 70, 71, 77, 84, 117, 140, 184, 271, 273; *Parsifal*, 64, 93, 94-5, 177; *Tristan und Isolde*, 65, 95, 218; *Siegfried*, 71; Prelude to *Die Meistersinger von Nürnberg*, 233
Waldeland, Hilda, 206
Walenn, Herbert, 15, 26, 51
Waller, Professor, 213

Walter, Bruno, 114, 116, 193, 194
Walton, Sir William, 38, 205, 233; *Belshazzar's Feast*, 132, 278; Viola Concerto, 165, 233
Warner, Oliver, *A Portrait of Lord Nelson*, 234
Washington Symphony Orchestra, 241
Watson, Henry, 243-6
Weber, Carl Maria von, 47; Overture to *Der Freischütz*, 29, 207
Webster, David, 200
Weinberger, Jaromí, *Švanda dudák (Schwanda the Bagpiper)*, 66
Weingartner, Felix, 26, 108, 158
Weldon, George, 28, 29, 210-11; arrangement of *Suo Gan*, 211
Westminster Hospital, 194
Wheeler, Sir Charles, 48
Whitaker, Dr., 155
White, John, 53
Whiteman, Paul, 54
Whitington, Richard, 29
Whittaker, George, String Quartet, 219
Widor, Charles-Marie, 218
Wilde, Oscar, 76
Williams, Austen, 34
Winter Gardens, Bournemouth, 98
Wolf, Hugo, 27
Wood, Sir Henry J., 28, 29, 130, 212
Woolhouse, Edmund, 14
Woolley, Frank, 54
World's Fair, New York, 240
Ysaÿe, Eugène, 26, 51

ALSO PUBLISHED BY THE BARBIROLLI SOCIETY

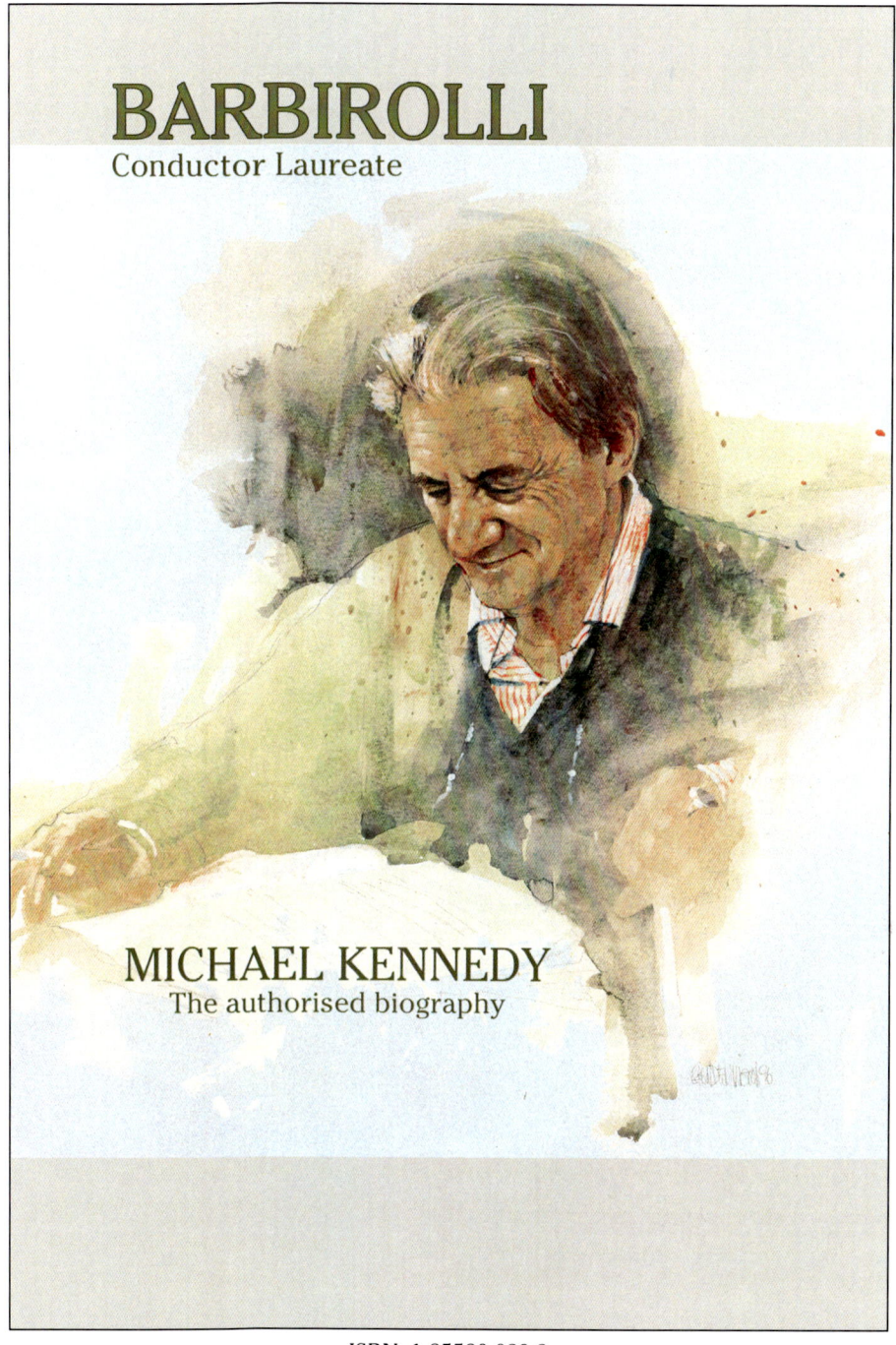

BARBIROLLI
Conductor Laureate

MICHAEL KENNEDY
The authorised biography

ISBN: 1-85580-029-2